To Stanley Dennison

a much valued teacher,
friend and colleague

Contents

List of Tables

List of Figures

Acknowledgements

Those who travel the academic road accumulate many debts. Here, only the biggest and most obvious are mentioned.

I am especially grateful to Eamonn Butler, Director of the Adam Smith Institute, who suggested to me early in 1989 that I should write on the topic of trade union reform. What I have produced is significantly longer than he expected, but nevertheless he has read every word of it in draft, and has made many helpful and constructive comments.

I thank Paul Marshall, one of my students at Newcastle University, for allowing me to use the diagram of strikes, etc., at the end of Chapter 1. This first appeared in one of his essays.

I am in debt to my immediate colleagues, including the library staff, at the University of Newcastle upon Tyne, who have put up with my eccentricities for many years and have generously helped me on many occasions.

Finally, I offer inadequate thanks to my wife and family, who often rescued me when I had almost lost patience with my word processor. But where would we be today without those marvellous machines?

Of course I am solely responsible for any omissions or errors which remain in the text.

CHARLES HANSON

Author's note: For the sake of convenience, the masculine pronoun is sometimes used in this book as a proxy for both men and women.

The author and publishers would also like to thank the following for permission to reproduce copyright material:

Employment Gazette and Paul Marshall, for Figure 1.1 (1990).

The Certification Officer for Trade Unions and Employers' Associations, for Table 6.1 from Annual Reports of the Certification Officer, 1980–89; and for Table 6.3, from Annual Reports of the Certification Officer, 1984–89, and for Table 9.4, from Annual Reports of the Certification Officer for 1985 and 1989.

ACAS, for Table 6.2, from ACAS Annual Report, 1987.

National Consumer Council, for Table 12.6, from *Consumer Concerns 1990: a Consumer View of Public Services* (1990).

Professor Patrick Minford, for Table 10.5 from Liverpool Macroeconomic Research Ltd, *Quarterly Economic Bulletin*, June 1990.

Kogan Page, for Table 16.7, from D. W. Bell and C. G. Hanson, *Profit Sharing and Profitability* (1987).

The Manpower Services Commission, the National Economic Development Council, and the British Institute of Management for figures on p. 164, from *The Making of Managers* (1987).

Abbreviations

ACAS	Advisory, Conciliation and Arbitration Service
AEFWU	Amalgamated Engineering and Foundry Workers Union
AUEW	Amalgamated Union of Engineering Workers
BR	British Rail
BT	British Telecom
COHSE	Confederation of Health Service Employees
CROTUM	Commissioner for the Rights of Trade Union Members
EETPU	Electrical, Electronic, Telecommunication and Plumbing Union
EC	European Community
GMWU	General and Municipal Workers Union
HMSO	Her Majesty's Stationery Office
HRM	Human Resource Management
IBM	International Business Machines
ICI	Imperial Chemical Industries
IPA	Involvement and Participation Association
IPM	Institute of Personnel Management
IR	Industrial Relations
LRC	Labour Representation Committee
MATSA	Managerial, Administrative, Technical and Supervisory Association
MORI	Market and Opinion Research International
NAFF	National Association for Freedom
NCB	National Coal Board
NGA	National Graphical Association
NHS	National Health Service
NUM	National Union of Mineworkers
NUPE	National Union of Public Employees
PA	Personnel Administration
PLC	Public Limited Company
RDW	Registered Dock Worker
SOGAT	Society of Graphical and Allied Trades
TFA	The Freedom Association
TGWU	Transport and General Workers Union

TQM	Total Quality Management
TUC	Trades Union Congress
TULRA	Trade Union and Labour Relations Act

Foreword

This instructive book by Charles Hanson grew up from two roots. One was his discussions with the publisher concerning the need for a good book on the economics of industrial relations which would reflect the fundamental restructurings that have taken place in the British economy in the 1980s. The speed of those changes has been so startling that many books on the subject now belong firmly to the past; many practitioners in the field cannot understand the present; and many employers remain unprepared for the future.

The second root was discussions with the Adam Smith Institute, which was also thinking about these changes. In January 1979, in the depths of the 'Winter of Discontent', the Institute had published a short but deeply influential book on the structure of trade union power, *The Trojan Horse*, by Professor John Burton. It argued that the special legal privileges enjoyed by trade unions had upset a delicate constitutional balance. Legislation to protect and promote trade unions had given them the leverage to expand their membership (voluntary and involuntary), which in turn increased their leaders' strike-threat power and gave them the strength to demand yet more favours from the policy-makers. Power bred power, and once the balance had been lost, the democratic structure began tottering perilously.

Yet within the decade, the balance had been pushed back again. No more beer and sandwiches in Downing Street, record *low* numbers of strikes, falling union membership, rising recriminations in the TUC, the ghostworking and restrictive practices of Fleet Street lying abandoned, and even union leaders accepting that the time had come to scale down their block vote at party conferences.

Was all this the intended result of a deliberate and planned war of attrition by a determined government? Or was it merely the outcome of a series of *ad hoc* measures that had no greater vision than the political expediency of the time? Had Mrs Thatcher learnt from Mr Heath's administration that the problem of union power was too big to be solved all at once?

Plainly, these questions called for a sequel to *The Trojan Horse*, and Charles Hanson agreed to merge the two projects, with this very happy result.

He starts by taking us back to the 'Winter of Discontent', the awful details of which are often blotted from people's memory. It makes us understand why trade union reform seemed so urgent at the time; and he traces out the step-by-step reforms taken by the incoming government and tries to judge whether they constituted a deliberate programme or a faltering series of steps that eventually, and after some diversions, brought the government to the point where it wanted to be.

From there the book analyses the roots of the power which the trade unions had accumulated by 1979, and how the various legislative reforms tackled them. There is, believes Charles Hanson, still a bit of work to do if the constitutional balance is to be restored to a precise level once again.

But what of the future? Here the author deploys his expertise as an analyst of human resource management so that, mindful of the past that he has sketched, business managers can evolve the new strategies they will need for the future. For the changing shape of our economy has made the traditional divide between the 'two sides' of industry as irrelevant now as it was sterile before; today's manager must harness the individuality of his workforce, recognise the motivational importance of raising product quality, and create the team spirit to achieve it. In this environment – in many cases a post-union environment – a new style of management must evolve.

Charles Hanson has done us all a service in pointing out just how stark is the divergence between the old ways and the new. Let us hope that our entrepreneurs have learnt from the industrial-relations history that he illustrates so graphically – and that the results prove to be just as divergent.

EAMONN BUTLER

Part I
The Thatcher Government's Employment Reforms 1980–90

1 The Winter of Discontent

> Now is the winter of our discontent
> Made glorious summer by this sun of York.
>
> W Shakespeare, *King Richard III*

The winter of discontent was long and harsh. It began on 28 September 1978 with a strike at Fords which lasted for nine weeks, and finally petered out in mid April 1979 as members of civil service unions brought to a close their series of sporadic strikes. There were six and a half months of industrial disputes culminating in eleven weeks of general misery and chaos, when it was often the weakest members of the community, including the terminally ill, who suffered most.

In June and July 1989 a series of one day strikes on the railways, the London underground and in the town halls, and a short national strike in the docks provoked talk of a summer of discontent, as if 1989 compared with 1979. But that was not the case. Over a period of ten years memories fade and past events, especially unpleasant ones, tend to be forgotten. We need to be reminded of the blatant abuse of trade union power which was the primary cause of the election of the Thatcher government in May 1979.

But why was that power abused? Hadn't the Wilson/Callaghan government of 1974–79 conceded all the trade union leaders' demands for legal privilege? Weren't the trade unions to all intents and purposes above the law by 1979? Couldn't the closed shop now be enforced without regard to the protests of those who preferred not to join a trade union? Wasn't it now possible to take an employer to court for not recognising a trade union? Didn't employees have a range of employment rights without any mention of duties, which would have been unthinkable in the 1960s? Didn't the members of the General Council of the Trades Union Congress regularly spend so much time in 10 Downing Street that they must sometimes have thought of it as their own home? And couldn't the electorate have been forgiven for thinking that the trade union leaders had taken over the job of government?

The winter of discontent, and the whole period 1974–79, indicate that governments do not necessarily win prestige by giving in to a particular interest group – in this case the TUC. Rather, the appetite of such a group grows with feeding. To say that is not to suggest that Prime Minister James Callaghan was solely responsible for creating this wretched situation, which had roots stretching back many decades. Instead, he just happened to be in charge when the whirlwind struck. But there was a certain poetic justice in the 1979 crisis, because in 1969 Mr Callaghan had led the rebellion against Harold Wilson's attempt to introduce a modest measure of trade union reform. On that occasion Callaghan had been the trade unions' champion, but in 1978–79 their sole aim seemed to be to humiliate him, even though in retrospect his policies seem so reasonable, totally in keeping with the consensus spirit which had prevailed since the famous White Paper on Employment Policy of 1944.

The Labour government had initiated its four stage incomes policy in July 1975 when inflation was getting completely out of hand. The first stage – a rigid, flat-rate increase of £6 a week – was simple and apparently effective. The rate of inflation fell from 24 per cent in 1975 to 17 per cent in 1976.

Stage Two was even more drastic, with a guideline of 5 per cent within a floor of £2.50 and a ceiling of £4. In 1977 the rate of inflation fell again to 16 per cent, and Stage Three of the incomes policy provided a guideline of 10 per cent. By 1978 inflation was down to 8 per cent and understandably the government wanted to maintain the downward trend. Hence the title of its White Paper *Winning the Battle Against Inflation* published on 26 July, which stated categorically that 'the increase in earnings for next year must be substantially lower' (than for the present year) and that 'The Government has therefore decided to adopt a pay policy to apply from August 1978 in which the guideline will be set at 5 per cent'.

The tone of the White Paper was one of sweet reason. And yet it was based upon two false assumptions which eventually led to the government's downfall. The first was that a corporatist consensus involving 'broad agreement between Government, unions and employers' would enable inflation to be kept under control. The second was that an incomes policy could be made acceptable for another year. Already the Stage Three guideline of 10 per cent had been so frequently breached that the average rate of earnings increase was about 15 per cent. All the indications were that the dam was beginning to break and that the rigidities imposed on the labour market by Stages One, Two and Three would soon be swept away. But the government preferred to indulge in wishful thinking instead of facing reality, especially when it was thought that an election might be only weeks away. Indeed, many commentators felt certain that Mr Callaghan would go to the country in October and soon after the turn of the year he must have bitterly regretted not taking that course.

THE BREWING STORM

Naturally the 5 per cent guideline was debated at the TUC in early September and at the Labour Party conference the following month. The TUC delegates heard the Prime Minister politely as he insisted that the guideline must be observed, gave him a standing ovation and then, on the following day, voted overwhelmingly against Stage Four of the incomes policy. The pattern was reversed at the Labour Party conference: on Monday the incomes policy was disowned by a majority of two to one and on the Tuesday Mr Callaghan received a standing ovation! The Transport and General Workers Union had already decided in favour of free collective bargaining and, by the time Mr Callaghan spoke at Blackpool, Ford's 57,000 manual workers (over half of whom were TGWU members) had been out on strike for four days. Actually the die had been cast during the holiday month of August. The TUC barons had brooded on Stage Four, decided they would not accept it and made their views clear at the September Congress. As *The Economist* reported with remarkable prescience on 9 September: 'Behind the TUC's glossy election veneer the real message from Brighton was that Britain is in for a winter of industrial discontent come what may'. But did the writer of those prophetic words really foresee the full scale of the impending storm?

It was the government's ability to achieve its aims, not its sincerity, which was in doubt. With the Prime Minister in the lead the Cabinet was united round the 5 per cent guideline. Cash limits had been imposed in the public sector and, as the White Paper had pointed out, some 30 per cent of the labour force worked in that sector. So it seemed that the government started from a position of some strength. But the cry for comparability was its Achilles heel. Once a few private sector settlements had breached the guideline, clearly others – and especially the low-paid public sector trade unions – would be seeking to follow their example and the government would be in acute difficulties. So the outcome of the dispute at Fords was critical for the whole economy, and in 1978, as today, Ford UK was a profitable concern, capable of raising wages by more than many other companies.

By late October it was plain that the Ford settlement would be in double figures. Management had offered 8 per cent plus a productivity deal which was expected to be worth another 4 per cent, but the offer was initially dismissed by the unions. The strike continued and by early November a 17 per cent pay settlement was agreed at Ford's – far worse than anything the government could have feared, a severe test of the threatened sanctions against companies which breached the 5 per cent guideline, and an open invitation to other trade unions to go for what they could get.

By the end of December it was difficult to believe that the 5 per cent guideline still retained any credibility. To begin with, Parliament on 14 December declined to support the government's arbitrary use of economic sanctions against companies which broke the guideline. The sanctions would probably have been ineffective anyway, but their existence at least suggested that the guideline had to be taken seriously. Once they had gone, the policy was in tatters. Then five other settlements, averaging around 12 per cent, drove a few more nails into the coffin. First, British Oxygen settled for a 10 per cent increase. Next the Central Arbitration Committee awarded BBC staff 12.5 per cent plus an extra 4 per cent for some technicians. Soon afterwards petrol tanker drivers were offered 15 per cent by Esso and other big petrol companies, but there were doubts about whether they would accept it. Meanwhile merchant seamen had accepted 8.75 per cent and the Agricultural Wages Board had given farm workers 13 per cent. As the 5 per cent guideline disappeared from sight the Prime Minister must have had an unhappy Christmas. But the real problems were yet to come.

1–21 JANUARY 1979

It would be wrong to describe the first three weeks of the new year as the lull before the storm, because there was a good deal of turbulence during this period. The turbulence was unpleasant but of no account in comparison with the onslaught by the public sector unions on Monday 22 January. It was on that day that the fate of the Labour government was finally sealed, even if it was not apparent at the time. Nevertheless, the preceding three weeks set the tone for what was to follow, as the secondary pickets went out in force.

To begin with, lorry drivers came out on unofficial strike in eleven of the country's eighteen regions on 3 January. The lorry drivers had refused a 15 per cent pay offer and were holding out for 23 per cent and shorter hours. Although only 30,000 out of a total of 180,000 drivers had stopped work, their dispute was greatly intensified by flying pickets who closed the docks and disrupted manufacturing industry. *The Economist* argued on 13 January that 'Picketing has now become such a powerful weapon that even workers with only limited industrial muscle can paralyse huge chunks of industry. Strong unions can go straight for the country's jugular, and every major strike can now have the impact of a general strike'. And the writer went on to say 'The whole issue of union power is now, rightly, back at the centre of political debate'. Meanwhile the water workers had rejected a 9.3 per cent offer and the going rate for increases in the private sector had risen to 15 per cent.

By mid January the Prime Minister was breaching his own 5 per cent guideline. First, he offered £3.50 a week to anybody for whom this was more than 5 per cent; then he offered public sector workers pay comparability with their private sector equivalent, leading to staged settlements beyond the end of the 1979 pay round. Those making public sector claims already included local authority manual workers, water workers, health service ancillary workers, ambulancemen, railwaymen, postmen, steel workers, gas and electricity supply workers and miners. The list seemed endless. The militancy of some of these groups was growing by the day, and the government's willingness to allow unconditional comparability awards meant that its pay policy was dead. But its major industrial troubles were only just beginning, even though the water workers accepted a 14 per cent pay deal on 19 January. The period of maximum misery was scheduled to start on 22 January.

22 JANUARY–19 MARCH 1979

The morning of Monday 22 January saw the biggest strike in Britain since the General Strike of 1926. About one and a half million public service workers stopped work for 24 hours, paralysing schools, hospitals, ambulances, rubbish collection, cemeteries and some municipal airports. Many of the strikers, including gravediggers and crematorium workers, indicated that they would stay on strike either indefinitely or at least for the rest of the week.

When some of the strikers returned to work on Tuesday 23 January, the railways came to a halt for 24 hours, with a second one day stoppage being called for the Thursday. The fact that many roads went ungritted in the sub-zero temperatures created an additional hazard for those who were trying to avoid the effects of the rail strikes. An RAC spokesman described it as 'dicing with people's lives'.

The four public sector unions involved in the Monday stoppage – NUPE, COHSE, the GMWU and the TGWU – were so encouraged by their members' response to the stoppage that they committed themselves to an indefinite programme of selective industrial action in pursuit of higher pay. They gave warnings of lightning stoppages by key individuals or groups of workers employed by town halls or hospitals, of official 'blacking' of specific tasks, of working to rule, and a commitment by members in some areas to 'working without enthusiasm'. In other words, the policy was to cause the maximum amount of inconvenience to the public with the minimum loss of pay for trade union members. With union membership of seventy or eighty per cent in much of the public sector such a policy was likely to be very effective, and the minority who preferred to work rather than strike could expect rough treatment from their colleagues.

One such public-spirited individual was Mr Michael Arundell, head porter at the Hospital for Sick Children in Great Ormond Street, London. By the end of February, after five weeks of intermittent strikes, he had resigned from NUPE and the TGWU, and knew that when his colleagues returned they might refuse to work with him. In a newspaper interview he agreed that pay and conditions in the Health Service were 'diabolical' but said 'enough is enough'. He realised that it might be difficult for him to continue to work within the Health Service as a non-union member and stated that 'what I am doing is not heroic – it is suicide'. Others like Mr Arundell would have been well aware of the likely consequence of continuing to work.

For its part the government was losing control of events. About the only thing which the Prime Minister and other ministers could do was to talk, and this they did, inside and outside Parliament. On 23 January, Mr Callaghan stated in the House of Commons that the unions were in danger of exhausting the nation's patience and saddling themselves with laws curbing their activities. By this he meant not that a Labour government would take any action against them, but that an incoming Conservative government might do so. At the same time he pointed out that there was nothing to stop any citizen crossing a picket line if he chose to, and that he would not hesitate to do it himself. Meanwhile the Prime Minister's chief aim was to negotiate some sort of agreement with the TUC as a face-saving substitute for his defunct pay policy.

Much the nastiest aspect of the public sector dispute, and indeed of the whole winter of discontent, was already apparent by Wednesday 24 January. On that day 65 cancer patients, and some expectant mothers, had to be sent home from the Queen Elizabeth Hospital, Birmingham, after NUPE pickets refused to allow food and medical supplies into the hospital. Their action sparked off a furious row between Mr William Bond, director of the hospital's radiotherapy unit, and the local officials of NUPE after he had vigorously denounced the union in colourful language and his colleague, Mr Malcolm Butler, administrator of eight hospitals in central Birmingham, had called the union's action 'totally heartless'.

The validity of these accusations may be assessed by the outcome of a meeting on the following day between the Area Health Authority and officials and shop stewards of NUPE and COHSE. Management had asked the unions to lift their ban on nineteen items which pickets had prevented from entering the hospital. In the event the unions consented to fourteen dispensations including food, surgical dressings, disposable nursing needs, medical and surgical instruments, laboratory equipment, medical gases and chemicals. But they refused to allow in fuel, laundry materials, spares and maintenance equipment and stationery.

On the following day (26 January) it was reported that NUPE members at the same hospital had refused to deliver food and medical supplies to the 25 patients on Ward East 1A for three days and had also declined to move two corpses from the ward. When asked to do so by Dr Hugh Bradley, Senior Registrar in charge of the ward, the head porter replied that he was taking orders from no one, and the bodies were later removed by nurses and medical students. Dr Bradley commented that 'Our requests bounced off the porter like a ball against a brick wall'.

Incidents like those which occurred at the Queen Elizabeth Hospital, Birmingham, took place all over the country and by the end of January almost half of the 2,300 state hospitals were providing emergency services only, and hardly a single ambulance system in Britain was working normally. The crisis was recognised by David Ennals, Secretary of State for Health and Social Services, who called Alan Fisher and Albert Spanswick, general secretaries respectively of NUPE and COHSE, to talks on 31 January. But even while he was urging the union leaders to keep their members under control, all but one of the forty hospitals in Birmingham were affected by strikes, and a union official said that a total breakdown of the city's health services could be imminent. Meanwhile the TGWU instructed members employed by local councils to intensify their 'guerilla actions', and strikes by cemetery and crematorium workers continued to prevent funerals in many areas. Liverpool, where two hundred embalmed bodies were stored in a disused factory and sixty other bodies awaited burial, was considering burying its dead at sea.

Nevertheless, 28 February was a turning point. On that day delegates at a TGWU conference voted 'reluctantly' to accept the offer of a 9 per cent increase plus £1-a-week advance on a pay comparability study and it was reported that members of the GMWU were voting strongly in favour. Three days later NUPE leaders in two areas also voted in favour and on 7 March NUPE announced that its local authority members had voted for acceptance by 227,591 votes to 150,455. But their NHS members had rejected a parallel offer by nearly 4 to 1, and ambulance men had also rejected it decisively. NUPE leaders immediately announced that they would spread industrial action, short of all-out strikes by hospital ancillary workers, and on 16 March a new surge of disruptive action engulfed hospitals in response to the government's encouragement to use volunteers to maintain essential services. This militancy petered out only on Monday 26 March when, at a meeting of the Ancillary Staffs Whitley Council, NUPE representatives were outvoted 12–4 by representatives of the other three unions present. There was a majority decision to accept the government's 11 per cent immediate pay offer plus a comparability study, and nine weeks of chaos and misery for health service patients finally drew to a close.

But the government's misery was far from over. Other unions were glad to take over when NUPE members returned to work, and union leaders of 500,000 civil servants called a one day strike for Monday 2 April. The response was moderately good, with perhaps half of the members obeying the strike call. While most went back to work on the Tuesday, a few continued or even stepped up their action. For example, customs officers threatened to wreck the Easter travel plans of many holidaymakers and the computer staff at the Lytham St Anne's computer centre stayed out. This meant that repayments of National Savings Certificates, Premium Bonds and some Government Securities had been at a standstill for more than five weeks. It should perhaps be mentioned that striking civil servants had also closed the Government Communications Headquarters in Cheltenham for a period in March.

THE GOVERNMENT–TUC CONCORDAT

By late January the government's primary aim was to reach an
agreement with the TUC which would end the unions' discontent.
To this end Denis Healey, Chancellor of the Exchequer, led a team of
senior ministers to Congress House, TUC headquarters, on 26
January. Three days later the whole General Council of the TUC
(all 42 of them) met the Prime Minister at 10 Downing Street in an
attempt to reach an 'understanding' designed to end the current strife
and restore stability to the economy. Finally, after further negotiations, the Prime Minister announced on 14 February that he had
reached an agreement with the TUC, but he refused to say what, if
any, bearing it would have on the present industrial troubles. In the
nineteen-page document entitled *The Economy, the Government and
Trade Union Responsibilities* there was no mention of the possibility of
legal restrictions on the closed shop, secondary picketing or unofficial
strikes and it was immediately dismissed by Mrs Thatcher as 'a
boneless wonder'. Its lack of teeth was not surprising, as among the
members of the General Council which agreed the document were
several trade union leaders publicly committed to causing the
government the maximum amount of embarrassment. In effect the
so-called 'concordat' was a re-run of the 'solemn and binding' promise
to mend its ways by the TUC to Harold Wilson's Labour government
in 1969, when the Prime Minister withdrew his 'In Place of Strife'
proposals to reform trade union law. In other words, it was a face-
saving gesture of no real substance at all.

28 MARCH–3 MAY 1979

The winter of discontent was by no means at an end on Wednesday 28
March. However, on that day Parliament decided that enough was
enough. In the late evening a motion of no confidence in the minority
Labour government was carried by one vote. For the first time since
1924, Parliament asserted its right to vote Her Majesty's ministers out
of office and on the following day Mr Callaghan announced that a
general election would be held on 3 May.

With hindsight, it might appear that the winter of discontent had
presented Mrs Thatcher with an election victory which was hers for the
taking. However, at the time the outcome looked much less certain.

Memories of Mr Heath's promise in 1970 to tame the trade unions, and the total collapse of his policies in 1974, were still fresh. Why should Margaret Thatcher succeed where Ted Heath had failed? She had to convince not only the electorate, but also many sceptics within her own party, that she had learned from her predecessor's mistakes and could do much better. Not only that, but she had to do much better with many of the cabinet ministers who had served under Ted Heath and had major reservations about their new leader's radicalism. And none of them was more hesitant that James Prior, shadow Secretary of State for Employment. The failure of the 1971 Industrial Relations Act was constantly on his mind. He was insistent that an ultra-cautious step by step approach to trade union reform must replace the disastrous 'big bang' of 1971, and he was determined that the first step should be a very modest one. But would the Tories get the opportunity to try their new approach? That question had to be answered first.

THE NEW AGENDA

In the event on 3 May the Conservatives found themselves elected to govern with an overall majority of 43 in the House of Commons. Commentators were generally agreed that the winter of discontent was the primary reason for the Tory victory and it followed that the foremost task of the new government was the effective reform of trade union law. That was the chief criterion by which it would be judged, and everything else really depended on the successful achievement of that aim. Chapters 2–6 indicate how that task was largely complete by 1990.

APPENDIX TO CHAPTER 1

The summary chart, Figure 1.1, on p. 13 shows the dramatic reduction in strikes, days lost through stoppages of work, and trade union membership between 1978 and 1989. It would be distinctly premature to claim that there has been a transformation of industrial relations in Britain, but the new framework of trade union law has provided the basis for such a transformation. How that can be achieved is set out in Part II of this book. There is no single statistical series which gives an accurate guide to the state of employment relations in the UK. But figures for the number of strikes and number of stoppages, taken

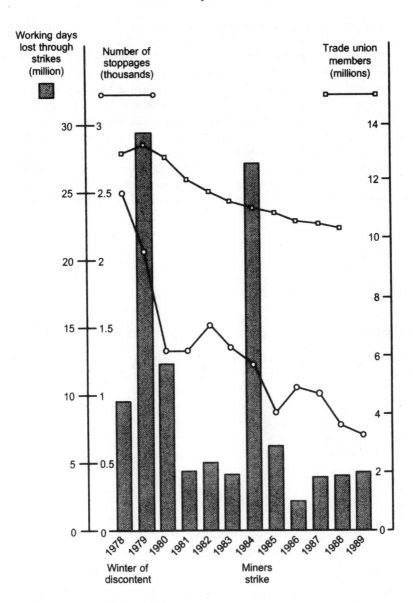

Figure 1.1   Working days lost through strikes, number of stoppages and trade union membership, 1978–89

Source: *Employment Gazette*, May 1990 pp. s44 & 260

together, are a good indicator and these figures show a marked downward trend since 1978–79. The similar trend in trade union membership is partly a result of the high unemployment 1980–86, but it also reflects the changing nature of the labour market and the contraction of the closed shop. Of course it would be possible to have an almost strike-free economy in which most people were working at half speed or less, so figures for comparative labour productivity are also important. But some of our main industrial competitors (eg West Germany) have higher labour productivity *and* are almost strike-free. Internationally the UK has been consistently in the middle of the strike league and this is sometimes regarded as cause for congratulation. Should it not rather be seen as a classic case of British complacency?

2 Step by Step Reform: An Outline of the Process

> The longest journey begins with a single step.
>
> Chinese proverb

Between 1979 and late 1989 five Bills to reform trade union law were presented to Parliament. But it would be quite wrong to suppose that they were all part of a major long-term strategy which had been completely thought through before the 1979 election victory. On the contrary, the failure of the mammoth 1971 Industrial Relations Act meant that the Conservatives were unwilling to think in terms of a comprehensive package of reforms, even if it was spread out. Perhaps it is fair to suggest that four main principles lay behind their approach to trade union reform early in 1979:

1 The process had to be step by step, with the next step only being taken when the previous one had proved its worth.
2 Apart from the first step, the policy was to be pragmatic. It had to be worked out in the context of prevailing needs and circumstances.
3 The distinction between Labour and Conservative policies should be emphasised. This was spelt out in a key paragraph of the 1979 Conservative Manifesto:

> Labour claim that industrial relations in Britain cannot be improved by changing the law. We disagree. If the law can be used to confer privileges, it can and should also be used to establish obligations. We cannot allow a repetition of the behaviour that we saw outside too many of our factories and hospitals last winter.

4 The first step, which would be precisely in line with the Manifesto commitment, would be given the highest priority in the legislative programme.

Taken together, these principles have meant that the Tory approach to trade union reform since 1979 has been pragmatic rather than strategic. Indeed a cynic might describe it as ad hoc, but this was the inevitable reaction to the 1971 fiasco. In this situation the personality and interests of the successive Secretaries of State for Employment were to have a marked effect on the legislative programme. Mrs

15

Thatcher was frequently criticised for interfering too much in the detail of government, but what happened over eleven years in the Department of Employment suggests that she gave her ministers plenty of room to show their initiative or otherwise.

It is not the purpose of this chapter to examine in detail the provisions of each of the five reform Acts, because the following chapters will do that according to the nature of the particular reform. Instead, the intention here is simply to give the reader an overview of the complex reform process, and the best way to do that is to set out the five Acts with the periods of office of the six Secretaries of State for Employment, together with a brief description of the contents of each Act:

Act of Parliament	*Secretary of State for Employment*
Employment Act 1980:	James Prior, May 1979–September 1981
Employment Act 1982:	Norman Tebbit,
	September 1981–October 1983
Trade Union Act 1984:	Tom King, October 1983–September 1985
	David Young, September 1985–June 1987
Employment Act 1988:	Norman Fowler, June 1987–January 1990
Employment Act 1990:	Michael Howard, January 1990–

The nature of the legislative process, in which a White or Green Paper usually precedes by about six months the introduction of a Bill to Parliament which takes six to nine months to become an Act, means that the initiatives of a Secretary of State may well come to fruition under a successor. For example, Norman Tebbit initiated the Trade Union Act 1984 which became law during Tom King's tenure of office, and Tom King, like his successor, took no new initiatives to expedite reform.

The legislative pattern is one of bursts of energy, which reached an intense peak during Mr Tebbit's term of office, interspersed by periods during which no legislative proposals were made. David Young, for example, showed no interest at all in trade union reform during his 21 months at the Department of Employment and was much more concerned with the reorganisation of the Manpower Services Commission and the provision of job training schemes for young people and the unemployed. Progress has been erratic, and for a time in 1985 and 1986 it seemed to have come to a halt altogether, with a feeling in some quarters that the task was complete.

The main provisions of each Act were as follows:

EMPLOYMENT ACT 1980

1 Modified the law on the closed shop to remove the worst excesses of the period 1974–79 by providing a proper conscience clause and making secret ballots obligatory before the introduction of new closed shops.
2 Made most secondary picketing illegal.
3 Removed immunity from *trade union officials* who organised certain secondary strikes.
4 Provided public money to cover the cost of secret ballots on strike action, elections for a union's executive committee or principal officers, rule changes and amalgamations.

EMPLOYMENT ACT 1982

1 Placed much stricter controls on the closed shop by providing that all *existing* closed shops had to be approved by a very large majority in a secret ballot every five years.
2 Narrowed the definition of a 'trade dispute' so that the immunity available to union officials acting 'in contemplation or furtherance of a trade dispute' was significantly cut back. The immunity was now only to be available in 'a dispute between workers and their employer which relates wholly or mainly to' the terms and conditions of employment and closely related issues. Thus politically motivated and demarcation disputes no longer enjoyed immunity.
3 Removed immunity from *trade unions* in four cases 'if, but only if, the act was authorised or endorsed by a responsible person', i.e. a trade union official. Trade union action was now liable if
   (a) it was not taken 'in contemplation or furtherance of a trade dispute' under the new, narrower definition of a trade dispute.
   (b) it involved unlawful picketing.
   (c) it entailed unlawful secondary action, or
   (d) it was taken to impose union membership (closed shop) or recognition requirements on another employer.

This direct removal of legal immunity from trade unions in particular cases was distinctly the most radical element in the whole programme of Conservative trade union reform, and the part most feared and hated by the unions. For the first time since 1906 they were brought fairly and effectively under the law instead of being above it. Some of Mr Tebbit's cabinet colleagues thought he was going too far with this measure, and that it would be unenforceable. Subsequent events proved them wrong.

TRADE UNION ACT 1984

1   Made all trade union legal immunities conditional upon the holding of a secret ballot and a majority vote in favour of industrial action.
2   Provided that every voting member of a trade union's governing body must be elected at least every five years by secret ballot of the members.
3   Laid down that unions must keep an accurate register of members' names and addresses.
4   Required trade unions with political funds to ballot their members at least every ten years on whether they wish their union to continue to spend money on party political matters.

EMPLOYMENT ACT 1988

1   Removed all statutory support for the closed shop by
    (a) making it unfair in all circumstances to dismiss an employee for non-membership of a trade union and
    (b) making it unlawful to organise or threaten industrial action to establish or maintain a closed shop.
2   Tightened up balloting procedures.
3   Gave union members the right
    (a) not to be disciplined by their trade union if they work during a strike, cross a picket line etc.
    (b) to restrain unballoted action whatever the terms of their union's rulebook
    (c) to have access to union accounting records.
    (d) to have the 'check-off' stopped in respect of their union dues
4   Established the office of Commissioner for the Rights of Trade Union Members to assist them to enforce their rights.

EMPLOYMENT ACT 1990

1 Attempted to eliminate the closed shop by making it unlawful to refuse employment on grounds related to trade union membership.
2 Made *all* secondary action unlawful.
3 Made unions responsible for unofficial strikes by making them liable for the acts of all their officials (including shop stewards) and committees unless they have been repudiated in writing by a senior official.

The implications of this massive and largely effective programme of reform are considered in detail in chapters 3–6 following. All that remains to be said here is that in only one area - the closed shop - has the government yet claimed that its task is complete. The implication is that further steps might be taken in the future. What those further steps could be is considered in chapter 9.

3 Trade Union Immunities: The Heart of the Matter

> There can be no salvation for Britain until the special privileges granted to the trade unions three-quarters of a century ago are revoked.
>
> F. A. Hayek, *1980s Unemployment and the Unions*, 1980

Quite understandably the term 'trade union immunities' is not calculated to set the heart pounding or the pulse racing. On the contrary, because it is a technical, legal term it is likely to cause all those who do not have some legal expertise to switch off abruptly. But such a tendency must be resisted, because the existence of unconditional and practically unlimited legal immunities for trade unions and their officials from 1906 to 1980 lies at the heart of the British trade union problem and, some would say, at the heart of the economic problem too.

DEVELOPMENT OF IMMUNITIES

Every democratic society has to attempt to find a solution to the problem of the right of association. As one writer put it

> The problem to be solved, either as a matter of theory or as a matter of practical necessity, is at bottom always and everywhere the same. How can the right of combined action be contained without depriving individual liberty of half its value; how can it be left unrestricted without destroying either the liberty of individual citizens, or the power of the government?[1]

In Britain attempts to solve this problem veered from one extreme to the other between the beginning of the nineteenth and the twentieth centuries. From 1799 to 1824 all trade union activity was outlawed under the Combination Acts. Later, public opinion began to change so that in the period 1871–75 parliament legislated more favourably for the trade unions, whose membership was growing steadily. But how far were they liable for strike action, especially when that action interfered with the contracts of employment of their members, as it

20

usually did? Could employers sue for damages which, if granted by the courts, would possibly destroy the union?

Parliament had not thoroughly settled these questions in the 1870s and some decisions in the courts left them open in the 1890s. Finally in 1901 the House of Lords decided in the Taff Vale case that trade unions were corporately liable for the acts of their agents and the Amalgamated Society of Railway Servants, which had been involved in a strike against the Taff Vale Railway Company, was obliged to pay a huge sum in damages and costs.

The basic principle involved in this case was that a wrongdoer should be made to redress his wrong. For their part, the unions argued that this principle made effective strike action impossible. The outcome of this dilemma was decided not by legal principles but by political lobbying led by the trade unions and their vigorous offspring, the newly formed Labour Party. The Trade Disputes Act 1906 conceded all the demands of the union lobby, and to all intents and purposes put trade unions above the law.

A. V. Dicey, the great constitutional lawyer, wrote that

It makes a trade union a privileged body exempted from the ordinary law of the land. No such privileged body has ever before been deliberately created by an English Parliament.[2]

and Sidney and Beatrice Webb, both strongly sympathetic to the trade union and Labour Party cause, said that the Act conferred upon the unions

an extraordinary and unlimited immunity, however great may be the damage caused, and however unwarranted the act, which most lawyers, as well as all employers, regard as nothing less than monstrous.[3]

The 1906 Act was one of the shortest and most important statutes affecting the trade unions between 1875 and 1971. In two crucial clauses it gave complete unconditional legal immunity to trade unions and comprehensive immunity to their officials. Section 3 provided that union officials should have immunity whenever they were acting 'in contemplation or furtherance of a trade dispute', but even more important was Section 4, which stated that

An action against a trade union... in respect of any tortious act alleged to have been committed by or on behalf of the trade union, shall not be entertained by any court.

In plain English this meant that trade unions were above the civil law; or, in other words, they could not be sued for damages, however much they damaged an employer's business during a strike. Even more, they could not be sued for committing other unlawful acts like negligence, nuisance, breach of duty and defamation. Thus Parliament decided in 1906 that British trade unions and their officials should be protected from legal action arising out of a strike by giving them comprehensive, unconditional, *legal immunities*, and a consensus view was quickly established that these immunities were sacrosanct, like the law of the Medes and Persians.

Since the introduction of their legal immunities in 1906, the trade unions have resisted even modest curtailment of them, and until 1980 they always got their own way. In 1969 they had swept aside the proposals of the Prime Minister, Harold Wilson, and his Secretary of State for Employment, Barbara Castle; and five years later they destroyed the Tories' 1971 Industrial Relations Act when a Labour government was returned to office. During the period 1974–79 every conceivable loophole in the immunities was filled in, so that by 1979 virtually all kinds of industrial action were protected. The decision of the House of Lords in the case of *Express Newspapers* v. *Macshane* (December 1979) indicated that trade union officials could spread an industrial dispute in any way which *in their view* would help them to win it. In other words, they could cause damage to business firms or other organisations in no way connected with the original dispute without any fear of legal redress.

THE LIMITS OF THE LAW

This legislative approach to the right of association was in marked contrast to that adopted in other countries, where positive rights to strike were provided, and trade unions were constrained by a framework keeping them within the law, and it meant that

> Contrary to popular belief English law does not recognize and has never recognized a right to strike, if that is taken to mean a legally enforceable right to walk off a job whenever the worker or his union thinks fit and return in due course without penalty.[4]

It must be remembered that the legal immunities were granted to trade unions and their officials. Parliament has never given protection to trade union *members*, and consequently if a strike is called, employers have normally been within their legal rights to sack the strikers. Of course it is extremely difficult for an employer to replace his entire workforce, many of whom may be highly skilled, but one exception which proves the rule occurred in January 1986. On that occasion 5,300 production and ancillary workers producing four national newspapers in central London for News International went on strike and the proprietor, Rupert Murdoch, sacked them all. He then hired a replacement labour force of 1,300 to produce the same newspapers in a new-technology plant at Wapping, East London.

THE CONSERVATIVES' POLICY

The policy of the Conservative government since 1979 has been significantly to cut back, but not to eliminate entirely, these extensive immunities, so that by late 1990 trade unions and their officials were unquestionably inside rather than above the law.

There are various facets to this process of reducing immunities. The reductions can apply to trade unions and/or their officials. They can apply to primary and/or secondary disputes and to particular kinds of such disputes, e.g. threats or action to establish or maintain a closed shop. So the process is not a simple or straightforward one, and sometimes it might seem more appropriate to consider a reduction in immunities under a different heading. For example the Trade Union Act 1984 made all immunities conditional upon a majority vote in favour of industrial action in a secret pre-strike ballot. That particular measure could be regarded as a change in trade union immunities, or it could be seen as part of the drive to increase trade union democracy. But the truth is that practically all of the most important reforms of the 1980–90 programme have come about through a reduction in trade union immunities, and it is this reform above all others which has curbed the abuse of trade union power.

THE REDUCTION OF TRADE UNION IMMUNITIES 1980–90

Each of the five reform Acts of 1980, 1982, 1984, 1988 and 1990 has cut back the immunities in one or more ways, and the process will now be examined in some detail.

The modest 1980 Employment Act removed immunities from trade union *officials* who organised certain secondary strikes, from pickets operating away from their own work, and from all those who organised industrial action to make trade union membership compulsory. *Trade unions themselves* retained the full range of immunities which they already possessed. It will be readily understood that the impact of this measure was likely to be small, because even if the offending trade union officials and pickets could be identified – not always an easy task – they would be incapable of paying substantial damages. Even then, secondary action by employees of customers or suppliers of the employer in dispute retained immunity and James Prior, Secretary of State for Employment at the time, justified this on the grounds that sympathetic action of this kind was traditionally acceptable. In arguing like this he seemed more concerned with past custom than the need for reform, and he was determined to proceed with the utmost caution, constantly bearing in mind that previous attempts at trade union reform in 1969 and 1971 had collapsed. It cannot be claimed that this first small step made a major change to trade union law, but it was an important step none the less because it marked the first successful reversal of the 1906 immunities, and it received widespread public support.

By comparison with Mr Prior's mouse, Norman Tebbit's 1982 Employment Act was an elephant, and in terms of the restriction of trade union immunities it was much the most significant step in the reform process. To begin with it abolished special arrangements which gave trade unions a wider immunity than trade union officials or other individuals. This means that since 1982 it has been possible to seek injunctions against, and sue for damages, trade unions as well as individuals if they commit unlawful acts or organise unlawful industrial action. Secondly, the Act redefined the term 'trade dispute'. This was of critical importance, because all those who organised industrial action which interfered with contracts were now only protected by the legal immunities if they were acting 'in contemplation or furtherance of a trade dispute'. Narrowing the legal definition of a trade dispute meant that several types of dispute were now unlawful including:

- disputes between groups of workers or trade unions, eg demarcation disputes.
- disputes which are not wholly or mainly about pay and conditions of work, eg political disputes.

- disputes between workers and employers other than their own.
- disputes which relate to matters occurring overseas.
- disputes between a trade union and an employer, where none of that employer's work-force are in dispute with him.

Thus since 1982 for a trade dispute, as legally defined, to exist

- there must be a dispute between workers and their own employer.
- the dispute must be wholly or mainly about such matters as pay and conditions, jobs, allocation of work, discipline etc.

But even if a trade dispute existed, individuals or trade unions would have no immunity if they were organizing unlawful secondary action or unlawful secondary picketing as defined in the 1980 Act, or attempting to impose union membership (closed shop) or recognition requirements on another employer.

The government recognised that to expose trade unions to the full rigours of the law might be to destroy them. Consequently it set upper limits to the damages which could be awarded by the courts, and these ranged from £10,000 for unions with less than 5,000 members to £250,000 for unions with more than 100,000 members. However, those who are damaged by unlawful trade union action, eg secondary picketing, are much more interested in getting the action stopped than becoming involved in a lengthy court case to win financial compensation. What business people want is to be able to get on with their business. So the first line of defence is usually to seek a court order (an injunction) to get the action stopped. If such an order is granted and the union quickly obeys it, that may well be the end of the matter. But if it is disobeyed, then those who sought it can go back to court and seek to have those concerned declared 'in contempt of court'. The consequence of being declared 'in contempt of court' is usually, first, a large fine (without an upper limit) and, if that is not paid promptly, 'sequestration' of the union's entire assets, when court officials take over and freeze all the union's property and bank accounts, making it impossible for the union to carry out its normal functions.

From this brief account of the 1982 Act it can be seen that Mr Tebbit's chief aim was to bring the trade unions back within the law, making them accountable for their actions, without bankrupting them through excessive damages and without trade union leaders being locked up in prison for organising unlawful disputes. The chief remedy was to lie against trade union funds *not* trade union officials. The strategy was very carefully thought through and executed with speed and boldness. But would it be effective? The trade unions had been above the law for 76 years and many prophesied that such a drastic change would be unenforceable. Would any employer be brave enough to test the new law? And if so, what would be the result?

MESSENGER NEWSPAPERS LTD v. *NATIONAL GRAPHICAL ASSOCIATION*

The first major test of the new legislation occurred at Warrington, Lancashire, late in 1983. Eddy Shah, chairman of the Stockport Messenger Group, which provided free weekly newspapers, decided to employ some non-union labour at his printing plant. This initiative was strongly opposed by the National Graphical Association (NGA), a union which is committed to the closed shop and other restrictive practices and includes most skilled print workers in the UK. Shah dismissed six NGA employees who objected to his new policy and they were soon joined on the picket lines outside his factory by many other NGA members determined to prevent the printing and distribution of his newspapers. This action, deliberately organised by the union, was a flagrant violation of the new laws which made secondary picketing unlawful.

Shah duly sought injunctions against the NGA to stop the mass picketing and to prevent the union from bringing pressure on advertisers to boycott the Messenger papers. Both injunctions were granted on 14 November 1983 but the unlawful action continued and three days later the Manchester Crown Court fined the union £50,000 for contempt. On 22 November the NGA national council decided not to pay the fine, and mass picketing with occasional violence continued at the Warrington plant.

On 25 November the High Court fined the NGA a further £100,000 and ordered the sequestration (confiscation by court officials) of £175,000 from the union to settle its debt. On the same day the union decided to call a two-day stoppage of national newspapers and seven national papers were subsequently granted a High Court injunction banning a repetition of the stoppage which occurred on 26 and 27 November.

Talks between Shah and the NGA came to a halt on 9 December when the union was fined £525,000 in the High Court. Finally on 18 January 1984 the union's national council decided to accept defeat and purge its contempt of court in order to unfreeze its assets of about £10 million which had been frozen since November. The total cost to the union of its unlawful action was about £1 million.

Thus quite quickly after its introduction the new legislation was shown to be completely effective. The consequences of this case were profound, because the NGA and its fellow union SOGAT (Society of Graphical and Allied Trades) have long resisted the efficient introduction of new technology in the national newspaper industry. Two years after his legal victory early in 1984 Mr Shah published a new national newspaper (*Today*) using all the latest technology, and many commentators believe that he was the catalyst which produced a revolution in that industry between 1986 and 1989. So legal reform had a rapid and far-reaching effect on the economy.[5]

The 1982 Act was a landmark, but the government had not yet touched a major problem which had been swept under the carpet for many years – the problem of trade union democracy. This is dealt with in more detail in chapter 6, but a few words must be said about it here because the Trade Union Act 1984 attempted to promote trade union democracy through the medium of reducing legal immunity.

THE PRE-STRIKE SECRET BALLOT

The approach of the 1984 Act was simple, direct and in some respects effective. All legal immunity for industrial disputes endorsed by trade unions was made conditional on a majority vote in a secret ballot in favour of the action by the union members involved. The only disputes not covered by this provision were unofficial ones, many of which were local and brief. The nature of the ballot was also prescribed in some detail – for example, ballots have to be held not more than four weeks before the start of industrial action – but these were subsidiary details in comparison with the Act's main provision.

Because this measure was widely supported by trade union members and the electorate as a whole, and because failure to comply would leave trade unions open to heavy damages, pre-strike secret ballots came into general use after the date laid down in the Act – 1 October 1985 – and hundreds of such ballots have now been held. The principle that trade union immunities should not be complete and unconditional, but rather should be restricted in order to modify trade union behaviour, was becoming established. However, the nature of this particular condition needs to be briefly considered.

The introduction of the pre-strike ballot seemed to be based on the assumption that union members are less militant than their officials. But will that always be the case? And is it not likely that the ballot will often be used simply as a tactic in negotiations? In providing that trade union immunities should be conditional on a successful pre-strike ballot, Parliament said nothing about the reasonableness or otherwise of the union's claim. Nor did Parliament provide that a strike should always be a last resort, after all other possible methods of settling the dispute had been exhausted. There is nothing in the law to prevent the members of a monopolistic trade union in an essential public or privatised service from voting in favour of a grossly excessive pay claim and then claiming immunity for their union as provided by Parliament. In fact, by making union immunity conditional on a pre-strike ballot, Parliament in effect transferred its legislative function in the area of industrial action to union members. There must be major doubts about the wisdom of this approach as a long-term legislative arrangement.

THE 1988 AND 1990 ACTS

The Employment Act 1988 was mainly concerned with providing rights for trade union members, but it did further restrict trade union immunity at one point. Until 1988 an employer could not take legal proceedings against a trade union which called or threatened industrial action to promote or maintain a closed shop among his own employees, provided that the union members had voted in favour of such action. Section 10 of the 1988 Act changed this by removing immunity from such action regardless of the members' views.

Two years later the Employment Act 1990 took three further steps to reduce immunities, after unofficial strike action on the London Underground had seriously inconvenienced millions of commuters in the south-east.

First, it removed immunity from the acts of all trade union officials (including shop stewards) and committees unless such acts were repudiated in writing 'as soon as reasonably practicable' by the principal executive committee or general secretary. This meant that unofficial action, if not quickly repudiated, would make a trade union legally liable, and it was intended to produce a marked reduction in the level of such activity.

Secondly, it removed immunity from *all* secondary action, apart from peaceful picketing at the pickets' own place of work, including action at customers or suppliers of the firm at which the primary dispute occurred. It will be remembered that in 1980 Mr Prior had insisted on retaining these exceptions on the grounds that sympathetic strikes of this kind were traditional. Nine years later Norman Fowler wisely decided to end that particular tradition.

Thirdly – and this was a relatively minor point – the Act made pre-strike ballots obligatory for those who work under contracts for services rather than contracts of employment.

The failure of the two attempts to reform trade union law in 1969 and 1971, together with the destruction by the trade unions of Mr Heath's government in 1974 and Mr Callaghan's in 1979, suggested that Henry C Simons was remarkably prescient when he wrote in 1944 about monopolistic trade unions:

> Here, possibly, is an awful dilemma: democracy cannot live with tight occupational monopolies; and it cannot destroy them, once they attain great power, without destroying itself in the process.[6]

In Britain significant reform of the trade unions in the 1980s depended on the substantial reduction of the unlimited, unconditional immunities which Parliament had so rashly provided in 1906. Once excessive privilege has been conceded, it is extremely difficult to claw it back. Fortunately in 1979 a change in public opinion coincided with the election of a new government headed by a Prime Minister who recognised what needed to be done and was determined to do it. The reduction of immunity, which has brought trade unions back within the rule of law, was central to the whole process of reform and has brought considerable benefits not only to the general public, but also to trade union members themselves.

4   The Closed Shop

It cannot be stressed enough that the coercion which unions have been permitted to exercise contrary to all principles of freedom under the law is primarily the coercion of fellow workers.

F. A. Hayek, *The Constitution of Liberty*, 1960

Trade union power, which usually goes hand in hand with coercion, does not develop in a vacuum. It is derived from changes in the law and in custom and practice which transfer responsibility from the individual employee to the collective body. The emphasis on trade union 'solidarity' produces a conviction that members of a trade union always have common interests and think and speak with one mind. But the members themselves know differently. Even when their interests are under attack, perhaps because of actual or threatened pay cuts and redundancies, there are substantial differences in opinion. The period 1980–83 saw severe redundancies in British manufacturing industry. Often the immediate reaction of trade union officials to the announcement of proposed redundancies was complete opposition. But quite quickly they had to back down as many employees came forward to accept redundancy, especially where it was accompanied by a silver handshake. This meant that frequently most redundancies were voluntary and only a minority of redundant employees were laid off against their will.

The problem for the full time trade union official, who gave up work at the bench or the desk years ago, is how to overcome these differences of opinion when the union goes to war, i.e. engages in industrial action. And the principal methods of ensuring that everyone falls into line are two: the closed shop and picketing.

The first thing which needs to be said is that if the closed shop in Britain grew rapidly in the 1960s and 1970s (as it did), there is nothing new about it. The Webbs stated that 'the exclusion of non-unionists is .... coeval with Trade Unionism itself'[1] and they went on to say

It is, in fact, as impossible for a non-unionist plater or riveter to get work in a Tyneside shipyard, as it is for him to take a house in Newcastle without paying the rates. This silent and unseen, but absolutely complete compulsion, is the ideal of every Trade Union.[2]

So the debate about the closed shop goes immediately to the heart of the debate about the proper nature of trade unionism in a free society, which Hayek has defined as 'that condition of men in which coercion of some by others is reduced as much as is possible'.[3] Petro put the same idea in a slightly different way when he wrote that 'The basic institution of the free society is personal freedom'[4] and of course personal freedom is incompatible with compulsory association. The man who has acquired a skill as a hole-borer, and then has to join the Amalgamated Society of Hole-Borers and accept its rules and discipline before he can exercise his trade, has given up an important part of his personal freedom. If ordered to strike he has to obey although he might be entirely satisfied with the pay and conditions of work on offer. It is difficult to see how there can be any meeting of minds between the collectivist, who regards the closed shop as a necessary and desirable aim for the trade union, and those who believe that personal freedom is the most important aspect of society, arising as it does out of our God-given free-will.

The second thing which needs to be said about the closed shop is that it cannot operate without agreement (implicit or explicit) from the employer. Consider how a non-union shop becomes closed. First the union organises a minority of employees. Second, the minority becomes a majority. Third, the union demands recognition and collective bargaining from the employer, with the demand being backed up by a strike-threat. So the employer concedes. Finally the union claims that non-members are benefiting from the collective bargaining and demands (once again backed by a strike threat) that the shop should be closed. Again the employer concedes, and he has now formed an unholy collectivist alliance with the trade union which ensures that union membership is an absolute condition of employment in that shop.

The trade union arguments seem so reasonable and plausible – yet they are based on a fallacy and the closed shop eventually does immense damage to the business. The chief fallacy lies in the union's final argument that non-members are benefiting from collective bargaining. The truth is that collective bargaining in Britain in the twentieth century has normally gone hand-in-hand with union imposed restrictive practices which reduce rather than increase output and profitability in the companies concerned. Lower profits mean lower investment, and in the longer term real wages fall. Collective bargaining also has the effect of causing employers to consider their employees en masse instead of as individuals with different abilities and talents. They tend to deal with them second hand, through a shop steward, and problems are exacerbated rather than solved. In other words collective bargaining, unaccompanied by regular appraisal of individual employees, is a lazy employer's way of dealing with his workforce. The closed shop adds compulsion to laziness and means that employers are less likely to get the best out of their most important asset – the people they employ.

Between 1963 and 1979 the number of employees covered by the closed shop in Britain increased from a minimum of 3.76 million to a minimum of 5.18 million.[5] In the light of the above analysis, it is not surprising that this large and rapid increase in compulsory unionism was accompanied by a severe deterioration in the performance of several major industries. Most obvious among these was the motor industry which until the 1950s had been a world leader, with the Japanese using some British designs in a rather feeble attempt to catch up. Yet by the late 1970s it had become a symbol of low quality and productivity at home and a laughing stock abroad.

*   *   *

Recognition of the importance of personal freedom as a key element in the achievement of the free society has been central to Mrs Thatcher's political philosophy. It is, therefore, understandable that turning back the tide of the closed shop, if not eliminating it altogether, was a high priority for her government in 1979. But how had the law encouraged the expansion of the closed shop before 1979? And how did the Thatcher government discourage it? These questions must now be explored.

THE CLOSED SHOP AND THE LAW BEFORE 1980

Before 1971 the question of the closed shop was more a matter of custom and practice than a bone of legal contention. Cases did arise, especially when the closed shop prevailed and trade unions either refused to admit new members or expelled existing members, but most closed shops were simply informal, unwritten agreements which continued because employers did not wish to challenge them. On the contrary, encouraged by academics like McCarthy who accepted 'the general justifiability of both the pre- and post-entry closed shop'[6] employers often preferred the closed shop as a convenient method of maintaining the fiction that the shop stewards could speak for the whole workforce. But 1971 was a watershed when the right not to be unfairly dismissed was introduced by the Industrial Relations Act. That development raised a straightforward question: was it 'fair' to dismiss an employee for not being a union member when a closed shop (technically a 'union membership agreement') existed? Most of the many changes in the law on the closed shop since 1971 have been connected with the different ways in which governments have answered that question.

There is no need to examine the complex closed shop provisions of the 1971 Act in detail because they were relatively ineffective and the Act was repealed in 1974. Suffice it to say that the intention was to produce a rough balance between the right to join a trade union (which has been consistently protected since 1971) and the right not to join. However, the strong tide of collectivism made the new law incapable of protecting the right not to join. Existing closed shops were maintained and new ones were formed, for example in the engineering industry. The aim of those who drafted the 1971 Act was to protect individual rights, but this aim was not achieved, and when the Labour Government was returned to office in 1974 the collectivist tide was soon in full flood.

The 1971 Act was repealed by the Trade Union and Labour Relations Act 1974 (TULRA), and, soon after the Labour Government achieved an overall majority, TULRA 1974 was supplemented by the Trade Union and Labour Relations (Amendment) Act 1976. The net effect of these two pieces of legislation was to maintain the right to join a trade union while eliminating the right not to join, where a closed shop existed, except for that tiny minority who could prove that they genuinely objected 'on grounds of religious belief to being a member of any trade union whatsoever'. These changes were not made inadvertently. They were an indication that the Labour Government was determined to give priority to collectivism at the expense of individual liberty and freedom of conscience.

The effect of TULRA 1974 and 1976 was to encourage a major expansion of the closed shop. Trade unions requested this and many employers conceded it. Among them was British Rail, who negotiated a closed shop with the National Union of Railwaymen, the Associated Society of Locomotive Engineers and Firemen, and the Transport Salaried Staffs' Association in 1975. At the time more than 90 per cent of BR employees were union members, but that still left several thousand outside the union. How were they to be treated? BR's policy was quite simple. Non-members were given an ultimatum: 'Join your appropriate union by the due date or be sacked without compensation'. When it is appreciated that the National Union of Railwaymen had as its slogan 'Workers of the world unite' (the concluding exhortation of the Communist Manifesto) and that the senior officials all had to be paid up members of the Labour Party, it can be understood that at least a few of those non-members were rather reluctant to join their appropriate union.

However, the position of these non-members must be considered. The truth is that victims of the closed shop have very few friends. By the trade union they are regarded as free-riders who pick up the benefits of collective bargaining without paying for them, while the employer sees them as trouble makers who upset the neat and tidy arrangement of compulsory unionism. Once the law had stripped these victims of legal redress through the Industrial Tribunals, it seemed that their plight was hopeless. But some help, at least, was at hand. A group of activists who were deeply concerned about the way in which individual rights were being suppressed met in July 1975 and in December of that year the formation of the National Association for Freedom (NAFF) was announced at a press conference. (Not long afterwards the slang word 'naff' with its derogatory overtones came into general use and the National Association for Freedom became The Freedom Association.)

The reaction to this announcement was understandably sceptical. One reason for this was that most of those who worked for the media were members of closed shop unions and had learned to live with this aspect of the prevailing collectivist philosophy. But it was easy to underestimate the tenacity of those who led NAFF, their small group of paid staff and the determination of the members. NAFF achieved a notable success in 1977 when it prevented a vast mob of flying pickets, with Arthur Scargill sometimes in attendance as 'marshal', from closing the north London factory of film processors Grunwick. But over the past fifteen years many of its most important successes have been relatively low-key, involving support for the otherwise friendless victims of the closed shop. Three of these victims, Messrs Young, James and Webster, had been dismissed by British Rail for refusing to join the appropriate trade union and in 1976 NAFF decided to assist them to appeal to the European Court at Strasbourg on the grounds that the existing UK law on the closed shop allowed for the infringement of Article 11 of the European Convention on Human Rights, and that such an infringement had taken place in this case.

Legislation is often expensive and slow. That is doubly true of cases before the European Court, which are heard as cases between the applicants and their own government. It was a full five years before the 21 judges of the Court ruled by a majority of 18 to 3 that the dismissal of the three railwaymen violated Article 11 of the European Convention on Human Rights, and another year before they were compensated. The applicants were totally vindicated and the Labour government's closed shop legislation was condemned. But the costs of the case were £75,000 and success would not have been achieved without The Freedom Association's support.[7] The fact is that between 1975 and 1981 The Freedom Association played a crucial role in tapping public sympathy for victims of the closed shop when it seemed that the well of support for personal freedom had practically run dry, and it still has a job to do.

Understandably the 1979 Conservative Manifesto included a promise to change the law on the closed shop, and the following words appeared on page 10:

People arbitrarily excluded or expelled from any union must be given the right of appeal to a court of law. Existing employees and those with personal conviction must be adequately protected, and if they lose their jobs as a result of a closed shop they must be entitled to ample compensation.

In addition, all agreements for a closed shop must be drawn up in line with the best practice followed at present and only if an overwhelming majority of the workers involved vote for it by a secret ballot.

This modest pledge was translated into law in Sections 4–10 of the 1980 Employment Act, and that legislation has subsequently been supplemented by the Employment Acts of 1982, 1988 and 1990, so that today the government's hostility to compulsory unionism is crystal clear. The progress of this programme of reform must now be reviewed.

THE EMPLOYMENT ACT 1980

With hindsight, the provisions of this Act appear extremely modest. That is not surprising as its architect, James (now Lord) Prior, had vivid memories of the failure of the 1971 Industrial Relations Act and was determined to avoid a repeat of that fiasco. Consequently his first step was hardly more than a soft shoe shuffle. The manifesto pledge quoted above was precisely fulfilled, but no attempt was made to reduce the numerous closed shops which existed. That was thought to be far too dangerous an assault on trade union power. Prior's policy was seen as cautious and wise, or simply 'wet', depending on one's point of view. The latter view could have been supported by that lengthy section in the accompanying Code of Practice which explained how to negotiate a new closed shop once the Act was in force. However, in contrast to 1971 the 1980 Act stuck, it provided the opportunity for some closed shop victims to pursue their cases successfully at the Industrial Tribunals, and it paved the way for the tougher 1982 Act. For these reasons alone perhaps it deserves to be rated as a successful initial onslaught on the large edifice of compulsory unionism. And its more vigorous successor was not long in making its appearance.

THE EMPLOYMENT ACT 1982

Although it happened in 1981, one wonders whether the Department of Employment has yet recovered from the shock of the appointment of Norman Tebbit to succeed James Prior. That Department has long been the supreme example of the proponent of 'consensus' policies, extremely loath to do or say anything which would upset the Trades Union Congress. Norman Tebbit was an inspired choice to implement Thatcherite policies and his tenure of office as Secretary of State for Employment was marked by a sustained onslaught on the closed shop as well as other collectivist policies.

To begin with, he showed his contempt for the dark days of 1974 to 1980 by providing compensation for people dismissed for non-membership of a trade union during that period when they had no redress in the UK. With the help of The Freedom Association several hundred people proved a valid claim. Then he prohibited 'union labour only' and 'union recognition' requirements in contracts. But most important of all, he introduced legal provisions to undermine existing closed shops. There were two main aspects of this policy. First, dismissal for non-membership of a union in the context of a closed shop became automatically unfair if the agreement had not been approved by an overwhelming majority of employees covered (80%

of those eligible to vote or 85% of those voting) in a secret ballot. Second, the level of financial compensation for unfair dismissal in closed shop cases was substantially increased so that in 1990 terms the victim of a blatant case might be awarded £30,000 or even more. The 1980 Act had already enabled employers to 'join' the appropriate trade union as a party to such cases and thus to make them wholly or partly liable for any compensation awarded. Clearly Norman Tebbit's intention was to make the level of compensation punitive on employers and unions who ganged up against individual employees who insisted on their right not to associate.

By 1986 as many as 116 closed shop ballots had been held and 91 of them achieved the necessary majority. But the fact that these 91 agreements covered only 30,000 employees[8] indicates that they were among small, tight-knit groups. The vast majority of employees covered by closed shops after 1st November 1984 (the date by which ballots had to be held) had not voted for them and consequently the employers and unions concerned would have found themselves in serious difficulties at an industrial tribunal hearing if an employee had been dismissed for non-union membership. The closed shop had been weakened. But was it dying? And if so, was this the consequence of the legislation or of other factors?

That the closed shop reached a peak in 1978–79 and started to shrink thereafter there is no doubt. Gennard's survey produced a figure of 'at least 5.2 million' employees covered in 1978, but Millward and Stevens estimated that by 1984 the figure had fallen to between 3.5 and 3.7 million.[9] However, as unemployment soared in the period 1980–83 it was exactly those industries and sectors in which the closed shop was most prevalent which suffered most heavily from redundancies, eg steel, mining, ship-building and manufacturing. But if the primary cause of the shrinkage in the closed shop was falling employment in some traditional industries, the change in public opinion, and the Employment Acts of 1980 and 1982 which were the public expression of that change, were important secondary causes. Employers and trade unions were now much more cautious about imposing compulsory unionism on groups of employees and some major employers publicly announced the abandonment of their closed shops.

The 1980 and 1982 Acts were encouraging the closed shop to shrink. But the government's attitude towards it was still equivocal. The government was still not saying that the closed shop was always an unacceptable infringement of personal freedom; only that it was unacceptable unless a large majority of the relevant employees had voted in favour of it. But in 1988 they took another step.

THE EMPLOYMENT ACT 1988

David (later Lord) Young had shown very little interest in employment law during his tenure as Secretary of State for Employment but his successor, Norman Fowler, knew from his own experience as a journalist on *The Times* about the impact of the closed shop. After a six year legislative lull in this area the 1988 Act went significantly further than its predecessors *by making dismissal for non-membership of a trade union (or action short of dismissal) unfair in all circumstances.* At the same time it removed immunity from trade unions which organise or threaten industrial action designed to establish or maintain a closed shop.

The nettle was now firmly grasped and the government's intentions were made clear – compulsory unionism is unacceptable, full stop. The argument that closed shops were traditional in certain (usually very inefficient) industries no longer cut any ice and for the first time the right *not* to join a union was put on a par with the right to join. But as has been suggested in this chapter, the closed shop is a plant (or perhaps one should say 'tree') with very deep roots, and it is extremely difficult to change overnight the custom and practice of decades or even centuries. A sample survey carried out by National Opinion Polls on behalf of the Department of Employment early in 1989 indicated that about 2.6 million employees still thought of themselves as covered by the closed shop and that half of these were covered by a pre-entry closed shop. In other words they either had to be a member of the appropriate union before being considered for the job; or they had to join that union before starting work. The Green Paper of March 1989 which revealed these figures went on to say that

> The pre-entry closed shop therefore remains widespread – indeed, significantly more so than previously estimated. There are concentrations in shipping, printing, manufacturing, the theatre and the London wholesale markets. It is also present in construction and road haulage and is found across all major sectors of the economy, largely reflecting its importance in the traditional craft occupations.[10]

It was time for another step.

THE EMPLOYMENT ACT 1990

In the House of Commons on 19 January 1990, moving the second reading of the Bill, Michael Howard, Employment Secretary, stated that the government were taking the final step in making the closed shop unlawful. The intention of Sections 1–3 of what became the Employment Act 1990 in October of that year was to end the pre-entry closed shop by giving to those who are refused employment on the grounds of membership or non-membership of a trade union the right to complain to an industrial tribunal, with the possibility of receiving financial compensation of up to £8,925. Tony Blair, Labour's employment spokesman in the Commons, found himself in acute difficulties over this proposal because in 1989 the Labour Party had warmly embraced the European Community's 'Charter of Fundamental Social Rights'. And Clause 11 of that Charter gives every employer and worker 'the freedom to join *or not to join*' (emphasis supplied) professional organizations or trade unions of their choice 'without any personal or occupational damage being thereby suffered by him'. Until December 1989 such an even-handed approach to the right of association was anathema to the Labour Party and many trade unions. But by a delightful irony the Social Charter acknowledges the importance of voluntary association. In this area at least the continental Europeans have a better understanding of freedom than their British counterparts.

The pre-entry closed shop is, of course, the toughest nut of all and it is still too early to say whether the 1990 Act will crack it. The government should survey the situation again in 1992 and take appropriate action if any traces of the closed shop remain.

CONCLUSION: THE IMPORTANCE OF THE CLOSED SHOP

Many of those concerned with human resource management may see the closed shop as a side issue which is blown up out of proportion by those who feel passionately about personal freedom. That is not the view taken here. Surely there is no more important issue in employment affairs than the question of whether an employer sees, and deals with, his employees directly as individuals or indirectly, through a shop steward, as trade union members. The introduction of collective bargaining suggests that an employer is taking the latter view, but so long as at least a few employees remain outside the union there is some obligation to deal with them as individuals. However, once the shop is closed, individual negotiation dies, the union members become subservient to a collective will which cannot possibly represent their individual aspirations, and the employer hands over a key part of the management function to the union. That arrangement then becomes part of the status quo and the conventional wisdom insists that reform is impossible.

So the existence or absence of a closed shop, in the context of the British economy, has been a touchstone of competent management. In some key areas like the national press, the docks and the motor industry, where closed shops existed for several decades, it was true to say not that management was incompetent but that it was non-existent. Thus the Thatcher government's determination to reduce the closed shop to minimal proportions has had a doubly beneficial effect. First, it has given several million actual or would-be employees the right to make a free choice about trade union membership. Second, and almost as important, it has forced managers to think about employees as individuals rather than trade union members bound by rules and restrictions over which they have no control. There are already signs that this different approach by management can produce a large increase in quality and productivity and, as the message that the closed shop is unacceptable is more widely received and understood, this favourable trend should develop further.

5　Picketing

To permit strikers to congregate at the scene
of the labor dispute is to invite violence.

S. Petro, *The Labor Policy of the Free Society*, 1957

Every aspect of trade union law is contentious, but none more so than that which relates to picketing. Picketing and strikes go together like bread and cheese, and this has been true for 200 years and more. The existence of pickets means that the strikers are aware that others would probably be willing to work for wages and conditions which they themselves find unacceptable. The objective of picketing is ostensibly to notify others that there is an industrial dispute in progress. But it often quickly deteriorates into a crude attempt to prevent those who want to work from doing so by threats, intimidation and sheer force of numbers. This problem was at the forefront of the minds of the nineteenth century reformers, who had a keen sense of personal freedom and readily understood that to legislate in favour of collective action at the workplace was always to run the risk of neglecting the interests of those who might prefer working to striking. In the twentieth century much has been written and spoken about 'the right to strike', but 'the right to work' is rarely mentioned.

PICKETING AND INTIMIDATION

The British approach has always been to make picketing unlawful whenever it involves any kind of violence or intimidation. This was so clearly spelt out in the Conspiracy and Protection of Property Act 1875 that doubts arose about the legality even of peaceful picketing. Consequently Section 2 (1) of the Trade Disputes Act 1906 provided that

It shall be lawful for one or more persons, acting on their own behalf or on behalf of a trade union or of an individual employer or firm in contemplation or furtherance of a trade dispute, to attend at or near a house or place where a person resides or works or carries on business or happens to be, *if they so attend merely for the purpose of peacefully obtaining or communicating information, or of peacefully*

41

persuading any person to work or abstain from working. (emphasis supplied)

Thus the intention of Parliament in the twentieth century has consistently been to allow pickets peacefully to explain what is going on, but *not* to obstruct those who wish to cross the picket line to go to work. Where it seems that an excessive number of pickets might prevent those who wish to work from doing so, it is the unhappy lot of the police to enforce the law. In so doing, they usually appear to be taking sides against the strikers.

During the 1970s, violent and intimidatory picketing, which was of course unlawful, became increasingly common. People with no direct connection with an industrial dispute (including perhaps a few Labour Members of Parliament) would appear on the picket line with the deliberate intention of preventing those who wanted to work from doing so. A classic case occurred at the firm of film processors Grunwick in north London in 1977 when the strike committee announced that

> The mass picketing will now be continuing until a settlement is reached. Our Union is asking for all Unions at national level to send large regular delegations and we are calling for the largest possible turnout daily from 6.30 am onwards. Please report to the Strike Headquarters at the address below.[1]

After this dispute had been settled the Scarman Court of Inquiry, which had been set up specifically to investigate it, reporting to the Secretary of State for Employment, stated that

> We . . . welcome your announcement in an answer in the House of Commons on 12 July that the Government has under review the law relating to picketing.[2]

But for a government minister to say that a particular matter is 'under review' often means, as in this case, that nothing will be done. Ministers and their civil servants are reviewing lots of matters most of the time.

Subsequently, the whole issue of intimidatory and secondary picketing came to a head during the winter of discontent. Thus it was not surprising that a section of the 1979 Conservative Manifesto was devoted to picketing and that it included promises to ensure that the protection of the law is available to those not concerned in the dispute but who at present can suffer severely from secondary action (picketing, blacking and blockading) and to make any further changes [in the law] that are necessary so that a citizen's right to work and go about his or her lawful business free from intimidation or obstruction is guaranteed.[3]

KEEPING THE PLEDGES

The 1980 Employment Act made secondary picketing – that is, picketing at a place other than a picket's own place of work – unlawful. At the same time the Act gave the Secretary of State for Employment powers to 'issue Codes of Practice containing such practical guidance as he thinks fit for the purpose of promoting the improvement of industrial relations' and a Code of Practice on Picketing was issued to come into effect in December 1980. That Code, which is a statement in plain English of the law on picketing, is still valid, but the law was amended in 1982 when it was made possible to sue trade unions as well as trade union organisers for unlawful acts.

Essentially the Code emphasises that only peaceful picketing is lawful – and there is nothing new about that. But it did introduce two new elements into the situation. The first of these was the one already mentioned, that only primary picketing is now permitted by the law.

The second was to limit the number of pickets who could turn up at the factory gates. This rule was contained only in the Code and does not, therefore, have the force of law but is admissible in evidence and may be taken into account in proceedings before any court or industrial tribunal.

The restriction on numbers is to be found in that section of the Code which is concerned with 'Limiting Numbers of Pickets', and begins with the statement that 'The main cause of violence and disorder on the picket line is excessive numbers'. Numerous incidents over the past twenty years testify to the truth of this remark. The fact is that mass picketing is *always* intimidatory and therefore unlawful. Most people go to work in ones or twos: to be faced with an ugly mob at the entrance to the workplace is extremely unnerving, especially when it is combined with spitting and abusive threats. Mass picketing by its very nature cannot be only for the purpose of peacefully obtaining or communicating information or peacefully persuading a person to work or not to work. Because this was recognised by those who drafted the Code, they included a statement that

> pickets and their organisers should ensure that in general the number of pickets does not exceed six at any entrance to a workplace; frequently a smaller number will be appropriate.

This part of the Code immediately raises the question: why was it not written in to the law instead of the Code? Presumably it was felt that there would be great difficulty in enforcing such a law. But if that is so, is it not an admission that the government is incapable of providing for purely peaceful picketing? And in that case, should not picketing be banned altogether?

The 1980 Act was soon supplemented by the Employment Act 1982, and the effect of the latter was to enable those damaged by unlawful (secondary) picketing to seek an injunction or damages against the *trade union* concerned. Under the earlier Act remedies could only be sought from the pickets or trade union officials, and some employers would have felt that such action was simply not worthwhile. The 1983 case of *Messenger Newspapers Ltd* v. *National Graphical Association*, discussed in chapter 3, was a classic example of the effective use of the new law. Mr Shah, as chief executive of Messenger Newspapers, would have had great difficulty in first identifying and then getting any satisfactory remedy from the pickets or their organisers.

Several years later, sections 3 and 5 of the Employment Act 1988 gave trade union members who want to walk through a picket line further protection. These sections provide that trade unions may not discipline members who

- go to work despite a call to take strike or other industrial action
- cross a picket line
- speak out against industrial action
- refuse to pay a levy to fund industrial action

and this was another major step in providing a genuine right to work. Not surprisingly this part of the Act produced outrage among those many senior trade union officials and Labour party politicians who do not recognise the existence of such a right.

HOW EFFECTIVE A LAW?

Finally, mention should be made of the massive campaign of intimidatory, secondary picketing deliberately carried out by the National Union of Mineworkers during their strike of 1984–85 (see chapter 8 for more detail). Was this not evidence that the new laws were ineffective? It was suggested at the beginning of this chapter that the law on picketing is especially contentious, and it is a matter for those who are damaged by unlawful industrial action, including picketing, to decide whether or when it will help them to use the law. The unlawful picketing from March 1984 onwards meant that the National Coal Board had an open and shut case against the NUM. In fact within a few days of the start of the strike Mr Justice Nolan had granted an injunction, at the request of the NCB, banning secondary picketing. The injunction was flagrantly defied, but for reasons which have never been adequately explained the NCB did not return to court for a declaration of contempt. Apparently Mr MacGregor, Chairman of the NCB, and the politicians most immediately connected with the dispute, especially Peter Walker, Energy Minister, took the view that such action would unite the whole trade union movement behind the NUM, and that it was too big a risk to take. Others, including the officials of the Police Federation, whose members bore the brunt of the mass, secondary picketing organised by the union over a period of ten months, were understandably disgusted by the NCB's failure to use a law which had been provided for exactly that kind of situation.[4]

A similar set of circumstances occurred at Wapping early in 1986, when News International dismissed its entire central London labour force and re-located its printing in a secret new plant. Rowdy, mass picketing took place over many weeks, despite a very large police presence and legal action against one of the unions concerned.

Perhaps the lesson to be learned is that the law is enforced with difficulty where the passions and emotions of hundreds or thousands of people are involved. But enforced it must be in a democracy which accepts the rule of law. And conceivably the marked reduction in mass picketing since 1986 means that respect for, and acceptance of, the new law is growing, and public opinion is coming to see that peaceful picketing should mean what it says. Since Mr Callaghan encouraged people to cross picket lines in 1979, his advice has been followed on numerous occasions.

6 Trade Union Democracy and the Role of the TUC

The fundamental problem of [trade union] democracy is the combination of administrative efficiency and popular control

S. and B. Webb, *Industrial Democracy*, 1902

Too many strikes and too much picketing were the most obvious symptoms of Britain's industrial relations problem in the 1970s. But why did employees strike so easily? Was it because they wanted to, or because they were forced to? After all, where closed shops existed, those who disobeyed union instructions were running the risk of expulsion from the union and loss of their jobs. The Conservative Party took the view that many strikes were caused by a minority of militants, often politically motivated, who dominated certain trade unions. Hence the statement in their 1979 Manifesto that

> Too often trade unions are dominated by a handful of extremists who do not reflect the common-sense views of most union members.

The truth of this dogmatic pronouncement would only be tested over a period of several years.

Because trade unions regularly accuse employers of acting in a high-handed, undemocratic way, one might expect them to be especially sensitive to the charge of acting undemocratically themselves. But that has often not been so. To begin with, the system of block voting so long employed at the Trades Union Congress and Labour Party Conference has long been widely criticised as inherently undemocratic. Senior officials of a trade union, who are supposed to represent the members, hold up a card representing so many thousand or million votes in favour of a motion – eg unilateral nuclear disarmament – about which none of the members have had the opportunity to express an opinion! Also, many unions, including some of the biggest, have sought extra members almost without regard to the problem of democracy, which grows rapidly as membership increases. The twin aims of political influence and administrative efficiency have pushed popular control into a poor third place. This became obvious in 1952 with the publication of Goldstein's classic book subtitled *A Study of Apathy and the Democratic Process in the Transport and General Workers Union.*[1]

The TGWU since its formation by Ernest Bevin in 1922 has set the tone of the Labour Party and the trade union movement. First, because of its large membership (more than 300,000 in 1922, reaching a peak of 2,086,281 in 1971) the TGWU has had the biggest block vote at the Trades Union Congress and the Labour Party Conference. Second, for 28 years after the opening in 1928 of Transport House in Smith Square, London, the union was host and landlord to the TUC and the Labour Party, and after the TUC moved to Great Russell Street in 1956 it continued as landlord to the Labour Party for another 24 years, until the latter's move to Walworth Road in 1980. And today the union sponsors several Labour Members of Parliament, including Neil Kinnock. So the TGWU's influence is all-pervasive in the Labour movement, and the presence or absence of the democratic process in that giant union is of crucial importance to the British political system.

Goldstein could not have written his study without the full co-operation of the members and officials of the union, including Arthur Deakin, the General Secretary, and the officers and members of 'Branch 1/AAA' in south London. In theory, union democracy operates through the participation of lay members in branch activities, including ballot elections for officials. Goldstein described how such an election for Area 1 Representatives to the General Executive Council took place in the 1/AAA Branch:

Sister Johnson, the Branch Secretary, received from Area 1 Office on behalf of the Branch, 1,000 ballot papers for distribution to approximately 950 eligible members. These ballots were divided into thirty packets each containing one ballot for each eligible member of the 'constituency' of the Shop Steward for whom the packet was designated. In all but a very few cases the distribution of these packets did not go beyond Brother Vinson, Convener of Shop Stewards and C.P. (Communist Party) member. Both Sister Johnson and Brother Vinson gave almost identical descriptions of the voting procedure that followed:

A few packets were distributed to Shop Stewards who might have been suspicious if they had not received them. A group of Shop Stewards, all members of the inner circle, gathered around a table one evening and with varied coloured pencils proceeded to place crosses by the names of C.P. candidates Papworth and Jones. To give the appearance of authenticity, only 432 of the 518 ballots cast in this way supported the Branch's favourites. This deceptive record indicates that approximately 55 per cent of the eligible membership participated in this election, while close to 1 per cent would be a more accurate figure.[2]

Comment on this episode is superfluous, and it is hardly surprising that at the end of his study Goldstein emphasised the apathy of rank and file members and argued that

> it becomes difficult to avoid the conclusion that the Transport and General Workers Union is an oligarchy at every level of its structure, failing to elicit the active participation of its members.[3]

If that was true in 1947 when the TGWU had 1,317,000 members, how much truer was it in 1979 when membership exceeded two million and the proportion of trade unionists covered by the closed shop had significantly increased. Compulsory membership means that union officials have even less incentive to take a serious interest in the views of ordinary members, who may be seen simply as subscription fodder and a supplement to the size of the conference block vote.

LEGISLATING FOR DEMOCRATIC TRADE UNIONISM

How far one can legislate for democratic trade unionism or democratic anything else in the face of apathy by the individuals concerned is a very nice question. Compulsory voting in a general election in Australia may be seen as an aid to democracy or an indication that democracy there is a fragile plant. The fact that between 70 and 80 per cent of the electorate regularly vote in a general election in the United Kingdom suggests that most people take their national responsibility seriously, but a turnout of only 40 per cent in local elections indicates a different view about local government.

However, if compulsory democracy sometimes seems like a contradiction in terms, compulsory membership of a state or organisation is surely the best indication that democracy is absent. The Berlin wall and the iron curtain, together with the knowledge that potential escapers would be shot, were an obvious sign that the German Democratic Republic belied its name. In the same way, the closed shop transfers power from the union members to the officials because the members can no longer vote with their feet except at great personal cost. Did employers understand that when they accepted a closed shop they were driving another nail into the coffin of trade union democracy?

It needs to be said that the reintroduction of the open shop, which goes hand in hand with the accountability of union officials to their members, is a key factor in the restoration of trade union democracy, because the Trade Union Act 1984 had nothing to say about ending the closed shop. Instead, this particular matter was dealt with in the Employment Acts of 1980, 1982, 1988 and 1990 and those measures were thoroughly discussed in chapter 4. So here the importance of the open shop as a contribution to trade union democracy is emphasised, but attention is concentrated on the government's other measures, and especially on the Trade Union Act 1984.

THE TRADE UNION ACT 1984 AND THE ATTITUDE OF THE TUC

The 1984 Act was divided into three main parts, all of which were designed to stimulate the interest of trade union members in their union's affairs. Much the most popular and best known part of the Act was that which obliged unions to ballot their members and to achieve a majority vote in favour before taking industrial action, so let us look at this first although it is Part II of the Act.

(a) Secret ballots before industrial action

The implications of this important measure have already been dealt with in chapter 3, but some further comments are in order here. The intention was clearly to eliminate situations in which union members were called out on strike without an opportunity to express a personal opinion about the dispute. As the Secretary of State said in the debate on the second reading of the Bill:

> It is still the case that most unions refuse to hold secret ballots before strikes and rely on rowdy open-air meetings which are a travesty of democracy.[4]

There was plenty of evidence that many trade union members were sick and tired of being ordered out on strike by shop stewards or full-time union officials, sometimes without even knowing what the dispute was about. Mr King referred to the case of the Inland Revenue Staff Federation which had recently conducted a survey of its 60,000 members. The response, which was given to the executive and delegates at a delegate conference, was that 94 per cent favoured pre-strike ballots. And yet the delegates rejected a proposal to change the union's rules to make such ballots obligatory.

Of course there were *some* unions in which such matters were dealt with democratically, but in others – including some of the biggest – democracy was dead or dying. In fact the trade union movement, which had originally been based on the principle of local democracy, was rather like an overripe pear which was rotting from the centre.

THE ATTITUDE OF THE TUC

From the day on which Mrs Thatcher became Prime Minister in May 1979, the TUC turned its back on the process of trade union reform. It not only refused to play any part in the normal consultative process with government minsters which takes place before a Bill is presented to Parliament, but it also tried to prevent TUC-affiliated unions from achieving any of the benefits of the reforms, however much their members desired them.

This total opposition to reform of every kind was seen most clearly in the TUC's hostility to secret ballots and the 1984 Bill and Act. For several years the TUC was opposed root and branch to the idea of compulsory ballots of every kind – they were regarded as an intolerable interference in trade union affairs, however undemocratic those affairs had become. Alongside the opposition to ballots was hostility to the use of public funds for ballots, despite falling trade union membership and accompanying financial difficulties.

It was the Trade Union Act 1984 which brought the matter of secret ballots, and the use of public funds to cover their cost, to a head. Public funds had been made available for ballots in the Employment Act 1980, but nothing was said there about ballots being obligatory. That fact, together with TUC opposition to ballots and the use of public funds, meant that the cost of ballots to the Exchequer was very small from 1980 to 1984. But the 1984 Act made them compulsory (a) before industrial action (b) to elect a union's senior officials and (c) for political funds (every ten years). Because the cost of a (postal) ballot can be up to £1 a head, large sums of money were now involved, as Table 6.1 shows.

Table 6.1   Public funding of trade union ballots

Year	Number of trade unions receiving public funds	Total amount paid out (£ million)
1980	–	–
1981	7	0.01
1982	12	0.03
1983	14	0.06
1984	13	0.07
1985	11	1.96
1986	30	0.74
1987	37	1.16
1988	38	0.87
1989	51	1.34

Source: Annual Reports of the Certification Officer, 1980–89.

The 1984 Act made ballots obligatory. But would the TUC retain its opposition to the use of public funds? The embargo was first breached by the second largest TUC union – the Amalgamated Union of Engineering Workers (AUEW) – early in 1985 when the union reported that it had received £1.2 million of public money in respect of ballots held between March 1981 and September 1984. Subsequently the AUEW balloted its members on this question and a clear majority voted in favour of their union's policy. Meanwhile the Electrical, Electronic, Telecommunications and Plumbing Union (EETPU) had followed the same route and by December 1985 its members, too, had endorsed the use of public funds.

What was the TUC to do? Should it expel two leading members for accepting the full implications of the government's pro-democracy measures? The outcome was a conference of TUC unions, held in February 1986 which showed 'very little inclination... for the General Council to take any further disciplinary action under Rule 13 against unions which seek or accept public funds for union ballots.'[5] Two months later the General Council decided that 'whether to apply for such funds under the 1980 Employment Act was a matter for the discretion of individual unions.'[6]

A growing number of unions, including TUC affiliated unions, received public funds for ballots between 1985 and 1989, but several major unions still refused to apply for them. The TGWU Biennial Delegate Conference held in June 1989 seemed to be a turning point, when it was decided that the TGWU should claim public funds in future. But was this the result of a genuine conversion to trade union democracy or simply a matter of financial expediency for a union which had lost 37 per cent of its members between 1979 and 1988?

Given the strong general support for the idea of trade union ballots, the groundswell of continuing opposition from the TUC and several major unions indicated either that senior union officials were still out of touch with their members or that they would not listen to what the members were saying. But Table 6.2 shows that by 1987, as the Trade Union Act 1984 came into full operation, pre-strike ballots had become commonplace, and over 90 per cent of them were going in favour of industrial action. Thus the claim that they spelt the end of trade union rights was shown to be a complete myth.

Table 6.2   Trade union pre-strike ballots 1986–89

Period	No. of Ballots	No. Won	No. Lost	No. Tied	Per cent Won
Up to the end of 1986	152	Nk[*]	Nk	Nk	–
1987	280	251	26	3	90
1988	331	305	23	3	92
1989	340	318	21	1	93.5
Total	1103				

[*] Nk = Not known.
Source: ACAS Annual Report 1987, p. 11, supplemented by further information from ACAS.

Early in 1990 ACAS commented that

> unions have been increasingly concerned to steer a careful course through the complex legal provisions which now bear on their actions.[7]

and they went on to say that

> While many unions, for example, acting in accordance with their
> rule books, had long undertaken secret ballots of members before
> considering industrial action, in our experience the practice is now
> universal.[8]

Following the spread of pre-strike ballots, in April 1990 the Department of Employment, with the authority of Parliament, issued *The
Code of Practice for Trade Union Ballots on Industrial Action*. This
advisory Code should be extremely helpful to union officials who have
the responsibility for organising pre-strike ballots and who want to
operate within a law which has become increasingly complex.

(b) Secret ballots for the election of every voting member of a trade union's governing body

Part I of the 1984 Act provided that every voting member of a trade
union's governing body (usually known as the National Executive
Committee or National Executive Council) must be elected by the
members in a secret ballot at least every five years. At the same time all
trade unions were obliged by law to keep an accurate register of their
members' names and addresses.

Like Part II, Part I was designed to bring unions which did not
observe this practice into line with those which did, and most members
welcomed the change. Considerable controversy centred on the
question of whether postal voting should be obligatory or not. It
was argued that it was the only way to ensure that votes were not
tampered with, but others insisted that in some firms and industries
workplace ballots produced a better response. In the event, the
government adopted a compromise by allowing workplace ballots on
stringent conditions, but they changed their minds in 1988 when postal
voting was made obligatory.

Of course apathy is still a problem, and in some large unions only 25
per cent of the members or less may return a vote. But Goldstein's
argument that 'the Transport and General Workers Union is an
oligarchy at every level of its structure' no longer holds any water.
The opportunity for democratic participation is there, even if a large
majority of members refuse to take it.

(c) Secret ballots for a political fund

The Trade Union Act 1913 provided that unions could use a political fund for (party) political purposes if the establishment of such a fund was approved in a ballot by a majority of the members voting. It was also laid down that members who did not wish to contribute to the political fund should be allowed to 'contract out' without being disadvantaged in any way as members. Subsequently many large unions established political funds and these have provided financial support for the Labour Party since 1913, so that the Party has never been short of money. In 1988 the income of the political funds in 47 unions was £12.1 million.

Many of the ballots in favour of a political fund had been held in the period 1914–40 and by 1984 practically all of the members who had taken part in those ballots had retired or died. So did the present members favour the continuation of such a fund? The evidence from unions like the Association of Scientific, Technical and Managerial Staff (ASTMS), where more than two thirds had contracted out of the political levy, suggested that the answer might be negative, and a Conservative government was naturally interested to discover whether this evidence pointed in the right direction. Consequently Part III of the 1984 Act required trade unions to ballot their members every ten years on whether they wish their union to continue to spend money on party political matters.

Table 6.3   Growth of trade union political funds, 1983–88

Year	No. of unions with political funds	No. of members contributing (million)	Total political fund income (£ million)	Fund at end of year (£ million)
1983	58	5.9	7.7	4.5
1984	53	5.7	8.5	7.0
1985	50	5.7	10.0	10.6
1986	41	5.6	10.3	12.4
1987	45	5.6	11.4	8.8
1988	47	5.6	12.1	11.9

Source: Annual Reports of the Certification Officer 1984–89.

Presumably the government expected that in some unions at least the vote would go against the continuation of the political fund. But if so, this particular piece of legislation seriously backfired, so that it ended up by encouraging rather than discouraging political funds which are frequently used to support the Labour Party in its political activities. Table 6.3 shows how the funds' income has grown since 1983.

The increase in political fund income is largely the result of a remarkably clever campaign by the unions and the TUC to persuade members to vote in favour of their funds once the 1984 Act came into operation, so that in its 1988 Report the TUC was able to claim that

To date 15 unions have established new political funds in addition to the 37 unions which have voted to retain their political funds under the requirements of Part III of the 1984 Trade Union Act.[9]

CONTRACTING IN TO OR OUT OF THE POLITICAL LEVY

The question of whether members of a union with a political fund should have to contract out of or in to the levy has been a major bone of contention ever since Parliament decided in favour of contracting out in 1913. Clearly this gives a boost to political fund income, as many apathetic non-Labour supporters do not bother to contract out. And in some cases unions have deliberately made it difficult for members to do so. So the arguments have gone back and forth. Contracting in replaced contracting out in 1927, but the Labour government of 1945–51 promptly reversed this when they came to office, and the Conservatives have let sleeping dogs lie since then.

During the debate on Part III of the Trade Union Act 1984 Mr King, Employment Secretary, was pressed by several Conservative back-benchers to re-introduce contracting in. His response was (a) to reach an agreement with the TUC that the right of all members to contract out should be respected and (b) to promise that, if this agreement was not honoured within two years, the unions 'must be prepared to face the consequences'. That promise was not kept, and this matter is looked at in more detail in chapter 9.

It will be understood that the Trade Union Act 1984, together with the measures contained in the Acts of 1980 and 1982 to discourage the closed shop, represented a major attempt to ensure that trade unions were distinctly more democratic and responsive to the wishes of the members. Parts I and II enjoyed a wide measure of popular support and have proved extremely successful from the government's point of view. (A side effect of these reforms has been the generation of a large amount of business for independent scrutineers who must oversee the ballots. Much of this work has been carried out by the Electoral Reform Society in an exemplary way).

Part III, by contrast, has probably been seen as a major success by the unions and the Labour Party! Whatever the outcome, by 1987 the government felt that there was a need to strengthen its measures to achieve trade union democracy. It was no longer a question of encouraging democracy, but rather of ramming it down the unions' throats.

THE EMPLOYMENT ACTS 1988 AND 1990: A MEASURE OF OVERKILL?

To begin with, as mentioned in chapter 4, the 1988 Act attempted to restrict the closed shop still further by removing immunity from all industrial action to establish or maintain any sort of closed shop practice and making dismissal for non-membership of a union unfair in all circumstances. This was intended to give all employees the right to resign from a trade union if they chose to do so.

Then, as mentioned in chapter 5, the Act introduced a wide range of new rights for union members, infringement of which by a trade union could be remedied by application to an industrial tribunal or a court.

Additionally, the Act established the office of Commissioner for the Rights of Trade Union Members (the CROTUM)[10], whose chief function is to give assistance to union members contemplating or taking court proceedings against their union. But is this office worthwhile? Its first full Annual Report was published in July 1990 and showed that only 29 applications had been dealt with at a gross cost of approximately £250,000. Of these 29 applications, 9 were outside the scope of the Commissioner's assistance and, of the remaining 20, only 5 produced positive results. Can such an expenditure of taxpayer's money really be justified to produce such a meagre harvest?

There is an even bigger question as to whether such an office can be justified when aggrieved members are now generally free to resign from their union if they choose to do so. It seems that in respect of the

CROTUM the government's drive for union democracy has overshot the mark. It would surely be best to terminate this particular experiment at the earliest opportunity and transfer the CROTUM's very modest duties to the Certification Officer for Trade Unions and Employers' Associations, who already has the responsibility, under the Trade Union Act 1984, for dealing with complaints about trade union elections. Meanwhile the government is going in the opposite direction, and the Employment Act 1990 attempts to expand the CROTUM's workload. There must be major doubts about the wisdom of this approach.

Some of the other provisions in the 1988 Act – for example, the right of members not to be unjustifiably disciplined by their union – also appear to be based either on the assumption that attempts to make union membership voluntary will fail, or on a misunderstanding of the way in which the ending of compulsory unionism transforms the relationship between the members and their union. Voluntary members have no reason at all to fear union discipline, because they are free to resign if they feel they are being treated unreasonably. And the right to resign means that they are much less likely to be treated unreasonably in the first place.

It might be said, then, that the Employment Act 1988 is like the curate's egg – good in parts. The closed shop and certain other measures can be warmly welcomed, but there must be doubts about the extent to which the law can make the trade unions (or any other organisation) democratic. Genuine democracy always depends to some extent on the determination of ordinary people to stand up for themselves. In respect of trade union democracy, the main effect of the 1990 Act should be to hasten the end of the closed shop by forbidding employers making trade union membership (or non-membership) a condition of employment. And it cannot be said too often that genuinely voluntary membership is much the most important condition for real trade union democracy.

Ministers in the Thatcher administration frequently insisted that their aim was to reform the trade unions, not to destroy them, and their attempts to make the unions more democratic suggest that this claim was sincere. No sensible commentator could deny that the extension of the closed shop combined with dubious voting procedures and an inclination by full-time officials to dictate to their members had made many unions distinctly unattractive by 1979. Today, most unions have significantly improved their administrative procedures and have come to terms with a legal framework in which pre-strike and other ballots are carried out as a matter of course. The availability of public money for these ballots has meant that they are costless from the union's point of view.

The success of most of these reforms is all the more commendable when it is remembered that they were carried through Parliament in the face of total opposition from the Labour Party. There are signs that the Labour Party is beginning to pay slightly more attention to the views of trade union members, many of whom are enthusiastic about some of the Tory reforms. But is the Party's conversion genuine, or is it simply a device to win electoral popularity? That question will be explored in chapter 10.

7 Deregulating the Labour Market, the Rise of Self-Employment and the Individual Contract of Employment

> The Government believe that a sustained programme of deregulation in the labour market is necessary if we are to secure the flexibility we need for further employment growth.
>
> *Employment for the 1990s*, HMSO, December 1988

As the British economy matured in the twentieth century the labour market became inflexible and sclerotic. Many people, encouraged by academic and other opinion, expected to find a permanent, well-paid job within easy travelling distance of the place where they were born and bred. And they relied on strike-threat trade unionism to secure a steady increase in their standard of living.

The prevailing philosophy, finally adopted by Parliament in the 1975 Employment Protection Act, was that more collective bargaining and an increase in statutory employee rights, without any mention of duties, would automatically produce a healthier economy and better industrial relations. Meanwhile British consumers were rapidly turning to Japanese and other imported goods, so that by the early 1980s even home demand for British products was shrinking fast.

As well as challenging the conventional wisdom in respect of trade unionism and collective bargaining, the Thatcher government has mounted a challenge to the notion that a fully comprehensive range of statutory employee rights is really in the interests of actual or would-be employees. This was part of a wider challenge to excessive regulation and bureaucracy contained in two White Papers: *Lifting the Burden* (Cmnd 9571), published in July 1985, and *Building Businesses...not Barriers* (Cmnd 9794), published in May 1986. The architect of these White Papers was David (later Lord) Young, who came into Mrs Thatcher's government as Minister without Portfolio before being appointed Secretary of State for Employment in 1985; but the scene for the White Papers had been set by the report *Burdens on Business*, published in March 1985.

Thus it is clear that in the period 1984–85 a decision was taken at Cabinet level to encourage an enterprise economy and dismantle unnecessary regulations which held back economic growth. The primary objective was to create more private sector jobs by business growth, and the two opening paragraphs of the 1986 White Paper compared a bureaucratic European economy, which had lost two million jobs over the past decade, with an entrepreneurial American economy, which had seen considerable employment growth over the same period. The same objective was set out in the opening paragraph of a new 'Mission Statement' of the Department of Employment, printed on the inside front cover of *Building Businesses ... not Barriers*, which read:

> The prime aim of the Department of Employment is to encourage the development of an enterprise economy. The way to reduce unemployment is through more businesses, more self-employment and greater wealth-creation, all leading to more jobs.

Interestingly, the first chapter of the 1986 White Paper was called not 'The End of Regulation' but 'Better Regulation'. Admittedly it was argued (in para 1.13) that the most straightforward method of better regulation 'is simple abolition'; but again and again this initiative was hedged about with 'buts' and other qualifications, so that readers might be excused for wondering how much would eventually be achieved. And, of course, as was stated in para 1.15: 'This [better regulation] is no easy task. It represents a profound change of culture for Government.' For politicians and civil servants to favour deregulation is rather like turkeys asking for Christmas to be brought forward. After all, regulation, not deregulation, is their business. To them regulation is meat and drink. Without it, their *raison d'être* disappears.

And so the report and the White Papers discussed about eighty deregulatory proposals across a wide field of government activity from planning and the environment to government and business. Only a small minority of these related to employment law, but in this, as in other areas, there was a general intention to deregulate rather than to introduce more regulations. Two specific changes made in 1985 and 1986 were the raising of the qualifying period for unfair dismissal complaints from one to two years for all businesses, and the removal of all those aged under 21 from the scope of Wages Council Orders.

In addition to these innovations, an Enterprise and Deregulation Unit was established in 1985, initially as part of the Cabinet Office. This moved into the Department of Employment in 1986 and then went with Lord Young to the Department of Trade and Industry in 1987. Since then the Unit has kept a very low profile and those who favour deregulation will be concerned about its health, especially after Lord Young's resignation as Secretary of State for Trade and Industry in 1989.

THE CHANGING LABOUR MARKET

Policies tend to be made by politicians and civil servants in their forties and fifties, whose opinions were formed a generation earlier. But the labour market has changed out of all recognition since the 1950s and 1960s, when the norm, for men at least, was a permanent, full-time job, often for life. Part-time and temporary work was considered second or third best, and the self-employed were sometimes regarded as an anomaly which would gradually disappear as economic planning spread the benefits of large-scale production.

Even today, the idea of self-employment is rather strange to many employees, especially to teachers and others like them who used to be cocooned in an employment system of nearly total security. Most teachers, one suspects, would be profoundly shocked by Charles Handy's suggestion that education needs to be re-invented with schools being turned into a shamrock 'with a core activity and everything else contracted out or done part-time by a flexible labour force.'[1]

Some university teaching is currently 'bought in' if a department is short-staffed. However, many dons, and especially members of the Association of University Teachers, would be appalled at the idea that this should be the norm rather than the exception. There is, then, a danger that those who influence the younger generation are out of touch with what is happening in the labour market.

A key development in the UK labour market over the past forty years, but especially in the 1980s, has been the rapid growth of 'the flexible labour force', which includes part-time and temporary workers and the self-employed. In answer to a Parliamentary question in May 1990, Tim Eggar, an Employment Minister, stated that in December 1989 there were 3.3 million people in self-employment in the UK, an increase of 70 per cent since 1979. The enterprise culture encourages rather than disparages the self-employed, and it is clear that there has been a response to this encouragement.

PART-TIME AND TEMPORARY EMPLOYEES

Closely connected with a higher participation by women (and especially by married women) in the labour force is the large increase in part-time and temporary work. In fact many UK organisations would quickly grind to a halt today without their part-timers and temps. It must be very likely that the flexible workforce, which now numbers about eight million employees, or 35 per cent of the total, will continue to grow as self-employment becomes more popular and even more women take paid work. So UK government and EC policy towards this large group is very important.

Basically there are two policy approaches towards part-time and temporary employees. The first, which has been endorsed by the Labour Party and a majority of the EC Commissioners in Brussels, is to provide them with employment rights as near as possible to those of full-time, permanent employees. This approach practically ignores the self-employed and the unemployed, who have no statutory employment rights. The second approach, endorsed by the Thatcher government, is to deregulate this area as far as possible, so that employers will be keen to create more jobs of this kind. It does not call for the elimination of all employment rights, but believes that each proposal should be considered on its merits, taking particular account of its effect on job creation. In fact, the most widely used UK employment right – the right not to be unfairly dismissed – was introduced in 1971 by a Conservative government, and the Thatcher administration never suggested that it should be abolished.

It is not too difficult to condemn the second, deregulatory approach as uncaring, but it has one great merit which easily outweighs all its disadvantages – the experience of the past ten years indicates that it is highly effective in creating many part-time and temporary jobs, so that by 1990 the UK unemployment rate was below the EC average. In addition, the deregulatory approach does not prevent business firms and other organisations from offering equal treatment on a pro rata basis for part-time staff if they wish to do so. Several major British companies, including Sainsbury's and the Halifax Building Society, have recently done this, and labour market pressures may persuade others to follow.

Actually, the contrast between the regulators and the deregulators is not quite so sharp as all this might suggest. For example, in the UK those who work less than 30 hours per week are regarded as part-timers for the purposes of employment statistics. But the right not to be unfairly dismissed is fully available to all who work more than sixteen hours a week. For those who work between eight and sixteen hours, the qualifying period of service becomes five years instead of two; and only those who work less than eight hours a week have no such right.

Without some lower limit, like eight hours a week, below which employment rights do not apply to part-timers, one would have a situation in which even a domestic cleaner, who did, say, five hours a week, might claim unfair dismissal by her employer from the very first day. Presumably that is what the Labour Party wants, because in its 1989 policy document it stated categorically:

> Everyone at work will have the same legal status. All workers, barring those genuinely running a profession or business on their own account, will be covered by the full range of employment rights. These rights will apply regardless of the number of hours worked, the length of time the individual has been with their employer, the size of the company or whether their employer calls them temporary, sub-contracted, self-employed or home workers.[2]

The effect of such a policy, under which every single employee would have a full range of employment rights, including the right not to be unfairly dismissed, from the first day of his or her employment, can easily be imagined. It would cause a substantial decrease in the number of part-time and temporary jobs on offer as employers moved to avoid their almost limitless liabilities. The regulators usually profess some concern for the unemployed, but the net effect of their policies would be to increase their number significantly. A further consequence would be a very large increase in the work of the Industrial Tribunals as the number of complaints about the abuse of employment rights soared. The whole situation would be a bureaucratic nightmare. In fact, as Professor Roberts has pointed out, the regulatory approach to part-time and temporary employees, like other European Community policies for 'social harmonisation', is 'the product of economic and social thinking that had its dirigiste origins in the first half of the 20th century and played a dominant role in the advanced industrialised economies after the second world war.'[3]

The approach is based on a fundamentally flawed analysis of a situation in which the wages of some groups (eg part-timers) and some nations (eg Portugal in the EC) are lower than those of others. Economists would see this as a comparative advantage which will attract investment and employment and lead to rising real wages for those who were previously low paid. A classic case is that of Japan, where real wages are now on a par with the best-paid Europeans.

The regulators, however, describe this comparative advantage as 'a distortion of competition' and try to legislate it out of existence, using several pejorative terms to buttress their case. The flexible workforce is described as 'atypical' and production in areas where labour costs are low is referred to as 'social dumping'. In fact these so-called 'distortions of competition' are differences which will be narrowed all the quicker if a competitive labour market is allowed to function. And attempts by the EC Commissioners to eliminate them by the Action Programme which is linked to the Social Charter are bound to damage the economies of poorer EC countries like Portugal and Greece.

Again, it is necessary to criticise these proposals in a thoughtful way. For example, it is obviously right that part-time and temporary workers should be fully covered by the same health and safety regulations as full-timers. Each extra proposal must be assessed on its merits and with proper regard to its overall effect on the creation of new jobs. As many small farmers leave agriculture, and big companies shed jobs to achieve increases in labour productivity, millions of new jobs are going to be needed in the EC in the near future.

SELF-EMPLOYMENT

Policies in the field of self-employment also point up the contrast between the regulators and the deregulators. For the latter, an increase in self-employment, with the prospect that some of these tiny firms will quickly grow and provide work for others, is to be warmly encouraged. But for the regulators the self-employed are simply an embarrassment. How can they be given employment rights against themselves? They just do not fit into the socialist model of planned industrial giantism. But they cannot be ignored because their number has increased so dramatically in recent years.

Some of these new recruits to the ranks of the self-employed have been trade union members for whom self-employment has offered the only prospect of a job. Understandably the unions are rather unhappy about the prospect of losing them for good. That explains why, in 1986, MATSA, the white collar section of the General, Municipal, Boilermakers and Allied Trades Union, established a Self-Employed Unit in Newcastle upon Tyne to cater for those members who had gone into business on their own account. Such a development would have been unthinkable a few years earlier.

The self-employed have a vital role to play in a market economy, and sensible taxation policies will warmly encourage this kind of activity. In the UK the income of employed people is taxed through the Pay As You Earn system under Schedule E, while the self-employed are taxed under Schedule D. Because of this distinction it may be that some people have difficulty in changing from employed to self-employed status, and that difficulty needs to be eliminated. This could be achieved by a short Act of Parliament and an appropriate Bill has already been drafted.[4]

THE INDIVIDUAL CONTRACT OF EMPLOYMENT

As already mentioned at the beginning of this chapter, a collectivist philosophy was encapsulated in parts of the Employment Protection Act 1975. For example Section 1.-(2) charged the Advisory, Conciliation and Arbitration Service (ACAS) with the particular duty 'of encouraging the extension of collective bargaining and the development and, where necessary, reform of collective bargaining machinery'; while Clauses 11–16 attempted unsuccessfully to establish a process operated by ACAS through which a trade union could achieve recognition by an employer against the employer's wishes. Meanwhile lawyers accepted that the individual contract of employment was 'the cornerstone of the edifice'[5] of labour law. So which was to be more important – the collective bargain or the individual contract?

Certainly in the period 1974–79 it seemed that the collective bargain would prevail, as the trade unions grew in numbers and strength and negotiated as equals with the government. But all that changed in 1979 and the unions now include only a minority (perhaps 40 per cent) of UK employees among their members. By the mid–1980s employers became less willing to recognise trade unions and some companies actually de-recognised them and introduced individual negotiations.

In its 1989 Annual Report ACAS suggested that union de-recognition 'remained rare and overall continues to affect only a relatively small number of employees'. At the same time they pointed out that trade union membership was highly concentrated in the public sector and stated that

> According to some sources membership density in private industry and commerce may now be no higher than 20 per cent, and a good deal lower in the private service sector.

In recent years a growing number of business firms have thought seriously about operating without a trade union and collective bargaining, and a growing number of employees have begun to think that individual contracts of employment might be in their best interests.

THE IBM EXAMPLE

The British subsidiary of International Business Machines (IBM) is the classic case of a non-union UK company. Of course it is often claimed that non-union companies operate in that way by brow-beating their employees to accept their policy. For IBM this claim was effectively scotched by an independent assessor in 1977, when ACAS conducted a survey among all their UK employees in response to a union request for recognition. Some 95 per cent of employees responded to the survey. Of the respondents, 91 per cent were against joining a trade union and 95.6 per cent were opposed to collective bargaining. Not surprisingly, ACAS recommended against collective bargaining despite its statutory terms of reference. Philip Bassett has written that 'IBM refuses to recognise unions, not because of their potential nuisance value, but because their collectivism runs wholly counter to the company's fundamentally individualist philosophy.'[6] The company believes that the individual approach produces better results, and its record in the provision of computer hardware and software offers more than a little support for that belief.

INDIVIDUAL CONTRACTS IN THE PUBLIC SECTOR

Despite the greater influence of trade unions and collective bargaining in the public sector, even there some organisations, including local authorities, are now breaking away from centralised, national negotiations, so that in May 1990 it was reported that nearly twenty councils had opted out of national bargaining for administrative and professional staff, and national pay talks would 'cover fewer councils than ever before'.[7] In addition some councils have introduced voluntary individual contracts for senior and principal officers, and out of 150 such officers employed by Macclesfield Borough Council, 92 per cent made the change to individual contracts.

Universities typically negotiate an annual, national pay bargain with the Association of University Teachers. But within that framework there is plenty of room for individual negotiation. For example talented researchers may be offered a permanent teaching post with very light teaching duties. This enables them to travel the world and produce a stream of publications while their colleagues, who sweat it out in the lecture and seminar room, reap some benefit from a high research rating for their Department.

THE MUTUAL BENEFITS OF INDIVIDUAL CONTRACTS

The feeling that even a skilled employee is at a permanent negotiating disadvantage with an employer, and therefore has to join a strike-threat trade union, is gradually giving way to an understanding that individual contracts may be beneficial for both parties. At a conference in London in April 1990, referring to the spread of individual contracts of employment in both the public and private sectors, Graham Mather, General Director of the Institute of Economic Affairs, mentioned local government workers, port employees, journalists, telecom employees, electricity supply workers and farm managers as being among groups which had been offered such deals in recent months; and he went on to say that 'the new contracts are usually accompanied by substantial improvements in pay and/or benefits'.[8] These contracts often include provision for individual appraisal and performance-related pay, a topic which will be looked at more closely in chapter 14.

It can, then, be seen that the movement towards all-embracing, national collective bargaining, accompanied by the development of (compulsory) trade unionism, which occurred in the period 1974–79, has been not just halted but reversed by the Thatcher government's determination to deregulate the labour market. However, the regulators have not gone away. At home they are just biding their time, while in Brussels they are absorbed with an Action Programme, linked to the Social Charter, which could destroy millions of actual or potential jobs in the European Community. It is certainly true to say that the price of a free UK labour market is eternal vigilance.

8 Some Economic Benefits of the Reforms

For many years now, newspapers have been produced in conditions which combined a protection racket with a lunatic asylum.

Bernard Levin, *The Times*, 3 February 1986

Parliament legislates, but some statutes quickly become dead letters while others have a significant and immediate effect on social and economic behaviour. In chapter 6 it was shown that the Trade Union Act 1984 quickly led to pre-strike and other ballots becoming universal. But how have the Tory employment reforms affected the economy? Is it possible to detect a positive connection between the reforms and the major improvement in labour productivity which occurred in the 1980s? In this chapter it will be argued that such a connection did exist, and the way in which legislative and policy changes have revolutionised working practices in three sectors of the economy, namely coal-mining, the national newspapers and the docks, will be examined. Also, the government's attempt to reform the legal profession will be assessed.

These sectors have been chosen for two reasons. First, they cover a wide range of activities. The work of a coal-miner has little in common with that of a barrister. Second, in 1979 most people who knew the ways in which miners, national newspaper printers, dockers and barristers worked would have insisted that radical changes in their obsolete practices were impossible because the trade unions, or, in the case of barristers, the Inns of Court, would never permit them. Producer organisations had these activities in an iron grip and they were absolutely unwilling to relax it.

Coal-miners produce the coal which generates most of the electricity in the UK, and the cost of energy, together with the reliability of supply, is a key factor for business firms and households. The UK has various energy sources and should be one of the lowest-cost producers of electricity in the world, but by the late 1970s that was not so because of the inefficiency of the coal industry. Would the National Union of Mineworkers permit reform?

The problems of Britain's *national newspapers*, most of which were printed in or near Fleet Street, were no less acute. It was well known that overmanning on all the newspapers was scandalous, but it was a story that no-one could publish, because any attempt to print it would have immediately caused a strike.

Britain has always been a trading nation and efficiency in *the docks* is, therefore, crucial to her economy. But by the 1960s most major ports were being slowly suffocated by the Dock Labour Scheme, introduced by the Labour government of 1945–51. Would any government be bold enough to act?

A small group of senior barristers has dominated *the legal profession* in Britain. But they had long been bound by self-made restrictive rules, some of which greatly increased the cost of litigation and worked against the client's interest. How could this situation be changed?

The total number of people involved in all of these four activities was distinctly less than 300,000 – a tiny fraction of the total labour force of about 25 million. And yet each of these groups had – and still has – an influence on the British economy out of all proportion to the numbers employed.

THE COAL MINING INDUSTRY

It was the National Union of Mineworkers (NUM) which caused the three-day week and destroyed Mr Heath's government early in 1974. It was well known that the maintenance of the supply of electricity depended on the members of the NUM producing enough coal, and in 1974 the oil crisis added to the strength of their position. In that dispute Arthur Scargill, a young official in the NUM, made his name by closing the Saltley Coke Depot, Birmingham, with thousands of flying pickets. The police were simply overwhelmed. It seemed clear that whatever laws were passed by Parliament after 1979, there would be no resolution of the trade union problem without a confrontation between Scargill, who was dedicated to fighting the class war, and the Thatcher government.

A major reason why so many thought that union reform could never succeed was the belief that in any such confrontation the government would lose. In addition to the members of the NUM, many others believed by 1979 that Scargill and the NUM were invincible, and this myth was fostered by the supporters who idolised him. Naturally the myth gained ground in February 1981 when the National Coal Board (NCB) proposed pit closures: the miners threatened a national ballot on strike action and the government backed down after senior ministers had decided that they could not win a trial of strength at that time. But they were determined that such a débacle should not recur, and strenuous efforts were made to increase the stocks of coal available at the power stations. 'From the summer of 1981 the statistics of stocks held by the generating boards were for the first time amongst those supplied to the prime minister for her weekly scan of key indicators.'[1] And when Arthur Scargill was elected president of the NUM a few months later it seemed clear that the union was on a collision course with the government.

As well as building up coal stocks, the government was determined to appoint a chairman of the NCB who was tough enough to deal with Scargill. Their choice was Ian MacGregor, who had proved his business competence on both sides of the Atlantic and had turned round British Steel between 1980 and 1983. He took up his post with the NCB on 1 September 1983, just before his seventy-first birthday. Soon afterwards Peter Walker was appointed Secretary of State for Energy, with the loss-making nationalised coal industry as one of his most important responsibilities.

The new chairman was immediately faced with the question of the industry's future which was bound to mean pit closures and redundancies (preferably voluntary) among the labour force. The level of redundancy pay had been increased, so that a married man aged 50 with thirty years' service who earned £180 a week (slightly more than the average) could receive £22,000 in lump sums and £75 a week as a mixture of pensions and benefit. But Scargill and the NUM were adamantly opposed to closures, especially on economic grounds.[2]

The election of Arthur Scargill and the appointment of Ian MacGregor meant that a major coal strike was almost inevitable. The only question was: how and when would it start? In the event it began on 12 March 1984 following an announcement on 1 March that Cortonwood colliery in South Yorkshire would close, and a meeting between the NCB and the NUM on 6 March at which MacGregor insisted that output of coal would have to be reduced and several (perhaps 20) pits closed. But would members of the NUM back the strike call? The union's Rule 43 stated flatly that a national strike could not be called without a 55 per cent majority in a ballot, and in March 1983, only 39 per cent had voted in favour of a strike. Had opinions changed one year later? That question was never to be answered, because Scargill and his friends on the NUM executive had decided that 'they would not be constitutionalised out of a strike'.

They refused to hold a ballot in accordance with union rules and chose mass picketing, not a democratic ballot, as the method of ensuring that the strike would be solid.

The picketing started on the first day of the strike and the chief aim of the Yorkshire pickets was to prevent the Nottinghamshire miners, who had voted in a local ballot against a strike, from working. The record number of flying pickets for an individual pit was 8,000 at Harworth on 2 May. But this time the government was prepared and a massive police presence in Nottinghamshire, co-ordinated by the National Reporting Centre at Scotland Yard, meant that the Nottinghamshire pits stayed open throughout the strike and produced a prodigious quantity of coal. It was this more than any other factor which prevented the NUM from defeating an elected government for the second time in ten years.

This secondary picketing was, of course, blatantly illegal under the Employment Acts 1980 and 1982. Would the NCB use the new legislation and if so would it stand up under the strain? Within a few days of the start of the unlawful picketing the NCB applied for an injunction against it and the injunction was granted on 20 March. But the picketing continued. All the NCB had to do to have the NUM heavily fined or more likely, because the union would probably have refused to pay a fine, to have all of its funds sequestrated, was to return to the court to ask for a declaration of contempt. But this step was never taken, and the reason is shrouded in mystery.

Adeney and Lloyd state that 'The Coal Board, and the other state industries, were positively forbidden to use the Employment Acts when they wished to: government, having advertised them as mild, balanced, 'step-by-step' affairs, found when the largest test for them came that they would be too inflammatory to be unleashed'.[3] Ian MacGregor, on the other hand, in his own account of the strike, stated that 'Our reasons for not going ahead with it (legal action) were simple – and, though I hate to disappoint the conspiracy theorists, nothing to do with the government'.[4] He said that there were two reasons. First, it was thought that legal action of this kind would unite other trade unions, including the railwaymen and the steelworkers, behind Scargill at a time when they were unwilling to offer him much tangible support. Second, it could well drive many of the Nottinghamshire miners and TGWU members who were digging coal for the NCB on open-cast sites back into Scargill's arms. So a policy decision was taken in March that the NCB and other nationalised industries should not use the law against the NUM. But nevertheless the law was used by others.

In April 1984 Read Transport of South Wales secured an injunction against secondary picketing by NUM members and in July the union was fined £50,000. Subsequently the sequestrators took control of £707,000 and the union backed down. More important was the common law action taken by two Yorkshire miners, Taylor and Foulstone, against the NUM for breaking its own rules by calling a national strike without a ballot. Mr Justice Nichols ruled in their case that the Yorkshire strike should not be called official and in another case brought by three Derbyshire miners he ruled that their strike was unlawful. Because the NUM took no notice of his rulings, he fined the union £200,000 and its president £1,000. When the fines were not paid, the High Court ordered the seizure of all the union's assets and the sequestrators found themselves looking for funds which had been moved to banks in Dublin and Luxembourg.

No one will ever be able to say whether or not the use of the law by the NCB would have had the effects which MacGregor predicted. What can be said is that the NCB's failure to use the law placed immense burdens on the police, who bore the brunt of the mass picketing, and on those individual miners who were brave enough to take their own union to court. The fact that the legislation was relatively new and that MacGregor had only been chairman of the NCB for six months before the strike started, may have been factors which deterred him from using the law.

In the event, by January 1985 the trickle of striking miners returning to work became a stream and by late February the stream had become a flood. Finally in March the NUM called off the strike and claimed victory for the union though most observers saw it as an unconditional surrender. The purpose of the strike was to prevent pit closures, but since 1985 the closure programme has significantly accelerated with the number of pits falling from 170 in 1984[5] to 69 in 1990[6] and the number of the NCB's (now British Coal's) employees falling from a total of 246,000 in 1984 to 80,000 in 1990. Sir Robert Haslam, who succeeded Sir Ian MacGregor as Chairman in 1986, claimed in 1989 that change in the period 1985–89, including a 90% improvement in labour productivity, 'represents a restructuring unmatched in depth and speed in any major UK industry in recent history'.[7]

Meanwhile, the Nottinghamshire miners broke away from the NUM to form the Union of Democratic Mineworkers and the NUM found itself facing severe financial difficulties.

It would be good to think that the restructuring carried out by the NCB in 1985–90 had produced a bright future for the British coal-mining industry, but that is not the case. The energy crisis of the 1970s is over, and there is now a world surplus of coal and oil, so that British-produced coal is about twice as costly as world-traded coal. Then there are environmental pressures which make high-sulphur British coal unattractive. Consequently in May 1990, Sir Robert Haslam spoke of another 7,500 job losses over the next three years, while Mr Colin Webster, commercial director of National Power, expressed doubt about whether the British coal industry had a future.[8] So the future is, at best, uncertain.

If Mr Scargill had won in 1984–85, the cost of the coal industry to the taxpayer would by now be gigantic. In addition the general use of mass secondary picketing to shut down any business operation which Scargill or other similarly minded union leaders disliked, would have frightened off practically all new foreign investment in the UK and done immense damage to the British economy.

It can reasonably be argued that use of the new employment legislation was not a major factor in Scargill's defeat. But what cannot be gainsaid is that his defeat was a vital part of the government's overall employment strategy. And now that the foundation of the new laws has been in place for several years, there is less reluctance to use them by major employers.

THE NATIONAL NEWSPAPER INDUSTRY

'Fleet Street' is perhaps the ultimate example of an industry which has been transformed during the Thatcher era, because it has virtually disappeared along with the absurd practices – 'ghost' working, 'blow' systems, 'double' working, 'fat' payments and 'fiddles' – which characterised our national newspapers. Some of the offices still stand as a memorial to the past, but letters to the editor now have to be addressed to Wapping and other unlikely places.

Despite the influence of television, newspapers still have a crucial effect on the tone of society because of their ability to comment in depth on people, policies and events. If the national newspaper industry is inefficient and badly managed, it is bound to have a detrimental effect on the whole economy as journalists take low standards for granted. By the early 1980s, there was more than enough evidence that, at least as far as its employment arrangements were concerned, the industry was extremely inefficient and very badly managed.

Leaving aside the journalists, employment matters were taken care of by the trade unions, mainly the National Graphical Association (NGA) and the Society of Graphical and Allied Trades (SOGAT), though the brotherly relationship between these two unions was often similar to that between Cain and Abel. If a vacancy arose the appropriate union would be asked to fill it and the employer would have to take whoever the union sent. This applied to office staff as well as compositors and printers. Charles Wintour's wife, who worked at the *Sunday Times* as an assistant editor, needed a secretary. 'After a long delay the union produced a Chinese girl who could barely speak English and was quite unable to understand the simplest telephone message, let alone use a typewriter. Somehow she had gained a SOGAT card and was therefore deemed by the chapel to be suitable.'[9] Now the story can be told, but until February 1986 an industry which was dedicated to the exposure of scandal in every other walk of our national life maintained a conspiracy of silence about its own mis-management.

However, others had lifted a corner of the veil from time to time. It was well understood that a healthy, independent, national press was a vital element of a democratic society, and after the second world war there was growing concern about the demise of some newspapers, including the *News Chronicle* and the *Daily Sketch*. Royal Commissions on the Press reported in 1948, 1962 and 1977 without any noticeable effect, there were reports from the Economist Intelligence Unit in 1966, from the Prices and Incomes Board in 1970 and from ACAS in 1976, and two books appeared in the mid-1970s.[10]

From these sources, and especially from Graham Cleverley's book, it is possible to find out in some detail what actually occurred in respect of employment practices.

'Double' working, whereby casual workers signed on for shifts with two papers at the same time, was just one of these tragi-comic practices. Usually this meant signing on at one place then leaving to work at another before returning to collect a (second) pay packet at the first place. Normally two names would be used and it seems that occasionally a casual worker would forget his alias. As Cleverley wrote in 1976:

A small, but noticeable, number of casual pay-packets once in a while go uncollected in Fleet Street offices. Which is difficult to account for except on the basis usually advanced by Fleet Street managers: that the man concerned had forgotten the name he had used to sign on.[11]

The truth is that Fleet Street employers had lost control of their employment arrangements and labour costs. One reason for this was connected with the nature of the industry – that national newspapers are prepared and printed between 8 pm and 1 am. Most managers preferred to be at home at this time, and it was pointed out in the Report of the 1962 Royal Commission on the Press that:

> One of the contributory causes of Management's apparent weakness in controlling labour is, in our view, attributable to poor communications, which almost inevitably arises through the lack of a really senior Management Representative actually present and in control when the paper is produced.[12]

There was a power vacuum in the industry, and the trade union organisers had moved in to fill that vacuum. Various estimates were made of the overmanning which existed. The management consultants retained by the 1962 Royal Commission reported that 'There is a very serious excess of labour in almost all departments of each of the Newspapers investigated'[13] and they concluded that 'overall, out of every three men employed, only two are really needed. This is a serious position representing a severe waste of manpower.'[14] But by 1986, when the industry was finally shaken out of its torpor, the situation was far, far worse. Two examples will suffice.

In January 1986, Rupert Murdoch dismissed the 5,300 employees of News International in central London when they went on strike, and printed exactly the same number of newspapers in his new-technology plant at Wapping with a staff of 1,300. Admittedly some of the central London staff were casuals, but overmanning must have been about 200% compared with the 50% figure mentioned in the 1962 Royal Commission Report. Other national newspapers were soon following Murdoch's example, and Wintour tells us that the numbers employed in London in the actual printing of the *Daily* and *Sunday Telegraph* 'was reduced from 1,559 in the year ended March 1985 to only 400 in 1989'[15]. Thus it seems reasonable to conclude that 200% was a fairly typical figure for overmanning on our national newspapers in 1985. But how, if at all, did the Thatcher government's trade union reforms contribute to this astonishing increase in labour productivity?

For the national newspaper industry the critical event was the move to Wapping by News International in late January 1986. After that nothing could be the same again. So how did Rupert Murdoch achieve the impossible? After all, the Thomson Organisation had sat out an eleven month strike at *The Times*, from December 1978, over the question of new technology, without achieving any significant gain.

The reasons for Murdoch's success are carefully analysed in Wintour's mini-biography.[16] First was his willingness to take a risk. That was fundamental, because the move to Wapping was perhaps the riskiest business operation of the 1980s. All the odds seemed to be against success, including the biggest problem of all – the trade union problem. Even if Murdoch could get his papers printed at the new location – and the chances of that seemed low – there was the additional problem of distribution in a system which was practically controlled by the unions.

According to Wintour the idea of the move to Wapping came from Bruce Matthews, Murdoch's fellow Australian and managing director of News International. He had seen a successful single union deal with the EETPU operating in a paper mill in North Wales and during his Christmas break in 1984 he began to think that something similar could be worked out at Wapping. Wintour continues:

> There were other factors. The new industrial relations legislation outlawed secondary action... Other Fleet Street employers had already used the law to good effect. Further, the miners' strike was failing to break the resistance of the Coal Board, and behind them, the government. Maybe they could work the plants after all. Maybe this was the time to break out. Matthews said as much to Murdoch in his telephone call from Australia to the States and was told he had better fly over.[17]

By late February, Murdoch had decided to move his newspapers to a fully equipped, new-technology plant at Wapping and the die was cast. Thus it seems that the reform of trade union law was a key factor in the minds of Murdoch and Matthews as they took this risky decision. On its own that would not guarantee success, but at least it meant that there was a possibility of such an outcome. In the event the law was used by News International, and soon after the move SOGAT '82's entire financial assets of many millions of pounds were sequestrated for its defiance of a High Court order to stop blacking the wholesale distribution of the company's newspapers. In June 1986 delegates to the SOGAT '82 conference were told that the dispute had so far cost the union £1.5 million and that this could rise above £3.9 million through claims for damages which the company had already been granted. Despite many months of mass picketing the papers were printed without interruption and Murdoch's plans to distribute them by means of his own road transport system proved thoroughly successful. By late 1986 three other national newspaper groups had plans to move to docklands and *The Guardian* had almost completed its Isle of Dogs printing works. For the Fleet Street trade unions the game was up.

THE NATIONAL DOCK LABOUR SCHEME[18]

A trading nation like Britain needs efficient docks. But by 1967 labour in about two-thirds of the ports was strictly regulated by the statutory National Dock Labour Scheme, which had developed in 1947 out of an attempt in Liverpool in 1912 to 'de-casualise' the industry and to eliminate the worst features of a primitive labour hiring system.

The main elements in the 1947 Scheme were:

- Joint control and management, including discipline
- A guaranteed weekly wage
- The determination of the size of each port's register by the National Dock Labour Board
- The legal definition of dock work and the reservation of such work for Registered Dock Workers (RDWs)

and the 1967 Scheme added a fifth element

- The allocation of all RDWs as permanent workers to registered employers (the so-called 'jobs for life' arrangement).

Of course these five statutory conditions taken together created in all Scheme ports rigid conditions of employment which became more anachronistic with every passing year. Meanwhile, as containers and other modern methods of cargo handling were introduced, the number of RDWs declined from 78,000 in 1947 to 9,221 at the beginning of July 1989. This shrinkage in the labour force was encouraged by a relatively generous redundancy scheme funded jointly by the employers and the government. By 1985 a redundant docker with long service could collect a cash sum of £25,000.

The 'Spanish customs' in the docks, broadly equivalent to those in Fleet Street, included 'ghosting', 'bobbing', 'moonlighting' and 'disappointment money'. 'Bobbing' meant that a certain number of dockers (actually twice as many as needed) were assigned to a task. Half of them worked and the others 'bobbed off'. Why didn't the employers eliminate the practices? Because, as in Fleet Street, they had lost control of labour arrangements. This was caused by the central pillar of the Dock Labour Scheme – the principle of joint control. This principle was enshrined in the constitution of the National Dock Labour Board and the Local Boards and meant that it was impossible for the employers to exercise discipline over their workforce and to manage their businesses in an effective way. So in this industry the root problem rested with the government, which had introduced and maintained this statutory principle, rather than the employers who were hamstrung by it.

It has to be said, however, that for several decades port employers seemed to feel that it was pointless to make a serious effort to persuade the government to repeal the Scheme, despite the fact that the cost per tonne of moving cargo in a Scheme port was about twice as high as elsewhere. The consequence of these high costs were exactly what one would expect – trade moved away from Scheme ports. It moved in two directions: first to the continent, where operations were far more efficient than those in the UK Scheme ports; and second, to the 35 non-Scheme ports in the UK. Foremost among the latter were Dover and Felixstowe. But surely a Conservative government committed to trade union and labour reform would listen to the complaints of the port employers who were getting increasingly restive? Surprisingly, the answer was 'No' until 1989.

After two dock strikes in 1984 the employers went to see the then Transport Secretary, Nicholas Ridley, and asked him to repeal or reform the Scheme. His reaction was negative. He would only consider reform if the employers and the union (the TGWU) jointly asked for it, and the union was totally opposed to reform. In fact their attitude was plain: any attempt by the government to change the Scheme would provoke a national dock strike. The government did not think the TGWU was bluffing and they were unwilling to face such a prospect.

But this time the employers were far more determined, and they refused to let the matter rest. In 1987 they decided that amendment of the Scheme was pointless and that their aim had to be outright abolition. A small project team of two full-timers (Nicholas Finney and Iain Dale) and one part-timer (Malcolm Purgavie) was established to campaign for the abolition of the National Dock Labour Scheme by every fair means, and the team approached this task in a highly professional way.

By the middle of 1988, a large majority of Conservative back-benchers had indicated their support for abolition of the Scheme and numerous articles in the press and elsewhere had commented on its most anomalous features. But still the government refused to budge in the face of continuing threats by the TGWU of a national dock strike. The turning point came in late 1988 and early 1989 when Sir Leon Brittan, Norman Tebbitt, Michael Heseltine and other senior Conservatives insisted that the government should act and on 6 April 1989 Norman Fowler, as Secretary of State for Employment, announced the government's decision to repeal the Scheme. This decision had probably been taken two or three months earlier, but kept secret because of the strike threat. Bearing that threat in mind the government acted with lightning speed and the Dock Work Act, which abolished the Scheme, came into effect on 3 July. It does not happen frequently that a radical measure of employment reform goes through the whole of the consultative and Parliamentary process in three months, but in this particular case the strategy was almost entirely effective, the TGWU was wrong footed, and the sting of a national dock strike was largely drawn.

To begin with the dockers' leaders took two weeks from 6 April to consider the legal, financial and tactical implications of a stoppage, which would, of course, have to be preceded by a strike ballot. The TGWU announced a strike ballot on 20 April, but on 8 May port employers began legal proceedings to have the threatened strike declared unlawful. Eleven days later the results of the ballot showed that the dockers had voted 3–1 in favour of a strike, but negotiations continued until 7 June when the Court of Appeal granted the employers an injunction banning the union from calling a national strike. The injunction was effective, as the TGWU was determined not to fall foul of the law. However, on 20 June, following an appeal to the House of Lords, the union was given permission to go ahead with a dock strike, but by then the May ballot had run out of time, as a strike has to take place within four weeks of the declaration of the ballot result. Another (successful) ballot was held, but by this time (7 July) the Scheme had been abolished; nobody could suppose that it would ever be re-introduced and most dockers knew that a strike was a futile exercise. Thus the new employment legislation had a crucial role in delaying a national strike and undermining the dockers' morale.

From the beginning of the strike on 10 July, enthusiasm for it was limited. At several Scheme ports local agreements were quickly made and normal work resumed after a token stoppage. In addition many dockers were attracted by the generous redundancy terms on offer (up to £35,000) and by 31 July 2,812 RDWs out of a total of 9,221 had left the industry. On the same date (31 July) the National Association of Port Employers reported that there were more dockers working (3,684) than on strike (2,725) and on 1 August the TGWU's executive committee voted by 18–12 to end the strike. A week later Liverpool dockers voted 3–1 to return to work after an impassioned plea by Ron Todd to do so. The strike was over and all the obsolete restrictive working practices disappeared as employers at Tilbury, Liverpool and other (previously Scheme) ports offered new employment contracts to those dockers who wanted to stay in the industry.

Because many dockers became self-employed, and working arrangements in many ports completely changed once the Dock Labour Scheme had been abolished, it is very difficult to estimate the overall improvement in labour productivity. But a survey of 15 former Scheme ports, carried out for the Department of Employment a year after the Scheme was abolished,[19] showed that at Liverpool, Hull and Tilbury productivity improvements of between 28 per cent and 100 per cent had taken place, and it was suggested that 'at the heart of the changes lies a radical restructuring of the labour force and re-definition of the work to be carried out in the cargo handling area'.[20] Perhaps most interesting of all were the favourable comments by managers *and* members of the workforce about the new arrangements. Brian Harding, a manager at Cardiff, said

> The new labour force, now that they are trained, have done a superb job. The quality of the cargo handling service has improved dramatically. There is significantly less damage to cargo and to expensive plant, equipment and gear. A whole better spirit exists through the more caring attitudes, greater dedication to the task and a feeling of all working together.[21]

Sentiments of this kind were endorsed by other managers and reciprocated by former registered dockworkers. Len Mitchell from Southampton said

> All right, we lost the fight. There is a change in the economic climate – we have got to live in this modern world and that is what we intend to do.[22]

Of course, the ultimate aim of abolishing the National Dock Labour Scheme was to provide better customer service. Had that been achieved one year later? Referring to the more aggressive competition

which followed the Scheme's repeal, Michael Everard, chairman of
E. T. Everard and Sons, a leading short sea European shipowner, said

> It's really good news for the consumer because the cost of
> importing/exporting goods through Britain's ports has been re-
> duced.[23]

One other great benefit of the increased competition between Britain's
90 or so ports could easily be overlooked – a national dock strike is
now virtually impossible. If the dockers at a particular port were
foolish enough to go on strike, others would be delighted to step in and
handle the cargoes.

THE COURTS AND LEGAL SERVICES[24]

Restrictive labour practices, based on a producer rather than a
consumer mentality, have not been limited to manual work but have
run right through society. Senior academics, with their lifetime tenure,
lawyers, doctors, and other professional people have been just as guilty
of these as coal-miners, newspaper printers and dockers, and the
denunciation of the trade unions by some professional people has
contained more than a dash of hypocrisy. The economic consequences
of professional restrictive practices were admirably analysed by
Professor Lees in 1966,[25] but very little notice was taken of his
criticism until the late 1980s. It is to the Thatcher government's great
credit that during its third term of office it attempted to shake several
of the professions, including teachers, medical doctors, opticians and
lawyers, out of their torpor. This should have persuaded all but the
most cynical that, rather than engaging in a class war, the government
was committed to an even-handed programme of employment reform.
    An attempt to achieve even a modest amount of reform in the
professions requires a high degree of political courage, because the
professions are experienced and skilful lobbyists and detest any
interference from outsiders, however much public money they
absorb. And the toughest opponent for any government is the legal
profession, which is deeply entrenched in the very process of
government and law-making. Until 1988, when Lord Mackay became
Lord Chancellor, it seemed as though the holder of that office, with his
ex-officio seat in the Cabinet, often saw his main role as the guardian
of tradition. Part of that tradition was that it was for lawyers to decide
what kind of legal system was best for the public who provided their

income, and the consumer interest played little or no part in their calculations. In this respect the 6,000 barristers, who had a monopoly of advocacy in all superior courts, were far worse than the 50,000 or so solicitors who came into regular contact with the public. As Lees wrote of the barristers: 'They are a law unto themselves. Those who administer and shape the law stand, as a profession, outside it,'[26] and he went on to say of their self-imposed restrictive practices, which in some cases at least doubled the cost of justice, that 'All this begins to make the London printers look like a high point of free enterprise.'[27]

The economic effects of this privilege were unfortunate. But far more serious for society as a whole was the fact that most citizens, who are neither poor – and thus eligible for legal aid – nor very wealthy – and thus not too concerned about the cost of justice – have been denied access to the courts because to lose their case would mean financial ruin. One reason for the lack of concern about this situation by senior barristers and judges might be that their own incomes are well above the average and there is, therefore, a danger that they simply do not appreciate the problems of Mr and Mrs Average in meeting the costs of litigation. Then the Inns of Court have a mediaeval atmosphere which is hardly conducive to conducting their business efficiently. Finally, barristers are expert at making a case and are quite prepared to defend the indefensible, especially when they think that their own interests are threatened. This helps to explain why they have so stoutly resisted many proposals for reform, including the termination of their monopoly of advocacy in the higher courts. But the Thatcher government eventually grasped even this sharp nettle in January 1989 when in three Green Papers Lord Mackay, the Lord Chancellor, recommended fundamental reform of the legal profession and the ending of this restrictive practice.

The tone of the main Green Paper *The Work and Organisation of the Legal Profession*[28] was set at the beginning of its first chapter where it stated that:

1.1 The Government's overall objective in publishing this Green Paper is to see that the public has the best possible access to legal services and that those services are of the right quality for the particular needs of the client. The Government believes that this is best achieved by ensuring that:

(a) a market providing legal services operates freely and efficiently so as to give clients the widest possible choice of cost effective services; and

(b) the public can be certain that those services are being supplied by people who have the necessary expertise to provide a service in the area in question.

1.2 The Government believes that free competition between the providers of legal services will, through the discipline of the market, ensure that the public is provided with the most efficient and effective network of legal services at the most economical price, although the Government believes that the public must also be assured of the competence of the providers of those services.

For those ordinary people who want to avail themselves of legal services, these truths would probably be self-evident. But for many barristers, used to making their own restrictive rules, they were revolutionary. It was not in the least surprising that, on the day following the publication of the Green Papers, Lord Hailsham, who had been Lord Chancellor for twelve years between 1970 and 1987, had nothing good to say about the proposals which, in his view, 'are not particularly well timed, not particularly well thought out, and some aspects, particularly the suggested compromise with contingency fees, are definitely sinister'.[29]

But *The Times* leader writer disagreed. He argued that 'The Lord Chancellor's [Lord Mackay's] logic scores a number of direct hits. There is little ground for denying solicitors access to the High Court bench. There is a sensible case for a limited "contingency fee" system.'[30] And the next day a senior barrister, Sir William Goodhart, QC, gave the Green Papers 'a cautious welcome' and of the key proposal to abolish the barristers' monopoly of advocacy in the higher courts he wrote 'On balance, I believe that the Bar does not need the protection of exclusive rights of audience. The Lord Chancellor's proposals on this front call for a cautious but positive response.'[31]

THE COURTS AND LEGAL SERVICES ACT

Battles against reform by professional groups are just as vigorous as those conducted by trade unions, but instead of the picket lines they are fought in more sober places, and words take the place of physical force. In the case of the proposals for the reform of the legal profession, including the removal of the barristers' monopoly of advocacy in the higher courts, the climax occurred in the House of

Lords on 7 April 1989, only ten weeks after the publication of the Green Papers.

It is unusual for the House of Lords to sit later than 3 pm on a Friday, But the leading proponent of reform, Lord Mackay, the Lord Chancellor, was determined to give his opponents every opportunity to have their say, and on this particular Friday the debate on the Green Papers lasted from 9.56 am to 10.41 pm. Lord Mackay opened and closed the debate and was present for almost the whole of it. Most of the 53 speakers were lawyers, and most of these, especially the barristers, were opposed to the reforms on various grounds. The leaders of the opposition were Lord Lane, the Lord Chief Justice, and Lord Hailsham, a previous Lord Chancellor. Lord Lane aroused fears of 'control by the executive [the government] of the principal means available to the ordinary citizen of controlling that same executive' and, likening the Green Paper proposals to the Nazi dictatorship, he went on to say:

> Oppression does not stand on the doorstep with a toothbrush moustache and a swastika armband. It creeps up insidiously; it creeps up step by step; and all of a sudden the unfortunate citizen realises that freedom has gone.[32]

Lord Hailsham was more restrained than Lord Lane. He was 'frankly appalled' by the content of the Green Papers and 'shocked' by the constitutional issue which they raised. But he did at least 'invoke the long and noble tradition of this country that one may differ sharply on policy without losing friendships.'[33]

So the judges and barristers, easily superior in the number and length of their speeches, had their say. And yet Lord Mackay emerged a clear winner from the 12½ hours of debate. One reason was that his few supporters, including Baroness Phillips, had the better of the argument. But perhaps even more important was his composure when under attack and his perfect courtesy towards his opponents, qualities which made Lord Lane's words seem thoroughly intemperate. By the end of the debate, given that Lord Mackay had the support of the Prime Minister and the cabinet, it was practically certain that the main proposals for reform would go through without serious amendment.

THE BILL AND THE ACT

A period of discussion on the Green Papers was followed by a White Paper in July 1989[34] and some months later a Bill was presented to

Parliament which received the Royal Assent in October 1990 and became the Courts and Legal Services Act. This massive piece of legislation carries into effect most of the original proposals, including the termination of the barristers' total monopoly of advocacy in the higher courts, and marks the biggest reform of the legal profession ever carried out. It is still too early to assess its effectiveness, but its intentions are certainly sound. However there is one short section which seems to run counter to the Act's statutory objective in Section 17-(1) of securing new or better ways of providing legal services 'and a wider choice of persons providing them, while maintaining the proper and efficient administration of justice'.

THE LEGAL IMMUNITY OF ADVOCATES

At a time when trade union immunities are fast disappearing, it is anomalous that Section 62 of the new Act gives statutory immunity from liability for negligence to all advocates who are not barristers, putting solicitors who are engaged in advocacy on a par with barristers who already have such immunity under the common law. One might rather have expected a short clause removing the immunity for barristers. How is this immunity justified? The brief argument of the main Green Paper was repeated in the White Paper where it was stated that

> The Government accepts that if advocates are to be able to carry out their overriding duty to the court in presenting cases fully, they must be immune from actions in negligence in respect of the conduct and management of a case in court, and the preliminary work intimately connected with that.[35]

Those (hopefully few) clients who lose their case as a result of their advocate's negligence will feel cheated by this special pleading and the immunities which accompany it. They will want to know how advocates who have been negligent in the preparation or presentation of their case can possibly have carried out 'their overriding duty to the court.' It will be poor consolation to them that negligent advocates might eventually be disciplined by their professional bodies, and Section 22-(7)(b) of the Act deliberately prevents the newly created Ombudsman from intervening in cases of this kind.

However, most major statutes require some amendment soon after they come into effect. The repeal of Section 62 and its substitution by a Section which removed barristers' immunity from liability for negligence would be a most desirable amendment to the Act. It would clearly indicate that the interests of consumers, so far as legal services were concerned, were indeed taking precedence over those of producers.

*   *   *

In this chapter an attempt has been made to show that the legislative programme of employment reform between 1980 and 1990 has had or will have a noticeable and beneficial effect on labour practices in four walks of life. This does not mean that the labour market as a whole is now working in a flexible and satisfactory way. The sclerosis of a lifetime is not cured in a few years. However, at least an environment has been created in which people can begin to feel that a cure is possible for what was previously thought to be an incurable disease.

9 Unfinished Business

Give us the tools, and we will finish the job
Winston S. Churchill, Radio Broadcast, February 1941

As indicated in chapter 2, the Thatcher government's programme of trade union reform developed in a thoroughly pragmatic way. Because a comprehensive strategy was never set out in 1979–80, it cannot be claimed that the task was completed, and no such claim was made either by Mrs Thatcher or her last Secretary of State for Employment, Michael Howard.

In fact radical reform in an area like employment and trade union law may never be complete, as the constantly changing environment requires changing policies. The Japanese approach to working practices in a car assembly plant, summed up in the word *kaizen* (continuous improvement) may be appropriate to legislative reform, where the British approach has usually been to 'leave well alone', despite strong evidence that existing laws were not working at all, let alone working well. The main danger now is that, without making an explicit statement that the job has been finished, there will be an implicit assumption to that effect in the Department of Employment, so that ministers and officials there ignore the labour market and trade union problems which remain.

The most obvious of the remaining problems are:

1. No answer has been found to the problem of disputes in essential services, so that in 1989 many people were deprived of an ambulance service for several months.
2. Unemployment is still over 6 per cent. Beveridge regarded 3 per cent 'as a conservative aim to set for the average unemployment rate of the future.'[1]
3. Unit labour costs in the UK are rising much too fast. What would happen if unemployment started to move down towards 3 per cent?
4. Labour productivity is still far too low, so that a British factory operative produces about half as much as his US counterpart.

5. The 1984 reform of the law relating to the political levy has partially failed, so that many thousands of non-Labour voters are still contributing to the Labour Party through their trade union political funds.
6. The TUC is still dominated by old-fashioned ideas about the structure of the labour market, and the only realistic, progressive trade union (the EETPU) remains outside the TUC.
7. At the root of all the above problems is the government's slowness in the public sector in moving away from the obsolete, collectivist approach to employment relations and switching the emphasis to the individual contract of employment, with pay being related to the performance of the individual employee.
8. The Advisory, Conciliation and Arbitration Service (ACAS) (a supposedly impartial body) is still charged by Parliament with the particular duty 'of encouraging the extension of collective bargaining'. While those words remain on the statute book there are bound to be major doubts about the government's commitment to a radical reform of the traditional system.

Of course a basic problem for any government is that cabinet reshuffles make it difficult to achieve real continuity of policy. But problems are there to be overcome. If a Secretary of State knows that he will probably be in a post for only two years, presumably he will be aware that his first few months in office are crucial. During that period there has to be a recognition of the problems which remain and an assessment of the best way to resolve them.

So what should be the next step in trade union and labour market reform? There are at least five areas where practical action could start now:

1. Trade union immunities, especially in essential services.
2. Picketing.
3. The trade union political levy.
4. Trade union democracy, including the closed shop.
5. Further deregulation of the labour market, including amendment of the terms of reference for ACAS.

These areas will now be considered in turn.

TRADE UNION IMMUNITIES – ESPECIALLY IN ESSENTIAL SERVICES

At the heart of the Thatcher government's reform of trade union law was its reduction of the wide-ranging immunities granted by Parliament to the trade unions and their officials in the Trade Disputes Act 1906 and extended even further by the Labour government's legislation of 1974 and 1976. What is most surprising about these immunities is not that they were grossly abused in the winter of discontent, but that for most of the period 1906–79 they were not abused. This suggests that ordinary British employees are fundamentally reasonable people who will do a fair day's work for a fair day's pay if trade union law is put into a proper state. But what is 'a proper state'? That is a question which usually provokes an emotional response based on the fallacy of labour's bargaining disadvantage, a fallacy which Professor Hutt exploded sixty years ago in his book *The Theory of Collective Bargaining*.[2]

The idea of 'compulsory' or 'slave' labour is abhorrent to western democracies. Consequently employment law is rightly based on voluntary contracts made between an employer and his individual employees. Usually a period of between one and three months notice is required of either party if they wish to terminate the contract, but in practice the employee is free to walk out without notice because the legal costs of enforcing this part of the contract are more than it is worth to the employer. In law and in practice all employees are volunteers, and the employer knows this. If the pay and other conditions which he offers are less than the going market rate, he will have a second- or third-rate labour force and his goods or services will not be fully competitive. The corollary is that no employee can properly grumble about his pay and conditions of work. If he is dissatisfied with what is being provided, an immediate remedy is available – to leave and find better-paid work elsewhere. However, often this is not what happens because the least competent employees are the ones who grumble loudest and longest. The most effective antidote to this kind of complaint is to ask the grumblers why they don't hand in their notice. Naturally it would be rather optimistic to expect a truthful answer to this question!

The enormous growth of trade unionism and collective bargaining between 1900 and 1979, together with the careless approach by many employers to the labour aspects of their businesses, obscured the fact that the basic contract of employment has always been between the employer and each individual employee. The trade union enters on the scene as a third party, and in the UK collective bargains as such have never had the force of law. This was made clear in the case of *Ford Motor Co.* v. *AEFWU* (1969), where Mr Justice Lane held that an agreement made between Fords and nineteen trade unions was binding in honour only, ie it could be broken immediately and with impunity by those who had just set their names to it. In other words, as one lawyer recently put it, 'agreements affecting the livelihood of millions of workers, and thence the prosperity of the country, are strictly speaking not worth the paper they are written on.'[3]

So by 1979 British trade unions had achieved an amazing and unique position in which (a) their legal immunities meant that actions which they took, including those which induced breach of employment and commercial contracts, were above the law while (b) the collective bargains which they signed were unenforceable. Clearly such an arrangement was quite incompatible with an efficient labour market and a properly functioning economy. But how does the situation differ today? What was the essence of the Thatcher government's programme of reform?

The unenforceability of collective bargains can be dealt with very briefly, because nothing has changed. Collective bargains in the UK are still unenforceable in a court of law and there is no sign at all that this situation is likely to change in the foreseeable future.

But as described in chapters 2–6 above, and especially in chapter 3, trade union immunities have been very substantially cut back, so that they are now only available in a primary dispute, as more narrowly defined, after a secret ballot among the members concerned has shown a majority in favour. In effect, Parliament is saying to trade unionists: 'Your union may have legal privileges (immunities) in primary disputes, however outrageous your demands, provided a majority of you have voted in favour of those demands'. Or, in other words, Parliament has given to trade union members themselves the right to decide whether or not legal immunities are available. It is as if Parliament had given motorists the right to decide an appropriate speed limit, or burglars to say that they should be immune from prosecution if the value of their haul was less than £10,000.

This policy must be based on a presumption that in all UK trade unions a majority of members who bother to vote in a pre-strike ballot are reasonable and moderate people who will never abuse the privilege which Parliament has given them. But is that a reasonable presumption? It was shown in chapter 6 that over 90 per cent of pre-strike ballots go in favour of strike action, and that is not in the least surprising because the union members concerned have nothing at all to lose by supporting the recommendation of their executive. In fact the number of ballots in favour of industrial action increased from 90 per cent in 1987 to 93.5 per cent in 1989 as the unions came to terms with the new rules of the game; and it might be expected that in a few years time it will come very close to 100 per cent.

Now it may be that in the process of step by step reform, which the Thatcher government adopted in 1979, it was necessary at some stage to make trade union immunities in primary disputes, including essential services, conditional upon approval of a trade union's demands in a secret ballot. But there must be a major question as to whether this is sustainable as a permanent policy. Since the 1950s the British economy has had a predisposition to wage inflation, which has led to an increase in unit labour costs well above that of its major competitors. The high unemployment of 1980–88 acted as a restraint to excessive wage claims and enabled the rate of inflation to be reduced from 18 to 4 per cent. But as unemployment continued to fall, pay demands began to accelerate so that by the end of 1989 the year-on-year increase in average earnings was nearly 10 per cent. At the same time the Amalgamated Engineering Union was winning a battle against several leading employers for a shorter working week, adding to the pressure on unit labour costs.

The trade unions best placed to exploit this situation are those in monopoly (or monopolistic) essential services, and it can surely be only a matter of time before they use the muscle which Parliament has given them. To give someone, or a particular group of people, a privilege is to encourage them to use it!

In most other countries it has been understood that certain services, necessary for public health and safety, must be protected against disruption, and their legislation reflects this.[4] It is, therefore, now appropriate for the British government to legislate for

    (a) a statutory duty to maintain the supply of a specified short list of essential services, including health, gas, water, electricity, telephone and fire services;

    (b) an obligation to provide compensation to customers when the above statutory obligation is not fulfilled, and

    (c) the removal of all trade union immunities in the relevant industries.

Those who currently work in these industries could receive cash compensation (say £1,000 each) for the change in their contract of employment. New entrants would be told at the recruitment stage that no trade union immunities existed in that particular industry. Removal of the immunities would be a strong encouragement to both parties in these industries to negotiate 'no-strike' deals, providing for external binding arbitration as a last-resort option for negotiations over pay and other conditions of employment. Once experience had shown that this arrangement worked well in this limited area, the way would be open for the abolition of all trade union immunity.

The complete abolition of trade union immunity will be seen by some, and even by some radicals, as one step too far. But as Professor Minford put it recently:

> This change then would in no sense be a draconian anti-union device, outlawing strikes. Rather it would return contracts to the private sector, and the law into its proper role of arbitration. Union law would, as an attractive by-product, be dramatically simplified, since the whole immunity tangle would go.[5]

The complete abolition of all union immunities must be the ultimate aim. But the step by step process has stood the test of time, and the next step should include the removal of immunities in essential services.

PICKETING

The proposal here, already adumbrated in chapter 5, is very straightforward. It is to transfer the restriction on the number of pickets (6) at an entrance to a workplace from the Code of Practice on Picketing to the statute book.

The only kind of picketing which is acceptable in our society is peaceful picketing; but mass picketing is always intimidatory and inclines towards violence. It follows that the number of pickets in any one place must be restricted by law. The fact that mass, intimidatory picketing has been common in the past, and especially in the 1970s, is no reason for permitting it in the future. The Thatcher reforms should have created a break with many (bad) past traditions of industrial relations in the UK and opened up the possibility of new thinking.

At the same time, in a Green Paper suggesting this and other reforms as legislative options, it would be wise to make the point that peaceful picketing, like trade union immunities, is a privilege granted by Parliament, and that Parliament always reserves the right to withdraw privileges which are abused.

THE TRADE UNION POLITICAL LEVY

The 1983 Conservative Manifesto contained a promise to

> invite the TUC to discuss the steps which the trade unions themselves can take to ensure that individual members are freely and effectively able to decide for themselves whether or not to pay the political levy. In the event that the trade unions are not willing to take such steps, the Government will be prepared to introduce measures to guarantee the free and effective right of choice. (p. 12)

And Tom King, as Secretary of State for Employment, duly carried out the first part of the promise. Following his discussions with the TUC, the TUC issued a statement of guidance to affiliated unions, requiring the unions to inform all of their members that they had a right to contract out of the political levy and telling them how to do so.

During the debate in the House of Commons on this part of the Trade Union Bill, Sir Nicholas Bonsor was one of several Conservative backbenchers who doubted that this agreement with the TUC would produce the desired result; and Mr King duly gave him an assurance that 'If the agreement is frustrated, let there be no doubt that the Government will not sit back. We will honour our undertaking to introduce measures such as those to which I have referred.'[6] But how is the government to know whether or not the agreement has been frustrated?

One suggestion might be that they should wait and see how many complaints there are from trade union members about not being able to contract out of the levy, which amounts to about five pence a week out of a total subscription of a pound. That suggestion should not be taken too seriously, because very few people grumble about paying such a small sum. Indeed, many contributors to the political fund are probably unaware that they are paying into it. A better measure is to consider the proportion of members who are paying the levy in the fifty or so unions which have political funds. Omitting the National Union of Scalemakers, which has only two members contributing to its rather small political fund, this proportion varies considerably, from 20.5 per cent in the Association of Cinematograph Television and Allied Technicians to 97.6 per cent in the National Union of Railway-men and the Transport and General Workers Union (1988 figures). Now it may be that both the NUR and the TGWU would insist that they are trying to keep their members informed about their right to contract out of the political levy. All one could say to that is that other unions are trying harder and with much more success. In fact Table 9.4 shows that in several major trade unions (a) the proportion of members contributing to the levy is suspiciously high, and (b) it has been rising rather than falling since the TUC issued its 'statement of guidance' in 1984.

Table 9.4 is strong *prima facie* evidence that some major trade unions have made it more difficult, not easier, to contract out of the political levy since the TUC issued its statement of guidance in 1984. This is not surprising, because (as Sir Nicholas Bonsor and his backbench friends understood, but not, it seems, whoever drafted this part of the 1983 Manifesto, nor Mr King) the TUC has no authority to enforce the terms of a statement of guidance of this kind on its affiliated unions. In fact the Secretary of State's negotiations with the TUC were a complete waste of time.

There is only one satisfactory answer to this problem: that is to substitute contracting in to the political levy for contracting out. The main purpose of this reform would be to ensure that no-one pays the levy involuntarily. But it would have the side effect of significantly reducing the total annual income of the trade union political funds, which might fall from about £12 million to £8 million. Nearly all Labour supporters and even some Conservatives would be dismayed by this prospect on two grounds. First, that it would be unfair because the Conservative Party is largely funded by business firms who do not have to get specific approval from their shareholders before they make such contributions; and second, that it would increase the probability of state funding for political parties in Britain, which few want.

The first objection can be dealt with quickly. Of course it is quite wrong that the directors of a company should be able to give away their shareholders' money to a political party without their specific approval at the company's annual general meeting, and company law should be changed to provide for this. The second objection seems more substantial; but on closer inspection it, too, falls away. Clearly it is unhealthy in a supposedly democratic society for major political parties to be funded by a few wealthy backers; but equally clearly the

Table 9.4   Subscribers to the political levy in ten major trade
          unions, 1984 and 1988

	Trade Union	Per cent of members subscribing in 1984	Per cent of members subscribing in 1988	Per cent change between 1984 & 1988
1	Amalgamated Engineering Union	73.4	96.2	+ 22.8
2	Confederation of Health Service Employees	91.7	92.2	+ 0.5
3	General, Municipal Boilermakers and Allied Trades	86.1	94.7	+ 8.6
4	Musicians Union	80.5	95.1	+ 14.6
5	National Union of Public Employees	97.1	96.7	− 0.4
6	National Union of Railwaymen	96.9	97.6	+ 0.7
7	Transport and General Workers Union	92.5	97.6	+ 5.1
8	Union of Communication Workers	93.0	94.7	+ 1.7
9	Union of Construction, Allied Trades and Technicians	77.8	85.2	+ 7.4
10	Union of Shop, Distributive and Allied Workers	91.3	92.1	+ 0.8

Source: Annual Reports of the Certification Officer for 1985 and 1989.

parties will not make a strenuous effort to reform the system so long as that backing is available. Already the Labour Party has tried to encourage individual party membership, and these efforts are bearing fruit, so that a report in September 1990 suggested that the number of individual members was not far short of 300,000[7], who were paying an annual membership fee of £10 each. It was expected that that fee would soon be increased to £20.

So a reduction in financial support from the trade unions for the Labour Party and from business firms for the Tory Party does not necessarily mean the introduction of state funding for political parties. On the contrary, by putting pressure on party organisers to increase individual membership it should improve the health of British politics. It follows that the arguments against the substitution of contracting in to the political levy for the current system of contracting out have little force.

TRADE UNION DEMOCRACY

There are two recommendations here. The first concerns the closed shop, and the second is to do with the 'overkill' policy which established the office of the Commissioner for the Rights of Trade Union Members (the CROTUM).

The Closed Shop

As shown earlier, the closed shop in Britain has deep and strong roots. The Thatcher government has attacked it on several occasions, but there can be no guarantee that these attempts to eliminate the closed shop, including the latest one contained in the Employment Act 1990, will succeed. The right policy, therefore, is to survey the situation again in 1992, when the 1990 Act has been in effect for about eighteen months. The survey should be directed especially at those difficult areas mentioned in the Green Paper of March 1989 *Removing Barriers to Employment*, and these areas include shipping, printing, manufacturing, the theatre, the London wholesale markets, construction and road haulage. If the 1992 survey was to show that the closed shop is still being practised in these and other areas, then even higher fines on employers and other tougher measures would be necessary.

The CROTUM

This proposal has already been dealt with in some detail in chapter 6. Experience has shown that the CROTUM is under-employed. The post should, therefore, be abolished and the CROTUM's duties transferred to the Certification Officer for Trade Unions and Employers' Associations. The Certification Officer might need one or two extra staff to cope with the additional work, but overall there would be a saving. The government will, of course, argue that this recommendation is premature because the 1990 Employment Act will provide the CROTUM with more work. In that case the situation should be kept under close scrutiny, and Tory backbenchers should force the Secretary of State to abolish the post if his prediction is proved false.

Further Deregulation of the Labour Market

Again, these policy issues were considered in some detail in the relevant chapter (7) and all that needs to be done here is to recapitulate briefly. The recommendations should be viewed against the background of a labour market which is still far too inflexible, mainly because the tradition of national collective bargaining is so strong.

The Terms of Reference for ACAS

Against the background of an inflexible labour market, and their rather ineffective attempts to loosen it up, the fact that the Thatcher government was in 1990 still instructing ACAS, a supposedly impartial body, to encourage 'the extension of collective bargaining' smacks of extreme carelessness. Actually this carelessness typifies the amateur approach to employment relations sometimes adopted by government and many employers. One is bound to wonder why employer representatives and independent members continue to serve on an arbitration body with such partial and obsolete terms of reference. It is impossible to take seriously other government policies for a more flexible labour market while these words remain on the statute book.

Self-Employment

The right policy for self-employment is to encourage it as far as possible, and that means ensuring that there are no taxation or other obstacles for those hardy souls who wish to move from employment to self-employment. Officials at the Department of Employment should work with members of the Deregulation Unit, situated in the Department of Trade and Industry, to keep the situation under constant review. If there is any hard evidence that the Inland Revenue are creating difficulties for those who wish to be taxed as self-employed, the government should promote a Parliamentary Bill to eliminate these difficulties.

In addition, it should be remembered that when employment affairs are being discussed, the interests of the self-employed are often ignored, because they are too busy running their businesses to spend time at the conference table. There must be a deliberate effort by EC and other policy makers to ensure that the interests of the increasing number of self-employed are taken fully into account.

Other Deregulatory Policies

The Thatcher government attempted to deregulate the employment market for several years, but the task is a Herculean one as the EC Commissioners generate an avalanche of documents as part of the 'Action Programme' of the Social Charter. Meanwhile, the socialist majority in the European Parliament applauds the Commissioners' efforts and the British Labour Party promises to go even further. It is an uphill battle for the deregulators as they attempt to rebut policies which are bound to have an especially damaging effect on job creation in the poorer areas of the EC, like Portugal, Greece and now East Germany. However, the re-unification of Germany might induce the Germans to offer the British deregulators some support, because as East Germany and other Eastern European nations move from a command to a market economy they will need to generate millions of new jobs, and many of these will be part-time and/or temporary. In these circumstances it would be foolish and hypocritical for the Germans to support a mass of unnecessary regulations which would damage the employment prospects of their own people.

Thus the right policy for the British government at the present time is to devote most of its efforts to refuting the greater absurdities of the 'Action Programme'. And all those individuals and groups which agree with the deregulatory approach should give the Secretary of State and his officials as much practical help as possible.

*   *   *

In this chapter an attempt has been made to show that trade union and labour market reform is still incomplete. When so much has been achieved, it would be tragic if complacency prevented the job from being carried forward towards completion.

10 What Would a Labour Government Do?

> While recognising the freedom not to join a trade union in the
> [European Social] Charter, we fully support and advocate
> 100 per cent trade union membership at the workplace.
>
> *Looking to the Future*, The Labour Party, 1990

Unless Parliament unexpectedly decides otherwise, there will be a general election before 9 July 1992, bringing with it the possibility that a Labour government will be returned to office. The purpose of this chapter is to explore, in a tentative way, the consequences of such an outcome for trade union and employment law and for the British economy. The task has been made easier by the publication in 1989 and 1990 of two Labour Party policy documents: *Meet the challenge, Make the change*, and *Looking to the Future*, the result of two years' intensive review of policy following the Party's defeat in three successive general elections. Together they contain about 140,000 words, and trade union and employment matters are given a fair coverage. Given the endorsement of these policies by the Trades Union Congress and the Labour Party conference in the autumn of 1990, it seems reasonable to assume that they contain an accurate indication of the way in which a future Labour government would legislate in this field.

The quotation at the head of this chapter suggests that the Labour Party is in a serious dilemma about its policy towards the closed shop, and the same may be true about its other trade union policies. The termination of the collectivist consensus by the Thatcher government, coming as it did with widespread popular support, has created an extremely difficult situation for a political party which was early on backed by the trade unions in order to provide their legal immunities, and which still receives from them very significant financial and other assistance. At this point a brief historical digression is necessary.

UNION ROOTS OF THE LABOUR PARTY

The function of the Trades Union Congress, which was founded in 1868, 'was mainly political and propagandist in orientation.'[1] However, it was not until the following year that a Parliamentary Committee was established, and that Committee only became effective in 1871, when several senior trade union officials were elected to it to watch over the passage of the Trade Union Bill. They set to work immediately, and within a few days of the Congress wrote a letter which was quickly printed and in the hands of every Member of Parliament. Together with a deputation which had been sent to the Home Secretary by the TUC the previous week, the letter produced a rapid and tangible response from government in the form of a decision to split the Bill into two parts, a decision which 'greatly helped the unions in the long run.'[2]

From the beginning, the TUC proved itself immensely effective in lobbying Parliament. That continued despite a change of government in 1874, so that with the passage of the Conspiracy and Protection of Property Act in 1875, the unions were convinced that the law was in an entirely satisfactory state, ie all their interests had been taken care of.[3] This situation was only upset by the decision of the House of Lords in the Taff Vale case (1901), already discussed in chapter 3. The trade unions were appalled to find that their immunities (privileges) were not so comprehensive as they had imagined. What were they to do when neither the Liberal nor the Conservative Party was willing to give them the complete legal immunity which they were asking for? The answer was to put more of their weight behind a newly established political party known as the Labour Representation Committee.

In fact the TUC had played a major part in the creation of the Labour Representation Committee in February 1900, following a resolution to that effect passed by a modest majority at the 1899 Congress. But the new political party was a sickly child. At the general election in November 1900 only two LRC candidates were elected, and only one of them – Keir Hardie – was a socialist. However, the result of the Taff Vale case put a totally new complexion on the LRC's future. The affiliated trade union membership rose rapidly, and serious preparations were made for by-elections and the next general election. After the general election of January 1906, the House of Commons contained thirty members of the LRC, with seventeen other members who had clear links with the labour movement. A month later the LRC changed its name to the Labour Party and the trade unions began to flex their political muscles.

But how did it happen that Sir Henry Campbell-Bannerman's Liberal government, with an ample overall majority, conceded complete legal immunities to the unions against its better judgement?

Early in 1906 a Royal Commission had reported on the state of trade union law, and had recommended that the unions should accept full responsibility for their own actions subject to some amendment of the law in their favour. The Webbs, who were intimately involved with these developments, described what happened next:

> When the Liberal Government brought in a Bill very much on the lines of the Commission's Report, there was a dramatic exhibition of the electoral power that Trade Unionism, once it is roused, can exercise in its own defence. Member after member rose from different parts of the House to explain that they had pledged themselves to vote for the complete immunity which Trade Unions were supposed to have been granted in 1871. Nothing less than this would suffice; and the most powerful government hitherto known was constrained, in spite of the protests of lawyers and employers, to pass into law the Trade Disputes Act of 1906.[4]

It can be seen, then, that the origins of the Labour Party within the trade union movement made its support for complete trade union immunities inescapable. Of course, much has changed since 1906, and even since 1979, but it does mean that, in matters of employment policy at least, these origins are still keenly remembered and exert a strong influence on Labour Party policy.

For example, trade union leaders have demanded, and have usually been able to assert, a large say over employment legislation when the Party has been in office. And despite recent changes to the Party's constitution, the trade unions still have a majority of the votes at Conference and on other key policy-making bodies, and sponsored 142 Labour MPs out of 230 in 1990, including 18 members of the shadow cabinet.[5] Furthermore, the fact that the trade union political funds now generate £12 million annually and still provide the greater share of the Party's income must give the unions a major informal source of leverage in addition to their constitutional position.

It is worth noting that every single part of the post-1979 reforms, including the popular pre-strike ballot, has been steadfastly opposed by the Labour Party in Parliament. Of the Bill which included that particular provision and duly became the Trade Union Act 1984, Mr John Smith, later shadow Chancellor of the Exchequer, said in the House of Commons:

> Because the Bill will do serious damage to both industrial relations and political fairness, we shall not only fight it with vigour and

determination but, when we come to power as we will, we shall repeal it and replace it with legislation that reinstates the principles that this government seek to abandon.[6]

These remarks were made of the piece of legislation which more than any other has saved the trade unions from themselves! However in respect of trade union ballots it seems that second and wiser thoughts have prevailed, because Labour's recent policy documents promise to preserve them.

The overall aim of the Labour Party in its recent policy statements seems fairly clear. It is to give the impression that the Party is now in control of the unions instead of the other way round, and that its policies would help to produce the more efficient economy which will be essential as competition increases inside and outside the EC. But whoever is calling the tune, what is actually proposed? The different aspects of policy will be considered under the headings already used in previous chapters, i.e. (1) Trade union immunities (2) The closed shop (3) Picketing (4) Trade union democracy, and (5) Regulating the labour market.

TRADE UNION IMMUNITIES

It seems that the trade unions have finally accepted that their legal immunities should not be unlimited and unconditional, and even a Labour government would not return to the 1906–79 situation. But the unions have exacted a price for this 'concession', as they see it, and that price is a high one. Union immunities will be extended significantly beyond those which currently exist, and there will be further legislative measures, some of them unprecedented, to advance the rights of individual employees, so that the package as a whole will be very damaging to the flexibility of the labour market. This change of policy will, of course, tend to reverse the markedly downward trend from 1979 to 1990 in the number of strikes and days lost through strikes.

Several specific proposals will encourage strikes. First – and this is an unprecedented move in the UK – individuals will be given the right not to be dismissed for going on strike after a majority ballot in favour. It is claimed that this will bring Britain into line with other European countries, but what is not mentioned is that other European countries generally have more responsible or much weaker unions than those in the UK. The introduction of such a right would be an open invitation to all trade unionists always to vote in favour of strike action. It would strip the pre-strike ballot of any real meaning.

Second, (and again the European example is speciously prayed in aid) certain sympathetic strikes will be legalised. These will include strikes against customers or suppliers of the company at which the primary dispute exists. In other words, there will be a reversion to a state of affairs in which an employer who has no dispute at all with his workforce may be deliberately involved in someone else's dispute, and suffer serious loss as a result, without redress.

Third, the courts will be forbidden to issue *ex parte* injunctions (injunctions which are granted without hearing the trade union point of view) to employers who are being damaged by illegal trade union action. In addition, where a court grants an interlocutory injunction, at the option of either party a hearing on the full merits of the case would have to follow immediately.

Finally, a Labour government would establish a new Industrial Court 'to deal with the whole area of industrial disputes'. This new Court

will have full powers of enforcement and damages – but [there is always a but] legislation will prevent the total sequestration of a trade union's income and assets in a way which paralyses the union in all its lawful business, such as paying benefits and representing other members.[7]

The effect of this proposal would be to take the sting out of sequestration, which is the ultimate penalty for contempt of court. It suggests that trade unions still have reservations about the rule of law in a democratic society.

THE CLOSED SHOP

The quotation at the head of this chapter exemplifies the Labour Party's dilemma over the closed shop, to which it gave wholehearted support during its period of government 1974–79. Once it is agreed that employees have the right not to join a trade union, then major doubts arise about the benefits or otherwise of trade union membership. This situation creates considerable difficulties for those trade union officials who believe that improvements in living standards arise through trade union activity alone. But the Labour Party's commitment to the European Social Charter seems to have eventually brought about an acceptance of the view that the right to join a trade union must include an equivalent right not to join. This conversion has been long drawn out, but it seems to be genuine.

PICKETING

Accompanying the recidivist approach towards certain sympathetic strikes, a Labour government would permit some secondary picketing.

TRADE UNION DEMOCRACY

Trade union members would continue to have a legal right to a secret ballot to elect the members of their union executive. In addition, they are promised:

> a new independent tribunal empowered to hear complaints from individuals which allege that their union has breached statutory provisions on strike ballots and ballots for the election of union executives.[8]

Again, it would seem that there has been some conversion here to the merits of a practice which is now operating well and is popular with union members.

REGULATING THE LABOUR MARKET

It will be noted that, for this topic, the word 'Regulating' has been substituted for chapter 7's 'Deregulating', because Labour's policy is in complete contrast to that of the Thatcher government. The proposed regulations are so numerous that the commentator hardly knows where to begin. Perhaps it is best to start with the tone of the Labour Party's policy.

It might appear from their proposals on the closed shop and trade union democracy that the Labour Party has been at least partiall converted from its adherence to collectivist employment policies based mainly on trade union representation. Careful study shows that this is not so. Again and again in the policy documents there is strong emphasis on trade union representation and collective bargaining. Two quotations make the point:

> Trade unions have an essential and positive role to play in achieving good industrial relations and in representing people at work. Labour therefore believes it is right to promote union membership and organisation, to encourage union recognition by employers for collective bargaining purposes and to develop and support stable and effective negotiating machinery.[9]

and a few paragraphs later:

> The Labour government will positively encourage the development of collective bargaining as an act of public policy.[10]

However, this collectivist emphasis most emphatically does not mean that individual employment rights are forgotten. As mentioned in chapter 7 above, a Labour government would not only implement fully the European Social Charter, but it would go much further. Every employee, without fail, would have the full range of employment rights from their first minute at work. And there is more. The *pièce de résistance* of Labour's policy is a national minimum wage, which will start at 50 per cent of male median earnings (equivalent to £2.80 per hour in 1989 terms) rising over time to two-thirds of male median earnings.

This is not the place to examine these proposed regulations in detail. All that needs to be said here is that for the vast majority of the several hundred thousand business firms in the UK, which are small firms, the proposals would create a bureaucratic nightmare. One might imagine that the proprietors of many small companies would prefer to close rather than attempt to comply with them and that at least half a million jobs would soon disappear, with the total number of job losses eventually reaching a million or more.

Those employment proposals of the Labour Party which most directly impinge on recent reforms have been briefly described. An attempt will now be made to assess their overall effect on the British economy.

THE ECONOMIC EFFECTS·OF THE PROPOSALS

Labour's trade union and employment policies are only one part of an extensive package which, in the Party's view, would benefit the British economy. Others beg to differ. Using the Liverpool Quarterly Model of the Economy, Patrick Minford and Paul Ashton have simulated the effects of Labour's economic and employment policies as recently published. Some of the economists' key predictions are contained in Table 10.5.

Table 10.5   Predicted effects of a Labour Government's economic and employment policies

Note: All figures show differences from base forecast

Year	Inflation[1] %	Average tax on employees[2] %	Unemployment (millions)	Output index of Gross Domestic Product %
1992	1.3	3.9	0.1	0.8
1993	4.5	7.2	0.4	1.4
1994	8.9	14.4	0.9	−0.9
1995	11.4	18.6	1.9	−6.9
1996	10.3	21.1	3.0	−10.1

[1] Consumer Price Index.

[2] Per cent of average earnings lost in taxes and NI contributions for a married man with two children.

Source: Liverpool Research Group in Macroeconomics, *Quarterly Economic Bulletin*, Vol. 11, No. 2, June 1990.

Like all models, the Liverpool Model is based upon certain assumptions. One of these is that the rise in union power is approximated by a 2 per cent rise in union density, an assumption which seems modest in the light of Labour's commitment to the union cause, discussed above. So what does the simulation predict?

The initial effects of the policies are encouraging, with output, consumption and investment all rising in year 1 (1992).

However even in the first year signs of strain are appearing in the financial markets...

> By 1993 or year 2, growth is declining and by the end of 1994, output is 3% lower than in the base as the effects of reversing the supply-side reforms of the 1980s come through. Unemployment climbs steadily, and by 1994 is running over 1 million higher than in the base. As the minimum wage rises and tax rates rise, the rise escalates to over 3 million in 1996.

> Inflation rises by over 5% within two years, and by 1994 is over 10% higher than in the base. This is the result of higher borrowing which by 1994 is growing sharply...It is this that compels a rise in general taxation (a rise of 6 pence in the standard rate), assumed to occur in 1995.[11]

So the economic scenario for the third and fourth years of a Labour government, which sticks to its policy pledges as presently published, is falling output, sharply rising unemployment, higher inflation and a significant increase in taxation for most wage and salary earners. This is not an attractive prospect. But is it realistic?

Actually, it seems possible that the Liverpool model might have underestimated the problems, and especially the problem of wage-push inflation, which the Labour policies would produce. Their promises to improve social security benefits and to introduce a national minimum wage rising to two-thirds of male median earnings would immediately push up the lowest wages, and create expectations of further increases well above the rate of inflation. Meanwhile at the other end of the income scale, income tax would rise from 40 per cent to 50 per cent and higher national insurance contributions would add another 9 per cent, so that all the well-paid would experience a substantial decline in their disposable income. How would they react? It is not unreasonable to suppose that they would seek, and probably achieve, a large increase in their gross income to restore most or all of the cut in their net income.

Thus the vast majority (about 80 per cent) of the working population, who are neither low-paid nor high-paid, would find themselves sandwiched between two groups, both receiving high pay increases. What would the majority do? Surely many of them would refuse to be left behind in the pay race, and their trade unions would submit large claims, backed up by strike threats, to ensure that they keep up with the rest. This development might be expected within 12–24 months of a Labour government coming to power.

The outcome of such a situation can readily be imagined. Mr Kinnock would face a situation very similar to that faced by Mr Callaghan in 1978. For a description of what happened then, the reader is referred back to chapter 1.

From the above analysis, the conclusion must be that the implementation of Labour's trade union and employment pledges, in conjunction with the Party's economic policies, would be very damaging to the British economy. To quote again Minford and Ashton:

> It hardly seems possible that they [the Labour Party] can so comprehensively ignore the lessons of the past decades.[12]

Epilogue to Part I

The thorough reform of trade union law, generally thought in 1979 to be impossible, was almost complete by 1990. Progress has been erratic and the policy has been pragmatic. Some Secretaries of State for Employment did a great deal; others made little or no contribution to the reform process. But behind her Secretaries of State stood a Prime Minister fiercely determined to resolve the problem which first brought her to office.

There cannot be any doubt that Margaret Thatcher deserves most of the credit for this remarkable achievement. As David Owen wrote in *The Times* on 19 April 1989, two weeks before the tenth anniversary of her premiership:

> Her most fundamental, far-reaching and sustainable success is the trade union legislation. Not only will that legislation stay on the statute book well into the 21st century, but, though she will hate the word, she has achieved a consensus in this area which embraces a far broader constituency than that of the Conservative voter. Paradoxically, she achieved these reforms not by a bold and radical stroke, but by a series of steps building upon each other in a logical and indeed evolutionary manner.

> But the legislation would, of itself, have been insufficient. A successful confrontation with mindless militancy was the essential buttress. Until Arthur Scargill was soundly and humiliatingly defeated, the spectre of 1979's winter of discontent hung over the country. It was Mrs Thatcher who, virtually alone, understood this.

Part II
New Employment Policies in the Enterprise

Introduction to Part II

Professor Hayek argued with conviction in 1980 that an economic recovery of Great Britain was impossible until the special privileges granted to the trade unions in the Trade Disputes Act 1906 had been revoked.[1] That task is almost complete, but Britain's economic recovery is at best partial and spasmodic.

It needs to be remembered that Hayek saw the removal of trade union immunities as a necessary, but not sufficient, condition for economic recovery. Allen had suggested a few years earlier that a more professional approach to the management of industry was a key factor in this process,[2] and it was seen in chapter 8 that there was some justification for this point of view. But until the Thatcher trade union reforms had taken place, business managers could always argue that their hands were tied so far as employment policies were concerned, because the unions were too strong. That excuse has now been invalidated. But will managers use their new opportunities in a constructive way?

Part 2 of this book is addressed primarily to business managers who understand that new opportunities now exist *and want to make the best use of them*. Britain is an open society. There is no lack of new ideas, but there is a reluctance to assess them critically *and to implement them*. Consequently these eight relatively short chapters are intended mainly for those managers who have executive responsibilities and want to introduce the best employment practices into their companies. Managers are busy people, and at this stage brevity is of the essence. If they are interested in the ideas sketched out in the following pages, they will find that further reading and advice is readily available from various sources, including those academics who are increasingly becoming involved in business problems.

11 From Industrial Relations to Human Resource Management

Britain and the world blamed the unions, and turned their backs on British Leyland products. But the real blame lay with management, for they failed in their duty to manage.

Michael Edwardes, *Back from the Brink*, 1983

In recent years the name of the academic discipline which covers the subject matter of this book has been changing from Industrial Relations (IR) to Human Resource Management (HRM). And in 1990 two new journals including the phrase Human Resource Management in their titles have been published.[1]

It might be thought that a change of name is not particularly significant. After all, the editors of these new journals were previously working in the discipline of Industrial Relations. How can the discipline have changed significantly if the same people are involved? Nevertheless, it could be that the change is real and fundamental, and will have profound consequences, because, as David Guest has put it, 'Adoption of HRM requires the capacity to think strategically and to manage innovative HRM policies.'[2] This is in contrast to the previous state of affairs in many companies, where it was accepted that multi-unionism and collective bargaining prevailed, that the shop stewards frequently made the rules and that management was powerless to alter the situation.

Another aspect of this change from IR to HRM is an understanding that managers are capable of influencing the attitude of employees towards their work, and thence working practices themselves, to improve quality and productivity in the workplace. As early as 1964, Allan Flanders showed in his classic text *The Fawley Productivity Agreements* how managers could achieve higher productivity, but the lesson was never taken to heart more generally. Many British managers preferred to ignore it, and in any case the law was heavily biased in favour of the trade unions. Now, in 1990, a different situation exists. How should managers use their new opportunities?

Some may see the new legislation as an encouragement to indulge in a crude bout of union-bashing, but this attitude would be unhelpful, to say the least, and it might bring a company into conflict with the law, because all employees now have a legal right to join a trade union and take part in its activities. The Thatcher government never suggested that this right should be removed, and the existence of independent trade unions (for example, Solidarity in Communist Poland) is usually seen as a hallmark of a free society. No, instead of attacking the union(s), it makes much more sense for managers first, to think carefully about the best ways to win loyalty and commitment from the whole workforce, and then to implement measures which will produce this result. That will be a taxing task; and it will be a task which is never complete. In fact it is better to think of it, like other management objectives, not as a task with a finite end but as an ongoing process for which the perfect method will never be achieved.

This process, as reflected in the change of name from IR to HRM, presents an intellectual as well as a practical challenge. There may be a feeling in some academic circles that success in business, including the human resource aspects of business, is more the result of sheer force than of thinking through a problem before tackling it. But as Peter Wickens has shown in his chapter entitled 'Commitment – Not Sickness – Determines Attendance'[3], low absenteeism in a car assembly plant is achieved not by a dictatorial, dogmatic management style, but by thinking hard about the best way to get people to work, regularly and on time, to do a tough repetitive job, week in week out, and then implementing those policies.

THE NEED FOR AN ORGANISATIONAL STRATEGY

Of course it is impossible for an organisation to win the commitment of its employees unless its aims have been spelt out and the employees have agreed with them. David Drennan described the problem well when he wrote recently

> Above all, management has got to get its goals clear and communicate them to employees in such a way that they understand them well enough to be able to help make the goals a reality.[4]

An increasing number of employers have attempted this task in the past few years, but many of the results have been unsatisfactory, to say the least. The goals must be set down in writing, but it should be remembered that most of us are not great readers. If the statement of goals is too long or complicated, it will be ineffective.

Goldsmith and Clutterbuck quote the statements of company objectives of Standard Telephones and Cables (STC) and H.P. Bulmer.[5] The former is 723 words and the latter 453. Both of these are far too long to be readily memorised. Much better is the summary of what it meant for STC to be the best company in its field, which contains 40 words.[6] It is significant that this was agreed by a series of committees all round the company, including shop floor people. Of course, a comprehensive statement of aims may be desirable, but if this is too long few will read it, and if it is much more than 100 words, a summary should be provided for general consumption. For the summary, about 100 words should be a maximum and within that length three or four aims are better than nine or ten.

Drennan was critical of a set of ten values recently approved by the Commissioner of the Metropolitan Police to guide police in their work. One of these ten values was 'to adopt the highest standards'. Drennan asked what that actually meant in practice, and, instead of the ten values, suggested three simple goals for the police:

- to reduce crime
- to make it safe for anyone to walk anywhere at any time in the UK
- to treat everyone fairly

Most members of the police force and most citizens might agree that these three aims include all the really important tasks the police have to do, and they have the great merit of being memorable and brief. Together they contain a total of 22 words. Every business firm and every non-profit-making organisation should have a similar short statement of its key goals, and every employee should know them by heart. Indeed, applicants for employment should be informed of these goals when they are invited for interview, and they should be asked at the interview if they accept them. A negative response to that question might mean the end of the interview. It is quite unreasonable for senior managers to accuse their employees of lack of loyalty or commitment if they have never set down in writing the goals of their organisation and ensured that every single employee is fully aware of them.

THE PROFIT MOTIVE AND EMPLOYEE COMMITMENT

At this point, it has to be said very plainly that profit-making organisations – mainly business firms – do have a fundamental problem when it comes to winning the commitment of their employees to their goals. Economists have long assumed that the overriding aim of a business firm is to maximise its profits. A contemporary company might paraphrase that as 'adding the maximum value for their shareholders'. But why should employees bother to help maximise profits or shareholder values if they receive no share in those gains? This basic problem has received remarkably little attention from economists since it was discussed by W. Stanley Jevons in a paper which he delivered in 1870 under the auspices of the National Association for the Promotion of Social Science. On that occasion Jevons examined two examples of profit sharing schemes which had worked quite well and he argued that

> The sharing of profits [with the employees] is one of those apparently obvious inventions, at the simplicity of which men will wonder in an after-age.[7]

Profit sharing was again warmly endorsed in 1928, when leading Liberal politicians, and some distinguished businessmen, economists and trade unionists who were broadly sympathetic to a Liberal point of view, published a programme for *Britain's Industrial Future*[8] as they called their report (which quickly became known as *The Yellow Book*). In the third part of that far-sighted report, entitled 'Industrial Relations', they insisted that profit sharing, as 'an addition to, and in no degree a substitution for' an employee's agreed wages, was an essential element in a sound system of remuneration, and in three important pages they spelt out the purposes of profit sharing and the conditions for its success. The following sentence is perhaps the most important of that section:

> The real purpose of profit sharing, in conjunction with the system of organised consultation which is described in the following chapters, is to show that the worker is treated as a partner, and that the division of the proceeds of industry is not a mystery concealed from him, but is based upon known and established rules to which he is a party.[9]

This 'partnership' element of profit sharing, which also lay at the heart of Jevons' 1870 paper mentioned above, explains why some advocates of profit sharing have refused to use the term on its own. For them, it had to be 'Profit sharing and Co-partnership', because the mere distribution of a profit share was meaningless unless it was linked to the intention to create a genuine partnership between labour and capital. Enough of profit sharing at this stage. More will be said about it in chapter 16.

STYLES OF HUMAN RESOURCE MANAGEMENT

Some may be uneasy about the setting of corporate goals, believing that it smacks of a Big Brother approach. Others, including trade union officials, will be concerned that the substitution of Human Resource *Management* for Industrial Relations will mean a dictatorial attitude by employers towards their employees, with employers indulging in what is sometimes called a macho-management approach. These concerns may occasionally be justified, but wise managers will seek to alleviate them. A dictatorial management style is likely to be damaging rather than helpful when it is increasingly understood that it is the operative on the shop floor who builds quality into a motor car, or the bank clerk at the till who satisfies the customer. Actually the technological developments of the past generation mean that dictatorial managers, who may know less about the latest computer than the junior who operates it, simply make themselves look ridiculous. If HRM is to mean macho-management, it will be a step back from IR rather than a step forward.

One way out of this impasse is to recognise that the word 'management' may have undesirable connotations, because it usually suggests a superior giving orders to an inferior. Now in all organisations there has to be a chain of command which means that orders are given and have to be carried out. But the employment contract is *voluntary*. Unlike soldiers in war, who may be shot for disobeying orders, employees are volunteers, not conscripts, and if they are consistently ordered around some of them (and probably the best of them) will leave. Actually the word 'administration' may often be more appropriate than 'management', although the latter is commonly used in English. In this respect it is significant that, in his foreword to the English translation of Henri Fayol's classic text *Administration industrielle et générale*, L. Urwick stated that it is a pity that Mrs Storrs [the translator] and Messrs. Pitman have decided to translate Fayol's word '*administration*' by 'management'. In the original English translation his title was translated directly 'administration'.[10]

And later Urwick states that

Fayol employs the word '*administration*' with *one* meaning and one meaning only. He uses it to describe a function, a kind of activity. And he is quite indifferent whether those exercising this kind of activity are described as 'Managing Directors' or as 'Charge-hands'. He is concerned with the function, not with the status of those who exercise it.[11]

CONCLUSION

Every organisation, however small, needs a strategy, and a key part of that strategy will relate to its most precious asset – its human resources. The strategy will be initiated by the chief executive and the board of directors, but it must be communicated to, and endorsed by, the whole workforce. The strategy will require regular review, and changes will also have to be agreed by the whole workforce. This will be a time-consuming process, but it will be much less costly and time-consuming than the strikes, go-slows and general bloody-mindedness which have characterised the British economy in the twentieth century. Until this is understood and implemented, the real benefits of the Thatcher employment reforms will not be experienced.

12   The Importance of the Customer

Jobs come from customers and from nowhere else.

Employment: The Challenge for the Nation, HMSO, 1985

A chapter on the customer may seem out of place in a book on employment policies. However, it is desirable because of the danger that those who are concerned with employment policies or human resource management see these activities as ends in themselves. They are not. Rather they are means to the end of serving the customer. As Peter Wickens has reminded us:

> Companies are not in the employee relations business, any more than they are in the cost control business, industrial engineering business etc. They are in business to sell profitably a product desired by the customer. Though employee relations might be exemplary, if the product is of poor quality, the design bad, or the market changes, the company can go out of business or the factory close.[1]

The truth is that the employer is not the real boss. He is simply an intermediary between the true boss in a market economy – the customer – and the employee. A wise employer will understand this situation and constantly react to it. And he will see that his workforce is well-informed about their need to meet the customers' demands.

UNDERESTIMATION OF CUSTOMER IMPORTANCE

Economics textbooks have long stated that, in a market economy, the customer is king; but it is doubtful that this extremely radical notion has been fully grasped even by teachers and students of economics. Appearances often suggest otherwise. Chief executives of large companies have such high salaries and seem to be so influential. Surely they have immense power? Can it really be true that if enough ordinary men and women walk past the doors of Marks and Spencer and choose to buy their everyday food and clothes elsewhere, that vast enterprise would close within weeks? Is it really the case that if shoppers buy more of brand X and less of brand Y, the firm producing brand X will boom, while the firm producing brand Y may go bust? Is it possible that if enough unorganised consumers, including housewives and pensioners, change their tastes, members of the strongest trade unions in the land will have to accept redundancies and pay cuts? It all seems so unlikely.

Then again, so many top people, including university dons, senior civil servants and others who have sought security in the public sector, see the market as a disreputable device which is to be avoided at all costs. The very idea that their salaries should be connected even remotely with the demands of ordinary consumers is deeply offensive to them. Why should such superior folk take any notice of what others want?

Then there are the churchmen, for whom the market is basically immoral, because it enriches those who satisfy consumer demands and fails to provide directly for the sick or those who do not update their skills. For these critics, Dr Johnson's dictum that 'There are few ways in which a man can be more innocently employed than in getting money' is the ultimate aberration.

So the market, which is certainly a common device because it serves the common people, has often had a bad press. But in 1990 it thrives as never before, spurred on by recent developments in Eastern Europe and reinforced by the determination of Japanese business leaders to provide consumers in all the world's major markets with the motor cycles, cars, cameras, hi-fis, televisions and videos that they want to buy.

PRIVATISATION, DEREGULATION AND THE CUSTOMER ETHIC

In 1983 Goldsmith and Clutterbuck examined the reasons for success of 23 leading British companies and argued that 'to say 'the customer is king' is an understatement for many of our successful companies.'[2] And yet the UK's fast diminishing share of world trade, and the ability of Japanese and other manufacturers to take a large slice of the UK home market, suggest that these are exceptional companies which prove the rule that too many firms have neglected the customer.

This is not surprising, because many of the largest UK business firms have been, until very recently, nationalised monopolies with a protected home market. This meant that they only had to pay lip service to the idea of serving the customer. In practice, the chief executive of these nationalised concerns was usually a man with some technical expertise relating to the supply of gas, telephone services or whatever, but his interest in customer service was limited. The organisation of these giant concerns was bureaucratic and hierarchical, and almost without exception they were heavily unionised right up to middle management level. Nor was this state of affairs confined to the nationalised industries. The clearing banks, for example, operated like a cosy cartel, with their branches normally open at times when their working customers were unable to use them. Only when the building societies began to threaten their market by extending their range of services and opening longer on weekdays, and on Saturday mornings, did the banks begin to take some notice of customer needs.

Thus it can be seen that the massive privatisation programme of the 1980s, which still continues, has been indispensable in forcing senior executives in previously nationalised industries to think far more carefully about the customer. But the level of competition in these privatised industries is still too modest. Consumers still have no choice in respect of gas, electricity, water and postal services. Elsewhere – in telephone services, for example – the rate of progress is slow. But slow progress is better than no progress. At least there is some movement in the right direction.

The policy aim should be straightforward: that every employee in every business and non-profit-making organisation should become customer conscious. Already some organisations have moved in this direction. For example, Northumbrian Water Group PLC, one of the newly privatised water companies, stated in its first Annual Report in August 1990 that '*Everyone* in the Group has attended a Customer First course' (emphasis supplied). The total number of employees in the Group on 31 March 1990 was 1,452. For British Telecom, with over 200,000 employees, a change in company culture following privatisation is a bigger task. However, in 1987 the company introduced a Total Quality Management (TQM) programme to make the culture more entrepreneurial, and in response to the competitive challenge from Mercury, BT has had to develop marketing skills. It is now even possible for customers to talk to British Telecom staff face to face in a telephone shop, although there is only one such shop in Newcastle upon Tyne, which is a major shopping centre. In that shop the absence of a queue is a rare event, and customers can stand for up to half an hour before being attended to. It seems that in British Telecom the concept of TQM has not yet brought its full benefit to the customer, who may still be regarded as a nuisance rather than the *raison d'être* of the company.

British Gas is another privatised concern which has attempted to improve service through its 'Banishing Gripes' campaign. As part of that campaign a booklet entitled *Commitment to our Customers* was published, which contained a letter to the customer from Robert Evans, Chairman of British Gas, opening with the statement 'The service we provide for you as a British gas customer is an important part of our business'. Many customers would perhaps prefer to think of it as *the most* important part of the business. After all, what else is as important as customer service?

However, the tone of this booklet, which includes a promise to pay compensation of up to £5,000 to customers who have been unfairly treated, suggests that British Gas is at long last trying to put its house in order. This is highly desirable, because individual consumers easily feel helpless when they are faced with a giant monopolistic organisation. And nothing is more essential, especially for elderly people in the winter, than heating.

Customers' views about the provision of several important services were brought together in the summer of 1990 in a MORI survey of 1,938 people nationwide, carried out for the National Consumer Council.[3] The response was analysed in terms of a net overall satisfaction index, which measured the difference between those expressing satisfaction with a particular service and those expressing dissatisfaction. By this standard a rating of 70 per cent or more must be considered good:

Table 12.6   Net overall satisfaction with certain cervices

	%
Electricity	77
*Gas	77
*Coach	76
Telephone	60
Water	58
Post Office Counter Service	54
*Bus	47
*British Rail	25

Base = All 1,938 respondents except for those services marked with a * which include only users of that service (Gas = 84% of sample, buses = 50%, rail services = 38% and coaches = 24%)

It would be interesting to compare these results with other goods and services provided by the private sector (say, food, clothing, milk and newspapers), but the clearest message from the survey is the considerable dissatisfaction with the level of service provided by British Rail. This is even more marked in London and the South East, where net overall satisfaction was as low as 14 per cent. In addition, 47 per cent of rail users thought that ticket prices were unreasonable, including many young people between the ages of 15 and 24. As the Report put it, 'There is a message for British Rail here.'

However, these figures provide no reason for complacency by suppliers of gas, electricity or coach services, although their net satisfaction rating looks high. The truth is that British consumers are rather easily satisfied with public and private services. How many people are willing to complain if a highly priced restaurant meal is almost inedible? Hosts do not want to embarrass their guests, and guests are certainly very reluctant to embarrass their host. So poor standards are tolerated – even though host and guests may make a mental reservation never to go near that restaurant again.

TURNING PRODUCERS INTO CUSTOMERS

It might be accepted that there is a need for shop assistants, service engineers and all others who have direct contact with the public to be trained in customer service. But many employees – for example those who work in a food processing factory or a car assembly plant – never see the customer. How can the importance of customer service be brought home to them? Progressive manufacturers are trying to achieve a state of affairs in which every work station sees itself as a customer and supplier of another. Thus the operatives check the quality of the work they receive and accept that their work will be checked at the next stage down the line. When this attitude is combined with a Just In Time approach to the manufacturing process, there is instant feedback on quality or quantity problems; otherwise the line stops.

Some companies, then, believe that the quality of service for their external customers depends to a large extent on the way in which employees deal with each other internally. The Nationwide Anglia Building Society has developed what it calls its 'Partnership Programme', which includes everybody in the company from the chief executive to the newest recruit. Tim Melville-Ross, the society's chairman, wrote recently:

> We believe that to be truly effective a customer care programme needs to address the service given to 'internal' customers too – it needs to be relevant to everyone throughout the organisation.[4]

THE OPPORTUNITIES

Well-managed organisations acknowledge the crucial importance of the customer at all times, but this can never be taken for granted. There are no infallible human beings, and that means that there are no infallible companies. But given the right attitude, mistakes can be turned into opportunities to create customer goodwill. Tom Peters tells the story of a customer at the American clothing retailer, Nordstrom, who needed some alterations to two suits he had bought at the Portland, Oregon, store.[5] The house rule is to have alterations ready the next day, but when the customer called to collect his suits before going on a business trip, they were not ready. The customer departed, but soon after he reached his hotel in Dallas, Texas, there was a parcel for him containing his two suits, an apology from the sales assistant and three silk ties by way of compensation. The assistant had telephoned his home, found out his itinerary from his family and spent $98 sending him the goods via Federal Express delivery service. When British employees start using their initiative like that, or better still make sure that the goods are always ready on time, their firms will not be short of orders.

The message is clear for those who are mainly concerned with human resource management: good HRM is chiefly a means to the end of excellent customer service, because without satisfied customers at home and abroad there will be no jobs.

13 Zero-Defect Quality and High Productivity

We aim to build profitably the highest quality car sold in Europe.

First sentence of philosophy statement of
Nissan Motor Manufacturing (UK) Ltd, issued to all employees

The younger generation take it for granted today that 'Made in Japan' is a guarantee of high quality. They would probably be surprised to learn that a generation ago it meant that a product was cheaply made and would quickly fall to pieces. Sadly the converse has been true for 'Made in Britain'. What was a stamp of quality in the 1950s had become a badge of shame by 1980, even for luxury goods like Jaguar cars. These two changing standards of quality can be illustrated diagrammatically thus:

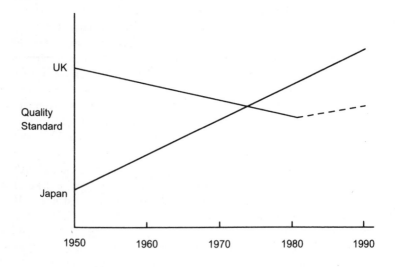

Figure 13.2   Changing quality standards of Japanese and UK goods, 1950–90

Japan is the best known example of a country which has dramatically and quickly improved quality, but it is not the only one. West

128

Germany's large balance of payments surplus owes much to her reputation for quality goods, and Hong Kong, Taiwan and Singapore have also acquired good reputations. Unless the UK can reverse the quality slide of 1950–80 and match, or better still beat, the standards of her international competitors, her economy has no future at all.

The Japanese example shows that quality standards can be revolutionised for the better over a period of about 30 years. There is no reason in principle why British manufacturers should not do as well, but improvements of this kind do not just happen. They require a tremendous effort, both nationally and, even more, at the level of the enterprise. And that effort has to be made *by everyone*. Zero-defect quality (which must become the only acceptable standard) requires that everyone in a company is pulling in the same direction, because the board of directors on its own is quite incapable of achieving this aim. In the car assembly plant it means that *every* weld has got to be right and that *every* part of the electrical system has got to be correctly wired up. The electrics are the nervous system of a modern motor car. A failure of that system at night on a motorway, caused by faulty wiring, is most unpleasant for the car driver. These jobs will not be correctly done on the shop floor *every* time, unless *the whole workforce* is committed to customer service and the company's success.

As well as the Japanese example in Japan, there are now numerous anglicised versions in the UK. More than twenty Japanese companies are now established in north east England and several more in other parts of the country, including Wales. Perhaps the best known is Nissan, which will be making more than 200,000 cars a year by 1992 at their state-of-the-art plant at Washington, near Sunderland.

THE STEPS TOWARDS IMPROVEMENT

By 1980, as well as a major quality problem, the UK also had a major productivity problem. Quality was not suffering because of a rapid work rate. On the contrary, poor quality went hand in hand with low output. The classic case was the Ford car factory at Halewood, near Liverpool, which makes Ford Escort cars. In 1981–82 it took twice as many man-hours to assemble an Escort car at Halewood as at Saarlouis in West Germany, and the quality was better at Saarlouis. Halewood was not the only British car plant at which both quality and productivity levels were appalling.

Since the early 1980s, there has been a significant improvement in quality and productivity in the British motor industry – indeed without such an improvement the industry would have died. But in British manufacturing industry generally (not forgetting services), there is still a need for a very large improvement in quality and productivity. Five steps will have to be taken before that improvement occurs.

The first step is to *recognise that a serious problem exists*. Certainly there has been some improvement since 1980, but other countries have not stood still and it is necessary to run, not walk, to keep pace with one's competitors, let alone to move ahead of them. Complacency has been a central element in the British disease. There is no place at all for it in an increasingly competitive world which has forgotten that Britain was the first industrial nation and had a great empire.

The second step is to understand that a choice does not have to be made between an improvement in quality and an improvement in productivity, but that, as the Japanese have shown so clearly, *better quality and higher productivity can go together and be mutually reinforcing*.

The third is to appreciate that, in the quest for better quality and higher productivity, quality must come first and *there is only one acceptable quality standard: zero-defect quality*. Customers whose car or television set breaks down soon after they have bought it will not be too pleased to be informed that the defect rate for that product is only one per cent. As far as they are concerned it is 100 per cent! *Every* task, however unpleasant or repetitive, has got to be done as if the operatives themselves were going to be the owner of that product. So all shop floor operatives have to be completely committed to quality; but, as Peter Wickens put it,

> the solution starts with top management commitment and that is not something that can be taught. We discovered this commitment by working with the Japanese, absorbing their values on quality and by determining that we would show the Japanese that the British could produce to Japanese standards.[1]

Top managers, and especially chief executives, in the UK have to be willing to absorb these values in the same way as Peter Wickens and his British colleagues. It seems that the values have to be caught rather than taught.

The fourth step is to *set ambitious quality and productivity targets over a reasonable time period, and be very persistent about the programme*. Roger Hale at Tennant Company in the USA observed in 1981 that there was about one hydraulic leak per 216 joints in the company's floor cleaners. Each machine had 150 joints, so almost every machine leaked. It took the company four years to reduce the leak ratio to one leak in 1,286 joints, and in that year not a single customer complained. In the following year they achieved a ratio of one leak per 2,800 joints. Persistence pays off.[2] Similar targets are necessary for productivity growth. Japanese companies adopt an annual target for improvements in labour productivity, probably in the range 10–15 per cent. Clearly British targets need to be at the top end of this range, or perhaps between 15 and 20 per cent per annum. That has to compared with an annual average increase, per employee in manufacturing, of 5.8 per cent in the period 1983–87. And this was an exceptionally high UK figure by historical standards.

British manufacturing and retail companies have a major problem when it comes to improving productivity because their expectations are so low. In a survey carried out in those sectors in 1988 by the PA Consulting Group and the Confederation of British Industry,[3] a large majority of companies expected less than a 20 per cent increase in productivity over the next five years, from existing resources and major new investments. This was equivalent to an increase of 2 per cent per annum, and less than 5 per cent of companies expected to increase productivity by more than 50 per cent over the next five years. These figures need to be turned upside down, with a large majority of companies expecting productivity increases of more than 50 per cent over the next five years, and the more ambitious going for 100 per cent.

Having set targets, the fifth and final stage is to *implement the programme*. Easier said than done, perhaps, but Japanese and other examples show that where there is a deliberate intention to move forward, much can be achieved.

A classic case was reported by Kevin Eason, motoring correspondent, in *The Times* of 3 July 1990, following a visit to Acco Cables of Stourport, Hereford and Worcester, a company which makes handbrake cables for the new UK Nissan car plant. John Young, managing director of Acco, agreed that the company's product used to be of 'mediocre quality, poor delivery and reasonable prices.' Three years later, Acco achieves 'superb delivery and high quality.' Productivity has gone up by 70 per cent, and while the defect rate is not yet zero (an unattainable ideal) it is moving fast towards it. Previously the defect rate on an assembly line manned by seven operators was far too high, but remedies proved ineffective. The breakthrough came when two

Geordies from Nissan, well versed in the ways of British industry but trained in Japan, visited Mr Young and his manufacturing team, examined the problems, and then left Acco to make the necessary changes. Massive improvements in quality and productivity quickly followed. The key to the improvements was the elimination of the gap between management and workforce. Mr Young commented that:

> We have bridged the gap between all sections of the workforce, so that we all know what we have to do to survive.

Perhaps the biggest barrier to many other companies quickly following this example is the reluctance of their chief executives to take a leaf out of John Young's book and admit that there is much room for improvement. Toyota (a bigger firm than Nissan) is now starting to build a car factory near Derby. Like Nissan, it will buy many of its components in the UK if British manufacturers can reach the required quality standards. They will have to be ready to learn!

Of course, the achievement of zero-defect quality depends to a large degree on discipline, without which learning is impossible. This discipline does not have to be unduly harsh or severe, and the best kind of discipline is self-discipline exercised in a climate which encourages it. That is the discipline of craftsmen who take a tremendous pride in the job; for them, second-best is just not good enough. Ideally a job is done right the first time every time, but human beings are not infallible. That has to be accepted and allowances made so that errors can be rectified, preferably by the person who made the error, at the earliest opportunity. When he is taking visitors round the Nissan car plant, Peter Wickens likes to point out that very little space has been allocated for rectifying faults. The philosophy is that they must be put right on the production line.

The Japanese invasion of the UK has created a golden opportunity for British manufacturers to equal, or even surpass, Japanese levels of quality and productivity. But the necessary improvements will not occur automatically. A pre-requisite for employers is the planning and implementation of a strategy to win the hearts and minds of all their employees (or better still, co-partners) both as individuals and as members of a team. How to do this is the subject matter of the next five chapters.

14 Recruiting and Motivating Individual Employees

> The essence of the psychological contract is that it is a
> mutual agreement between individual and organisation.
>
> Peter Herriot, *Recruitment in the 90s*, 1989

It was argued in chapter 7 that the employment contract is basically between the employer and the individual employee, even when many of the terms and conditions of employment are settled by collective bargaining. The example of IBM as a non-union firm was discussed, and mention was made of particular groups of employees who had improved their terms and conditions by moving from collective bargaining to individual negotiation. But how does this approach fit with the emphasis on teamwork which is to be found in many Japanese companies? Does an organisation have to choose between an individualist and a collectivist approach to its human resources?

The answer to this question is 'Yes and No'. Clearly all companies, and especially those which are setting up on a greenfield site, have to make choices. Collective bargaining which includes the recognition of numerous trade unions in one organisation is now thought of as an anachronism, so the choice for a greenfield site is a single union deal or no union recognition. This particular policy decision and many others have to be made. But organisations do not necessarily have to make a straight choice between individualism and collectivism. It is possible both to emphasise the importance of the individual by providing, as Herriot puts it, a suitable 'psychological contract' for him or her,[1] and at the same time to emphasise strongly the importance of teamwork in the organisation and a corporate culture. So the emphasis on the individual in this chapter does not have to be set against the stress on teamwork in the next. It is possible to combine the two in a fruitful way.

Even where hundreds of people are doing virtually identical work in a large factory or office, no two of those people are identical. People need to be valued and respected as individuals, and from the organisation's point of view it is vitally important that for some of the time, at least, they should be treated as such. It is generally accepted that human resources are an organisation's most precious asset, but that will only be true if round pegs are fitted into round holes. People should be working where their own particular qualities and gifts can be best used.

Consider a typical situation. The supervisor of a work-group retires and a new appointment has to be made. Should it be an internal or an external appointment? The answer to that question will depend to some extent on whether a suitable internal candidate is available, which means that someone has to be reasonably well informed about the strengths and weaknesses of the possible internal candidates. They must be known as individuals. Even then, it would be wise to put them through a selection process to check that the necessary leadership qualities are present. Managing people is a totally different task from doing an ordinary job of work.

It has been said that an army is only as good as its officers, and in the same way a business firm is only as good as those in supervisory and managerial positions. But the right appointments can only be made if people are known as individuals. It follows that to treat a workforce *en masse*, as if they were all alike, is a disastrous policy. People need to be treated as individuals both for their own sake and for the good of the organisation.

RECRUITMENT

First impressions are important, and the first contact between an employee and his or her employer takes place during the recruitment process. In fact it may be true to say that the quality of an organisation's human resource programme can be assessed by the way in which it recruits its staff. If that is done in a casual or haphazard way, how can anything else work well? Few UK companies have recently recruited on the scale of Nissan, which took on nearly 3,000 new staff between 1984 and 1990, and that company insisted at the beginning that their supervisors would be a key element in their organisational structure. So they advertised for supervisors and received 3,500 applications for 22 jobs! After a two stage process, this number was reduced to 75, and they then spent over 100 manager days selecting 22 from these 75.[2]

Once they had some supervisors in post, they could start to advertise for 300 'manufacturing staff'. On this occasion their advertisements attracted some 20,000 applications, and these were reduced to 1,900, of which 1,100 went through exhaustive mental and physical aptitude tests before the final selection was made. This alone indicated the thoroughness of their procedures, which contrast rather favourably with the pre-1986 Fleet Street arrangements discussed in chapter 8. But there is one aspect of this selection process at Nissan which deserves a special mention: the role of the supervisor, who is thoroughly involved in recruitment, makes the final decision, telephones the successful applicant to offer the job and then meets him for a chat. As Peter Wickens puts it, this has two significant effects:

> It makes the Supervisor committed to his staff – if there are problems he has only himself to blame and will work harder to rectify the situation. Second, it starts the bond between the employee and the Supervisor – at the very least he respects the Supervisor's judgement. There can be no better way of starting the team building process.[3]

This is a classic example of the way in which treating individuals with respect in the recruitment process promotes their respect for the company and their inclination to want to work with a good team.

There is no need to labour the point about careful and thorough recruitment. Wise employers will accept that it is basic to company performance.

TRAINING AND EDUCATION

Zero-defect quality and much higher productivity will never be achieved without a well-trained workforce, and there is very widespread agreement that the whole area of education and training in the UK leaves a great deal to be desired. In the schools, nearly a half of all pupils are leaving after eleven years' compulsory education without any kind of worthwhile certificate, and far too few are going on to higher education. In the workplace, the system of craft apprenticeship is now defunct, but it has not yet been replaced by other, more suitable methods of training.

Professor Sig Prais and his colleagues at the National Institute of Economic and Social Research have now done enough comparative studies to show beyond any reasonable doubt that the UK suffers severely because of an under-educated and under-trained workforce, especially at the intermediate level. Some of the most important of these studies were drawn together and published in December 1989 in a single volume.[4] They show that vocational training in several important sectors of the economy is significantly better in France and West Germany than in the UK, and this helps the continental Europeans to achieve considerably higher quality and productivity. In one study, carried out in 1983–84, 25 British firms in the category of 'general jobbing engineers' were compared with 20 similar West German firms in the same category, and of this sample 'The specifications of products made by six pairs of firms were sufficiently similar to warrant a simple comparison of labour productivity.'[5] The comparison showed that the average differential was 63 per cent in favour of the German firms. In addition the researchers 'discerned a tendency for the German products to be technically more advanced and of higher quality,'[6] and they stated that 'Perhaps the most important overall implication of this study is that lack of technical expertise and training, rather than a simple lack of modern machinery, is the stumbling block.'[7]

Of course this problem of comparatively low UK labour productivity is not new. Graham Hutton dealt with it at length in his book *We Too Can Prosper: The Promise of Productivity*, published in 1953 and quickly reprinted. The trouble in the last few decades in the UK has not been that serious problems have gone unrecognised; on the contrary, they have been written about and discussed *ad nauseam*. The trouble is that the words have not been translated into appropriate action, because until the Thatcher government took over, British managers had become talkers rather than doers.

The problem of inadequate and unsuitable technical and vocational training is intimately related to the inadequacies of the country's educational system, where low standards have too easily been accepted as the norm by politicians, parents, school governors and teachers, and where there has been an anti-business sentiment among some teachers in the higher education system. This naturally tends to be reciprocated by the business community, so that an unhealthy gap has existed between those who are teaching the brightest young people and those who will employ them. The fact that students have expected their fees and living expenses to be funded entirely by their parents or the state has exacerbated this problem.

Sir Claus Moser, president of the British Association for the Advancement of Science, touched a raw spot when he stated at the Association's meeting in August 1990 that 'Hundreds of thousands of children have educational experiences not worthy of a civilised nation', but there was less support for his call for a Royal Commission on education which would be 'all-embracing, visionary yet realistic'. There are many who share Mrs Thatcher's view that such official investigative bodies tend to keep minutes and waste hours, and in any case some good work has already been done in analysing the problem, making recommendations, and even beginning to make some sensible progress.

Two of the most valuable recent reports on education and training are *More Means Different: Widening Access to Higher Education* by Sir Christopher Ball, published by the Royal Society for the Encouragement of Arts, Manufactures and Commerce in 1990, and *Britain's Real Skill Shortage, and what to do about it* by John Cassels (Policy Studies Institute, 1990). In respect of sensible progress, mention might be made of the plan to test all school children at the ages of 7, 11, 14 and 16, and the increase in the number of university places which should become available between 1991 and 1995. The British educational and training system does sometimes move in the right direction, but it does so too little and too late.

However, the best reason for not setting up a Royal Commission of the great and the good to investigate Britain's educational problems is that, as Claus Moser himself stated, it is a mystery why education carries such low esteem in England and Wales (in contrast to Scotland, where it has always been highly regarded). It is unlikely that a Royal Commission would resolve this mystery, but until there is a generally greater regard for education and training in the UK *and a willingness to translate that greater regard into hard cash to pay for a better system*, no major improvements will occur. One suspects that most people would be appalled at the idea of foregoing an overseas holiday or a new car to pay for education and training. That is the kind of psychological barrier which has to be overcome.

APPRAISAL

All progressive organisations which want to develop their staff as individuals as well as members of the team, will operate an annual appraisal system under which people are appraised on their past year's performance and targets are set and agreed for the coming year. The question is not whether such a system should be introduced, but how it will operate. The details will naturally vary from one organisation to another.

The first question which has to be answered is whether the system should apply to everyone or only to selected groups, for example management staff. In the UK only a minority of companies appraise blue-collar workers, but the practice is growing. Clearly, a system which applies to all must be relatively simple and straightforward, and not too time-consuming. Above all, standards must be properly applied, so that a large majority of staff are not rated 'above average'.

Then there is the question of whether the appraisal system should be used for individual pay increases and promotion. Again, there is no simple answer. Perhaps there will be no direct link, but it might be foolish to state that an appraisal return, which should always be agreed between the appraisee and the appraiser, will never be used for such purposes.

As individual appraisal spreads throughout the economy, resistance to the practice can be expected to diminish, even among blue-collar workers. Meanwhile the traditional British situation of resistance to a proposal to do something new, followed by acceptance if the proposal is implemented in a sensible way, will probably prevail.

PROMOTION

Economic reasons for going to work are not the only ones, but they are very strong. It follows that individuals will be powerfully motivated by the possibility of promotion which brings with it a pay increase. When pensions are linked to pay on retirement, this incentive remains right up to the year in which an individual retires. It is probable that many organisations do not make the best use of promotions to work towards certain objectives which they regard as desirable.

For example, universities are in the business of teaching and research. However, it is well known that most appointments and promotions are made on the basis of published research, and it follows that teaching and course development tend to be Cinderella activities. Having spent several years at Balliol College in the 1740s, Adam Smith wrote that 'In the university of Oxford, the greater part of the public professors have, for these many years, given up altogether even the pretence of teaching.'[8] And still today the quality of teaching in some of our universities leaves a great deal to be desired, despite the fact that more than 50 per cent of the public funds allocated to universities are for teaching purposes. Can anyone doubt that if a university announced that 50 per cent of its promotions would, in the future, be biased towards teaching rather than research, more members of the academic staff would behave as though teaching was an activity of considerable importance?

PAY

The issue of pay is closely linked to that of promotion. There is a movement towards performance-related pay on an individual basis, and this is to be welcomed, especially for senior executives.[9] But this movement has to be seen against the background of an economy in which for several decades, unit labour costs have been rising much too fast, because at every level pay increases have been too high, with chief or senior executives being among the worst offenders. Two examples, one from the private sector and the other from the public sector, will suffice to make this point.

At the Midland Bank in 1989, pre-tax profits before exceptional charges fell by 11 per cent. After exceptional charges a profit of £693 million in 1988 became a loss of £261 million in 1989. And yet the chairman had a salary increase of 25 per cent, and the highest paid director's salary rose by 13 per cent to £725,844.

The latest results at British Coal were even worse. For the year 1989–90 the previous year's operating profit (after interest charges) of £66 million became a loss of £441 million, and taking into account exceptional items the loss of £203 million in 1988–89 became a loss of £5,076 million in 1989–90. By ordinary accounting standards the company was bankrupt, and yet the chairman had a pay rise of 6.5 per cent in 1989–90 and several other board members still received a performance bonus of 5 per cent of salary.

The overall results for these two major companies were quite appalling, and yet in both cases the chairman had a pay increase. What is perhaps most worrying is that the annual general meetings of major British companies come and go, usually without the major shareholders, the institutions, taking the directors to task for their excessive pay increases.

The lesson to be learned from this sorry situation is that while performance-related pay may be desirable in theory, in the context of generally excessive British pay settlements it is often far too loosely operated, especially for senior executives. In fact it is essential that the performance-related elements of remuneration for directors should be very clearly set out in the annual report, so that shareholders can see precisely how the change in their total remuneration relates to company performance, including profitability and earnings per share. Company law should be amended to make this obligatory, but at the end of the day it is up to shareholders to protest much more vigorously when those who are meant to be running the company in their interest help themselves to too big a slice of the cake.

CONCLUSION

It is essential for all organisations to take great care over recruitment and then to encourage the talents and abilities of individual members of the workforce. That can be done in a variety of ways, and some of the more important have been briefly discussed in this chapter. These policies should be seen as complementary, not contradictory, to those which promote teamwork, and the promotion of teamwork is the subject of the next chapter.

15 Creating a Team Spirit

Teamwork and commitment permeate every aspect of the Nissan approach.

P. Wickens, *The Road to Nissan*, 1987

Business firms like IBM may base their employment philosophy on concern for the individual, but that is only one side of the picture. Unless there is a team spirit in an organisation, it is simply a collection of individuals following their own inclinations, and such an organisation will quickly disintegrate. But where a group of well-trained, enthusiastic people work together to further a common goal, the sum is greater than the parts and far more can be achieved than was thought possible.

There is a vast pool of untapped talent and productive potential in the British economy. The best proof of that occurs at moments of crisis, as during the three-day week early in 1974, or during the Falklands campaign of 1982, when rates of output were as much as double those in normal times. So how can a team spirit like this be engendered when there is no crisis? That is obviously more difficult, because it has to be sustained over years and even decades. The huge Nissan manufacturing investment in the UK, which will not produce any financial return in its first five years, must be profitable in the 1990s and well into the twenty first century. How can an effective team spirit, which does not stifle individual initiative, be maintained and even developed over the long term? Clearly, achieving that aim calls for considerable leadership and managerial skills.

GAINING ACCEPTANCE OF A TEAM-BUILDING STRATEGY

Managers in companies which have previously operated in a traditional, confrontational way, negotiating only with shop stewards and leaving others on one side, may feel that moving to a more participative approach, which involves the whole workforce, is just too difficult to be attempted. They may fear that such a move would be opposed by the trade unions, and that the costs would be higher than the benefits. These managers will find helpful the Code of Practice for Employee Involvement and Participation in the UK,

141

devised by the Involvement and Participation Association (IPA) and the Institute of Personnel Management (IPM) in 1983. The IPA is supported by trade unions as well as employers, so the great strength of this Code is that it can be said to have bi-partisan backing. Part 2 of the Code contains an Action Guide to help organisations develop suitable participation arrangements and procedures, and it also includes a checklist which should prevent the omission of some vital element of a more participative strategy.

Two other sources which should be helpful to those who want to build up a team spirit are Chapter 4 of Goldsmith and Clutterbuck's *The Winning Streak Workout Book* – 'Winning through Involvement' (1985) – and the recent Department of Employment publication *People and Companies* (1989). The former provides some down to earth advice on how to develop successful employee involvement policies, and the latter contains examples of the ways in which 25 successful British companies have done just that. These examples suggest that, for employee involvement and participation, variety is the spice of life. Nevertheless, there are certain common elements to such a programme, and four of these will be discussed here. They are: a corporate culture; 'single status' arrangements; communication and consultation; and financial rewards.

A CORPORATE CULTURE

Every organisation has a corporate culture and that culture, which may be strong or weak, plays a key part in binding together those who work for it. Deal and Kennedy have reminded us[1] that the early leaders of American business such as Thomas Watson of IBM, Harley Procter of Procter and Gamble, and General Johnson of Johnson & Johnson believed that strong culture brought success. The same writers found that still today US companies with a strong culture are usually outstanding performers, and they argue that a major reason for Japanese business success is their strong national culture.

A corporate culture may be expressed in particular obvious ways, for example in the company logo or in a uniform, but its most important aspect is shared values – and they may not be so immediately obvious. These values are set by top management, but should permeate the whole organisation so that they are shared by every single employee. Corporate culture will be influenced by national culture, but the corporate culture of a multi-national company will to some extent transcend national cultures.

Major Japanese corporations in Japan, with their life-time employment, company songs, and exercises before work, provide the extreme case of a strong corporate culture. Most of these arrangements, including life-time employment, are not acceptable in Western countries where it is thought that the best way to get promotion is to move around. But many leading US and Western European companies have developed a corporate culture appropriate to their environment. A classic UK example is that of Marks and Spencer, who have gained a national reputation for the quality of their clothes and the freshness of their food. Their readiness to exchange goods which do not satisfy, or to give customers their money back, set a standard which other major retailers soon felt obliged to follow. Everyone who works for M & S knows that these standards must be maintained, and the well-paid staff are provided with excellent welfare facilities to encourage them to give of their best.

Clearly, the existence of a reasonably strong corporate culture makes it easier for all employees of an organisation to work together as a team. A very weak culture suggests that the directors may be uncertain about the organisation's values, and that is not a happy state of affairs.

SINGLE STATUS

Over the past thirty years, there has been a policy revolution in some progressive organisations about status differentials. Previously, bigger desks and offices, thicker carpets, longer and more alcoholic lunches, separate dining rooms and reserved car parking spaces were thought to be some of the essential accoutrements of seniority. Now it is understood that these status symbols not only create barriers between white- and blue-collar staff and between managerial staff and others, but that they also tend to produce an hierarchical bureaucracy which is more concerned with its own status differentials than with running the business in an efficient way. So in some organisations the reserved parking spaces have gone, the single cafeteria has replaced the graded dining rooms, open-plan offices have been substituted for separate rooms and so on. There has been a deliberate attempt to eliminate all inessential distinctions.

Of course single status does not mean complete equality of status and rewards. It means removing all the unnecessary distinctions, like those which have implied in too many British companies that white-collar employees, with their monthly pay and longer holidays, are a naturally superior breed to their blue-collar counterparts.[2] Experience shows that this kind of change can be made successfully on existing, brownfield sites, but like all such innovations it is more easily introduced on greenfield sites where people are not set in different ways. On brownfield sites the strongest resistance to single status may come not from the trade unions, but from managers who already enjoy certain privileges and are looking forward to more. The abolition of such privileges will require a strong lead from the chief executive and a willingness on his or her part to set a good example.

COMMUNICATION AND CONSULTATION

It goes almost without saying that a team spirit cannot exist if most employees are treated like mushrooms – fed on muck and kept in the dark. And yet Wallace Bell wrote recently that:

> there are still very many employees who know little or nothing about their employer's business and, in general, appear not to be at all concerned about it.[3]

In some firms this situation exists because management does not see any point in communicating, whereas in others an effort is being made to communicate, but it is just not producing the desired result. Companies which have an effective communications system are probably a small minority of the whole.

Too often, a communications system is seen as a method by which managers tell employees what they think they should know. In fact, an efficient system is two-way and even four-way. Managers need to listen as well as to speak; feedback is essential, as is communication *across* an organisation. And it may be that the informal grapevine is as important as, or even more important than, the formal system which is providing more information than most people can absorb. It has been well argued that the key to effective communications is not providing information in full to everyone – almost thrusting it on them – but making it available when requested and answering questions readily and frankly.[4]

There are more and more ways to communicate, including videos and other modern methods, but there will never be a substitute for the face-to-face meeting, and this should be the preferred method for all really important news – both good and bad. Peter Wickens insists that in a car assembly plant there is no substitute for the five minute meeting at the beginning of every shift, and that this contributes more than anything else to team building and commitment. Every organisation sometimes has bad news as well as good, and it may be that the way in which bad news is communicated is the real test of the communications system. As John Harvey-Jones put it:

I suppose the organization which fails to make it happen is best characterized by a lack of truthfulness and opennness. Truthfulness and openness without fear of the consequences is a most difficult trick to turn within a large group of people. It is not that large outfits inevitably seek to recruit liars. It is a tribute I suppose to the English language that there are so many forms of circumlocution that it is remarkably easy to persuade yourself that you have made a bold statement, or conveyed the bad news, whilst in reality there is no conceivable possibility that the recipient has actually understood what you are talking about.[5]

Consultation, which goes hand in hand with communication, implies a willingness to listen to employees' views *before* decisions are taken. It could consist of discussions with all employees individually, but for any organisation where they exceed a dozen or so that would be a time-wasting process. So genuine consultation requires a consultative council, or similar body, on which all sections of the workforce are represented and at which all important issues are discussed before plans are implemented.

In West Germany there is a legal obligation for all companies with more than four employees to establish such a council, and the law obliges the employer and the Works Council to 'work together in a spirit of mutual trust...for the good of the establishment.'[6] Practically all German employees and many employers believe that these works councils are beneficial to employment relations at plant level, and one commentator has written that the system 'is a sane piece of industrial democracy that ensures that grievances are nipped in the bud.'[7] British employers are adamantly opposed to a compulsory system of works councils along German lines, but progressive firms have recognised the value of such bodies and have already introduced them.

FINANCIAL REWARDS

It was suggested in the previous chapter that pay is a crucial factor in motivating individuals. It is also crucial in creating (or destroying) a team spirit. If everything else is right, but the pay system is wrong, there will be antagonism instead of co-operation between groups of employees.

To a limited extent, organisations can set their own internal pay relativities, except that base rates of pay cannot be far below the market rate for a particular job. At any time there will be a market rate of pay for a competent secretary, motor mechanic or solicitor in London, Newcastle upon Tyne or Aberdeen, and the biggest multi-national corporation will have to pay that rate to attract good labour. It may be that the chief executive (himself an engineer) of an engineering firm has a good view of engineers and a poor view of accountants, but he will quickly find that the market in the UK dictates that accountants have to be paid as much as, or more than, engineers, because they always seem to be in short supply.

Most UK organisations will have an annual or bi-annual pay review and the whole workforce will expect and receive an increase close to the rate of inflation, regardless of organisational performance. That habit, which destroys the motivational effect of a pay increase, needs to be broken. Pay settlements should reflect an organisation's success, measured by the relevant criteria, always accepting that if the level of pay falls much below the market rate, recruitment will be difficult or impossible, and the best employees will leave.

Employees are naturally interested in the absolute level of pay. They are also interested in pay relativities. For example, in a manufacturing plant, how does a pay increase for white-collar workers compare with that for blue-collar workers? Is it more or less the same, and if not, why not? Presumably differential pay increases would not occur without a reason, and the most likely reason would be market forces. In schools, pressure is mounting to award maths and science teachers a differential pay increase because of the severe shortage of such teachers in some parts of the country, and in higher education it is becoming almost impossible to recruit for disciplines like Accounting and Law. It seems that without special pay awards to reflect these shortages, the situation will simply grow worse.

Differential pay awards as a result of labour market pressures may initially be resented in some parts of the enterprise, but eventually they will probably be accepted. Most people can understand that if certain essential skills are not adequately rewarded, there will be a shortage of key personnel which will damage the organisation. But high pay increases to a particular group, unrelated either to market forces or to the group's performance, will cause widespread dissatisfaction and adversely affect morale in other departments. It is not easy to define precisely 'a fair day's work for a fair day's pay', but the British have a keen nose for arrangements which are manifestly unfair because they are unrelated to skill or effort.

CONCLUSION

A good team spirit in an organisation is complementary to, not incompatible with, a concern for the interests of individual employees. It can be fostered in various ways, and that it should be fostered in every organisation is more important than the particular ways in which it is fostered. But if the primary objective of the board of directors is to maximise a business firm's profitability, surely the existence of a profit sharing scheme is necessary to achieve the full commitment of all employees to the company's aims. The implications of profit sharing, preferably linked to employee shareholding, are worked out in the next chapter.

16 Profit Sharing and Co-Partnership

> We only need to throw aside some old but groundless prejudices, in order to heal the discords of capital and labour, and to efface in some degree the line which now divides employer and employed.
>
> W. S. Jevons, *On Industrial Partnerships*, 1870

So far in this book the terms 'employer' and 'employee' have been used frequently, suggesting that organisations, including business firms, consist of two sides whose interests are often opposed. This becomes most apparent when collective bargaining takes place about wages and conditions of work. The employer wants a low pay increase in order to keep down his labour costs, while the employees want as high an increase as possible – and may be prepared to back their claim with a strike threat. Stanley Jevons suggested 120 years ago that we should abandon this kind of thinking, and surely it is time to follow his advice.

A CO-PARTNERSHIP APPROACH

If Britain is to catch up with, let alone move ahead of, Japanese and other competitors, the time for tinkering with the British system of industrial relations/human resource management is over. What is needed now in business firms is some radical thinking and action in which the idea and practice of a team of co-partners supersedes two opposing sides. But what would this involve? And why should it be more acceptable today than when Jevons and others proposed industrial partnership in the nineteenth century?

Like all important ideas, the essence of co-partnership is very simple. It involves changing only one small word when discussing the employment relationship. Instead of A working *for* B (who may be an individual or a company) A is said to work *with* B. At the same time, A is thought of as a colleague, or rather a co-partner, instead of an employee with an inferior status to B, the employer. If this change in status is genuine, the change in terminology will be accompanied by other tangible and visible signs which back it up.

Some of these changes will be similar to those which create a team spirit, as described in the previous chapter. But however well done, on their own these changes will not bring about co-partnership. As a growing number of firms emphasise in their philosophy statements, business firms are primarily about making profits. It is, therefore, impossible to achieve genuine co-partnership until most members of the workforce are sharing in those profits in a predictable and intelligible way.

Profit sharing has grown quietly in the UK since the 1860s, so that today as many as many as two million co-partners may be participating in about a thousand schemes. It has recently been defined as:

> the distribution to employees of part of a company's profits, determined by reference to a formula known to the employees at the start of the profit period, and the profit share is in addition to a fair level of remuneration for the job.[1]

So profit sharing is *not* profit and loss sharing. For the co-partners it is a one-way bet, and it is not surprising that they like it. An extensive survey among 2,703 participants in twelve UK profit sharing firms in 1983–84 showed that 70 per cent thought that it was an excellent idea and another 21 per cent were in favour, while less than 0.5 per cent were opposed.[2] But what about the whole body of shareholders? How might they respond to an arrangement in which 5 per cent, or thereabouts, of the profits are allocated to the co-partners? Perhaps they might agree to it as an experiment, but what about the longer term?

Of course, if profit sharing damages the interests of the providers of risk capital, the shareholders, it cannot be in the company's interests. In his 1870 paper, Jevons had argued that one of the favourable effects of the 'partnership principle', as he called it, would be 'to increase the average profit in some degree'[3], but that forecast could not be tested in the UK until the 1980s because profit sharing was not sufficiently widespread. The recent increase in profit sharing has enabled several researchers to show that Jevons' prediction was indeed correct, and that profit sharing companies are either more productive, or more profitable, or both, than non-profit sharers. The most extensive of these studies was carried out by Bell and Hanson in 1987.[4] They compared the financial results of 113 profit sharing companies with the results of 301 similar non-profit sharers over the period 1978–85. Some of the main results of their research are contained in Table 16.7.

Tabln 16.7   Comparative performance of profit sharing and
Non-profit sharing companies 1978–1985 (annual
average % performance over 8 years)

Financial Ratio	Profit Sharing Companies	Non-Profit Sharing Companies	% Difference: Profit Sharers above Non-Profit Sharers
Return on sales	8.4	5.6	50.0
Return on capital	20.6	15.5	32.9
Annual sales growth	15.5	13.7	13.1
Annual profit growth	13.6	9.7	40.2
Annual investor returns	24.8	18.0	37.8

Source: Bell and Hanson, 1987, p. 58.

Perhaps even more impressive than the figures in Table 16.7, was the comparison of cumulative investor returns over the eight years. In the profit sharing companies returns were 474 per cent, while in the non-profit sharers they were 226 per cent. Thus it became clear that profit sharing could be very good for all the shareholders, not only the co-partners. But a word of caution is necessary here.

It is very difficult to separate the effects of profit sharing from the effects of the consultative and other arrangements which normally exist in profit sharing companies. Profit sharing is only a part of the co-partnership approach, and it is dangerous to claim that it leads to increased profitability on its own. It is better to see it as a key element in a participative policy which produces good long-term results for shareholders, managers and co-partners.[5]

PROFIT SHARING AND EMPLOYEE SHAREHOLDING

Many of the profit sharing pioneers in the period 1870–1910 refused to talk about profit sharing on its own. For them the phrase was 'profit sharing and co-partnership', and this involved allocating the profit share in the form of shares in the company, so that the participants became shareholders in, or members of, the company. Since 1978, there have been tax concessions for participants who receive their profit share in this form, so that several hundred UK companies now practise profit sharing and co-partnership, and several hundred thousand employees have become co-partners, even if that term is rarely used.

Clearly, to allocate the profit share in the form of shares, especially if those shares are retained, is different in principle to allocating it as cash. To begin with, when the participants become and remain shareholders there is a significant change in their status, and they acquire the right to attend the annual general meeting and to vote for or against the appointment of directors. In addition, they get a taste of what risk capitalism is all about as their shares fluctuate in response to forces which may be completely outside the company's control. And if the company prospers and a number of share allocations are retained over a period of several years, a substantial capital sum may be accumulated.

By contrast, a cash allocation will probably be seen as just another pay bonus, to be spent on a holiday or a new car. It will be gladly received, but the recipient does not become a full co-partner in the same way as a colleague who receives and retains an allocation of shares.

GOVERNMENT POLICY

In 1978, a Labour government, under pressure from the Liberals, first introduced tax concessions to encourage share-based profit sharing. In other words, the concessions were only applicable to the kind of whole-hearted co-partnership described above, in which a majority of employees received a packet of shares as their profit share. Furthermore, these employees remained shareholders, because it was a condition of the tax concessions that the shares had to be held by trustees for a minimum period before they could be sold. These concessions were continued and enhanced by the Thatcher government, so that share-based profit sharing has continued to grow steadily. But still only a small minority of private sector employees participate in profit sharing, and of these only about half receive their allocation in shares.

PROFIT RELATED PAY

From 1978 until 1987, government policy was reasonably clear: profit sharing was to be encouraged; share-based profit sharing was to be particularly encouraged by tax concessions, because employee share-holding was a desirable development. Then in his 1987 budget, Mr Lawson, as Chancellor of the Exchequer, introduced tax concessions for profit related (cash) pay. This innovation cut across employee shareholding, because it was very unlikely that any company would operate both a profit related pay scheme and share-based profit sharing. Thus since 1987 the emphasis on employee shareholding has diminished and the message from government has been that any kind of scheme which links financial rewards to a company's profitability is desirable. Meanwhile the take-up of profit related pay, despite the tax concessions, has been disappointing. It seems that businessmen are much less enthusiastic than Mr Lawson about the scheme.

SHARE OPTION SCHEMES

In addition to the tax concessions for share-based profit sharing, concessions were made available for all-employee savings-related share option schemes in 1980, and for selective share option schemes in 1984. The latter are usually restricted to the directors of a company and a few other senior executives, although they can be extended to most employees. In practice the proportion of employees who subscribe to the so-called all-employee schemes is usually quite small – perhaps a fifth. The remainder are deterred by the complexity of the scheme and the need to save a regular monthly sum over five years. In a manufac-

Table 16.8   Inland revenue approval of profit
sharing and share option schemes

Type of Scheme	Year in which Introduced	Approximate Number of Schemes Approved by 1990
Share-based Profit Sharing	1978	900
All-Employee Savings-related Share Option Schemes	1980	900
Selective (executive) Share Option Schemes	1984	4,500

Source: Figures supplied by the Inland Revenue.

turing company, the number of blue-collar staff who subscribe to the scheme may be negligible, so it is difficult to see that these option schemes, on their own, have a major impact on the workforce.

However, the figures for approval by the Inland Revenue of the three different kinds of schemes make interesting reading (see Table 16.8).

It will be readily seen that directors and senior executives are very much quicker to take advantage of tax concessions for themselves than to use them for the benefit of other employees. But this enthusiasm by top managers for their own share options provides an ideal opportunity to speed up the spread of profit sharing which, at the present rate of progress, will not have a major impact on the British economy until well into the twenty-first century.

THE FURTHER EXTENSION OF CO-PARTNERSHIP

It has been argued here that profit sharing linked to employee shareholding is a necessary, if not a sufficient, condition for co-partnership, which is usually beneficial to company performance. Encouraged by tax concessions it is spreading slowly in the UK. How can the pace be speeded up? There are at least three possible policies.

First, the UK government could follow the French example, where profit sharing was made obligatory by statute in 1967 for all companies with over 100 employees. A version of this is to be found in *Citizens at Work*, the Liberal Democrats' Green Paper published in August 1990, where it is recommended that all employees should be given several individual rights, including the right to participate in a profit sharing scheme. These rights would be exercised, if desired, by employees and enforced by a government agency. A heavy-handed policy of this kind would be opposed by many employers, and their opposition would cause the government agency considerable difficulties. For this reason it is not to be commended.

Second, the tax concessions for share-based profit sharing could be increased. For example, corporation tax could be reduced for the first three years after the introduction of an approved profit sharing scheme. No doubt this would speed up the spread of profit sharing, but it would also give the impression that, to be worthwhile, profit sharing needs tax concessions, and that is not so. Jevons argued in 1870 that it would pay for itself, and several hundred schemes were operating in the UK before tax concessions were made available in 1978. This option, too, should be rejected.

In the current UK situation there is a third policy option which would be extremely effective while avoiding the disadvantages of those already discussed. It is to make the tax concessions for selective (executive) share option schemes conditional upon the introduction of an approved all-employee profit sharing scheme. From Table 16.8 above it can be seen that the directors of some 3,600 companies would quickly have to decide whether to give up their own share options or to offer share-based profit sharing to a majority of their employees. A significant proportion would probably choose the latter course of action and there would be an immediate, large increase in profit sharing and employee shareholding. Ministers in the Thatcher government frequently gave approval to profit sharing and employee shareholding. If they share this view, the Major government will adopt this third policy option at the earliest opportunity.

THE SPIRIT OF CO-PARTNERSHIP

Changes in the law, or new or altered tax concessions, can help to turn employers and employees into co-partners. Compulsion and persuasion can be to some extent effective. But how much better it is for developments of this kind to be voluntary; to come about because employers and employees notice good practice elsewhere and decide, of their own accord, to introduce it into their own company. This is an area where the spirit of the law is just as important as the letter, and a government agency can only enforce the letter. If an employer is unconvinced that profit sharing will work, and feels that it has been imposed upon him against his will, no government agency, however well funded, will ever produce real co-partnership in that company.

17 The Open Shop and the New Trade Unionism

Everyone has the right to freedom of peaceful assembly and to
freedom of association with others, including the right to form
and to join trade unions for the protection of his interests.

Article 11 (1), European Convention on Human Rights

Considering their reluctance to converse when travelling by train, the
British have an astonishing capacity to form voluntary associations of
every sort, from clubs for leek-growing and all kinds of sporting
activities to a wide variety of charitable and welfare organisations.
Closed shop trade unions have, of course, been compulsory rather
than voluntary associations, but as one writer has pointed out 'A trade
union, like a trade association or a lawn tennis club or the Junior
Carlton club, is characterized in English law as a voluntary,
unincorporated association'[1]. Now the Thatcher government has
legislated firmly against the closed shop, making it awkward for an
employer to attempt to introduce or maintain this arrangement. At the
same time the open shop has been endorsed by the European
Community in the Social Charter and this policy has been accepted
by the Labour Party. It seems, therefore, reasonable to assert that the
closed shop in Britain is dying and is unlikely to be revived. How
should employers react to this new situation, and what does it mean
for the trade unions?

EMPLOYERS AND THE OPEN SHOP

It was suggested in chapter 4 that the closed shop, which cannot exist
without agreement from the employer, was the lazy employer's way of
dealing second-hand with most of his employees through a trade union
official. So the ending of the closed shop should force these employers
to think more carefully about the way they relate to their workforce,
and it might quite quickly lead to a major change in practice.

Consider a situation in which a closed shop previously existed and
all communication and negotiation in that workshop was conducted
via the shop steward. Now, mainly for legal reasons, the employer

announces that new recruits will be encouraged, but not compelled, to join the union and existing members may resign if they wish to do so. After a few months trade union membership has fallen from 100 per cent to 95 per cent, and the employer begins to see that he must deal with the 5 per cent of non-members directly, on an individual basis, because the shop steward no longer represents them. Clearly he then faces certain problems. For example, should he always deal with the non-members individually, or are there some matters about which it would be better to speak to their representatives? And if the latter, how are those representatives to be chosen? Or would it not be better to consult with representatives *chosen by the whole workforce, union and non-union*?

The main point is that the existence of even a small proportion of non-unionists in a workforce should oblige an employer to establish a communication, consultation and negotiation system based on the cornerstone of good human resource management – the individual contract of employment – and once that has been done, he has regained the initiative which had been lost. The employer then has to decide how far to use this new approach *with union members as well as non-members*. It might be thought strange, say, to send a personal letter about re-organisation in the company only to non-members. Shouldn't the members have a copy too, even if previously they expected to get this kind of information through the shop steward? Thus it can be seen that the ending of the closed shop should compel previously closed shop employers to re-think the way in which they deal with the whole workforce, and not just with non-unionists.

In the same way, the fact that the closed shop is no longer an option may make it less likely that an employer will recognise a trade union for bargaining purposes. He knows that even if a majority of the workforce has joined a union, and he recognises that union, he will still have to negotiate individually with a minority. He may, therefore, decide that instead of recognising a union, he will put more effort into developing positive employment policies which divert his employees' (or better, co-partners') loyalty from the trade union to the company. And those 'positive' policies need not include underhand methods of discouraging union membership, which suggest that the employer has little confidence in himself.

The truth is that a progressive employer, who has thought carefully about his human resources, understands that they are the key to driving the organisation forward, and provides adequate training and other facilities as well as fair financial rewards, has nothing to fear from those of his staff (probably a minority) who join a trade union. In a democratic society they have a legal and moral right to take that step, and that right should be respected. But what does the future hold for the trade unions, which achieved an all-time membership record of 13.3 million in 1979 and have lost about 4 million members since then, with the decline still continuing?

THE FUTURE OF TRADE UNIONISM IN THE UK

The ending of the closed shop is only one of several factors which make it more difficult for the unions to stem, let alone reverse, the severe decline in their membership. Other factors which are working against them include (a) structural economic changes, like the decline of employment in the coal-mining, railway and steel industries, (b) the change from national collective bargaining to local or individual negotiations, (c) the move from full-time to part-time and temporary work, and (d) the growth of self-employment. All of these trends seem set to continue, so does it not follow that if union membership declines at a rate of 250,000 a year, the unions in Britain will be almost extinct by the year 2020?

It is certainly true that, as competition intensifies from inside and outside the EC, there is no future at all for old-fashioned, class-based, politically-motivated, strike-threat trade unionism of the kind which was so strong in the 1960s and 1970s. Even most union members are now very wary of strikes and picketing, as they appreciate that the kind of militancy which produced devastating results for the coal-miners could have equally devastating results on their own firm and trade union.[2]

Meanwhile, national collective bargaining is in decline and it is rather unlikely that even the election of a Labour government, with the promise that it 'will positively encourage the development of collective bargaining as an act of public policy'[3], could reverse this trend. The labour market is moving in the opposite direction, and those who try to oppose market trends usually find themselves in some difficulty. As union members come to see that they can be better off negotiating their own individual contracts of employment, why should they continue to pay £1 a week to organisations who still see their main function as collective bargaining?

There are those in the TUC and elsewhere who have begun to understand that the function of the trade unions is changing, and they are wooing members with credit cards and other similar attractions. However, the problem for the unions is that they have no monopoly of these goodies and they are operating in a market where their competitors have more experience than they do. So have the trade unions, whose members will be volunteers, not conscripts, anything to offer which will provide them with a long-term future? The answer to that question is 'Yes, but it seems unlikely that they will be keen to provide this particular service because of their commitment to collectivism'.

As developments in human resource management encourage employers to place more emphasis on the individual contract of employment, employees or co-partners may be glad to pay a modest sum, which they see partly as an insurance premium, to assist them in negotiating a favourable contract. Many people feel out of their depth in legal matters and find even a relatively straightforward contract rather baffling. The industrial tribunals were set up in such a way that ordinary people could make their own case, but the law on unfair dismissal has become so complicated that, however reasonable the members of the tribunal try to be, applicants who do not have legal representation may find themselves at a disadvantage if they are up against a skilful lawyer. And yet no legal aid is available for those who claim unfair dismissal, despite the fact that many of them will be unemployed.

The trade unions, for more than a century, have enjoyed great success in assisting their members, often by hiring the best lawyers, in cases of industrial injury. They have used their specialised knowledge of the workplace to good effect, and their similar knowledge of current employment practices could be used to equally good effect, preferably in negotiating suitable contracts, but also, when things have gone wrong, at the industrial tribunals. Of course, employees could always go directly to a solicitor, but their hourly rate may be £50 or more, so a few hours of consultation would be the equivalent of several years subscription to a trade union or professional association. And if the union's advice led to better terms of employment or a bigger redundancy payment, the subscription would have paid off handsomely.

This, then, must be the best way forward for the trade unions, although it will not be an easy way. The Electrical, Electronic, Telecommunication and Plumbing Union (EETPU) set out down this path some years ago, but its membership fell from 394,000 in 1984 to 370,000 in 1988. The truth is that there is no easy way ahead for the trade unions, but this is the only way which will give them a reasonably secure future. However, the prognosis is not good, because policies based on serving the individual member will only succeed if they are given the highest priority, and there is little evidence that most unions intend to do this.

To begin with, there is the emphasis in current Labour Party policy on collective bargaining. Then there is the regular applause at the annual congress of the TUC for the left-wing extremists and the boos for the moderates. This reached its apogee in 1988, when in an act of folly the TUC voted by an overwhelming majority to expel the EETPU, which has shown itself to be the only major union capable of coming to terms with reality. It is a pre-requisite of the TUC's willingness to be equally realistic that it should re-admit the EETPU. Until it takes this step, it is reasonable to assume that it prefers to live in the past.

Thus it is fair to conclude that the trade unions could still play a useful and important part in employment affairs, but at the moment it seems that they have set their collective face against so doing.

18 A New Style of Management

The essence of a board working together is that
it should be like Nelson's 'band of brothers'.

John Harvey-Jones, *Making it Happen*, 1988

Human resources will not achieve their potential in any organisation
without a new style of management. The primary requirement for the
managers of the future is that they should be able to think and act
strategically. In addition they will need to approach their job in a more
participative way; decisions will be implemented more quickly and
effectively if they have been agreed beforehand. To operate in this way,
managers will have to be better trained. And finally, because they will
be much more effective and productive, there will be fewer of them.
These four aspects of a new style of management will now be briefly
explored.

STRATEGIC MANAGEMENT

Too much of British management in the past has been ad hoc, crisis
management, because a strategic plan has been lacking. As Sir John
Harvey-Jones put it, following inside experience as a non-executive
director in several companies,

> most boards of directors have no provision at all to review the
> general strategies and directions in which businesses are going, and,
> apart from intervention in individual decisions of investment, play
> only a small role in strategic direction.[1]

But business firms have not been alone in lacking a strategic sense. For
example, few, if any, universities had a strategic plan before the 1980s.
   In public and private organisations, as chief executives came and
went, so the strategy changed without any formal announcement that a
major change had taken place. Because middle and junior managers
were unclear about long-term policies, much of their work consisted of
fire-fighting, or dealing with crises instead of achieving strategic goals.

Often this approach was commended, because the crises were overcome without total disaster. The classic national example was Dunkirk, which has usually been regarded as a triumph when surely it would have been better if the soldiers had not found themselves on the beaches in the first place. Perhaps the comment which Marshal Bosquet made about the charge of the light brigade – 'C'est magnifique, mais ce n'est pas la guerre' – should also be said about Dunkirk. The same might be broadly applied to the way in which the British have responded to the recent Japanese threat to dominate the world in the provision of certain goods and services. They have tended to carry on as if the threat did not exist.

It was mentioned in chapter 16 that recent research has indicated that, generally speaking, profit sharing firms are more profitable than non-profit sharers. The same kind of results are true for research into the effects of strategic planning. After surveying several studies, Hofer and Schendel wrote in 1978 that 'there is growing evidence to suggest that the use of formal approaches to strategy formulation is associated with superior organizational performance, especially for manufacturing companies.'[2] Thus there is good reason for business firms and other organisations to have a strategic plan.

Of course such a plan must be based on expected demand, and because this cannot be predicted with certainty, the plan must be as flexible as possible and regularly reviewed. The time period of the plan will vary according to the nature of the industry. For the electricity supply industry, the strategic plan will have to look at least five years ahead, but for a small company in a service industry, it may only be possible to plan one or two years ahead. However, those organisations which do not have a plan at all will tend to be in a permanent state of crisis, and they may be overwhelmed by a particularly bad turn of events.

To argue for a strategic plan is not to deny the view that managers have to adapt continuously to changing customer demands and be ready to meet difficulties which cannot possibly be predicted. The oil price shocks of the 1970s and the food scares of the late 1980s are just two problems which planners could hardly have foreseen. But these unpredictable events make it more important than ever that a strategic plan exists and that the long term objectives are known throughout the organisation. Once that preliminary exercise is complete, a regular review, probably on an annual basis, provides an opportunity for everyone to see how well they have performed over the past year and where they are expected to go in the next.

Good management must include a sound strategy, and organisations which lack a strategy are drifting. Too many British business firms and public sector organisations have no real sense of direction and that problem can only be remedied by top management. A key element of a sound strategy will be concerned with the management of human resources, and it will be understood that every employee or co-partner has a part to play in achieving the organisation's objectives. This will require a participative approach which, like all other effective policies, must start in the boardroom.

PARTICIPATIVE MANAGEMENT

Much has been written about employee participation and employee involvement, and there is growing support by employers and their organisations for involving employees in decisions which affect them, and for employee shareholding. However, this is sometimes seen as an arrangement by which top management communicates directly with office and/or works staff, by-passing intermediate managers and supervisors. Nothing is more likely to undermine the authority and damage the morale of middle managers and supervisors, and such an approach is a recipe for organisational disaster.

Instead, effective participation, which taps the latent abilities and skills of the whole workforce and makes everyone more productive has to start in the boardroom. Communication is too easily thought of as a one-way (downwards) process. Of course it should be at least two-way (upwards as well as downwards). But *lateral* communication is just as important as, and perhaps more important than, vertical communication and serious weaknesses can so easily exist on this plane. The most obvious example is when two senior people have fallen out and hardly speak to each other. That must be very damaging to the organisation. Perhaps just as damaging, but less noticeable, is a situation where senior managers do not fully share their skills and knowledge with their colleagues, so that they are not fully effective. This may arise not because people are deliberately stand-offish, but because they are not used to sharing ideas, except occasionally and rather specifically.

One of John Harvey-Jones' first actions as the new chairman of ICI was to arrange for himself and the other executive directors to spend a week away together to discuss how the board should lead the company, and how they should organise their work.[3] It would be interesting to know how his colleagues received this radical announcement, but it might have been with a mixture of shock and horror. How could one possibly tolerate one's immediate colleagues for more than a few hours? Needless to say, it seems that the event passed off without incident, and a decision was taken that the directors wanted 'a very open, flexible and friendly organisation, where we would have to accept that each of us was contributing in each other's fields almost continuously, and this meant trust, clarity and the perception of priorities.'[4] Following on from these initial discussions, it was decided that the executive directors should meet two or three times a year for two days in a conference centre outside London, and we are told that 'The quality of these meetings is of a different order, even from those that are held in the informally set-up boardroom in the main office.'[5]

The participative approach to management should be contrasted with the control-dominated system which relies on status and established hierarchy. The two approaches differ in quite fundamental ways, but two things should be said about participative management: (a) It does not mean that management loses responsibility or control. On the contrary, one imagines that ICI's board under Sir John Harvey-Jones was more responsible and had better control than before. But the control is of a different kind – more flexible, more understanding and more effective, because decisions are now only made after the fullest possible discussion and consultation; and (b) It does not mean that individuals have to submerge their personalities in 'group-think' or 'group-action'. That is clear from the ICI experience, because no leading British businessman has retained his individuality better than John Harvey-Jones. As suggested in chapters 14 and 15, creative individuals and good teamwork should be complementary, not incompatible.

Once the board of directors has begun to operate in a more informal, participative way, this approach can be deliberately spread throughout the organisation, but like all new ideas, it will meet with resistance. And the strongest resistance will probably come from management. Jerome Rosow warns that:

Managers have subtle ways to resist, especially when there is clear danger of further reductions in management control and layers of management. Their resistance is a serious obstacle to the achievement of managerial participation in light of the events of the last 10 years.[6]

So the chief executive who is committed to the new approach will have to be very determined, even perhaps to the point of losing some managers who will not, or cannot, adapt their style. Like all innovations, it will be easier on a greenfield site. But they are a minority – managers on brownfield sites will have to try harder.

BETTER TRAINED MANAGERS

Professor Allen wrote in 1979 that

> in comparison with other industrial countries, industry in Britain has not attracted a high proportion of the country's first-rate ability. The inclination of the best graduates is still to prefer an academic career, research, the Civil Service or the professions to jobs in industry. The mentors of the young must bear a share of the responsibility for this choice. They have been disposed to deflect their most promising pupils from employment in business to what they regard as worthier activities.[7]

Anti-business attitudes in schools and higher education are only part of the reason why British managers are under-trained for their work; the other main part is that top managers have had too poor a view of the importance of education and training. The cult of the amateur has died very hard in Britain, with a serious effect on business performance. One study based on 1975–76 data showed that, in a sample of 2,637 British managers, 52 per cent had no qualifications at all, and only 3 per cent were university graduates.[8] This situation might have improved slightly by the mid-1980s, but two reports published in 1987 drew attention once again to the comparatively very poor record of Britain in management education. The following figures from one of these reports make the point:

Country	Top managers with degrees (per cent)
Britain	24
France	65
Japan	85
USA	85
West Germany	62

Source: *The Making of Managers*, A Report commissioned by the Manpower Services Commission, the National Economic Development Council and the British Institute of Management, 1987, p. 2.

In a summary of its findings, the other report[9] stated categorically that 'Britain's managers lack the development, education and training opportunities of their competitors' and that the great majority of the 90,000 people who enter management roles each year 'have no prior formal management education and training.' The authors went on to say that 'It is estimated that UK managers receive an average of about 1 day's formal training per year. This figure hides a wide average. The majority of managers receive no formal training.'

The two 1987 reports sparked off an intensive debate about UK management education and training, and some action. But more does not always mean better. Second-rate training courses are a complete waste of time. Top managers should be able to assimilate information at a rapid rate, and short courses of between half a day and three days will usually be more valuable than longer periods. And there is no place for academic teachers who see themselves as superior in every respect to their students. Often a main part of the 'teacher's' job is to create a forum in which the 'students' can learn from each other. Finally, it needs to be remembered that there will always be natural entrepreneurs who have learned their trade exceedingly well in the 'university of hard knocks'.

A major question in the expansion of management education relates to the provision of funding. It is difficult to see why the state should fund courses for practising managers. Presumably they take such courses because they and their employers expect them to be beneficial. Consequently it is reasonable for the beneficiaries to pay for the courses themselves. But there is one area – that of undergraduate courses – where the market does not work because of the expectation that the state will provide fees for all UK undergraduates at universities and polytechnics. This attitude may be changing, but it will be at least five years before it changes fundamentally.

UK universities have been too slow to meet the significant increase in demand by some of the best sixth-formers for single and joint honours degrees (and especially sandwich degrees)[10] in business management. The consequence is that this demand is unsatisfied and many of these applicants have to settle for second-best. The only remedy is an injection of public finds for the expansion of this particular kind of course, to be bid for by universities which have already shown some inclination to move into this field and are keen to expand. A specific injection of this kind would have the desirable side-effect of creating a more enterprising spirit in the universities. These institutions have moved a little since 1979, but some of them still have great difficulty in coming to terms with the enterprise culture.

FEWER MANAGERS

Operating more participatively in an organisation with an agreed strategy, better trained managers will be considerably more productive. It follows that there will be fewer of them. Today, Tom Peters is the leading advocate of eliminating management bureaucracies, and chief executives pay attention to his views. He insists that five layers of management should be the maximum for the largest multi-national corporation, and three layers for any single facility such as a plant or distribution centre.[11] He quotes a recent McKinsey report which concluded that:

> The first step in accomplishing successful plant floor implementation of new manufacturing approaches is the clearing out of *all* the middle managers and support service layers that clog the wheels of change. These salaried people are often the real barriers to productivity improvement, not the hourly workers on the floor. (emphasis supplied)[12]

In fact this process, sometimes known as 'de-layering', is already taking place in some major British companies, including Boots, British Home Stores, British Petroleum, British Telecom, Hanson Trust, the Stock Exchange and the Trustee Savings Bank. The announcement in May 1990 that British Home Stores was shedding 900 management and support jobs came after it was found that only three out of every five employees were actually engaged in selling. It was well known that British Telecom was over-staffed, but it took the board of the privatised company several years to pluck up the courage to announce (also in May 1990) 5,000 managerial redundancies, accompanied by generous silver handshakes, among those earning £20,000 to £30,000 a year. There can be no doubt that this slimming exercise will make BT more efficient and lead to better customer service, and the same will usually be true of similar exercises elsewhere. Many major companies drastically slimmed head office staff in the 1980s, but there is scope to take this further and to trim the bureaucracy in every part of the organisation. And on the factory floor fixed rules about the span of control are becoming obsolete, as better-trained operatives take more responsibility for managing themselves, and supervisors become responsible for teams of a hundred or more.

CONCLUSION

The climate for managers in the 1990s and twenty first century will be increasingly competitive and invigorating. But it is now clear that the trade union tiger can be tamed, and the experience of Japanese-owned companies shows that the very best levels of quality and productivity can be achieved in Britain. All that is needed is for British businesses to set themselves, and to accomplish, equally high standards – and then to improve on them. There is now no reason in principle why 'Made in Britain' should not become again a cause for pride and a mark of excellence.

References

1 The Winter of Discontent

The main sources for this chapter are:
The Economist, July 1978–May 1979.
The Times, July 1978–November 1978.
The Daily Telegraph, December 1978–May 1979 (*The Times* was on strike for a year, beginning in December 1978).

2 Step by Step Reform: An Outline of the Process

The main sources for this chapter are the Acts themselves and the various Guides published by the Department of Employment.

3 Trade Union Immunities: The Heart of the Matter

1 A. V. Dicey, *Lectures on the Relation between Law and Public Opinion in England during the Nineteenth Century*, Macmillan, 1963, p. 468.
2 *Ibid*, p. xlvi.
3 S. and B. Webb, *The History of Trade Unionism*, Authors' Edition, 1920, p. 606.
4 M. Whincup, *Modern Employment Law*, Heinemann, 6th Edition, 1988, p. 92.
5 For a more extensive discussion of the relationship between legal reform and economic change, see Charles G. Hanson, 'Economic Significance of British Labor Law Reform', *Cato Journal*, Winter 1987, pp. 851–868.
6 H. C. Simons, 'Reflections on Syndicalism', *Journal of Political Economy*, March 1944, p. 4.

4 The Closed Shop

1 S. and B. Webb, *Industrial Democracy*, Longmans Green, 1902, p. 214.
2 *Ibid*, p. 215.
3 F. A. Hayek, *The Constitution of Liberty*, Routledge and Kegan Paul, 1960, p. 11.
4 S. Petro, *The Labor Policy of the Free Society*, Ronald Press, 1957, p. 25.
5 These figures arose from surveys carried out by W. E. J. McCarthy and J. Gennard. They are discussed in C. Hanson *et al.*, *The Closed Shop*, Gower, 1982, pp. 65–70.
6 W. E. J. McCarthy, *The Closed Shop in Britain*, University of California Press, 1964, p. 260.
7 Costs of this order would not be incurred today because (a) legal aid is available, and (b) applicants can represent themselves and costs are not awarded against them if they lose.

8 *ACAS Annual Report 1986*, p. 13.
9 N. Millward and M. Stevens, *British Workplace Industrial Relations 1980–1984*, Gower, 1986, p. 107.
10 *Removing Barriers to Employment*, Cm 655, HMSO, 1989, p. 5.

5 Picketing

1 From a leaflet issued by the Strike Committee
2 *Report of a Court of Inquiry under the Rt Hon Lord Justice Scarman OBE*, Cmnd 6922, 1977, p. 24.
3 *1979 Conservative Manifesto*, p. 10.
4 See I. MacGregor, *The Enemies Within*, Collins, 1986, pp. 216–18, and M. Adeney and J. Lloyd, *The Miners' Strike 1984–5*, Routledge and Kegan Paul, 1986, pp. 100 and 157–9.

6 Trade Union Democracy and the Role of the TUC

1 J. Goldstein, *The Government of British Trade Unions*, Allen and Unwin, 1952.
2 *Ibid*, p. 213. In 1949 the rules of the TGWU were changed to forbid members of the Communist Party from holding office. However, Goldstein points out that in the branch which he studied the leadership remained in the same hands, as members of the CP resigned from the Party in order to retain their office.
3 *Ibid*, p. 271.
4 *Official Report*, House of Commons, 8 November 1983, Vol. 48, c 157–8.
5 *Trades Union Congress Report 1986*, p. 30.
6 *Ibid*, p. 31.
7 *ACAS Annual Report 1989*, p. 30.
8 *Ibid*.
9 *Trades Union Congress Report 1988*, p. 35.
10 In the second reading debate on the Employment Bill 1990, Mr David Clelland MP (Tyne Bridge) suggested that CROTUM 'would be a rather unfortunate acronym if we ever got a senior commissioner for the rights of trade union members.' *Official Report*, 29 January 1990; Vol. 166, c. 82.

7 Deregulating the Labour Market, the Rise of Self-Employment and the Individual Contract of Employment

1 C. Handy, *The Age of Unreason*, Business Books, 1989, p. 169.
2 *Meet the challenge, Make the change: A new agenda for Britain*, The Labour Party, 1989, p. 22.
3 B. C. Roberts, *DELORS versus 1992? A review of the cost of social harmonisation in the European Economic Community*, The Bruges Group, Occasional Paper 1, 1989.
4 For the form of such a Bill see C. G. Hanson and G. Mather, *Striking out Strikes*, Institute of Economic Affairs, 1988, p. 51.
5 O. Kahn-Freund, *Legal Framework*, in A. Flanders and H. A. Clegg (Eds), *The System of Industrial Relations in Great Britain*, Blackwell, 1954, p. 45.

6   P. Bassett, *Strike Free: New Industrial Relations in Great Britain*, Macmillan, 1986, p. 164.
7   *Financial Times* article by D. Summers, 14 May 1990.
8   Reported in the *Yorkshire Evening Post*, 20 April 1990.

8   Some Economic Benefits of the Reforms

1   M. Adeney and J. Lloyd, *The Miners' Strike 1984–5: Loss Without Limit*, Routledge and Kegan Paul, 1986, p. 2.
2   Hence the sub-title of the above book.
3   *Ibid*, p. 6.
4   I. MacGregor, *The Enemies Within*, Collins, 1986, p. 217.
5   British Coal Corporation, *Report and Accounts 1988–89*, p. 29.
6   *Financial Times article* by D. Thomas, 31 August 1990.
7   British Coal Corporation, *Report and Accounts 1988–89*, p. 3.
8   *Financial Times article* by D. Thomas, 31 August 1990.
9   C. Wintour, *The Rise and Fall of Fleet Street*, Hutchinson, 1989, p. 244.
10 K. Sisson, *Industrial Relations in Fleet Street*, Blackwell, 1975, and G. Cleverly, *The Fleet Street Disaster: British national newspapers as a case study in mismanagement*, Constable, 1976.
11 G. Cleverly, *op cit*, p. 86.
12 *Report of the Royal Commission on the Press 1961–62*, Cmnd 1811, HMSO, September 1962, p. 216.
13 *Ibid*, p. 210.
14 *Ibid*, p. 215.
15 C. Wintour, *op cit*, p. 246.
16 *Ibid*, Chapter 11, pp. 215–37.
17 *Ibid*, p. 217.
18 This section draws on my article 'Time to End the Dock Labour Scheme', *Economic Affairs*, June/July 1988, pp. 34–36.
19 *The Peaceful Revolution: A progress report on changes since the repeal of the National Dock Labour Scheme*, Employment Gazette, July 1990, pp. 360–4.
20 *Ibid*, p. 362.
21 *Ibid*.
22 *Ibid*, p. 361.
23 *Ibid*, p. 364.
24 This section draws on my article 'Reform of the Legal Profession: The Biggest Bang of All', *Economic Affairs*, June/July 1989, pp. 23–25.
25 D. S. Lees, *Economic Consequences of the Professions*, Institute of Economic Affairs, 1966.
26 *Ibid*, p. 35.
27 *Ibid*, p. 37.
28 Cm 570, HMSO, January 1989.
29 *The Times*, 26 January 1989.
30 *Ibid*.
31 *The Times*, 27 January 1989.
32 *Official Report*, House of Lords, Vol. 505, 1988–89, c. 1331.
33 *Ibid*, c 1332–3.

34 *Legal Services: A Framework for the Future*, Cm 740, HMSO, 1989.
35 *Ibid*, para 10.10, p. 33.

9 Unfinished Business

1 Lord Beveridge, *Full Employment in a Free Society*, Second edition, Allen and Unwin, 1960, p. 128.
2 W. H. Hutt, *The Theory of Collective Bargaining*, P. S King, 1930, revised and re-issued as *The Theory of Collective Bargaining 1930–1975*, Institute of Economic Affairs, 1975.
3 M. Whincup, *Modern Employment Law*, Sixth edition, Heinemann, 1988, p. 34.
4 G. S. Morris, *Strikes in Essential Services*, Mansell, 1986, pp. 7–9.
5 P. Minford, 'The Medicine is Working', Liverpool Research Group in Macroeconomics, *Quarterly Economic Bulletin*, June 1990, p. 7.
6 *Official Report*, House of Commons, 2 April 1984, Vol. 57, c. 754.
7 Article in *The Independent* by B. Clement, 17 September, 1990.

10 What Would a Labour Government Do?

1 B. C. Roberts, *The Trades Union Congress 1868–1921*, Allen and Unwin, 1958, p. 51.
2 *Ibid*, p. 65.
3 See C. G. Hanson, 'Craft Unions, Welfare Benefits, and the Case for Trade Union Law Reform 1867–75', *Economic History Review*, Second Series, Vol. 28, May 1975, for an analysis of the way in which some trade unionists misled public opinion about the real nature of their activities.
4 S. and B. Webb, *The History of Trade Unionism*, Authors' edition, 1920, p. 606. Sidney Webb was a member of the Royal Commission on Trade Disputes and Trade Combinations which reported in 1906.
5 *Labour and the Unions*, Conservative Research Department, 1990.
6 *Official Report*, House of Commons, 8 November 1983, Vol. 48, c. 173.
7 *Looking to the Future*, The Labour Party, 1990, p. 34.
8 *Meet the challenge, Make the change*, The Labour Party, 1989, p. 26.
9 *Ibid*, p. 24.
10 *Ibid*.
11 P. Minford and P. Ashton, *Labour's Economic Policies*, Liverpool Research Group in Macroeconomics, *Quarterly Economic Bulletin*, June 1990, p. 43.
12 *Ibid*, p. 44.

Introduction to Part II: New Employment Policies in the Enterprise

1 F. A. Hayek, *1980s Unemployment and the Unions*, Institute of Economic Affairs, 1980, pp. 58 and 64.
2 See, for example, G. C. Allen, *The British Disease*, Institute of Economic Affairs, 1976, passim.

11 From Industrial Relations to Human Resource Management

1 The *International Journal of Human Resource Management* and the *Human Resource Management Journal.*
2 D. E. Guest, 'Human Resource Management: its implications for industrial relations and trade unions', in J. Storey (ed.), *New Perspectives on Human Resource Management*, Routledge, 1989, p. 46.
3 Chapter 7 in P. Wickens, *The Road to Nissan*, Macmillan, 1987.
4 D. Drennan, 'How to Get your Employees Committed', *Management Today*, October 1989, p. 121.
5 W. Goldsmith and D. Clutterbuck, *The Winning Streak*, Weidenfeld and Nicolson, 1984, pp. 182–5.
6 *Ibid*, p. 22.
7 W. S. Jevons, 'On Industrial Partnerships', in *Methods of Social Reform*, Macmillan, 1883, p. 121.
8 *Britain's Industrial Future*, being the Report of the Liberal Industrial Inquiry, Ernest Benn, 1928 (reprinted 1977).
9 *Ibid*, p. 199.
10 H. Fayol, *General and Industrial Management*, Pitman, 1961, p. xii.
11 *Ibid*, p. xiv.

12 The Importance of the Customer

1 P. Wickens, *The Road to Nissan*, Macmillan, 1987, p. 5.
2 W. Goldsmith and D. Clutterbuck, *The Winning Streak*, Weidenfeld and Nicolson, 1984, p. 88.
3 *Consumer Concerns 1990: A consumer view of public services*, National Consumer Council, 1990.
4 T. Melville-Ross, 'Marriage of Two Minds', *Management Today*, October 1989, p. 5.
5 T. Peters, *Thriving on Chaos*, Pan Books, 1989, p. 90.

13 Zero-Defect Quality and High Productivity

1 P. Wickens, *The Road to Nissan*, Macmillan, 1987, p. 64.
2 T. Peters, *Thriving on Chaos*, Pan Books, 1989, p. 73.
3 *UK Productivity – Closing the Gap*, The PA/CBI UK Productivity Survey, 1988.

14 Recruiting and Motivating Individual Employees

1 P. Herriot, *Recruitment in the 90s*, Institute of Personnel Management, 1989.
2 P. Wickens, *The Road to Nissan*, Macmillan, 1987, pp. 171–174.
3 *Ibid*, p. 91.
4 *Productivity, Education and Training: Britain and other countries compared*, (preface by S. J. Prais), National Institute of Economic and Social Research, 1989.

5 *Ibid*, p. 110.
6 *Ibid*, p. 111.
7 *Ibid*, p. 118.
8 A. Smith, *Wealth of Nations*, Cannan Edition, Methuen, 1904, Vol. II, p. 284.
9 A comprehensive text on this topic is R. T. Greenhill, *Performance Related Pay*, Director Books, 1988.

15 Creating a Team Spirit

1 T. Deal and A. Kennedy, *Corporate Culture*, Penguin, 1988, p. 5.
2 The Department of Employment continues to publish its wage statistics under the separate headings of 'manual' and 'non-manual'. Surely it is time to abolish this invidious distinction.
3 T. Wilkinson (ed.), *The Communications Challenge*, Institute of Personnel Management, 1989, p. 25.
4 *Ibid*, p. 27.
5 J. Harvey-Jones, *Making It Happen*, Fontana, 1989, p. 69.
6 1972 Works Constitution Act of the Federal Republic of Germany, Part 1, 2-(1).
7 E. C. M Cullingford, *Trade Unions in West Germany*, Wilton House, 1976, p. 22.

16 Profit Sharing and Co-Partnership

1 R. T. Greenhill, *Performance Related Pay*, Director Books, 1988, p. 174.
2 D. W. Bell and C. G. Hanson, *Profit Sharing and Employee Shareholding Attitude Survey*, Industrial Participation Association, 1984, p. 24.
3 W. S. Jevons, *op cit*, p. 139.
4 D. W. Bell and C. G. Hanson, *Profit Sharing and Profitability*, Kogan Page, 1987, p. 58. See also C. G. Hanson and R. Watson, 'Profit Sharing and Company Performance: some empirical evidence for the UK', in G. Jenkins and M. Poole (eds), *New Forms of Ownership*, Routledge, 1990, pp. 165–182.
5 D. W. Bell and C. G. Hanson, *Profit Sharing and Profitability*, p. 68.

17 The Open Shop and the New Trade Unionism

1 C. Grunfeld, *Trade Unions and the Individual in English Law*, Institute of Personnel Management, 1963, p. 9.
2 The wariness of the members is echoed by some trade union officials, including Norman Willis and John Edmonds. See C. G. Hanson and G. Mather, *Striking out Strikes*, Institute of Economic Affairs, 1988, p. 34.
3 *Meet the challenge, Make the change: A new agenda for Britain*, The Labour Party, 1989, p. 24.

18 A New Style of Management

1 J. Harvey-Jones, *Making it Happen*, Fontana, 1989, p. 274.
2 C.W. Hofer and D. Schendel, *Strategy Formulation: Analytical Concepts*, West Publishing Company, 1978, p. 11.
3 J. Harvey-Jones, *op cit*, p. 260.
4 *Ibid*, p. 264.
5 *Ibid*, p. 281.
6 J. Rosow, 'New Roles for Managers', *Involvement and Participation*, Summer 1990, pp. 19–20.
7 G.C. Allen, *The British Disease*, Institute of Economic Affairs, Second Edition, 1979, p. 55.
8 G. Crockett and P. Elias, 'British Managers: A Study of Their Education, Training, Mobility and Earnings', *British Journal of Industrial Relations*, March 1984, pp. 34–46.
9 *The Making of British Managers*, A Report for the BIM and CBI into management training, education and development, 1987.
10 Only those tutors with direct experience of sandwich courses will know about the dramatic effect which a good industrial placement has on a student. This must be the way forward for management education at the undergraduate level.
11 T. Peters, *Thriving on Chaos*, p. 359.
12 *Ibid*, pp. 355–6.

Index

175

THE TROPIC of
SERPENTS

THE TROPIC *of* SERPENTS

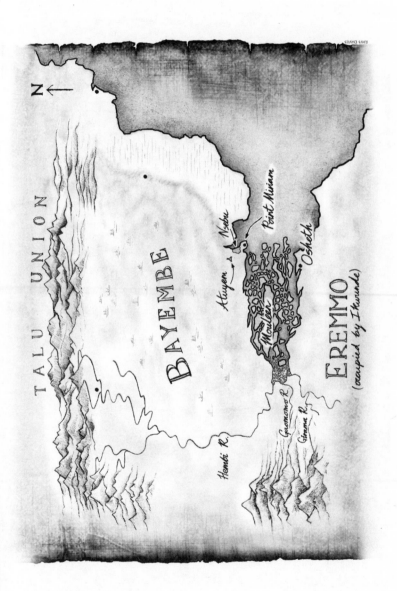

N ←

TALU UNION

BAYEMBE

Hembi R.

Atuyem • Nsebu

Point Miriam

Mouleen

Osheth

EREMMO
(occupied by Ikwunde)

Gaomomo R.

Girama R.

PREFACE

Public opinion is a fickle thing. Nowadays I am hailed from one end of Scirland to the other as a testament to the intelligence and derring-do of our race; indeed, if I am not the most famous Scirling woman in the world, I daresay I give Her Majesty the Queen a good fight. I would not go so far as to presume I am universally loved, but if any news-sheet sees fit to mention me (as they do not so often anymore, on account of my signal failure to make any new shattering discoveries in the last decade, nor to nearly get myself killed in suitably gruesome fashion), chances are good that mention will be favorable in tone.

It was not always so. Though few are old enough to remember it, and even fewer rude enough to bring the topic up, I was once reviled in the scandal-sheets. But I have no compunctions about washing my dirty linen in public—not when the linen in question is so very old and wrinkled. Some of the errors I was accused of were entirely baseless; others, I confess, were entirely fair, at least insofar as my own opinion may be trusted.

As I have not yet finished composing my memoirs, I cannot say with certainty that this, the second volume in the series, will be the most gossip-ridden of them all. That honour may belong to a later period in my life, before my second marriage, when my interactions with my future husband were grist for a very energetic mill both at home and abroad. I am still considering how much of that I will share. But this volume will be a fair contender, as it was during these years that I found myself accused of fornication, high treason, and status as the worst mother in all of Scirland. It is rather more than most women manage in their lives, and I own that I take a perverse sort of pride in the achievement.

This is also, of course, the tale of my expedition to Eriga. The warnings delivered in my first foreword continue to apply: if you are likely to be deterred by descriptions of violence, disease, foods alien to the Scirling palate, strange religions, public nakedness, or pinheaded diplomatic blunders, then close the covers of this book and proceed to something more congenial.

But I assure you that I survived all these things; it is likely you will survive the reading of them, too.

Lady Trent
Amavi, Prania
23 Ventis, 5659

PART ONE

In which the memoirist departs her homeland,
leaving behind a variety of problems
ranging from the familial to the criminal

ONE

*My life of solitude—My sister-in-law and my mother—
An unexpected visitor—Trouble at Kemble's*

Not long before I embarked on my journey to Eriga, I
girded my loins and set out for a destination I considered much more dangerous: Falchester.

The capital was not, in the ordinary way of things, a terribly
adventurous place, except insofar as I might be rained upon there.
I made the trip from Pasterway on a regular basis, as I had affairs
to monitor in the city. Those trips, however, were not well-
publicized—by which I mean I mentioned them to only a handful
of people, all of them discreet. So far as most of Scirland knew
(those few who cared to know), I was a recluse, and had been so
since my return from Vystrana.

I was permitted reclusiveness on account of my personal
troubles, though in reality I spent more of my time on work: first
the publication of our Vystrani research, and then preparation for
this Erigan expedition, which had been delayed and delayed
again, by forces far beyond our control. On that Graminis
morning, however, I could no longer escape the social obligations

I assiduously buried beneath those other tasks. The best I could do was to discharge them both in quick succession: to visit first my blood relations, and then those bound to me by marriage.

My house in Pasterway was only a short drive from the fashionable district of Havistow, where my eldest brother Paul had settled the prior year. I usually escaped the necessity of visiting his house by the double gift of his frequent absence and his wife's utter disinterest in me, but on this occasion I had been invited, and it would have been more trouble to refuse.

Please understand, it is not that I disliked my family. Most of us got on cordially enough, and I was on quite good terms with Andrew, the brother most immediately senior to me. But the rest of my brothers found me baffling, to say the least, and my mother's censure of my behaviour had nudged their opinions toward disapproval. What Paul wanted with me that day I did not know—but on the whole, I would have preferred to face a disgruntled Vystrani rock-wyrm.

Alas, those were all quite far away, while my brother was too near to avoid. With a sensation of girding for battle, I lifted my skirt in ladylike delicacy, climbed the front steps, and rang the bell.

My sister-in-law was in the morning room when the footman escorted me in. Judith was a paragon of upper-class Scirling wifehood, in all the ways I was not: beautifully dressed, without crossing the line into gyver excess; a gracious hostess, facilitating her husband's work by social means; and a dedicated mother, with three children already, and no doubt more to come.

We had precisely one thing in common, which was Paul. "Have I called at the wrong time?" I inquired, after accepting a cup of tea.

"Not at all," Judith answered. "He is not at home just now—a meeting with Lord Melst—but you are welcome to stay until he returns."

Lord Melst? Paul *was* moving up in the world. "I presume this is Synedrion business," I said.

Judith nodded. "We had a short respite after he won his chair, but now the affairs of government have moved in to occupy his time. I hardly expect to see him between now and Gelis."

Which meant I might be cooling my heels here for a very long time. "If it is not too much trouble," I said, putting down my teacup and rising from my seat, "I think it might be better for me to leave and come back. I have promised to pay a visit to my brother-in-law Matthew today as well."

To my surprise, Judith put out her hand to stop me. "No, please stay. We have a guest right now, who was hoping to see you—"

I never had the chance to ask who the guest was, though I had my suspicions the moment Judith began to speak. The door to the sitting room opened, and my mother came in.

Now it all made sense. I had ceased to answer my mother's letters some time before, for my own peace of mind. She would not, even when asked, leave off criticizing my every move, and implying that my bad judgment had caused me to lose my husband in Vystrana. It was not courteous to ignore her, but the alternative would be worse. For her to see me, therefore, she must either show up unannounced at my house . . . or lure me to another's.

Such logic did little to sweeten my reaction. Unless my mother was there to offer reconciliation—which I doubted—this was a trap. I had rather pull my own teeth out than endure more of her recriminations. (And lest you think that a mere figure of speech, I should note that I *did* once pull my own tooth out, so I do not make the comparison lightly.)

As it transpired, though, her recriminations were at least drawing on fresh material. My mother said, "Isabella. What is this nonsense I hear about you going to Eriga?"

I have been known to bypass the niceties of small talk, and ordinarily I am grateful for it in others. In this instance, however, it had the effect of an arrow shot from cover, straight into my brain. "What?" I said, quite stupidly—not because I failed to understand her, but because I had no idea how she had come to hear of it.

"You know perfectly well what I mean," she went on, relentlessly. "It is *absurd,* Isabella. You cannot go abroad again, and *certainly* not to any part of Eriga. They are at war there!"

I sought my chair once more, using the delay to regain my composure. "That is an exaggeration, Mama, and you know it. Bayembe is not at war. The mansa of Talu dares not invade, not with Scirling soldiers helping to defend the borders."

My mother sniffed. "I imagine the man who drove the Akhians out of Elerqa—after two hundred years!—dares a great deal indeed. And even if *he* does not attack, what of those dreadful Ikwunde?"

"The entire jungle of Mouleen lies between them and Bayembe," I said, irritated. "Save at the rivers, of course, and Scirland stands guard there as well. Mama, the whole point of our military presence is to make the place safe."

The look she gave me was dire. "Soldiers do not make a place safe, Isabella. They only make it less dangerous."

What skill I have in rhetoric, I inherited from my mother. I was in no mood to admire her phrasing that day, though. Nor to be pleased at her political awareness, which was quite startling.

Most Scirling women of her class, and a great many men, too, could barely name the two Erigan powers that had forced Bayembe to seek foreign—which is to say Scirling—aid. Gentlemen back then were interested only in the lopsided "trade agreement" that sent Bayembe iron to Scirland, along with other valuable resources, in exchange for them allowing us to station our soldiers all over their country, and build a colony in Nsebu. Ladies were not interested much at all.

Was this something she had attended to before, or had she educated herself upon hearing of my plans? Either way, this was not how I had intended to break the news to her. Just how I *had* intended to do it, I had not yet decided; I kept putting off the issue, out of what I now recognized as rank cowardice. And this was the consequence: an unpleasant confrontation in front of my sister-in-law, whose stiffly polite expression told me that she had known this was coming.

(A sudden worm of suspicion told me that Paul, too, had known. Meeting with Lord Melst, indeed. Such a *shame* he was out when I arrived.)

It meant, at least, that I only had to face my mother, without allies to support her in censure. I was not fool enough to think I would have had allies of my own. I said, "The Foreign Office would not allow people to travel there, let alone settle, if it were so dangerous as all that. And they *have* been allowing it, so there you are." She did not need to know that one of the recurrent delays in this expedition had involved trying to persuade the Foreign Office to grant us visas. "Truly, Mama, I shall be at far more risk from malaria than from any army."

What possessed me to say that, I do not know, but it was sheer idiocy on my part. My mother's glare sharpened. "Indeed," she said, and the word could have frosted glass. "Yet you propose to go to a place teeming with tropical diseases, without a single *thought* for your son."

Her accusation was both fair and not. It was true that I did not think as much of my son as one might expect. I gave very little milk after his birth and had to hire a wet-nurse, which suited me all too well; infant Jacob reminded me far too much of his late namesake. Now he was more than two years old, weaned, and in the care of a nanny. My marriage settlement had provided quite generously for me, but much of that money I had poured into scientific research, and the books of our Vystrani expedition— the scholarly work under my husband's name, and my own inane bit of travel writing—were not bringing in as much as one might hope. Out of what remained, however, I paid handsomely for someone to care for my son, and not because the widow of a baronet's second son ought not to stoop to such work herself. I simply did not know what to do with Jacob otherwise.

People often suppose that maternal wisdom is wholly instinctual: that however ignorant a woman may be of child rearing prior to giving birth, the mere fact of her sex will afterward endow her with perfect capability. This is not true even on the grossest biological level, as the failure of my milk had proved, and it is even less true in social terms. In later years I have come to understand children from the perspective of a natural historian; I know their development, and have some appreciation for its marvellous progress. But at that point in time, little Jacob made less sense to me than a dragon.

Is the rearing of a child best performed by a woman who has

THE TROPIC OF SERPENTS

done it before, who has honed her skills over the years and enjoys her work, or by a woman with no skill and scant enjoyment, whose sole qualification is a direct biological connection? My opinion fell decidedly on the former, and so I saw very little practical reason why I should not go to Eriga. In *that* respect, I had given a great deal of thought to the matter of my son.

Saying such things to my mother was, however, out of the question. Instead I temporized. "Matthew Camherst and his wife have offered to take him in while I am gone. Bess has one of her own, very near the same age; it will be good for Jacob to have a companion."

"And if you die?"

The question dropped like a cleaver onto the conversation, severing it short. I felt my cheeks burning: with anger, or with shame—likely both. I was outraged that my mother should say such a thing so bluntly . . . and yet my husband had died in Vystrana. It was not impossible that I should do the same in Eriga.

Into this dead and bleeding silence came a knock on the door, followed shortly by the butler, salver in hand, bowing to present a card to Judith, who lifted it, mechanically, as if she were a puppet and someone had pulled the string on her arm. Confusion carved a small line between her brows. "Who is Thomas Wilker?"

The name had the effect of a low, unnoticed kerb at the edge of a street, catching my mental foot and nearly causing me to fall on my face. "Thomas Wil—what is *he* doing here?" Comprehension followed, tardily, lifting me from my stumble. Judith did not know him, and neither did my mother, which left only one answer. "Ah. I think he must be here to see me."

Judith's posture snapped to a rigid, upright line, for this was *not*

how social calls were conducted. A man should not inquire after a
widow in a house that wasn't hers. I spared a moment to notice
that the card, which Judith dropped back on the salver, was not a
proper calling card; it appeared to be a piece of paper with Mr.
Wilker's name written in by hand. Worse and worse. Mr. Wilker
was not, properly speaking, a gentleman, and certainly not the
sort of person who would call here in the normal course of things.

I did what I could to retrieve the moment. "I do apologize. Mr.
Wilker is an assistant to the earl of Hilford—you recall him, of
course; he is the one who arranged the Vystrani expedition." And
was arranging the Erigan one, too, though his health precluded
him from accompanying us. But what business of that could be so
urgent that Lord Hilford would send Mr. Wilker after me at my
brother's house? "I should speak with him, but there's no need to
trouble you. I will take my leave."

My mother's outstretched hand stopped me before I could
stand. "Not at all. I think we're all eager to hear what this Mr.
Wilker has to say."

"Indeed," Judith said faintly, obeying the unspoken order
woven through my mother's words. "Send him in, Londwin."

The butler bowed and retired. By the alacrity with which Mr.
Wilker appeared, he must have sprang forward the instant he was
welcomed in; agitation still showed in his movements. But he had
long since taken pains to cultivate better manners than those he
had grown up with, and so he presented himself first to Judith.
"Good morning, Mrs. Hendemore. My name is Thomas Wilker.
I'm sorry to trouble you, but I have a message for Mrs. Camherst.
We must have passed one another on the road; I only just missed
her at her house. And I'm afraid the news is unfortunate enough

that it could not wait. I was told she would be visiting here."

The curt, disjointed way in which he delivered these words made my hands tighten in apprehension. Mr. Wilker was, quite rightly, looking only at Judith, save a brief nod when he spoke my name; with no hint forthcoming from him, I found myself exchanging a glance instead with my mother.

What I saw there startled me. *We're all eager to hear what this Mr. Wilker has to say*—she thought he was my lover! An overstatement, perhaps, but she had the expression of a woman looking for signs of inappropriate attachment, and coming up empty-handed.

As well she should. Mr. Wilker and I might no longer be at loggerheads the way we had been in Vystrana, but I felt no romantic affection for him, nor he for me. Our relationship was purely one of business.

I wanted to set my mother down in no uncertain terms for harboring such thoughts, but forbore. Not so much because of the sheer inappropriateness of having that conversation in public, but because it occurred to me that Mr. Wilker and I were engaged in *two* matters of business, of which the Erigan expedition was only one.

Judith, fortunately, waved Mr. Wilker on before I could burst out with my questions unbidden. "By all means, Mr. Wilker. Or is your message private?"

I would not have taken the message privately for a hundred sovereigns, not with such suspicions in my mother's mind. "Please," I said. "What has happened?"

Mr. Wilker blew out a long breath, and the urgency drained from him in a sudden rush, leaving him sagging and defeated. "There's been a break-in at Kemble's."

"Kemble's . . . oh, no." My own shoulders sagged, a mirror to his. "What did they destroy? Or—"

He nodded, grimly. "Took. His notes."

Theft, not destruction. Someone knew what Kemble was working on, and was determined to steal it for their own.

I slumped back in my chair, ladylike dignity the furthest thing from my mind. Frederick Kemble was the chemist Mr. Wilker had hired—or rather *I* had hired; the money was mine, although the choice of recipient was his—to continue the research we ourselves had stolen in the mountains of Vystrana, three years ago. Research that documented a method for preserving dragonbone: an amazing substance, strong and light, but one that decayed quickly outside a living body.

The Chiavoran who developed that method was not the first one to try. What had begun as a mere challenge of taxidermy—born from the desire of hunters to preserve trophies from the dragons they killed, and the desire of natural historians to preserve specimens for study—had become a great point of curiosity for chemists. Several were racing to be the first (or so they thought) to solve that puzzle. Despite our best efforts to maintain secrecy around Kemble's work, it seemed someone had learned of it.

"When?" I asked, then waved the question away as foolish. "Last night, and I doubt we'll get any time more specific than that." Mr. Wilker shook his head. He lived in the city, and visited Kemble first thing in the morning every Selemer. This news was as fresh as it could be, short of Kemble having heard the intruder and come downstairs in his nightclothes to see.

I wondered, suddenly cold, what would have happened if he

had. Would the intruder have fled? Or would Mr. Wilker have found our chemist dead this morning?

Such thoughts were unnecessarily dramatic—or so I chided myself. Whether they were or not, I did not have the leisure to dwell on them, for my mother's sharp voice roused me from my thoughts. "Isabella. What in heaven is this man talking about?"

I took a measure of comfort in the irreverent thought that at least she could not read any hint of personal indiscretion in the message Mr. Wilker had brought. "Research, Mama," I said, pulling myself straight in my chair, and thence to my feet. "Nothing that need concern you. But I'm afraid I must cut this visit short; it is vital that I speak to Mr. Kemble at once. If you will excuse me—"

My mother, too, rose to her feet, one hand outstretched. "Please, Isabella. I'm dreadfully concerned for you. This expedition you intend . . ."

She must be concerned indeed, to broach such a personal matter before a stranger like Mr. Wilker. "We will speak of it later, Mama," I said, intending no such thing. "This truly is a pressing matter. I've invested a great deal of money in Mr. Kemble's work, and must find out how much I have lost."

TWO

Frederick Kemble's—Synthesis—The symposium—Lord Hilford—
Natalie's prospects—Two weeks

B eing a recluse is not good for one's conversational agility.
I was accustomed to thinking over my words, revising
them, and writing fair copy before sending the final draft
of my letter to its recipient. My comment accomplished its intended purpose—she let me go at last, with Judith's polite farewells to fill in the awkward gaps—but my satisfaction faded
rapidly as I went out into the street. "I fear I will regret that," I
admitted to Mr. Wilker, pulling on my gloves.

"I don't think you've lost much of your money," he said, raising
his hand to signal a hansom on its way to the nearest cab stand.

Sighing, I drew his arm down. "My carriage is across the street.
No, I don't mean the investment; I don't regret that in the least.
Only that I said anything of it to my mother. She is determined to
see bad judgment in everything I do nowadays."

Mr. Wilker did not respond to that. Although we were on more
cordial terms by then, we were not in the habit of sharing our
personal troubles with one another. He said, "All is not lost, though.

Kemble took his current notebook upstairs with him last night, so that he could read over his thoughts as he prepared for bed. His wife may deplore the habit, but in this instance it's been a godsend."

(To those of my readers who flinch at minor blasphemies of this sort: I must warn you that there will be more ahead. Mr. Wilker restrained his language around me in our Vystrani days, but as we grew more comfortable with one another, he revealed a casual habit of naming the Lord. If I edited his language here, it would misrepresent his character, and so I pray you pardon his frankness, and mine. We were neither of us very religious.)

Mrs. Kemble was no resentful housewife; she worked alongside her husband, handling the practical matters of ordering and measuring chemicals, while he spent hours staring at the wall and chewing on the battered tail of his pen, mind lost in theoretical matters. But she believed in a separation of work from daily life, and I—who, you may have noticed, am more of Frederick Kemble's mind—blessed her failure to break him of his habits.

I said as much to her when we arrived at Kemble's house and laboratory in Tanner Fields, and got a dry look that did not entirely hide the nervous aftereffects of the intrusion. "I appreciate that, Mrs. Camherst, but I'm afraid it didn't save the glassware."

"May I see?" I asked. Mrs. Kemble led us into the cellar, presently in a state of half gloom, the only light coming in by the street-level windows. It was enough to show the destruction: shattered glass everywhere, measuring instruments bent and smashed. A chemical stink flooded the air, despite the open windows and a boy outside cranking a device to ventilate the room. They had not merely taken Kemble's notes; they had also done what they could to delay his further progress.

I held my handkerchief over my nose and said, "Mrs. Kemble, I am so very sorry. If you send a letter to my accountant, I'll see to it that you're reimbursed for what you've lost. It can't restore your peace of mind, but—" I gestured helplessly. "It can at least replace the glassware."

"That's very good of you, Mrs. Camherst," she said, mollified. "Kemble is upstairs; I needed him out from under my feet while I sort out what's broken and missing. Lucy will make you some tea."

Mr. Wilker and I went obediently up to the parlour, where we found Frederick Kemble scribing furiously onto a loose sheet of foolscap. Others like it were scattered across the table and the floor, and Lucy, the Kembles' remaining unmarried daughter, was trying to find a clear space to set down a tray containing not only tea but a stack of blank paper. She saw us come in and touched her father's elbow. "Papa—"

"Not now—let me—" He jerked his head in a motion I thought was meant to stand for a wave of his hand, his actual hands being occupied in note-taking.

Lucy retreated to our side. "What is he doing?" I asked, not daring raise my voice above a murmur.

"Writing down as much as he can remember," she said. "From the notebooks that were taken."

After three years' work, the process for preserving dragonbone must have been engraved on the inside of his eyelids; *I* had it memorized, and I was not even chemist enough to understand what most of it meant. As for the rest—"Mr. Wilker said the most recent notebook was not taken, yes? So long as we have that, the older notes do not matter half so much." Most of them were obsolete by now, documenting failed experiments.

Lucy spread her hands. "He says even the old notes are important—that he likes to look over them from time to time."

She went off to fetch more teacups, and then Mr. Wilker and I settled in at the far end of the parlour to hear Lucy's account of the break-in and the investigation thus far. By the time she finished, Kemble was ready to pause in his work and acknowledge the rest of the world.

"If they'd come before the Sabbath . . ." he said, clearly grateful they had not. His daughter presented him with a cup of tea, which he took and drained absently. "I was looking back through the old notebooks during lunch on Eromer, and something there caught my attention. Last year, I—"

Mr. Wilker, who had long since learned to recognize the warning signs, cut him off before he could descend into a thicket of scientific language I would not understand in the slightest. The body of our collective knowledge has grown so rapidly in my lifetime that although I am accounted an extremely learned woman, there are whole fields I know very little of; chemistry is one such. It was not a part of young ladies' curricula in my youth, and my self-education had gone in other directions. Mr. Wilker therefore diverted our chemist to the points he knew I would care about. "You said something about that this morning, yes. It gave you an idea?"

"I think so," Kemble said. "It's only a thought so far; it will take a great deal of testing. But I may have an idea for synthesis at last."

Had that not been the fifth time I heard those words from his mouth, I would have been more excited. It was, after all, the purpose for which we had hired Kemble. We knew how to preserve dragonbone; that was no longer a challenge. But Mr.

Wilker and I, discussing the matter three years ago, had seen the peril in that knowledge.

Quite apart from the desire of hunters to preserve their trophies, and the desire of natural historians to study their subject at leisure *post mortem,* the qualities of dragonbone made it attractive to other kinds of person. Its mechanical properties were far superior to those of iron and steel, being both lighter and stronger—and as the easily accessible iron deposits in Anthiope and other parts of the world began to run dry, the value of any alternative grew by the year.

I could enumerate at length the drawbacks to the industrial use of dragonbone. Indeed, I had an article already prepared on the subject, ready to send at a moment's notice to all the reputable publications. Dragons were even rarer than iron, and while it was true that they reproduced (which ore was not known to do), any widespread demand for their bones would lead to mass slaughter, perhaps even to extinction. The irregular shape of many bones rendered them less than ideal for the construction of machines, which would result in a great deal of waste. The expense and hassle of harvesting them from dead dragons (many of whom lived in locales as foreign and distant as those still rich in iron) rendered the prospect less than entirely profitable. It went on for pages, but the entire thing was flawed in its basic assumption, which was that people would consider the matter rationally before making their decisions.

The truth was that the idea would bring speculators flocking like vultures to a dead horse, ready to pick the bones clean. And if I tried to persuade myself that I was exaggerating—that such a doom-filled scenario would never come to pass—I had only to consider the Erigan continent, where the lure of iron had led several Anthiopean states to involve themselves in the affairs of the nations there. If Thiessin was willing to conquer Djapa, and Chiavora to encourage revolution in Agwi, and Scirland to insert itself between the Talu Union and the military might of the Ikwunde, for the sake of being able to build new steam engines, we would not hesitate to sacrifice a few dumb beasts.

I sighed and drained the last of my tea. "With all due respect, Mr. Kemble, I would almost welcome another set of eyes on the matter. I have every confidence that you can solve this riddle, given sufficient time—but that, we may not have. Sooner or later *someone* will figure out Rossi's method, even without your notes. If we are to avert chaos, we need a way to satisfy the demand for this substance that does not involve butchering dragons."

"I doubt we'll be that lucky," Mr. Wilker said, sounding bleak. "With the eyes, that is. How many people will go to the amount of effort you and I have, just to spare animals? We already butcher elephants for their ivory and tigers for their skins, and those are only decorative."

He was likely right. Sighing, I said, "Then we had best hope the police recover the notebook—small hope that it is. Do we have any notion who took it?"

By the grim silence that fell, the answer started with "yes" and got worse from there. Mr. Wilker replied obliquely. "You know about the symposium, I think."

A gathering of scholars, hosted by the Philosophers' Colloquium, the preeminent scientific body in Scirland. Mr. Wilker had not been invited to attend, because he was not a gentleman. I had not been invited to attend either, because although my birth was gentle, I was not a man.

But we knew someone who met both of those requirements. "If it was one of the visitors, Lord Hilford might be able to find out."

"He won't have much time," Kemble said, coming out of the reverie into which he so frequently lapsed. "Doesn't that end this week?"

It did, and the scholars would be returning to their homelands. "Indeed. Then I suppose I know what I am doing with my afternoon."

I was at the door to Lord Hilford's townhouse before I remembered that I had promised to pay a visit to my relatives by marriage. I knocked on the door anyway, thinking to ask the earl whether I might send them a note. As it transpired, he was not yet home from a lecture, and so I had more than enough time while I waited for him in the drawing room.

If you find yourself thinking that I had enough time to make good on that promise, you would be more or less correct. The Camhersts lived not far from Lord Hilford, in Mornetty Square, and it would not have taken me above twenty minutes to get there and back. But I did not know how long they would keep me, and it was of the utmost importance that I warn Lord Hilford about the intruders at Mr. Kemble's as soon as possible. If any of the visitors to the symposium were behind this outrage, we had limited time in which to find out—even more limited time in which to do anything about it.

So I told myself, at least. The truth is that, although I had told my mother that Matthew, my brother-in-law, had agreed to take in little Jacob while I was gone, I had neglected to mention his lack of enthusiasm for the entire plan. His wife did not mind the addition of a temporary child, but Matthew minded very much the possibility of keeping him permanently. He might have even been the one who spilled the secret of the Erigan expedition where my mother could hear. Drained by my morning confrontation and by the dreadful news of the break-in, I was not minded to face anyone I did not consider a good friend.

I therefore wrote out an excuse and had Lord Hilford's boot-boy run it to Mornetty Square. Then I linked my gloved hands together and paced, and worried, and made a hundred different (and useless) plans, until Lord Hilford came home.

When I heard his booming voice in the front hall, I did not trouble to wait in the drawing room. He saw me as I came to the door, and the white tufts of his eyebrows rose. "Not that it is anything but a pleasure to see you, Mrs. Camherst—but I judge by your expression that whatever has sent you here is not good."

"It is not," I confirmed, and explained while he divested himself of overcoat and hat. His cane he kept; over the years it had become less of an affectation, more of a necessity, as his rheumatism worsened. Lord Hilford followed me into the drawing room and lowered himself into a chair with a sigh.

"Mmmm," he said when I was done. "Makes me wonder if someone has been to Vystrana. I've heard nothing from Iljish in Drustanev, but you know what the post is like. And someone might have slipped past them."

The villagers were supposed to protect the nearby cavern from curiosity-seekers. It was the preserved dragonbone in that great cemetery which had given the first clues to the role of acid in that process. "We said nothing of it in the book," I reminded Lord Hilford, referring to the monograph we had published after our expedition. "Only that the dragons tore apart their deceased kin and took the pieces to a certain cave. No one could assume preservation from that—nor could they find the cave."

The flapping of the earl's hand reminded me I was saying nothing he did not already know. "Still, it's a possibility, and one we have to consider. Another possibility: Kemble talked."

"If he had talked, would they have smashed up his laboratory?" I said indignantly. Then I saw the flaw in my own logic. "Ah. You are not accusing him of selling the secret—only of letting slip some hint that might have allowed another to guess what he's doing."

"Any of us might have done it," Lord Hilford admitted. "Including me. I'd like to think I'm discreet, but—well. Scholars drink a great deal more than anyone thinks, and I don't hold my liquor as well as I once did."

I thought that I, at least, was unlikely to have betrayed our secret. Not out of any particular virtue; only from lack of opportunity. I hardly spoke to anyone who didn't already know. But it would do no good to say that, and so I said only, "Is there anyone among the Colloquium's visitors that you would suspect? Or among its members, I suppose."

Lord Hilford grunted. "Several, unfortunately. There's a ratty Marñeo fellow I don't trust in the slightest; he's been accused of passing other people's research off as his own. Guhathalakar openly admits he's working on the issue of preservation. No one in the Bulskoi delegation is, but they have more opportunity than most to go poking around in Vystrana. The Hingese . . . I'm sorry, Mrs. Camherst, but without more to go on, all I can do is guess."

"Well, Mr. Wilker is still at Kemble's, and they've spoken with the police; we can hope for some kind of lead." I got up and paced again, fingers twisting about one another. "I *wish* I could do something to hurry the research along. Money is only helpful to a point; it cannot make Frederick Kemble's brain work faster."

"Attend to your own research," Lord Hilford said, very reasonably. "You may find something of use there; or if you do not, then every bit we know about dragons is one more bit we can use to protect them. But, ah—if I may shift us from one nerve-wracking topic to another—"

It was enough to stop me pacing. I tried to remember the last time I had heard the earl so wary, and could not think of a single time. When I turned to look, he was chewing on the drooping end of his moustache. I waited, but he did not speak. "Oh, out with it," I said at last, quite sharply. "My nerves are no less wracked for being forced to wait."

"Natalie," he said, reluctantly. "Or rather, her family."

His granddaughter was not ordinarily a topic of any tension at all. Nor were her family, but—"Let me guess," I said with a sigh. "They have decided I am not fit company for her. Well, everyone else in Scirland has come to the same opinion; I am not fit company for *anyone.*"

"That isn't precisely it. They think you eccentric, yes, but for the most part harmlessly so. The trouble is that an eccentric is not good company for an unmarried young lady—not if she wishes to change that state."

I frowned at him in surprise. "But Natalie is only—" My arithmetic caught up with my words, and stopped them. "Nearly twenty," I finished heavily. "I see."

"Quite." Lord Hilford sighed, too, studying the head of his cane far more closely than it warranted. "And so her family is quite adamant that she should not accompany you on this expedition. You are likely to be gone for six months at least, likely more; it would be ruinous to her marital prospects. Old maids and all that. I've argued, truly I have."

I believed him. Lord Hilford had progressive notions of what ladies might do, and he doted on Natalie besides; but in the end he was not his granddaughter's guardian. "Have you spoken with her?"

"She knows how her family feels. I was hoping you might approach her—woman to woman, you know—and see if you can't reconcile her to the situation. They aren't intending to shackle her to some brute."

If she did not look herself out a husband soon, though, she might have trouble finding anyone other than a brute. "I will see what I can do."

Lord Hilford sounded relieved. "Thank you. You'll have to be quick about it, though. I was intending to write this afternoon, but now I can tell you in person: the schedule has moved up. Can you and Wilker be ready to depart in two weeks?"

Had I been holding anything, I would have dropped it. *"Two weeks?"*

"If you can't, then say so. But it may be another delay otherwise. There's going to be a changeover at the Foreign Office, and the incoming fellow is not very keen on travellers going to Nsebu, not with the unrest in the area."

"Unrest?" I echoed, my mother's comments rising to mind.

"Ah, yes—that hasn't reached the papers yet," Lord Hilford said. "I had it from our man in the Foreign Office. A group of Royal Engineers were ambushed while surveying the south bank of the Girama, which is territory that is supposed to be firmly in our control. It seems Eremmo has quieted sufficiently under the Ikwunde yoke for the inkosi to start looking outward once more. It has certain people rather worried."

As well it should, given the military success the Ikwunde had enjoyed in the last fifty years, under one warlike inkosi after another. Still, I had faith in our soldiers there; and besides which, the river region between Bayembe and Eremmo was clear on the other side of the country from Nsebu. "One scare after another," I sighed. "I am beginning to think this expedition will never happen."

"It will, Mrs. Camherst, if we move quickly enough. Otherwise we'll have to argue the new fellow around."

We had already spent months arguing the previous fellow around. I reviewed the state of my affairs, and suppressed the unladylike desire to curse. I had counted on Natalie to be my companion on this journey. Would it be worse to travel alone—with an unmarried man, no less—or to find some other woman on short notice? Or rather, would suffering the latter be worse than suffering the consequences of the former?

Either way, I could not let it change my answer to Lord Hilford. "I can be ready, yes. You will have to ask Mr. Wilker yourself."

"I know what Tom will say." The earl levered himself up out of his chair. "Two weeks it is, then. I'm sure you need to prepare. And in the meanwhile, I will look into the matter of this break-in."

THREE

Natalie's wings—The merits of a husband—
Keeping promises—Ladies at supper—Lord Canlan

Miss Oscott is here," the footman informed me when I returned home. "I believe she is in your study, ma'am."

Natalie. I would have preferred to delay my promise to Lord Hilford, but if I was to leave in two weeks, I simply could not spare the time. "Thank you," I said, distracted, and went upstairs.

My study had been my husband's study, once. The servants had called it *the* study for a good two years after his death; it was not the sort of room women normally laid claim to. But eventually their speech had shifted. No doubt that owed a great deal to the amount of time I spent there, often in the company of Natalie Oscott.

She was indeed there, tacking a sheet of paper onto the piece of corkboard we had hung for the purpose. "Oh, good heavens, Natalie," I said when I saw the figure drawn on it. "*That* again?"

"I've improved it," she said, flashing a grin at me over one shoulder. "On advice from an enthusiast in Lopperton. He thinks

I'm a lad named Nathaniel—I do a very good boy's hand, when I put my mind to it. On account of falsifying my brothers' workbooks, when they had not written the exercises our tutor had set. What do you think?"

The sheet of paper bore a large diagram, whose predecessors I had seen several times before. A wing spread across the page, with measurements carefully marked out, and annotations I could not read from where I stood. Even at range, though, one difference was apparent. "Are the wings curved?" I asked, curious despite myself.

"Yes, he thinks that would work better than a straight line. And he suggested an alteration to the harness, too, which he is going to try for himself as soon as he can get it built."

To be perfectly honest, I thought they were both mad. True, as I said in the previous volume of my memoirs, I had been obsessed with dragon wings since I was a small child, and the idea of being able to join them in the sky was attractive. But a human being cannot possibly achieve the pectoral strength necessary to fly by flapping artificial wings—that having been Natalie's first notion. The best he (or she) can hope for is to glide, and even then, I had my doubts.

But Natalie found the notion an intriguing challenge. For her, the puzzle was intellectual: was it possible to engineer such a thing? In pursuit of that question, she had taught herself a great deal of mathematics, most of which I understood not at all. She had also entered into correspondence with others, for she was not the only one with an interest in the matter.

Natalie had not yet attempted to construct or test any of her designs, for which I was grateful. Although my husband had called me the queen of deranged practicality, putting into practice ideas others would never think to attempt, even I have my limits. Those limits may, as this narrative will show, lie further out than I claim (and honestly believe)—but I never know that until I pass them. And that, I invariably do under circumstances in which going further seems to be the only feasible course of action. It is only afterward that the "deranged" part of "deranged practicality" becomes apparent to me.

Besides, I was less sanguine about others' foolishness, and I should not like to lose my closest companion to a broken neck. Natalie had been a great source of comfort to me since Jacob died. It made my heart all the lower, thinking that I could not bring her with me to Nsebu.

She saw my fallen countenance, but mistook the cause. "I promise you, Isabella—I have no intention of committing my own bones to the tender mercies of physics. At least not until after Mr. Garsell has conducted enough tests of his own to assure me the design is sound."

"That isn't it." I sighed and went to my desk—Jacob's desk, once—in front of the broad windows overlooking the back garden. The surface was cluttered with books and stray pages, my preserved sparkling Greenie standing guard over them all; I had forbidden the maid to touch anything there, even to dust. Maps of Eriga, travellers' reports, a draft of an article I was considering asking Lord Hilford to submit for me, under his own name. The Colloquium would not accept a paper from a woman.

Perhaps it was the reminder of the Colloquium's requirements that made my voice more bitter than I intended. "I spoke with your grandfather today. About your family."

"Oh." That one word might have been a valve, letting out all

the air and vitality that had made her so animated.

I lowered myself into the familiar leather of my chair. "You know, then. That they don't want you to go to Eriga."

"They want me to stay here and find a husband. Yes." Natalie turned and paced a few steps away.

Her deficit of enthusiasm was plain enough that I could read it without seeing her face. "It needn't be bad, Natalie. You have your grandfather on your side, and from what you tell me, your family has at least some understanding of your interests. My father consulted a matchmaker to obtain a list of unmarried men who might share their libraries with me. I am sure you can go further, and find yourself a husband who will support you in your work."

"Perhaps."

She did not sound convinced. Before I could muster the words to develop my argument, however, Natalie spoke again. "It is an untenable situation, and I know it. One way or another, I must be dependent upon *someone*. If not a husband, then one of my brothers, or—" She caught herself. "I cannot ask that of them. But how much less can I ask it of some stranger?"

I had not missed that *or*. She had been about to list a third option, and had stopped herself. I could guess why. Rather than approach it directly, though, I said, "Do you not *want* a husband? Presuming you could get a good one."

She stood very still; I think she was considering my words. Then she turned to face me, and answered in the tone of one who had never realized her true reply until this moment. "No," Natalie said. "I don't."

"Not for security," I said. At that time the Independent Virtue movement had not yet taken shape, but its arguments were beginning to be spoken, in hushed, half-scandalized whispers. If a woman traded her marital favors for financial support, did that not make marriage a form of prostitution? "But for companionship, or love, or—" Now it was my turn to stop shy of my final words.

Natalie blushed, but answered me. "Not for any of those. I welcome the friendship of men, of course. But childbirth is dangerous, and motherhood would demand too much of my time; and I have no interest in the, ah, *activity* for its own sake. What is left?"

Very little, really. Except, perhaps, for an end to her family's nagging—and that could be gotten in more than one way.

It would have been wiser for me to wait until I had examined the state of my own finances. But I was to leave for Nsebu in two weeks, and had no desire to waste my time or Natalie's on the wrong preparations. "If you must be dependent on someone," I said, "and if your conscience will permit it, then be dependent upon me. Widows often take on companions, and you have very nearly been mine these past few years; certainly you have been a dear friend. We might make it official."

The hitch in her breath told me I had struck my mark precisely. Still, she protested. "I could not do that to you, Isabella. If I do not marry, I will be a burden forever. What if you change your mind, two or ten or twenty years down the road? It might poison our friendship, and I would never wish for that."

I laughed, lightly, trying to ease the desperate tension in her eyes. "A burden forever? Piffle. Stay with me, and I will qualify you for a life of independent and eccentric spinsterhood, supported as you choose by your learning and your pen. Other ladies have done it before."

Not many, and few in the sorts of fields that Natalie had proven herself drawn to. Historical scholarship was more permitted to women than the designing of crazed glider-wings. But I had formed the resolution to live my own life as my inclinations demanded, and furthermore to do so with such zeal that society could not refuse me; it would be the height of hypocrisy for me to preach feminine obedience to Natalie now. She knew the obstacles and the cost: she had seen how I lived.

By the growing light in her eyes, the obstacles were trivial and the cost not even worth mentioning. Her mouth still spoke protest, but only because of her commitment to logic. "My family will take some convincing, I fear. Possibly a great deal of it."

"Then you have two choices," I said, rising from my desk. At this time of day, the light through the windows at my back would frame me with a kind of halo; I was not above using that for dramatic effect. "You may stay in Scirland and work on convincing them, and I will welcome you at my side once that is done. Or you can inform them of your intentions, leave for Nsebu with me in two weeks, and let them work through it on their own."

"Two weeks?" Natalie said, her voice going faint. "You are leaving in—oh, but—"

I waited. My words were sincere; I would welcome her company whether she had to join me later, or wait for my return to Scirland. It would not be fair to importune her with my preference.

Besides, I knew her well enough to guess her answer. Natalie's shoulders went back, and her chin rose. "I had promised to come with you to Eriga," she said. "A lady should keep her promises. I will inform my family at once."

I had never thought Maxwell Oscott, the earl of Hilford, to be a sadist. His chosen method for smoking out the thief, however, had me reconsidering the matter, with conclusions not favourable to him.

The symposium whose attendees comprised our most likely suspects was, as Mr. Wilker had said, scheduled to end that week. With the police turning up nothing of use in their examination of Mr. Kemble's laboratory, Lord Hilford settled upon a more direct method of looking for the guilty party, which was to invite everybody to supper and see if anyone flinched.

To this end, he arranged, on vanishingly short notice, to rent out the upper hall at the Yates Hotel, and made certain that all those we suspected would attend. His excuse for this event was that the Colloquium, which would be hosting a formal banquet the following night to mark the end of the symposium, did not permit women within their hallowed walls, and he was most determined that the gentlemen attending should meet various ladies of education and merit—chief among them, though he did not advertise this fact, the widowed Mrs. Camherst.

I suffered Lord Hilford to put me in the limelight because it would aid in our efforts, but under my mask of cooperation, I was petrified. At that time, the only monograph attributed to my name was *A Journey to the Mountains of Vystrana,* which was hardly a scholarly work; I had laid no claim to *Concerning the Rock-Wyrms of Vystrana,* being concealed in the small print line "and Others" that followed Jacob's name. The few articles I had published regarding my research on sparklings had not gone to scholarly journals. Furthermore, I had been a confirmed recluse for going on three years. The prospect of attending a dinner party with a crowd of intelligent strangers made me so ill, I could hardly eat.

But if my spine weakened, I had only to think of the dragons who risked slaughter if the secret of dragonbone preservation became widely known, and my resolve returned to me on the spot.

The upper hall at the Yates blazed with candles that night, their light reflecting from polished wall sconces, crystal chandeliers and glasses, and the silver cutlery laid in precise ranks along the table. The men who filled the room were a mixed lot: northern Anthiopeans in their black-and-white suits, southern Anthiopeans in calf-length caftans, Yelangese in embroidered silk robes, Vidwathi with gems pinned to the fronts of their turbans.

It was not a proper dinner party, such as Mrs. Gatherty would approve of; the gentlemen outnumbered us ladies by more than three to one. But Lord Hilford had done an admirable job, given the short timeline, of organizing female guests, so that Natalie and I were not the only women present. The noted ornithologist Miriam Farnswood was there, as was the mathematician Rebecca Norman; the others, regrettably, would mean little to a modern audience, as their work has not survived history's forgetting.

I pasted a smile on my face, took Lord Hilford's arm, and sallied forth to see who flinched.

He introduced me, one by one, to the individuals we considered to be possible culprits. Nicanor de Androjas y Reón (the "ratty Marñeo fellow," whose nose did give him an unfortunately rodentlike profile), Bhelu Guhathalakar, Cuong Giun Vanh, Foma Ivanovich Ozerin. Mr. Wilker was with us throughout. None of us expected our interlocutors to have broken into Kemble's laboratory themselves—that was undoubtedly the work of some hired criminal—but surely the thief would, by now, have glanced through Kemble's notes. Both Mr. Wilker and I were mentioned in abundance. The connection between that work and our names could not be missed.

Cuong dismissed me immediately as beneath his notice, directing all his conversation to Lord Hilford and Mr. Wilker. Ozerin gave me more attention than I wanted, but entirely of the wrong kind; I extracted myself from that situation as soon as possible. De Androjas y Reón did indeed flinch, but he flinched at everything. (I daresay that man was even less comfortable in such a crowd than I was.)

By far my best experience was with the Vidwathi chemist Guhathalakar, though not, at least initially, for any reason useful to our investigation. He was a younger man than the others, thirty at most, and of a type I have met countless times in my life, which I confess is one of my favourites: so powerfully interested in his subject that trivial considerations such as the sex of his conversational partner are quickly forgotten. I might have been an orang-outang, for all he cared; what mattered was that I showed an interest in chemistry, and could respond to his statements with intelligent questions (even if I did not understand the answers). It took no encouragement at all to get him expounding at length, his voice growing louder in his enthusiasm.

It took only slightly more encouragement to steer his exposition in the desired direction. "Dragonbone, yes," he said, his Vidwathi accent thickening as his mind raced ahead of his Scirling. "I think it is on the anvil. With so many working on the problem, and the new equipments we have now, we will have answers soon."

He showed no sign of secret knowledge, no coy hint that he knew more than he said. Even as I responded, I transferred my attention to the milling guests around us. Guhathalakar's voice carried well enough that soon the entire room would know we were discussing the preservation of dragonbone. "It would be a tremendous breakthrough, if so. But I confess myself troubled as to the potential consequences, once the problem has been solved. My own interest being in natural history, I cannot be easy with anything that might encourage men to butcher dragons."

An indulgent chuckle from my left heralded the arrival of Peter Gilmartin, marquess of Canlan and vice president of the Philosophers' Colloquium. "But did your own party not butcher a dragon for study in Vystrana, Mrs. Camherst? Indeed, I believe the drawings of that carcass were your own work. Surely it would be beneficial if natural historians could keep dragon skeletons for study, rather than having to obtain a fresh specimen each time they have a new question."

His words were sensible, but his patronizing tone ruffled my feathers the wrong way. Still, deference for his rank forced me to moderate the reply I wanted to make. "It is not natural historians who concern me, my lord, but others, who would likely not be satisfied with a handful of skeletons. Humanity is not known for its moderation."

"And yet, think of the advances that might come from this discovery. Should we put the well-being of savage beasts above our own?"

I had an entire article's worth of reply ready for that, but Lord Canlan gave me no chance to begin. He turned instead to Guhathalakar, leaning forward with a friendly and conspiratorial air. "I should like to talk with you tomorrow, when we are in more scholarly surroundings. Your work interests me a great deal, and I believe I may be in a position to help it along."

Had a Vystrani rock-wyrm breathed on me in that moment, I would not have been more frozen. While Guhathalakar made his reply, my gaze was pinned to Lord Canlan, unblinking, as if by sheer intensity of stare I could prove or disprove the sudden suspicion in my mind.

The marquess was in no position to exploit Kemble's research himself; his primary interest was in astronomy. But that did not mean he could not benefit in other ways. For example, by selling Kemble's notes to the highest bidder.

Did I imagine it? Was the smile he directed at me before moving onward merely more patronizing courtesy, or did it send a private, gloating message that he had what I had lost, and intended to profit thereby?

He was a marquess, above even Lord Hilford's elevated station. I could hardly accuse him where he stood—though shock nearly overrode my better judgment and sent the words flying out by reflex. And he had said nothing I could even begin to construe as evidence, let alone expect anyone else to accept.

I fulminated on this through dinner, for there was no opportunity to step aside with any of my own friends and give them my suspicions. Afterward, though, while Lord Hilford was bidding his guests farewell, I pulled Mr. Wilker into a corner and delivered the tale in a rush.

"It's a thin reed," he said when I was done, and frowned across the room at where Lord Canlan stood.

Although the words of his reply were scarcely encouraging, I took heart from them nevertheless. There was a time when Thomas Wilker would have scoffed at my fears and chalked them up to an overactive imagination. Now he gave them due thought—even if that thought did not lead him to agree.

"I don't know how he would have learned about Kemble's research," I admitted. "But you have met him before—is he the sort of man who would flaunt his coup in front of me like that?"

Mr. Wilker's grimace gave me my answer. "When it is the project of a woman and a man like me . . . then yes. He loves nothing more than to put his lessers in their place."

An unpleasant personality hardly constituted proof, though. "Will you be at the dinner tomorrow night?" Mr. Wilker shook his head, mouth set in a hard line. Of course not: his sex might grant him entrance to the Colloquium's premises, but the son of a Niddey quarryman would not be invited to their celebratory meal. "Lord Hilford will have to watch, then. Lord Canlan may be offering the notes for sale, or at least sounding out his prospective buyers. Given how chatty Guhathalakar is, it won't be difficult to encourage him to say."

A muscle tensed in Mr. Wilker's jaw. "It doesn't offer very good odds for stopping him, though. We can't ask Lord Hilford to make a scene."

"It's the best we can do for now," I said. And left unspoken the rest of my thought: that we might not have any chance to do better.

FOUR

Farewell to Jacob—My brother-in-law—
Lord Denbow is distraught—Natalie's escape—
Scene at the docks—A woman's wishes

I can only blame myself for the incident that occurred prior to my departure from Scirland.

The rush to depart left me with several dozen matters to take care of, ranging from soothing family to receiving Lord Hilford's report on the final dinner of the symposium. (He did indeed question Guhathalakar, but to no avail; Lord Canlan had ignored the man all night, much to Guhathalakar's disappointment.) One matter in particular had me more distracted than most.

On the afternoon before my departure, Mrs. Hunstin, the nanny, brought my son downstairs to await his uncle and his aunt, who would be caring for him in my absence. Jacob was dressed in a toddler's tunic, but his hair, a sandy shade that had not yet darkened to his father's rich brown, was presently bare of the cap clutched in his free hand. The other was clinging tightly to the nanny's thumb, his eyes fixed on the staircase, which he descended one careful step at a time.

My mother had accused me of heartlessness, abandoning him
to go gallivanting (her word) off to foreign parts. Her accusation
was only the first of many, as that judgment eventually spread not
only to others in our social circle, but to complete strangers and
even the news-sheets. There is no reason anyone should believe
me, justifying my behaviour at so late a date, but since I cannot
move on without addressing this subject, let me say: a pang went
through my heart at the sight of my son.

I had not been close to him during his rearing; he was not a
fixture of my life the way children are for more involved mothers.
I found more satisfaction in scholarly work than in the day-to-day
tasks of feeding, cleaning, and comforting him. In hindsight, a
part of me does regret missing such events—but even then, my
regret is an intellectual one. The development of children from
soft, formless infants into adults is a complex process, and one I
have come to appreciate on account of my dragon studies. (If you
read that comparison as demeaning, please understand that, for
me, it is not. We, too, are animals: the most wondrous and
fascinating animals of all.)

Despite that distance, however, I was not without feelings for
my child. Indeed, I imposed that distance in part *because* of my
feelings. Jacob's serious expression, focused on the challenge of
navigating the stairs, reminded me profoundly of his namesake.
As people had told me, again and again, he was in some sense a
piece of my husband, something left behind by Jacob the elder. I
was not always prepared to deal with the reminder of that
connection. And so a part of me chose instead to flee.

But it does a disservice to my own life to claim the Erigan
expedition was motivated by fear. It is equally true, if not more so,

to say that I was running *toward* something, as well as away. Jacob and I had shared a love of dragons, and if leaving his child behind was a betrayal of his memory (as so many people assured me it was), staying home would have been a betrayal as well. We had agreed, on a mountaintop in Vystrana, that caging me in the life expected of a Scirling gentlewoman would be the death of me: spiritually, if not physically. I had been caged for three years, caught in a trap of my grief and obligations as well as society's expectation, and the work I did on paper granted me only partial freedom. Enough to make me long for more, but not enough to satisfy.

And yet I *was* leaving behind a child. An innocent toddler, bereft even before his birth of one parent; now I proposed to subject myself to any number of potential calamities that might rob him of the second.

I cannot say whether, given the chance to revisit that choice, I would change my mind. I know now, to a very precise measurement, how great the dangers would be, and how narrowly I escaped them. But I also know that I survived. Little Jacob was not left orphaned, as so many had direly predicted.

Did I have the right to undertake such risk? I can only give the same answer I gave then: that I have, and had, as much right as any widower in the same situation. Few question the widower's decision, but everyone questions the widow's.

On that day, I buried all such thoughts beneath the press of business. (Almost all of them. The aforementioned pang was real, nor was it alone.) When little Jacob had finished his conquest of the stairs, I knelt on the cool stone of our front hall, putting myself closer to his eye level, and held out my hands. He came to them, hesitantly, after a nudge from Mrs. Hunstin.

"You must be very good," I told him, trying and failing to affect the tone I had heard others use with toddlers. "Nanny H will be coming with you, so you must mind her as you always do, even if you are in a different house. I shall write to you often, and she will read you my letters; she will write to me of how you are doing. And I shall be home before you know it."

He nodded obediently, but I doubt he grasped the import of my words. That I should go away for a few days was a thing he had experienced many times; that I should go away for months or a year was beyond his comprehension.

I heard the crunch of gravel before the ringing of the bell. My brother-in-law Matthew had arrived, and his wife, Elizabeth, with him. They came into the hall, and I gently shooed Jacob toward Bess, with Mrs. Hunstin close behind.

Matthew sighed, looking at Jacob, and shook his head. "I know it's too late to talk you out of this. But still—"

"You're right," I said, before he could finish that thought. "It *is* too late. I am profoundly grateful for your assistance, Matthew; never doubt that. But I am going to Eriga."

His jaw shifted, briefly giving his face the air of a bulldog facing an unwelcome target. "I never would have predicted that Jacob would marry so obstinate a woman."

I wanted to say, *then you did not know him very well.* But in truth, I'm not certain Jacob himself would have predicted our match, in the years before we met. Antagonizing Matthew would accomplish very little, and so instead I said nothing; I merely kissed my son on the head, admonished him once more to be good, and waved them off down the drive.

Their carriage, departing, passed another on its way in. The coat of arms painted on the door was familiar; it was the white stag's head on a blue field of Hilford. The carriage, however, was not the earl's. I stood in the entrance, frowning, and so had no chance to hide when the door flung open (almost before the carriage had stopped) and emitted the angry form of Lewis Oscott, the Baron of Denbow—and the earl of Hilford's eldest son.

"Where is she?" he demanded, striding across the gravel to confront me. "Bring her out here at *once*."

"She?" I repeated dumbly, for my tongue had not yet caught up with my brain.

"Natalie!" His bellow made my ears ring. "I have tolerated her association with you; until now it did little harm. But this is beyond the pale. You will give her up this *instant*."

My brain had only got as far as knowing who "she" was. Why else would Natalie's father be here, if not because of his daughter? But the rest still escaped me. I had not seen Natalie in several days—a fact which, in retrospect, should have concerned me. We left for Eriga on the morrow, after all. I had been too distracted to think of it, though, assuming (when I considered it at all) that she must be with her grandfather.

A foolish assumption, and one that was now having some very unfortunate consequences.

"My lord," I said, collecting my thoughts, "I cannot give you what I do not have. Natalie is not here."

"Don't lie to me. Where else would she be, if not here?"

The accusation set my back up. "With her grandfather, perhaps? I take it she spoke to you about her intentions."

He snorted in disgust. *"Intentions.* It is madness, and you know it. A position as a companion is all well and good for women who cannot do better, but Natalie has perfectly good prospects, so long as she is here to take advantage of them. And you will not want her with you forever. When you tire of her—or get yourself killed, which is entirely possible—what will become of her? No, Mrs. Camherst, I will not allow you to ruin my daughter's future for your own benefit." Setting his shoulders, he strode forward.

I slapped my hand against the doorjamb, barring his way with my arm. "Your pardon, Lord Denbow," I said, with icy politeness. "I do not recall inviting you in."

This sudden and brazen resistance startled him, but he did not let it slow his tongue. "I am here to collect my daughter, Mrs. Camherst, with your permission or without it."

"If she were here, I would be glad to broker some kind of negotiation between the two of you. As she is not, you will have to seek her elsewhere. I will not suffer you to rampage through my house regardless."

He was not so far gone as to try and shove me aside, though he very easily could have done so. His fury thwarted for the nonce, he resorted to persuasion. "Mrs. Camherst, please, see reason. You are determined to put yourself in danger, regardless of the consequence to your family; very well. I have no authority to command you to better sense. But I *can* protect my daughter, and I will."

"Lord Denbow," I said, moderating my own tone to suit his. "I have told you, she is not here. I have not seen Natalie in days. Should I see her before I leave, I will tell her you came, and advise her of your concerns. That is all I can promise."

He deflated visibly, like the punctured bag of a caeliger. "I am sure she is coming here. Please, might I—"

"I will tell her you came," I said firmly. Had he not attempted to thrust his way into my house, I might have been more tolerant; as it was, I wanted him gone. "If I see her."

With that, he had to be content. By then the footman was hovering behind my shoulder, looking distressed at the prospect of having to forcibly evict a baron from the premises, but determined to do so if necessary. (Clomers was a very good footman, the best I ever had.) Half-fuming, half-dejected, Lord Denbow returned to his carriage, and so away.

Once he was well down the drive, I deflated a bit myself. "If he comes back, do not let him in," I said wearily to Clomers; and, having received his stout agreement, I went upstairs to my study.

Natalie was sitting in front of my desk.

I very nearly swallowed my own tongue at the sight of her. While one part of my brain sorted out the contradictory impulses of gasping, shrieking, and demanding an explanation of her, the rest noted certain details: the open window on the side wall, overlooking a fine (and easily climbed) oak tree; the fierce and frightened look in Natalie's eyes; the small valise on the floor at her feet.

"He locked me up," she said, sounding almost as if she could not believe it. "We argued for days, and when I told him I was going whatever he said, he locked me up. Him and Mama. I am sorry to have made you a liar."

"She only lies who tells a falsehood knowingly," I said, as if such distinctions were at all the most relevant thing at hand.

Natalie drew in a breath, and the unsteadiness of it advertised her distress. "I fear I have made a great deal of trouble for you. I came here intending to go with you tomorrow—but if I do, Papa will be infuriated."

If she did not, then she would have little choice but to return to her family. And while they might have what they perceived as her best interests at heart, the disjunct there was severe enough to send Natalie up my tree and through my window, and who knows what else before that. Her actions, more than any words, told me that return was simply not to be borne.

Her grandfather might protect her against the worst of it—but a better protection would be to go beyond her family's reach. "Your father will have to be infuriated in Scirland," I said, the dryness of my tone covering for any temporary quailing of spirit. "He doesn't have a visa for Nsebu, and isn't likely to get one anytime soon."

Hope kindled new life in her posture. "Do you mean—"

"The ship leaves tomorrow," I said. "We must think of how to get you on it."

We smuggled her on board by way of the workers' gangway, where her father would never think to look. With Natalie dressed in the clothes of a laborer (yes, trousers and all) and a sack of potatoes on her shoulder, Lord Denbow never had the slightest chance of spotting her.

He was there, of course, and made a great protest, insisting to the gathered members of my family (Paul and Judith; my mother and father; my favourite brother, Andrew; Matthew and Sir Joseph, who was my father-in-law) that I had kidnapped Natalie.

"I have *not* kidnapped her, my lord," I said, covering my nervousness with irritation. In his distress, he had not yet thought to ask me outright whether I had seen his daughter. If he did, I would have to make up my mind whether to lie, and a sleepless night of pondering that very question had failed to supply me with an answer.

I had kept my word, if only halfheartedly, talking with Natalie of his concerns. The conversation had failed to divert either of us from our course. My one source of apprehension was that I had no opportunity to speak privately with certain individuals, namely, Mr. Wilker and Lord Hilford. The former would be coming with me on this expedition, and the ear not occupied by Lord Denbow's furious expostulations was being filled with my mother's insistence that in addition to it being madness for me to go abroad, it was even *more* mad to do so without any kind of female companion. Marriage had provided me with a mystical shield against impropriety, one not entirely lost with widowhood, but she still feared rumour. (In fairness to her, I must say she was right to do so. But I get ahead of myself.)

Lord Hilford, I thought, had guessed something of what was going on, though whether he knew I was actively helping Natalie, I could not say. I did, however, see him draw Mr. Wilker aside upon his arrival, and whatever he said turned Mr. Wilker's face to stone. That done, Lord Hilford set himself to diverting his son as best he could. They went together to examine my cabin, to satisfy Lord Denbow that Natalie was not there; I hoped she had found a good place to conceal herself until we were well away from shore.

Andrew, to my pleasure and relief, set himself the same task with our mother, and accompanied me on board when the time came, as he had done when I departed for Vystrana. "So, where are you hiding her?" he asked as we crossed the deck.

A heavy step brought my head around. Mr. Wilker had joined us, pacing to my right, leaving me feeling trapped between them. But Andrew was grinning as if it were all a tremendous lark, and the grim set of Mr. Wilker's jaw told me he would not be surprised by anything I might say.

"She is hiding herself," I said. "I honestly don't know where. This was her decision, you know, though I support her in it."

"Miss Oscott is even less sane than you are," Mr. Wilker said.

"Then she's in good company," I said lightly. That would not be the end of it, I knew; but Mr. Wilker would not go against Lord Hilford's clear wish, that his granddaughter be permitted her escape. He was too loyal to the earl, and owed him far too much. What arguments we would have—and oh, did we have them—would come later.

Our ship was the *Progress,* the famed steamship that for many years formed the primary link in the Scirling-Erigan trade. Built from Erigan steel and fueled with Scirling coal, it was a symbol of the partnership inaugurated by the Nsebu colony—at least, it was seen as a partnership on our side of the ocean, though the truth was less balanced than that word implies. The bulk of its capacity was given over to cargo, some of which would be scattered through various ports like seeds as we made our journey, the rest traded in Nsebu before the holds were filled once more with iron, gold, ivory, and more. But the *Progress* was the jewel of that sea route, and so it also had passenger cabins, well equipped for the comfort of the dignitaries who occupied them. The three of us were hardly dignitaries, but Lord Hilford qualified, and had arranged for us to travel in style.

We met him emerging from my cabin with Lord Denbow behind him. Or rather, Lord Hilford emerged; his son charged, backing me against a wall. "Enough of this, Mrs. Camherst! You will tell me where my daughter is, or—"

My brother was already stepping to defend me. I was very glad that Lord Hilford intervened, before I had to discover what

Andrew would do. "Lewis! Control yourself. Or do you *want* the crew to drag you bodily off this ship? You are making a scene."

All hail that bane of the upper class, *a scene*. The spectre of being publicly shamed was enough to check Lord Denbow. It was not enough to calm him, but with his momentum broken, the baron knew he could not prevent the ship from departing. And if he attempted to detain me, he would face any number of consequences. He could not decide what to do before his father took him firmly by the arm and dragged him away, not quite by force.

Still, he indulged in one final accusation, shot over his shoulder. "You will ruin her life."

"I have not ruined my own, Lord Denbow," I called after him. "Trust your daughter to find her own way."

Natalie emerged when we were out of Sennsmouth harbor, and once she was properly attired, I called Mr. Wilker in.

He shook his head at the sight of her. "I would ask whether you have any notion what you've just done. But you're the earl's granddaughter, and I know you've inherited at least a portion of his intelligence. So I will only ask you, in God's name, *why*."

"Because I had to," Natalie said.

I understood her meaning, but Mr. Wilker clearly did not. Yet we required some degree of comity, or this expedition would be doomed before we arrived in Nsebu. "Mr. Wilker. I am sure you endured hardships of your own, gaining your education, forcing those of higher station to accept you as their intellectual peer. Why did *you* do it?"

"This will rebound on her family," he said, ignoring my question.

"And were there no consequences for your own family, when you left Niddey for university?"

It was a guess, but not a blind one; I knew Mr. Wilker was the eldest son of his line. His indrawn breath told me I had struck my mark. Belatedly—as usual for me, I regret to say—I wondered whether his sensitivity on this matter was *because* of his own experience, rather than in spite of it.

"When you came to Vystrana, it was different," he said, as if appealing to me for reason. "You came with Jacob, and with his blessing."

"Are a woman's wishes only fit to be considered when blessed by a male relative?" I asked sharply. "If so, then take Lord Hilford's for Natalie, and let us be done with it."

He flushed, and left soon after. It was not the last time we argued the matter, but my words had lodged under his skin like a barb, and their effect became apparent in due course.

PART TWO

In which we arrive in Eriga,
where we achieve both success and scandal,
and embroil ourselves in various conflicts

FIVE

Sea-snakes—The port of Nsebu—Faj Rawango—
Half-naked men—Nsebu and Atuyem—We are no threat

E ven at the reliable pace of a steamer, the journey to
Nsebu was not short. We stopped in various ports for
trade; we battled foul weather; once three boilers broke
down in concert, and the *Progress* made no progress at all until
they were repaired. We were at sea for a month altogether, and to
alleviate my boredom (for we soon completed the plans for our
research, and there are only so many hands of whist one can play
without going mad) I began observing the sea life.

Fish and whales, sharks and seabirds; the latter held the most
interest for me, as I had not lost my childhood partiality toward
wings. But despite its lack in that regard, I was most captivated
by the great sea-snake we saw one afternoon near the end of
our voyage.

We were entering Erigan waters, crossing the latitude known as
the Tropic of Serpents, so named for the large numbers of sea-
snakes found there. This was the only one we got a good view of,
and all the passengers (and half the crew) crowded to the rails to

observe it. "People argue about whether they should be considered dragons," I said to Natalie, watching the great coils rise above the water's surface and slip away once more. "Your grandfather doesn't believe the Prania sea-snakes should be, but I wonder about these beasts. There are so many creatures around the world that seem partially draconic in nature, but they lack wings, or forelimbs, or extraordinary breath. I think sometimes that Sir Richard Edgeworth's criteria may be wrong—or rather, too strict."

"Another thing to study," Natalie said, amused. "Will you ever be done?"

I smiled into the sun, one hand holding my bonnet against the firm grasp of the wind. "I should hope not. How dreadfully tedious that would be."

Four days later, with all the passengers lined up at the rail once more, the *Progress* steamed past the rocky outcrop of Point Miriam and into the deep harbor of Nsebu.

Because the geography of this region will be of great relevance later, I should take a moment to describe it now. The land of Bayembe lies on the northern side of the Bay of Mouleen, mostly along a plateau lifted above sea level, but beneath the mountains that form their northern border with the Talu Union. Their eastern border and part of the southern are ocean; the rest was, at the time, the disputed territory between the Girama and Hembi rivers, and the edge of the great, sunken swamp of Mouleen, whose streams spill into the bay at a thousand points.

Mouleen is born from an eccentric quirk of geology. It would, in the normal way of things, be a great river delta, as the Girama, the Gaomomo, and the Hembi converge only a few hundred kilometers inland, the culmination of their long rush to the sea.

But a fault in the underlying rock dropped the region nearly to sea level at what should have been the confluence, with the result that all three rivers tumble over a cliff and drown the land below. Furthermore, the prevailing winds at that latitude blow from the east, funneling much of the atmospheric moisture into the low channel formed by that geologic fault, and therefore much of the rain. The resulting morass is the impenetrable jungle of Mouleen—more colloquially known as the Green Hell.

But that was not yet my destination. Although I spared a few glances for the emerald band that marked the western edge of the bay, the bulk of my attention was on the town perched just off its corner, over which the fort at Point Miriam stood guard.

Neither words nor images suffice to communicate what greeted me as we came into port, for even the best artwork is a static thing of the eye alone, and words are by their nature linear. I can tell you of the smells that assaulted my nose: the salt sea, the coal smoke of other steamers, the fish and shellfish that even today make up a brisk part of the port's local trade, the spices whose aromatic vibrancy is all out of proportion to their quantity. Unwashed bodies and tar, fresh-cut tropical lumber, the greasy stench of lunch being fried for dockworkers and hungry travellers alike. But I can only tell you of one scent at a time, and I cannot present those to you at the same time as I give you the sounds and the sights, the mad clamour that was my first experience of Eriga.

With the knowledge I have now, I can give the proper names to what I saw then only as a bewildering array of peoples. There were Scirlings among them, of course, merchants and soldiers, there to protect our interests in iron production. Nor were we the only Anthiopeans, despite tensions with our rivals over their involvement elsewhere in Eriga; there were Thiessois, Chiavorans, a cluster of Bulskoi looking exceedingly uncomfortable in the heat. Pigtailed Yelangese bustled around their ships, and Akhians were nearly as common as Scirlings.

But it was the Erigans who dazzled my eye, for they were new to me, and formed the bulk of the crowds.

Amongst themselves, they displayed a hundred different modes of dress and adornment, a hundred different details of physiognomy that mark one people as distinct from another. I saw complexions ranging from inky blue-black to bronze, mahogany, and dark amber, sharp chins and square jaws, high foreheads and low, full lips and wide mouths and cheekbones that rode flat or stood out like the arches of a bow. The people wore their hair in loose braids or braids close to the scalp, in beads or strips of fabric, in soft clouds and corkscrew curls and sharp ridges held in place by white or red clay. There were Agwin veiled from head to toe and Menke in little more than loincloths, Sasoro in silver and Erbenno in embroidery, Mebenye and Ouwebi and Sagao and Gabborid in variations on the folded wrap, whose subtleties of color and arrangement communicate a great deal to the knowledgeable eye, but escaped my understanding entirely that first day. And, of course, there were countless Yembe, the dominant people of that land.

I had studied the Yembe language (from a reference grammar, which is an abominable teaching tool), but it had in no way prepared me for the social language before me now. Staring out at the docks, I understood, for the first time, that I had left behind the familiar commonalities of Anthiope, and crossed the oceans to a different continent.

Mr. Wilker put his hand under my elbow, which tells me I must have reeled. "It will be a little while before we can go ashore," he said. "You might want to go below until we do. The sun can be brutal, for those not used to it."

Once he would have phrased it as "you *should* go below." Disagreements over Natalie's presence aside, we had indeed made great strides in our relationship with one another. "The sun does not bother me," I said absently, digging in my satchel for my sketchbook. I'd done little drawing since leaving Scirland, the pitch and roll of the ship wreaking havoc on my ability to place a precise line, but I could not pass up this opportunity to sketch the docks.

I could feel him wrestling with the answer he wanted to make to that, before finally swallowing it—for the sake of harmony, I suspect. "I will make certain our trunks are being seen to," he said, and went away.

I had only put the broadest outlines of the scene down on paper when a popping noise sounded behind me, and then my page was in shadow. "Natalie," I said, annoyed.

"You'll burn otherwise," she said, all practicality as usual. "Grandpapa warned me. About the sun, *and* about you—that you wouldn't take sufficient precautions."

"The sun here is strong, yes. It was strong in the mountains of Vystrana, too, and I had little trouble there." I had suffered more from dryness of skin than from sunburn.

Natalie laughed. "Yes, because you were cold all the time. You covered up and spent much of your time indoors to get away from the wind. But carry on with your work; this parasol is shading us both."

I hadn't needed her exhortation to continue. Line by line, the

people were taking shape beneath my pencil, surrounded by crates and ropes and warehouses and shops, with little boats bobbing in the water at the lower edge of the scene. Drawing at speed was something I'd practiced these past few years; the images I produced lacked the polished elegance of my youthful art, but I'd improved greatly in my ability to capture the subject accurately in a short span of time.

By the time Mr. Wilker returned, I had enough of it down that I could fill in the remainder without trouble later on. "Is it very far to our hotel?" I asked, tucking my pencil away and closing my sketchbook. Certainly there would be other sights worth seeing beyond the docks, but I hoped to manage some individual portraits. Sailors the world over are a visually fascinating lot.

"Actually," Mr. Wilker said, "it seems our plans may have changed. See that fellow at the corner there, beneath the yellow awning? The short one, with the band of gold around his forehead? He's a messenger from the palace, sent to watch for our arrival. The oba has invited us to be his guests."

I blinked at him in startlement. "At the palace? Surely not."

"It seems so," Mr. Wilker said. "And we're expected to come straight on. The messenger brought horses, and he says we needn't worry about our trunks."

No doubt the gesture was intended to be helpful, but in my travel-frayed state, it struck me as faintly sinister. "What is this messenger's name?"

"Faj Rawango," Mr. Wilker said, with the careful air of one who doesn't trust his tongue not to trip over the unfamiliar syllables. He too had studied the language, but Faj Rawango was not a Yembe name. Was the man a foreigner, or did he hail from one of the other peoples that made up the nation of Bayembe?

I didn't realize Mr. Wilker and I had both fallen into a brief silence until Natalie broke it by saying, "Well, we cannot refuse such an honour."

"No, of course not." I replaced my sketchbook and drew the satchel up onto my shoulder. "And I suppose there isn't much to be gained by delaying. Come, let us go meet this Faj Rawango."

We descended to the ship's longboat and were taken in to shore, disembarking on the salt-stained wood of the docks near where Faj Rawango stood. He was, as Mr. Wilker had spotted, a small fellow by the standards of those around him; in fact, he was a bit shorter than I. His skin, though still dark, was lighter and more reddish in tone than many of those around him.

Lacking a better option, I greeted him in the Yembe manner, touching my heart, and received the same in return. Natalie and Mr. Wilker echoed us both. But once the formal greetings were done—a rather lengthier process among the peoples of that region than among Scirlings—Faj Rawango spoke in our own tongue. "The oba regrets putting you to the trouble of a further journey, but you will rest in more comfort in the royal palace, in Atuyem."

"That's very kind of him," Mr. Wilker said. "Our arrangements are for rooms in a hotel near Point Miriam. We had hoped to perhaps gain an introduction on some future date, but had no thought of imposing on his time and generosity so soon after our arrival."

Faj Rawango dismissed this with a wave. "It is no imposition. He has met many Scirling merchants and soldiers, but no scholars. He is very curious about your work."

The last time a foreigner with a title had taken an interest in our work, it had not ended well. That, more than anything in the messenger's words, put apprehension in my heart. But what could we do? As Natalie said, we could not refuse this invitation. I cursed the politicking that preceded our journey. Necessary though it had been to procure our entrance to Nsebu, it had apparently drawn rather more of the oba's attention than I wanted.

Our horses waited beneath a striped canopy not far away, in company with enough others that I understood the place to be some kind of waiting room for equines. Ours, however, stood out from the crowd, not only for their quality, but for the grandness of their equipage, beaded and gilt. No fewer than four soldiers stood watch over this wealth, who clearly would form our escort.

I call them soldiers, but at the time I had difficulty attaching the term to them, despite the Scirling rifles they bore. To my mind, a soldier was a man in uniform. I thought of these men instead as warriors, for their garb looked nothing like the uniforms I was accustomed to—stiff wool in solid colors—being drapes of cotton tied about their waists and dyed in some intricate pattern, with leopard skins hanging down their back like cloaks. Wool, I suppose, does little to protect one against a rifle ball or a cavalry sword, but such logic did not prevent me from fearing for the men's bare and unprotected flesh.

As I turned to mount, I saw Natalie blushing. Until that moment, it had not even occurred to me, in more than an intellectual sense, that the men were half-naked. Then, unfortunately, I could think of nothing else. My own cheeks heated, and I fumbled my rise to the saddle, catching my shoe in the hem of my divided skirts. (My self-conscious embarrassment was somewhat mitigated by seeing Mr. Wilker a bit pink in the ears himself—likely more for ladies being exposed to such a thing than for his own sake, as gentlemen see one another bare in many contexts. We had all known this would happen, the climate of the region being what it is, but knowing and experiencing were separate things.)

To cover for my loss of composure, I questioned Faj Rawango as we rode out of the dockside district and through Nsebu proper. Or rather, that was my intention; it soon devolved into a polite argument wherein each of us tried to insist upon using the other's native tongue, with the result that he spoke to me in Scirling and I responded in Yembe. Languages have never been my *métier*, so I fear he had the better of me in the comparison of skill, but my experience in Vystrana had taught me that there is nothing like using a language on a regular basis to better one's skill. I therefore persevered until Faj Rawango bowed in the face of my stubbornness and began answering me in Yembe.

We conversed on a variety of topics then, exploring as widely as my limited vocabulary and Faj Rawango's instructions from his royal master would allow. The former was more of a restriction than the latter, but I soon discovered (through my customary curiosity and lack of discretion) that the political climate of Bayembe was not a suitable subject. The man did not chastise me for asking, but he showed a marked disinclination to speak about the movement of Ikwunde troops that had so spooked the new man at the Foreign Office, or even more generally about the expansionist ambitions of the inkosi, their ruler. Nor would he speak of the Talu, the "union" to the north that was, in truth, an empire by another name, assimilating its neighbours one by one. Clearly such matters were not for the likes of him to share with Scirling outsiders—even outsiders here for non-political purposes.

(Yes, I thought my stay in the region would be non-political. When you have finished laughing, you may proceed.)

We spoke instead of the men and women we passed, Faj Rawango giving me my first education in distinguishing one people from another, which in retrospect was at least as valuable to me as his political opinions would have been. Physical distinctions are, of course, often muddied by intermarriage, but enough patterns persist in that region to be of moderate use, and of course the apparel and ornament of each people has its variations. Nowhere, however, did I see anyone resembling Faj Rawango himself, and he deflected me when I asked. My suspicion that he was of foreign birth grew, but I did not press.

In this manner did we ride through the fortified gates of Nsebu and into the grass beyond.

These days the two places have run together into one indistinguishable city, but back then Nsebu and Atuyem were quite separate. The former had a small port district that had, up until fifty years ago, been all there was of the town. Increased trade had spurred its growth, and then the alliance between Scirland and Bayembe had seen the construction of the fort at Point Miriam, with the colony following soon after. Now Nsebu was a strangely hybrid place, creeping across the open ground toward the more aristocratic precincts of Atuyem.

These sit above Nsebu both socially and physically, on a plateau high enough to enjoy cooling winds, but near enough to the port to benefit from the trade; which is why Bundey n Mawo Nsori, the reigning oba a century before, had moved his primary residence there. Atuyem is further stratified between the lower town and the upper, which perches atop a rocky, flat-topped hill, the better to command a view of the surrounding countryside. The walls of the oba's fortified residence rose higher still, a crown surmounting that stony head, and they shone gold in the afternoon light.

Much of that gold was metaphorical, an illusion created by the color of the soil used in building the walls and the warm glow of the sun. The highest tower within the complex, however, gleamed too brightly for mere dirt. The stories were untrue, that the oba of Bayembe lived in a palace of solid gold; but one tower, at least, had been plated in the substance.

It was a suitably impressive display of wealth—though one the oba perhaps regretted in a time of such conflict and greed. Then again, Bayembe's gold was not what attracted interest from Satalu, Ikwunde, and Scirling alike. Iron was the prize those three lands sought to claim.

Around that central fortress spread the courtyards and compounds of his chief nobles, patriarchs of the various lineages that made up the aristocracy of Bayembe. These had, over the years, grown too numerous and extensive, crowding all others off the small hilltop, exiling the common folk to houses and shops gathered around the rocky skirts of the hill. Our little party attracted a great deal of attention as we rode through, for our escorts were clearly royal warriors, and Faj Rawango a high official; nor had Scirlings become so common here as to be unworthy of remark, as they were in Nsebu. Natalie and I drew particular commentary, Scirling *ladies* being very uncommon in any part of Bayembe.

I rode self-consciously, feeling the burden upon me of representing my race and my sex to these people. My clothing—travel wear that was simple to the point of tedium by Scirling standards—seemed fussy and overcomplicated here, designed for sensibilities and a climate foreign to this place. I knew my face was flushed and damp with sweat, and likely sunburnt despite the protection of my bonnet, and the gritty dust of these grasslands clung to me all over. As representatives went, I felt like a shabby one indeed.

We circled the base of the hill along what was clearly the main road, until we came to a gate built in the style of these lands: hard-pounded earth, decorated with bright tiles, and studded regularly with wooden struts that were, as I understood it, both internal supports and climbing aids for when the exterior needed repair. Here Faj Rawango conversed briefly and incomprehensibly with a guard, making it apparent just how much he had slowed and clarified his speech for my sake. Thus interviewed, we rode onward, and began our ascent of the hill at its gentlest point.

The Atuyem we traveled through now was entirely different. Instead of the clamour and crowds of the base, we passed the near-faceless walls of the lineage compounds, whose decorative tiles communicated a message beyond my skill to translate. Guards stood at the gates, and servants traversed the roadway, some of them bearing the shaded palanquins of their masters. Where the curtains were gauzy, I could glimpse dark shadows within, that sometimes stretched out gold-laden hands to twitch the fabric aside and study us directly. These stares were different from the ones before: to the nobles of the heights, we were not mere curiosities, but new variables in the political equation of their land. Whether our effect would be positive or negative had yet to be determined.

It was both a relief and a fresh source of tension to ride through the mighty gates of the oba's own fortress, away from those measuring eyes. We dismounted in a front courtyard and were met by kneeling servants who offered up bowls of fresh, cool water with which to cleanse our faces and hands. Our escort stood at attention while we conducted our ablutions, then saluted and jogged once more out the gates.

In their place came a pair of what I guessed to be upper servants, one male and one female. "Rooms have been prepared," our guide said. "These two will show you."

The presence of *two* servants gave me a hint as to what we might expect. "Are our quarters separate?" I asked.

Faj Rawango nodded, with an impassivity I read to mean he had anticipated the question, but still thought me a simpleton for asking. "Men and women do not lodge together in the royal palace."

I wondered what they would have done had Jacob been alive, and here with me. Were married couples given joint quarters, or did husbands have to arrange to call upon their wives? But that was hardly the sort of question I had come here to ask. "We intend to spend much of our time together," I said instead. "Our work requires it."

"Of course," Faj Rawango said, all courtesy. "There are public areas."

Where we could be watched, I supposed, for any hint of improper behaviour. I had hoped to leave that sort of thing behind in Scirland.

We suffered ourselves to be led away, Mr. Wilker in one

direction, Natalie and I in another. Our new guide was an older woman, her hair faded to an iron-grey that reminded me of Scirland's interests in this region. She led us through a honeycomb of courtyards and colonnades, until at last we climbed a set of stairs to a cool and airy room tiled in blue.

By now I was tired enough that my brain had become sulky about handling a foreign tongue, but I understood from the woman's words that this was to be a shared residence for Natalie and myself. It was sparsely furnished by Scirling standards, with a few padded benches and stools of the kind that can be folded out of the way when not in use, and chests for our belongings. The bed was draped with gauzy curtains, the better to keep out troublesome insects while still allowing cooling breezes through. After the cramped conditions of the ship and the rigor of a long ride, it seemed to me like a small corner of heaven.

While Natalie asked after the bathing arrangement, I explored. One set of windows, covered with wooden laths hung on string, faced west, and looked out over a section of the palace that, by what I could see of the bustle therein, was a working area for servants. We had not, it seemed, been given terribly desirable quarters, however elegant the tiling.

The windows on the opposite side overlooked another of the myriad of courtyards that made up this palace. (Indeed, I was not far wrong in thinking of the place as a honeycomb; it was composed as much of open space as enclosed, and virtually everything of substance seemed to take place in the former. In a country as hot as Bayembe, fresh air is not only pleasant but necessary for survival.)

Our servant departed, and Natalie collapsed with a sigh on the bed—the benches there being far less suitable for collapsing upon than sophas and divans. "I promise I will say this only once," she remarked, "but good *Lord,* the heat."

(With all due respect to Natalie, whom I love as my own self, she lied. If I took a sip of gin every time she said that during the expedition, my liver would be *foie gras*.)

I gave in to temptation, sitting down on a bench and unlacing my boots. The coolness of the tiles beneath my bare feet was a blessing. "I can't decide whether this is a good development or a bad one," I said. "Has the oba brought us here to offer his assistance, or is he going to interfere?"

"Why would he interfere?" Natalie asked, reasonably. "I can't see what he would gain by it, and he would risk antagonizing our fellow countrymen."

"That might be reason enough. It would be minor antagonism at worst—I doubt the military and industrial gentlemen have much concern for our research—and so it would be a relatively safe way for the oba to show that he won't be pushed around by Scirlings." I scratched my fingers vigorously along my scalp. "One thing is certain; he has quite neatly separated us from most of our countrymen. Perhaps he thinks we'll be less of a danger that way." My fingers came away covered in sweat and grit, and I grimaced at them.

Natalie rolled over to regard me directly. "But we aren't any kind of threat, are we?"

"No," I said. "I don't see how we could be."

Later I would recall those words with a great deal of irony.

SIX

Meeting the olori—M. Velloin—My views on hunting—
The uses of M. Velloin—Dinner at Point Miriam—Sheluhim—
The worship of dragons

True to Faj Rawango's words, there were public areas in which we could socialize with the opposite sex. Before we found them, however, we had to run a gauntlet of women. The next morning (having dined alone and retired early the night before), Natalie and I sponged ourselves off, dressed in fresh clothing, and went downstairs in search of Mr. Wilker. Trying to follow what we thought was the proper path, we found ourselves in a courtyard full of ladies, all of whom fell silent at the sight of us.

We were, I own, shockingly out of place. Everyone else in the courtyard was Erigan, and dressed in patterned cotton wraps that looked a good deal more comfortable in that weather than our own stays and long-sleeved dresses. Such exotic creatures as a pair of Anthiopean women must, of course, draw attention. But there was, I felt, more to it than that: we had now entered waters not only foreign but political. We were not merely strangers; we were, as I had thought before, new variables.

It soon became apparent whose responsiblity it was to address
the change in the local calculus. A woman sat on a low stool at the
far end of the courtyard, watching us, and by the disposition of
the people around her, she was clearly the most important in the
group. Her features were of the sort Faj Rawango had identified
to me as characteristically Mebenye: a low forehead and rounded
jaw that gave her broad face an almost circular appearance. It was
a friendlier shape than a more angular face might have been, but
the set of her full mouth and the sharp regard of her eyes warned
me not to read personality into physiognomy.

She gestured, and another woman approached us. Speaking in
Yembe, she said, "Olori Denyu n Kpama Waleyim bids you come
speak with her."

Then I knew who had snared us. "Olori" was the title given to
the oba's lesser wives; we might translate it as "princess consort,"
the position ranking below that of his principal wife or queen,
who had the title ayaba. The current oba had three wives, I knew,
but that was where my knowledge ended. Information on them
had been hard to come by in Scirland, and what little I'd gleaned
had to do with Idowi n Gemo Tagwi, the queen.

The only way to learn was to proceed. Natalie and I approached,
until the olori held up one hand for us to stop, about four paces
from her. She sat beneath a canopy of beaded and embroidered
fabric, and her hair was braided with gold, a match for the jewelry
that burdened her every limb.

I curtseyed to her as I might to the queen of Scirland, hoping
either that other Anthiopean women had been here before me, or
that the olori would independently recognize it as a gesture of
respect. Scarcely had I risen from this, and Natalie beside me,

when the woman spoke. "You are here alone?"

"No, olori," I said, hoping I was unlikely to go wrong if I addressed her by her title. "Miss Natalie Oscott here is my companion, and we also came with a gentleman named Mr. Thomas Wilker."

The pursing of her lips did not look impressed by this answer. "Your name. It is Isabella Camherst."

"Yes, olori." We must have been a topic of gossip before our arrival.

"Women of your people take the lineage name of their husband, yes? Then this man is not your husband. You came here alone."

Too late, I understood. "I'm afraid my husband is dead."

Her gaze flickered across my body. Looking for signals of mourning or widowhood, I supposed. "And his brother did not marry you?"

I thought of Matthew, and narrowly avoided laughing at the thought. "That is not our way, olori." Tardily, the recollection came that Bayitists in some countries faithful to the Temple still followed such practices—often the ones who also took multiple wives—but I did not trust my command of the language to address so complicated a topic, nor was it particularly relevant. Scirlings did not do such things; that was enough.

"Mmmmm." The olori showed no sign what she thought of this. She was, I suspected, a deeply political creature, who never showed much of anything unless it might bring her gain. I did not like her, but whether that was because her reserve hid any impulses I should fear, I could not tell.

Then she asked the question—the same question I have gotten dozens, nay, *hundreds* of times in my life, always with that same air of faint disbelief. "You are here for . . . dragons?"

"Yes." She could be reserved all she liked; I made no effort to hide my enthusiasm. "We are scholars of dragons." It was the closest I could come to saying "natural historian" in Yembe.

"What is there to study? They are not gods or great heroes. They are not even livestock, or beasts of war. You cannot train them to be useful. Are you hunters?"

"Gracious, no!" The words burst from me. "That is—we *have* hunted dragons, Mr. Wilker and I have, though I suppose it would be more precise to say he did the hunting. I only drew the body afterward. But we are not hunters as I think you mean it, olori, killing them for sport or for trophies. We seek to understand them: their nature, their behaviour."

Ordinarily this is the thread my conversational partners pursue, the (to them) incomprehensible question of why understanding the nature and behaviour of dragons is worth so much effort, if not for the purpose of killing them. Olori Denyu n Kpama Waleyim had other things on her mind. "Draw them? Then you are an artist?"

"I suppose so," I answered, taken aback. "I'm much more of a scholar, really, but I do draw and paint. For my work."

For some reason, this appeared to please the olori, though I could not imagine why. She put her hands on her knees with a self-satisfied air, nodding. It seemed to be a signal that our interrogation was done: other women began to speak then, and Natalie and I passed a pleasant (if mentally taxing) half hour conversing in Yembe. We only escaped by pleading the necessity of finding Mr. Wilker.

This gained us a guide, who showed us through the royal

honeycomb to a more public courtyard. We found Mr. Wilker there, beneath the shade of a spreading tree, deep in conversation with another man.

I was not sure whether I should be surprised that his companion was Anthiopean. Foreigners were not all confined to the colonial districts of Nsebu, of course, but I had not expected them to seek us out so quickly. Or had Mr. Wilker sought him out?

He did not appear to be a military man. Blond of hair and reddish of whisker, he wore loose, practical clothing made out of the fabric the Isnatsi call *khaki,* not a woolen uniform. His fair skin was weathered to a solid brown, much seamed with lines, though I judged him not to be above forty. He had the fit look of an athlete, and I had no idea who he was.

Mr. Wilker did not leave me long in suspense, of course. Rising from his stool, the other man a heartbeat behind him, he said, "Ah, Mrs. Camherst, Miss Oscott. I'm glad you could join us. May I introduce M. Gregoire Velloin?"

M. Velloin's hand was solidly calloused, with thick, blunt nails. A working man's hand, I thought. When he spoke, I was surprised to find his voice tinged with an Eiversch accent, instead of Thiessois. "Mrs. Camherst, a pleasure. Miss Oscott, very nice to meet you. There has been much gossip in advance of your arrival. You are not what I expected."

"Oh?" I said, mildly nettled for no reason I could discern. Perhaps my audience with the olori had put me out of sorts. "What did you expect?"

"Someone older and plainer," he answered, with bluntness that was likewise much more Eiversch than Thiessois. "I had heard you were a widow."

Now, at least, I had reason to be nettled. "I am, sir. But my late husband's passing has no bearing on my age or appearance."

Rather than taking offense, he laughed. "Oh, indeed. But that is rumour, is it not? Making assumptions with no basis, just to fill the time. I am sure gossip will be more accurate, now that you are here."

Based on my experiences thus far, I sincerely hoped I would not be there for long. I had far rather be out in the bush, pursuing dragons, than dealing with the people in Atuyem, be they Erigan or Anthiopean. "What brings you here, M. Velloin? You cannot be with any Scirling delegation, and I note your accent—and yet you affect a Thiessois title of courtesy."

"And a Thiessois name, too. My father was of that land; he was born in Fonsmartre. You know of it? Quite near the border, yes. He emigrated in his youth, and married an Eiversch woman. But I am *monsieur* instead of *Herr* because I have made my home in Thiessin for ten years now, and it is owing to the generosity of a Thiessois patron that I am here."

I frowned. "You have not yet answered my question, *monsieur.*"

"M. Velloin is a hunter," Mr. Wilker said, intervening.

Thinking back over my words, I winced; the hostility I was showing to our Anthiopean companion held some echoes of my early behaviour toward Mr. Wilker himself. I made an effort to moderate my tone. "I see. Is it the elephants you are here for, or the leopards?"

Velloin smiled, as if our conversation had been friendly all along. "I do not discriminate, Mrs. Camherst, except to choose only the most dangerous of prey. There is no challenge, without risk. I have hunted tigers in Rematha, bears in Kaatsedu, and mammoths in Siaure. Here I will hunt the elephant and the leopard and the dragon."

So much, I thought, for friendliness.

Natalie laid a restraining hand on my arm; she knew what the stiffening of my posture meant. It did not stop me from speaking. "The dragon. Indeed. In that case, I cannot honestly wish you luck in your endeavours. I have little fondness for sport hunting in the first place, and less in the case of dragons. You may not be aware, sir—unless you make a habit of reading scientific monographs, which I doubt—but on our Vystrani expedition—"

"You discovered mourning behaviour among Vystrani rock-wyrms." Velloin's mouth had compressed, though he maintained a good approximation of his amiable tone. "I do read monographs, Mrs. Camherst, where they concern the great beasts. A good hunter must know his prey."

"They are more than prey," I said, biting the words off. "That you should see them so, for the mere prize of teeth and claws, is a very great pity."

Pity fell far short of what I truly meant, but Scirling politeness restrained my tongue. Now, years after the fact, I have no compunctions about telling you what I truly felt.

It is true, yes, that my companions and I have killed dragons in the course of our research, and sometimes even for the purpose *of* that research. But even before I developed reservations about such practices, I had an utter loathing for trophy hunting, which was (and in many places still is) considered a wonderful expression of masculine virtue. Rarely do such men hunt verminous creatures, of the sort that truly plagues the common people; if they foxhunt, it is with a fox captured for the purpose and released in a pleasant park, not the one eating the chickens of the peasant outside that park.

No, the beasts they hunt are the splendid ones, the majestic kings and queens of the wild, and they do so for no better reason than because a splendid trophy is far more glamorous than a scrubby one. The occasional hunter will test his courage by going after a hippopotamus, which is as dangerous as it is comical looking, but most prefer those with pelts or hides they can display after the fact. To kill a creature simply to decorate one's study is repellent to me, and I cannot help but be repelled by those who engage in such activity.

And that abhorrence is redoubled when the hunter's target is a dragon, for I, as all the world knows, am partisan to their kind.

Velloin seemed unconcerned by my disapproval. Why should he be? I could do nothing but seethe. "Teeth and claws are prizes, yes, but hardly the only ones. I have captured animals, too—even a dragon, once. You may have seen it yourself."

"What dragon?" I asked. The question came out sharp, for a dreadful suspicion had taken shape in my mind.

"A Moulish swamp-wyrm," he said. "Took it from near the coast; only safe place to go, really, and hardly even then. The creature was a runt, but it made its way into the menagerie at Falchester."

He was watching me as he spoke, and I could not hide my reaction. I had indeed seen that dragon, along with two other runts, on the very day that I met my husband. Without those dragons, I might never have married Jacob, with all the consequences, both good and bad, attendant upon that decision. The thought of owing even a fraction of my happiness to a man like Velloin was infuriating.

Casually, he added, "I hope to try again, in the jungle or out in the savannah. Buyers are much harder to find for full-grown dragons—too difficult to keep them caged—but still, the challenge is the thing."

It would be hypocritical for me to wish him luck in that endeavour. It would also, however, be hypocritical for me to condemn him, given the joy I had derived from seeing those captive dragons. In the end, I clamped my jaw shut and let others take the conversation onward.

Unfortunately, it transpired that Mr. Wilker had engaged us to dine with the bloodthirsty M. Velloin that afternoon. He was on good terms with a number of people at Point Miriam, which served not only as a defensive fortification but also as the home of Nsebu's colonial government. Given that we were newcomers to the royal palace, unfamiliar with the rhythms of life there and (thus far) ignored by the oba who had invited us in the first place, it made all the sense in the world that we should accept Velloin's invitation. But I did not like the idea, and regretted that I saw no acceptable way to beg off.

On the contrary, our plans rapidly expanded from a single meal to a full day in the man's company, exploring the lower town of Atuyem before riding back down to Nsebu. As we left the royal compound, Natalie making light conversation with M. Velloin, I seized hold of Mr. Wilker's sleeve and dragged him back, so that I might hiss my words without being overheard.

"How could you put us in the company of such a man? And with no warning? You know quite well my feelings on the matter." I glared at M. Velloin's broad back.

Mr. Wilker freed his sleeve from my grasp with an irritated jerk. "I did so because he can be useful to us. Or would you rather kill *more* dragons, for the purpose of our tests?"

We had passed under the arch of an unfamiliar gate and out into a street, whose surface was not so well maintained as the one that led us in. At Mr. Wilker's words, I stumbled over an uneven bit of stone. We had agreed, when this expedition was first planned, that one of our tasks must be to test Rossi's preservation process on the bones of an Erigan dragon, to determine whether it was effective only on Vystrani rock-wyrms, or for a broader selection of species. And for that purpose, indeed, we required a dead dragon.

"Then——" M. Velloin's back had taken on an entirely different cast in my eyes. "You mean to steal his kills."

"Once he has his trophies, there's no reason for him to deny us the rest. We can tell him we're trying to make plaster casts of the bones; it's a reasonable enough excuse for us to take them."

Plaster casts had, before the preservation method, been the only means of keeping dragon bones for study. It did not work very well—encased in plaster, the bones deteriorated more rapidly than usual—but Elia Paradino had improved the process a bit. Mr. Wilker was right; it made a very good cover.

Still, I sighed. "It will require us to be in his company. Quite apart from his hobby, I do not like the man."

"No one is asking you to marry him, Mrs. Camherst."

Three years had passed; my grief for Jacob was no longer an open wound. Or so I had thought. But I was tired, and vexed with M. Velloin, and above all, I was on an expedition to study dragons. Bayembe was a vastly different place from Vystrana, but the fact remained that it had been on such an expedition that Jacob died.

This time I did not stumble. I stopped entirely. Only for a

moment—then I forced my legs into motion once more—but it was enough to tell Mr. Wilker he had erred. He stopped, too, and turned to face me, so that I had to halt again.

"I'm sorry," he said, and I think it was not the heat alone that had flushed his face red. "I—I didn't mean that as a jab. It was supposed to be facetious, but I didn't think before I said it. Please, forgive me."

I wondered, irrelevantly, how long our relative harmony would have to last before I stopped reflecting on the change from our early interactions. But for that harmony to last, I had to do my part, which did not consist of standing in the middle of a street reflecting on such things, while Mr. Wilker's apology hung in the air. "Forgiven," I said. "I did not take it as an insult; it simply— well. You understand."

We had, of course, attracted the attention of the other two, who had paused in the street up ahead. "Is everything all right?" M. Velloin called.

"Yes, quite," I called back, and offered Mr. Wilker a reassuring smile before going to join the others.

Dinner at Point Miriam was oddly disorienting. The heat and scent of the air were inescapably Erigan, but the house in which we dined had been built according to the standards of my people. The table was laid as if it stood in some lady's country house, and beforehand we enjoyed *hors d'œuvre* in a drawing room that might have been a small piece of Scirland transplanted onto foreign soil. The effect might have been intended to reassure, but it made for a sweltering evening; our architecture is not suited to the climate.

The composition of the group was quite as unbalanced as Lord Hilford's snare-setting meal had been. There were only three ladies in attendance: myself, Natalie, and a married woman from Uaine named Erynn Anne Kerwin, who was there with her husband.

"Such a relief it is to have other women here," she said upon our introduction. Her accent was much like Mr. Wilker's, but stronger. Uaine, lying as it does to the north of Niddey, is the most isolated of the large Scirling Isles; it is isolated even now, and was more so then.

"I take it you don't find much company among the Yembe," I said, which was perhaps not the most politic response.

Mrs. Kerwin did not take offense. "Oh, I spend a mort of time with them—but that's work, not leisure."

Despite my having come to Eriga for work of my own, I had assumed Mrs. Kerwin was here as an adjunct to her husband, whose profession I had not yet determined. Embarrassment leashed my tongue, and so it fell to Natalie to say, "What work is it that you do?"

"We're sheluhim," Mrs. Kerwin said.

Embarrassment had put a leash on my tongue; startlement took it off again. "What—do you mean to say that you're proselytizing to the *Yembe?*"

"That is precisely what we're doing," Mrs. Kerwin said. If her warm smile had cooled somewhat, I could not blame her. "We have brought the sacred fire of the Temple to this land, and will carry it to all peoples. Already a number of men and women here have chosen to become the Chosen of the Lord, following His laws. Sure I am that number will only grow."

It was unfair of me to be so startled. Sheluhim have been traveling all over the world since men invented ships safe enough not to drown their passengers in the ocean; it was only that I had never encountered any myself. There were a few Bayitist sheluhim in Scirland, trying in vain to convert Magisterials back to the old ways, but the proselytizers of both major sects devoted the bulk of their efforts to lands where Segulism held no sway in any form.

Mrs. Kerwin was almost certainly a Temple-worshipper herself, being from Uaine. The Magisterial reforms in Scirland never penetrated that island very deeply. I had dealt with her co-religionists in Vystrana, but theirs was a rural theology, not the sort that sought to convert others to its way. And no Magisterial sheluhim had yet taken it into their heads to convert the Vystrani.

This, however, was a land of heathens, and with the Scirling presence, prime territory for such efforts. I should have expected to find her kind here.

"Erigans worship their ancestors, do they not?" Natalie asked. She and I had both done a certain amount of reading during the preparation for this expedition, but very little of it had been devoted to religion.

"Together with idols of nature, yes," Mrs. Kerwin said primly. "They are entirely lacking in scriptures of any sort, and of course what few of the laws they follow, they follow by accident."

Had I known more about Erigan religion at the time, I would have pointed out to her that what they lacked were scriptures of *our* sort. At the time, however, I was both ignorant of such matters and distracted by a different thought. "Have you gone down into the swamp at all?"

Mrs. Kerwin looked horrified. "You mean into Mouleen? Certainly not. We wouldn't survive two days there. Wild beasts, fevers, not to mention the natives—"

"I take it they don't welcome visitors?"

"They have the Ikwunde on one side and the Yembe on the other." M. Velloin had overheard our conversation. "And the Satalu lurking in the wings, hoping to snatch up Bayembe for themselves—though to what extent the Moulish are aware of that, who can say? They trade occasionally with the peasants along their borders, forest ivory for food, that sort of thing. But those who go deeper into the swamp never return."

I wanted to shift away from Velloin, but he was clearly somewhat informed about the region, and I could not pass up the chance to ask. "There are stories about the Moulish, that say they worship dragons as the Draconeans once did."

We were gathering quite the audience now: not only Mr. Wilker, but Sir Adam Tarwin-Bannithot (who was then the governor of the Nsebu colony) and a man whose sober dress and Uaine accent marked him as Mr. Kerwin. The latter said to me, "I take it you've read the work of Yves de Maucheret."

By M. Velloin's expression, so had he. "Yes," I said, "though he was writing two hundred years ago, and not everything he put to paper has proved to be true. Still, it's enough to intrigue the mind, isn't it? Dragons rarely tolerate human company well, and Moulish swamp-wyrms are not known to be the most approachable of breeds. If the Moulish do indeed worship them, do they do so from afar? Or are they able to partially tame them, as the Draconeans are said to have done?"

"They are nothing like the Draconeans," Mr. Kerwin said, dismissing the notion with a wave of his hand. "That ancient civilization—well, it was a *civilization*. They built great temples, developed art, administered territory across multiple continents.

The Moulish bang on drums and run about naked. They may worship dragons, but there is no reason to suppose their manner of doing so bears any resemblance to Draconean religion."

"And yet, it would be closer to Draconean religion than any other example we have before us today," I said. "Do not ethnologists use modern evidence to analogize to the past? We might learn a great deal from the Moulish, regardless of their musical traditions and sartorial habits."

I spoke with the assurance of a young woman who thought her experience with natural history and *ad hoc* education in other subjects more than qualified her to hold forth on topics she knew nothing about at all. The truth is that any such comparison is far more complicated and doubtful than I presented it that evening; but it is also true that no one in my audience knew any more about it than I did, and most of them knew less. My assertion was therefore allowed to stand unchallenged.

For those who wonder why I showed such interest in the Draconeans, whose works I dismissed in the previous volume of my memoirs, do not think this meant I had undergone any great change of heart in the intervening years. I still at that time cared little for their ruined temples and stylized art; my interest was in living things, not dead civilizations. But as I said to Mr. Kerwin, the Draconeans were said to have tamed dragons. *That* was of great interest to me indeed, and so if Moulish religion was able to shed any light on the matter, then it, too, fell within the sphere of my attention.

Of course, there was the minor problem of the Green Hell being one of the deadliest regions on earth. But my interest was, that evening, still academic; my purpose in coming to Bayembe was to study the dragons of their arid plains. Moulish swamp-wyrms were a minor note—in much the same way that a fisherman's lure is a minor note in the world of a fish.

Sir Adam said, "I wouldn't waste much time or thought on the Moulish, if I were you. Whatever you might learn regarding dragons cannot possibly be worth the risk, and as for learning anything about humans—feh. That swamp is a backwater, in every sense of the word."

"A backwater which is presently protecting this country, is it not?" I said.

He shrugged. "For now."

A brief silence fell, broken a moment later by Sir Adam's uncomfortable cough and too-loud amendment. "Besides, you won't get into the swamp, not without the oba's permission. And he won't give it."

There is nothing in the world so enticing as that which you have been told you may not have. "Whyever not?" I asked. "Or rather, why should I need his leave in the first place? Mouleen is an independent state, is it not?"

Mr. Kerwin muttered something about not dignifying that festering pit with the name of "state," but my attention was on Sir Adam. He said, "At times like these, with the Ikwunde interfering with our work at the rivers, we must keep a careful eye on our borders."

Which was not much of an answer, but it was all that I could get from him, in the wake of that momentary lapse. Sir Adam had taken a bit too enthusiastically to the prescribed regimen of gin and tonic, with which we all held the malarial fevers at bay, and had said something he should not. Why would the Green Hell cease to protect Bayembe? Were the Moulish looking to ally themselves with the Ikwunde on the other side?

I did not know, but Sir Adam's slip had made me wary. I wanted only to study dragons, but first I had to get past the humans, and I feared they might be a greater danger to me than all the fevers of the tropics combined.

SEVEN

A certain taboo—The agban—*Galinke—Matters of lineage—
Natalie joins me—Making use of M. Velloin*

I must warn my male readers that I am about to address a topic
which may be deeply discomfiting to them, taboo as it is for
their sex.

When I awoke a few mornings later, I found my bedding
stained with traces of blood. I clicked my tongue in annoyance;
caught up in our affairs, I had not monitored the days as closely as
I should, and my menses have never been the most reliable
besides. But this was, I thought, only a minor irritation. I wet a
cloth, washed myself clean, changed into a fresh chemise, and
called for a servant.

When she came, I gestured at the stained bedding, washcloth,
and chemise, indicating that she should take them away to be
laundered. "And I will need rags," I said—as yet blissfully
unaware that in many parts of the world, rags are not employed,
but other, less comfortable alternatives.

(Indeed, for those young ladies who wish to follow in my
footsteps, I must warn you that this inconvenient fact of our sex is

one of the most vexatious aspects of being a lady adventurer. Unless you contrive to suppress your courses through pregnancy—which, of course, imposes its own limitations—or through strenuous exercise and privation, you will have to handle this necessity in many circumstances that are far from ideal. Including some, I fear, where the smell of fresh blood is a positive danger.)

Returning to the moment at hand: the serving girl's eyes widened at the sight of the stains, and she darted out of the room almost before I had finished speaking. So rapidly, in fact, that she left the laundry behind. I sighed, wondering if the fault was with my imperfect command of the language, or whether she—being prepubescent—was the sort of silly nit who bolted at the sight of blood. Well, I thought, if it came to that, I could sacrifice the rest of the stained chemise for rags.

The girl returned with equal speed, though, this time accompanied by a much older woman, who went to gather up the bedding and other articles. The girl herself approached me and draped an undyed robe over a bench, indicating shyly that I should wear it.

I saw no rags. "Thank you," I said, "but I have my own clothing; I only need something to stanch the bleeding."

The older woman—who was, by the look of her, well past the age of bearing herself—said, "Put it on; Lebuya will take you to the *agban*."

This was not a word I had encountered, either in my studies or my time there. *"Agban?"* I repeated.

She indicated the soiled items. "Until you are clean."

My first thought was that she meant a bath. But I knew the word for "bath"—that was where Natalie had gone, while I

worked on rousing myself to wakefulness—and had she meant
such a thing, would she not have said "where you can wash
yourself"? Suspicious, I asked, "How long will that be?"

By her reaction, I might have been as young and ignorant as
Lebuya, needing an older female relative to explain the basic
matters of womanhood to me. "Seven days."

I recoiled. She did not mean blood on my skin; she meant
impurity. It was not a topic that concerned us much in the relaxed
Magisterial traditions of Scirland, and although I had encountered
traces of it in the Temple-worshipping environs of Vystrana,
many of the finer points of religious doctrine there had been
whittled down to accommodate local practicality. The women of
Drustanev could not afford to seclude themselves for the duration
of their "impurity."

But I had not expected to find evidence of the Kerwins' success
here in the oba's own palace. Startled, I said, "I didn't realize you
were Bayitist."

She frowned at me. "What is Bayitist? You are unclean; you
cannot stay out here, where you will pollute others. Go with
Lebuya. She will show you."

No, this was not the work of the sheluhim; it had the sound of
a standard practice, and surely I would have heard if the entire
ruling class of Bayembe had converted to Segulism. But I could
no more afford to lose a week of my life than the women of
Drustanev could. (Or at least I was not willing to; that, I think, is
the more accurate statement, though it benefits from hindsight.) I
planted my hands on my hips, drew myself up like a proper
Scirling lady—taking Judith and my mother as models—and
said, "Nonsense. I have gone about in this condition once a

month for my entire adult life, and never polluted anyone."

The old woman made a gesture I thought was probably a ward against evil and said, "Then the oba will throw you into the Green Hell—if he does not have you executed for witchcraft." She picked up her bundle and left.

My certainty that the oba would do no such thing faded when I looked at Lebuya, who would not meet my eyes. She had avoided them, as she avoided touching me, placing the robe on a bench rather than handing it to me directly. She had brought an old woman to take away the stained fabric—someone past her own bearing days. The implications I saw there might be my own invention, but I did not doubt that *some* manner of significance clung to those actions. Whether the oba punished me or not, I would not be able to carry on my work as usual; it would be all around the palace before lunchtime that I was unclean, polluting everything around me. The consequences would damage us far more than a week of enforced idleness would.

Had we stayed at our hotel down in Nsebu, or better still among the Scirlings at Point Miriam, I might have avoided this difficulty. Since I had yet to see any particular benefit from being housed in the royal palace instead, it was with no little annoyance that I picked up the robe and put it on. The thing was shapeless cotton, draping to the floor, the sleeves long enough to cover my hands; there was even a hood for me to draw up over my impure face. Lebuya produced a pair of rough sandals and set them on the floor for me to don. I wondered if someone would come into the room after I was gone to purify it, and thought they probably would.

Natalie chose that moment to return, saving me the confrontation of insisting that, impure or not, I would go nowhere until I spoke with her. Her eyebrows rose at my explanation, and when I was done, she sighed. "Unless there's an exemption for unmarried women—which I doubt—then I'll be taking your place in this *agban* of theirs just as you're ready to leave. How can we be expected to get any work done, if one or the other of us is locked away two weeks out of every four?"

It would not be that much time—as I said before, my courses have never been fully regular—but I brooded upon Natalie's question as I followed Lebuya out. We might escape the restriction by going into the bush for an extended period of time; even then, though, we would need porters to assist us, and what if they rebelled against serving impure women? Perhaps we could hire foreigners from the docks. But they would not know the bush as the locals did, and lack of experience on that front might prove very dangerous.

With the hood blocking the edges of my vision, I could not see our path clearly, but it was not one I had traced before. We left the women's wing by what I suspected was a back entrance, passed through a low wall—not leaving the palace, but entering a new region of it—and came at last to a modest building that seemed almost like an ordinary house.

I did not need Lebuya's pointing arm to tell me where I was to go. This, obviously, was the *agban*: the prison for menstruating women. And I was to remain here for seven days? I should have brought my notebooks—presuming, of course, that they would not be irredeemably contaminated by such use.

Sighing, I muttered a thank-you to Lebuya that was not very heartfelt, and went inside.

The interior was pleasant and not at all prisonlike. It was, after all, where palace women spent one week out of every four; I suspect servants had their own *agban* elsewhere, as neither Natalie nor I ever saw one there. The front room had benches and hooks along the walls, one of which held a robe like mine, with the sandals beneath. I took this as a sign that I could discard my own. Thus freed, I ventured onward to a small courtyard, where a woman I judged to be around my age lay on a carpet beneath a tree, reading a book.

She looked up as I entered and smiled, showing only a little surprise. "I have not seen you before. You must be one of the new guests, those who came to study dragons."

"Isabella Camherst," I said. "I'm afraid you have the advantage of me."

The woman rose, laying her book aside, and touched her heart in respect. "Galinke n Oforiro Dara. I'm glad you came. It's pleasant to have time to read, but after a day or two I find myself eager for company."

"We're allowed to have things with us, then?" I said, gesturing at her book. "I was afraid they would burn my notes if I brought them here."

Galinke laughed. "No, no. We would go out of our minds if we couldn't have distraction! But why would you work, when you could relax?"

I joined her under the tree and discovered that, to Yembe women, and those of other Erigan peoples who engaged in similar practices, seclusion was not an exile, but more in the nature of a holiday. The other three weeks out of the month, they were obligated to work at various tasks—not the backbreaking labor of the peasant in the field, certainly, but weaving, child rearing, and other duties suitable to highborn women. When their impurity sent them to the *agban,* they could enjoy complete leisure. (They could also enjoy a respite from their husbands, which for some of them was even more valuable.)

Galinke herself was not married. "For now," she said with a sigh. "My brother would make a match for me, but he has to wait, in case it ends up being necessary for me to wed the mansa."

"The *mansa?*" I repeated, sure I had misunderstood the Yembe sentence. That was the title given to the Talu leader.

She nodded. "He has one wife from each of his subject peoples—as our ancestors had to do, when Bayembe was young. Even now, my brother has a Mebenye wife and a Sagao one, to keep the different peoples happy."

Had she been Scirling, I never would have blundered in such fashion. We trace descent through the paternal line, and pass on family names in the same manner; the Satalu do likewise, as do societies in many parts of the world. But the Yembe and the other peoples of their country are matrilineal: individuals belong to their mother's lineage, not their father's, and inheritance therefore passes from a man to his sister's son.

Galinke's lineage name was Oforiro Dara, which is to say she came from the Oforiro branch of the Dara line, as her mother had before her. Her mother, clearly, had been a lesser wife of the man who wed the mother of the current oba of Bayembe—whose lineage was Rumeme Gbori—and Galinke herself was the oba's half sister.

(I say "clearly" as if understanding came to me in an elegant flash. It didn't; I sat openmouthed for a solid minute while my brain struggled to bend itself around a system of kinship and inheritance utterly foreign to my way of thinking.)

"But—" I said, still working through the implications. "If you wed the mansa, would that not mean your children would have a claim on Bayembe?" The feud between Talu and Bayembe was an old one, as old and as bitter as that between Thiessin and Eiverheim, and it had only grown worse in recent decades. Anthiopean influence to the north had encouraged several Erigan kingdoms to band together against them, though their Union had swiftly transformed into something much more like an empire, with the others in a client-state role to the mansa of Talu.

Over time the Union had begun to intimidate their neighbours into joining them: a less violent approach to conquest than the Ikwunde used, but still not very appealing. Getting a claim on the rule of Bayembe would be exactly the sort of tactic the mansa might use, and I did not think the oba would be so foolish as to allow it.

"How could he have a claim?" Galinke asked, politely baffled at the wrongheadedness of my question. "I'm not Rumeme Gbori. Only our sister Nsami's sons can inherit."

Nsami, presumably, being the oba's full sister. Give me dragons any day; I understand their ways far better than those of my fellow human beings. We make our world much too complicated.

"I thought your brother detested the mansa," I said, then winced. "Forgive me. This is turning into gossip, and I have no business talking of such things."

Galinke waved my apology away. "What else does anyone in this place talk about, other than politics? You are right. But a wise ruler must be prepared to do what is necessary for the well-being of his people. Even if that means giving his sister to a man he detests."

Or inviting foreign soldiers to come defend his land—but I kept a better leash on my tongue this time, and did not say it. Still, the entire point of Bayembe's alliance with Scirland was to make sure this land would not have to give in to Talu pressure, just to defend themselves against the Ikwunde. If the oba was keeping Galinke in reserve, it suggested that he was less than entirely confident in our aid . . . or less than entirely pleased with it.

Galinke seemed matter-of-fact about the possibility of marrying the enemy, which is more than I could have managed in her place. I said as much to her, and she shrugged, looking philosophical. "Such trades are common. Not with the Satalu, perhaps, but others, to join one lineage to another. I have always known my marriage would be arranged."

I squelched the urge to tell her I had helped Natalie flee Scirland, that she might avoid any marriage at all. "I hope the good efforts of our soldiers can at least spare you *that* particular fate," I said. "I have heard rumours that the Ikwunde are moving their forces toward the rivers, which means we may have a chance to prove our use quite soon."

The words were as much a test as conversation, and I think Galinke knew it. Her full mouth curved in a hint of a smile. "The Ikwunde can never stay still for long," she said. "No sooner do they digest one meal than they go in search of another."

So she, unlike Faj Rawango, was permitted to discuss politics with me. I pressed the advantage. "You are fortunate to have Mouleen defending most of your southern border. I am told that anyone who tries to venture beyond the edge of the swamp is never seen again. Is that why the oba restricts travel there? To protect his people from the Moulish?"

Galinke laughed. "Few people wish to go there in the first place, except for hunters, sometimes. But my brother must keep a close eye on his borders in these troubled times, until we can build better defenses for them."

The only defense we had built thus far was Point Miriam. Were we planning another, or more than one, for points along the border? I had no chance to ask her; a servant entered then with food, and in the course of dealing with that, Galinke turned the conversation so deftly that I did not even notice until hours later.

I came to know her rather well over the four days we were in the *agban* together, and liked what I saw. Although we never returned to the specific matter of the Ikwunde, I learned a great deal about Bayembe politics from our conversations. This I absorbed more out of duty than anything else, for while Galinke seemed to view such things as a puzzle, an engaging challenge for her intellect, I could not bring myself to enjoy them in the same way. I had not been raised to such a life, and was grateful indeed for my freedom.

In retrospect, I wonder about those conversations. Galinke had not been forbidden to discuss politics; had she been *instructed* to do so? Certainly my time with her changed my view of the alliance between Scirland and Bayembe, which until that point had largely been shaped by the news-sheets of Falchester. Those sheets spoke glowingly of economic opportunity, and disapprovingly of the rapacious behaviour of Bayembe's neighbours, from which we were nobly protecting them.

This was not inaccurate, but it lacked nuance. From Galinke, I began to understand the unequal nature of the "alliance"—which is why I scar it with quotation marks—and the extent to which that economic opportunity favored Scirland. She spoke obliquely, of course; at no point did she tell me outright that her half brother resented the dependent condition of Bayembe, which he had inherited from his predecessor, the last oba of the previous royal lineage (and a less than competent ruler). Nor did she spill details of our government's plans, though I think she knew them. She did not even say that the aggressive movements of the Ikwunde and the Talu Union were driven by a desire to build strength against Anthiopean influence; that, I think, is something she did not think of consciously, as both nations were the enemy to her, and she was uninclined to view their behaviour in a tolerant light. Galinke merely talked, in the delicate and subtle manner of a well-trained courtier, and the ship of my thinking heeled slowly over to a new course.

Despite all the trouble that came of it, I thank her for that work, whether it was carried out on her brother's orders or not. Had she not laid those foundations in my mind, I might have failed to grasp the significance of later hints, and the course of history might have been very different.

After Galinke departed, I had two days in which I shared the *agban* with three women I did not know, with whom I made polite but uninteresting conversation, and otherwise devoted myself to my work. The leisure time might have been pleasant if I had been tremendously busy prior to my seclusion, but by the time Natalie arrived on my final day, I was more than ready to get back to my affairs.

"Mr. Wilker was less than pleased to hear where you'd gone," she said with a wry smile. "And even less pleased when he realized this would be a regular occurrence."

She had arrived at lunchtime, and joined me for the plain but nourishing food that in Bayembe was considered suitable for impure women: eggs and fufu (a doughy mass made from yams). "I imagine Mr. Wilker was unhappy to be discussing the subject at all," I said; he was unmarried, and so had never yet been forced by domestic necessity to consider that aspect of women's lives. "I'll see him straightaway tomorrow. What has happened, while I languished in here?"

"In terms of work, very little. I have met more of the palace ladies, and Mr. Wilker has spent much of his time at Point Miriam, talking to the Royal Engineers stationed here. They've been surveying the countryside, which may be of use in helping us chase dragons—though of course that is not why they're doing it. They are planning a railway, and a dam in the west, too, if the Ikwunde can be pushed back. Did you know that someone has developed a turbine which can use water to generate power? Like a waterwheel, but far more efficient."

I laughed. "*Which* one of you has been speaking to the engineers?"

Natalie ducked her head in sheepish acknowledgment. "I have more to converse about with them than with the palace ladies."

Given that the Royal Engineers are the unit responsible for building and/or destroying anything the army needs or wishes removed, I doubted they were accustomed to young women quizzing them on their work. "What of M. Velloin?" I asked. "Is he still in Atuyem?"

"Yes, though he intends to go out hunting soon."

This was precisely what I wanted to hear. The next morning I presented myself to the old priestess who oversaw the *agban*; she purified me by means of prayer and rolling an unbroken egg down my arms and legs and back, and then I was on my way. (No, I do not know the significance of the egg, except that it is a symbol of fertility, and therefore considered to be good luck.)

Mr. Wilker was not in the palace. I sought him down in the lower town, where some kind of festival was under way, with a boisterous parade wending through the narrow streets. Many of the people I attempted to question were drunk; I could discern only that the festival was religious in nature, as evidenced by the finely carved masks worn by the dancers at the heart of the parade. After days of quiet in the *agban,* the noise and movement were jarring; I was on the point of abandoning my search when I finally saw a handful of Scirling soldiers at the side of the road, and Mr. Wilker among them.

"There you are," he said when I arrived. "It's going to be damned inconvenient, Mrs. Camherst—pardon my language—if you and Miss Oscott must be locked away like this."

"I will see if anything can be done," I said. "In the meantime—is there any chance we could join M. Velloin's hunting party?"

"If we can persuade him to wait until Miss Oscott is free, then yes. Or if we are willing to leave her behind."

I was not willing to leave Natalie, but Velloin agreed to postpone his departure, and so we made plans to join him, combining our research with his hunt for trophies. Credit where credit is due; Mr. Wilker was right in suggesting it. Indeed, without M. Velloin to assist, we might have had more difficulty in beginning our work.

EIGHT

Into the bush—Okweme and his interest in me—The watering hole—
My first savannah snake—Hunting tactics—We study the carcass—
Chemicals and plaster—An awkward conversation—
An even more awkward interruption—Rumours

We made quite a cavalcade as we headed out into the grasslands the following week. In addition to the usual necessities of food, water, tents, and so on, plus the guns and ammunition for the hunters, our scientific expedition, which had attached itself to M. Velloin's group like a barnacle, carried a great deal of equipment. There were no fewer than four pack mules devoted to our notebooks, scalpels, measuring devices, plaster, tubs, and so on, along with a tent to do all the work in—not to mention, of course, the chemicals for preserving bone, which was our true purpose in coming.

It was by then the first week of Gelis—a fact which I consistently forgot, despite my assiduous care in recording the date in my journal every day. It did not feel like Gelis. The Days of Light were drawing near; the weather, my instincts insisted, should have been settling into the kind of damp, aching cold that

made one glad even for a candle's flame. Instead it was as hot as a
Scirling summer day, with not a cloud in the sky. Bayembe was
firmly in the grip of its long dry season; the intermittent wind
kicked up veils of dust from the hard ground, and the stiff grasses
rattled as our horses and mules moved through them.

I have not been to Bayembe in nearly twenty years, but my
memory of it remains as fresh as yesterday. Not the factual details,
but the experience of the place: the enormous quality the sky
seemed to take on, and the vast stretches of dry grass rustling in
the breeze. Scattered umbrella thorns spread their branches like
flat clouds above the ground; I caught occasional movement in
the grass that told me small creatures had taken advantage of the
shade beneath.

I had put on a bonnet for the ride, of course. My shipboard
argument with Natalie aside, I knew better than to ride all day in
the tropical sun with a bare head. But compared with the damp
chill that had greeted me in Vystrana, this warmth seemed a
friendly welcome, a promise of good things to come. I did not yet
realize how brutal the heat would become—though even then, I
would choose that heat above an equal or even lesser degree of
chill. The evidence of natural history points to a tropical origin
for our species, and I believe it to be true.

M. Velloin rode with a rifle tucked into one arm, its barrel lying
across the pommel of his saddle. I nudged my mare up to join
him and asked, "Do you expect to have need of that, this close to
Atuyem? I would think there are too many people about for your
sort of game to show their heads."

He laughed easily, teeth flashing predatorily in his tanned face.
"One never knows, Mrs. Camherst. Besides, in these troubled

times, it isn't only beasts we need to watch for."

"The Ikwunde?" I asked, skeptical. "I have heard they are threatening, but even if they overran our troops at the rivers, we would know of it long before they got this far."

"Single men can be as dangerous as armies, Mrs. Camherst, in the right place. But no, the truth is only that I like to keep my hand in. There are small beasts about that make good target practice—and good eating, too, some of them."

He was not wrong about the small beasts. I had field glasses with me, and put them to frequent use as we rode; it allowed me to see the creatures keeping a wary distance from our noisy herd. Low disturbances in the grass were occasionally visible as rock hyraxes, while larger ones were the rangy, rust-furred wild dogs endemic to the area. A cloud of dust marked the passage of a herd of zebra. An odd lump on a distant tree proved, upon examination, to be the recumbent body of a leopard, draped elegantly along a branch with its tail curving below. "Keep your distance," I murmured under my breath, as much for the leopard's safety as our own.

I had spoken in Scirling, and did not expect to have an audience. But from behind me, a voice said in Yembe, "I would like to learn your language."

Turning in my saddle, I found my interlocutor was a tall, well-made young man, one of the Yembe who had joined us for this excursion. Not a porter; the richness of the cloth wrapped about his hips and the gold braided into his hair made his status clear. He rode with easy grace, and his horse was, if I did not miss my guess, an Akhian stallion of breeding as good as his own.

"I would be a poor teacher, my lord," I said, defaulting, in the absence of his name, to a generically polite address. "I have struggled three years to acquire any ability in your language. Such things do not come easily to me, I fear."

He smiled broadly and touched his hand to his heart. "I am Okweme."

"Of what lineage?" I inquired. "If it is not impolite to ask."

"It is not impolite. I belong to the Kpama Waleyim."

My mare danced beneath me at my involuntary start of surprise. After meeting Galinke, I had vowed to learn more about the various lineages, and now that vow was bearing fruit. "You are the olori's son!"

"I am," he said, still smiling. "But here, in the bush, I am only Okweme."

Only a prince, as we would consider such things. A prince, and the son of the woman who had examined me on my first day in Atuyem as if I were a beetle under a magnifying glass.

But he had nothing of his mother's calculating manner. Okweme was a font of information about the savannah and its creatures, which he did not hesitate to share with me as we rode. His familiarity came from long experience as a hunter, but he did not put me off as Velloin had, for he seemed little concerned with the glory of his trophies. Or perhaps it was merely that he was a far more personable man.

Okweme took our plain supper with us when we stopped for the night, and traded delicate corrections to our Yembe grammar for some basic instruction in Scirling. Afterward, while Natalie and I helped one another dress for bed inside our tent, I said, "He seems a friendly sort. I'm surprised he's taken an interest in us, though. Aren't we far beneath his station?" Galinke had talked to me, but that was because we were locked in the *agban* together.

Natalie laughed. "An interest in *us?* I only saw interest in one person." She poked me in the side.

"Me?" I said, twisting to face her. "What? Why?"

"Oh, let me think," she said, turning so I could undo her buttons. "A handsome young man, an available young woman . . ."

Her description took me aback. I was not accustomed to thinking of myself as young, for all that I was barely twenty-three. I had been married; I was a widow, and had a son. In the eyes of society, all those things put me firmly into the category of "mature," and not the sort of woman with whom handsome young princes would trouble to flirt.

But what were Yembe views of widows and their marriageability? It was not something I had thought to research before coming, and now I felt the lack most acutely.

Fortunately, I soon had other things to occupy my attention. The following day we moved into a region too arid for agriculture, and here flourished the kind of game that attracted M. Velloin's eye.

In terrain of that sort—an arid mosaic of grassland and savannah, which is a kind of loose woodland—watering holes are everything. Their number is few, and a wide array of creatures must come there to drink; but the predators know this, and lie in wait for their prey. The approach to a watering hole is therefore perilous, and the beasts remain in a state of heightened alertness while there.

M. Velloin had not come this way before, but Okweme and the other Yembe with us knew the area well. They directed our group to a stony hillock, lesser cousin to the one upon which Atuyem stood. It lay downwind from the watering hole, which was as great a benefit as its elevation; if we did not make very noisy spectacles of ourselves, we could observe the area at our leisure, and make plans for further work.

I dismounted on the lee side of the hillock and immediately began scrambling up its slope. M. Velloin would be not far behind me, I was sure, and I wanted the chance to see this for myself, without his presence spoiling the moment. Nearing the top, I dropped into the grass and (silently cursing the long skirt of my dress) crawled the remainder of the way, until at last I could see what we had come for.

My gaze went first to the elephants. They were simply too large to overlook. A group of six had come to the far side of the watering hole; the rest of their herd stood a little more distant, perhaps keeping guard. The largest of those at the pond's edge, whom I judged to be an old cow, was showering a juvenile with water while he splashed in the shallows. For all that I am partisan to creatures with wings, a delighted smile spread across my face at the sight. The playfulness of the pair was undeniable, and charming. (I may also say that their large, flapping ears would very nearly serve as wings—an exaggeration, but one that crossed my mind whenever I saw the beasts.)

The watering hole itself was a kidney-shaped pond, muddy and reflective under the bright sun. It was, I later learned, fed by a tiny spring, which kept it present year-round; others wither to a tiny puddle or vanish entirely during the dry season. Even with the spring, I could see the hard-packed dirt where the waterline had receded; it would withdraw farther still before the rains came again.

A herd of gazelles had arrayed themselves not far from the elephants, presumably seeing their fellow herbivores as no threat,

despite their great size (against which the gazelles seemed positively tiny). Frogs spotted the water's edge like brown, restless lumps, and flies and other insects made a haze a little distance above. Several pairs of Erigan geese floated near the middle of the pond, muttering amongst themselves and occasionally setting up a great ruckus with their wings, the shading of whose red and grey feathers at rest resembled nothing so much as the scaled back of a Hakkoto carp.

Out of both wariness and eagerness, I looked about for predators, but saw none. Lions, of course, prefer to hunt at dusk and at night; leopards and hyenas are the same. Cheetahs will hunt during the day, but they are less common in that region— their niche being occupied by a Certain Other Beast.

My eye, I am not ashamed to admit, was simply inadequate to the task.

Their business at the watering hole done, the gazelles were loping away, their delicate legs flickering through the grass. Then something else flickered, too, that was most decidedly *not* a gazelle.

It came low and fast through the cover, at an angle to the herd that caused them to startle and veer in their course. Then, with a surge that caused my heart to give a great leap, it sprang into the air: an Erigan savannah snake.

The dragon's wings seemed to go on forever. Long and narrow, they are incapable of sustained flight, but they work excellently well for the species' chosen method of hunting. On the ground, with their wings folded in tight to their bodies, savannah snakes can very nearly equal the speed of a cheetah. Once they come within range, though, they leap upward and spread their wings, gliding above the panicked herd until a suitable target presents itself. Then they swoop down, long necks extended, and bite down hard upon the spine of their prey. If the dragon has gauged his attack well, he retains enough momentum to drag the beast sideways out of the main herd, whereupon the rest thunder off and he may enjoy his meal in peace.

So it was on that occasion. The entire incident was over with shocking speed: a few seconds of the dragon in gliding flight, followed by a bellow and a confusion in the rushing mass of gazelles. Then they were gone, leaving their dead brother or sister behind.

In repose, the savannah snake is not the most prepossessing of dragons. Compared with the Vystrani rock-wyrms I had known before, it seems almost laughably small; the largest specimen on record today weighs ninety-eight kilograms. Its scales are dull, shading to green during the rainy season and dun in the dry, and the elongated structure of its body, along with the contrast between its deep chest and narrow waist, conspire to give it the appearance of a serpent that has recently swallowed a very large meal. But its wings are a glory: slender and maneuverable, their translucent membrane glowing gold when the sun shines through them. (A sight most commonly available to their prey, who do not much appreciate the aesthetics. But I once had the pleasure of seeing a savannah snake airing its wings after being tumbled into water.)

"Ah, she's a beauty."

I had a smile on my face and words of agreement on my lips before I realized the remark had come from M. Velloin. At some point—I did not know when—he had crawled up to join me on the hilltop. He had brought field glasses, and raised them to better study the feasting dragon. Beneath that, his expression was not one of wonder, but rather of calculation, and I could guess what equations were in his mind.

On the other hand, I *had* come here to take advantage of the fruits of his hunt, and could hardly fault him for doing that job. I merely disliked him praising the beauty of the savannah snake with such a purpose in mind.

"They are solitary hunters, yes?" I asked, determined to make use of his knowledge.

"The females are, like that one there. Males will hunt together sometimes, in pairs or trios, occasionally quartets. Especially if they're brothers. If you hunt males, you must be *certain* how many there are, or that last one will be on your head while you're taking aim at the others."

(I must confess my imagination presented me with a picture of M. Velloin shrieking and running about with a dragon attached to his scalp. The reality, of course, would have been bloody and not at all amusing, but the image entertained me.)

I tugged my hat forward to better shade my eyes. "How do you hunt them? With a rifle, I presume—but do you chase them, or lie in wait?"

M. Velloin snorted. "Good luck chasing them; they can outpace an Akhian without trying. If the terrain allows it, lying in wait works very well. Unfortunately this hill is too distant to be of any use, unless the snake drives its prey right past us." He put down his field glasses and gave me a predatory smile. "Let me show you how it is done."

The showing took several days. Even an experienced hunter like M. Velloin is not successful on every outing—not in bagging dragons, at least, though there was not an afternoon in which he failed to bring back *some* kind of carcass. We dined that first night on roast waterbuck, and he took two zebra the following day, whose striped hides our servants were set to defend from scavengers attracted to the smell. Okweme and his companions went out at dusk in pursuit of lions, but had no luck.

M. Velloin's tactic for dragon hunting was this: He would watch from the hilltop until he saw a cloud of dust advertising the approach of some group of medium-sized herbivores (antelope or other such ungulates—never anything so large as an elephant). Then he and the others would ride to intercept it, close enough to the watering hole to be within a savannah snake's likely orbit. The arrival of men on horseback would invariably spook the herbivores, which in turn could sometimes be relied upon to provoke the snake, if present, into striking. Then M. Velloin, galloping along with the herd, would attempt to shoot the dragon from the sky.

This is, of course, a hazardous undertaking. Like all species then considered to be "true dragons," the savannah snake possesses extraordinary breath, in this case a corrosive mist. On the first instance of M. Velloin successfully flushing a dragon, he failed to shoot the beast, and one of the other men took the retaliatory spray across his right arm and shoulder, even up to his face. This immediately raised painful blisters, which soon after burst; and in a tropical environment such as Bayembe's, open wounds of that sort are extremely dangerous. They attracted midges and flies, and despite our best care, soon became infected. The man ultimately survived, but he was scarred thereafter, and much weakened in body.

Yet such perils do not deter hunters from their goal. M. Velloin was not the only one to ride out again after the man was wounded, and two days later, he met at last with success. And, as per our arrangement, he immediately quit the field and dragged the body back to where we had set up camp.

Almost immediately. He had, I saw, taken the time to claim his trophies, prising the teeth and claws free. I scowled at him. "I should like to have seen those in place, M. Velloin. We are not *only* going to make casts of the bones; there is a great deal to be learned by studying the specimen as a whole. How am I to understand its swift running, when you have taken away the claws?"

He looked abashed, and also like he was trying to use his abashment to mollify me. I refused to be mollified, and ordered him out of the way as we got to work.

The routine will be familiar to those who read the previous volume of my memoirs. My words to M. Velloin were true; I had every intention of extracting as much data from this carcass as possible. I therefore set to work sketching, while Mr. Wilker and Natalie took measurements, which I would use to correct my anatomical drawings when I produced the finished images.

We had quite an audience at first, some of whom were even willing to assist rather than getting in the way. M. Velloin, I must grant, was among those who chose to help. But our work is not exciting to watch, and so before long most of the observers drifted away. I was on my knees in the dirt beside the snake, flexing and twisting its hind foot to consider how it ran, when I realized that one was still present and watching very closely: Okweme, the oba's son.

"Can I help you?" I asked, too distracted by my task to address him as politely as I should have.

He slid one of my sketches from beneath the rock pinning it down and studied it. "You are indeed an artist."

"Had you any reason to doubt it?"

Okweme shrugged, returning the paper to its place. "Women sometimes exaggerate their skill, to attract a better husband."

It was very fortunate that Mr. Wilker was undertaking the task of butchery, severing and defleshing a wing on the far side of the carcass. Had the knife been in my hand, I might have cut myself. Was Natalie right? Was he evaluating me as a potential marriage prospect?

Among the Mebenye and the Yembe alike, creativity and artistic talent are considered great virtues in a wife: well, I was an artist. I was also a widow with many fertile years ahead of her, and that is not a thing they tend to leave at loose ends in their society. And this might explain the olori's interest, when I told her of my work. But surely a prince like Okweme was not so bereft of prospects that he needed to court the first unmarried woman who wandered by, artistic talents notwithstanding. Why should he be interested in a Scirling, anyway?

I had to answer him. "I am hardly a professional," I said, realizing too late that a disclaimer of skill is a sign of modesty, and also attractive. Was there nothing I could say that would not dig me in deeper? In desperation, I rose up to lean over the snake's body. "Mr. Wilker, is the wing ready? Ah, excellent. We should take the casts now, if Natalie has mixed the plaster."

She had indeed, along with other materials none of us mentioned aloud. We retired into our tent with the wing bones: long things, so slender it seemed they must snap beneath their own weight. But of course they did not, for that is the virtue of dragonbone. "The solution is under the cot there," Natalie said in a low voice, then went out, pulling the flaps shut behind her.

Mr. Wilker took the bones over to the cot. Between the two of us, he was the superior chemist (I being not much of a chemist at all), and better qualified to run the process that should, at least in theory, preserve savannah snake bones as well as those of rock-wyrms. I busied myself with the plaster, which would suffer an unfortunate miscarriage of procedure in the next few hours, resulting in no usable casts at all. The prospect of mockery for my error hardly pleased me, but we had agreed that it would arouse less suspicion than if Mr. Wilker were blamed for the loss. And we did not want anyone giving much consideration to the question of why we had no casts—not when we would, we hoped, be busy hiding the actual preserved bones.

We worked in silence for about a minute. Then Mr. Wilker cleared his throat. "He has one wife already."

Savannah snakes, as I have said, are not large beasts. Of course Mr. Wilker, on the other side of the carcass, had heard every word. I flushed and answered him sharply. "Is that meant to deter me? I am not looking to make him my new husband."

"I didn't think you were," he said. Then he fell silent: perhaps because he was attending to the task of dripping one chemical solution into another at a steady pace, or perhaps because he was thinking. Either way, when the dripping was done, he went on. "But you haven't exactly been dissuading him."

"Instruct me in how to dissuade a prince in a fashion that will not offend him and cause us trouble soon after," I said, "and I will do it with a glad heart. Until then, I must go on trying to be polite, for the sake of our expedition."

Mr. Wilker laid the last of the bones in their chemical bath and sealed the top, to protect them from both dust and prying eyes. We would need to remain here for at least three more days before they could be moved; I hoped M. Velloin would not take it into his head to shift his camp. Then my companion stood, looking at me. "Do you *want* to remarry?"

My hand on the edge of a plaster-filled tub almost overturned it, which would have made a very nice answer for why the casts had failed. "I fail to see how this has any relevance for our work, Mr. Wilker."

"I should think it's obvious, when you attract marital interest wherever we go."

"One princeling hardly justifies that description."

It would have been wiser for me to leave the matter there. But I made the mistake of looking at Mr. Wilker, whose expression I could not read. With the flaps closed, it was stiflingly hot inside the tent, and I was all too conscious of the need to keep our voices low. Natalie was supposed to be keeping watch outside, but canvas makes a very poor barrier to sound. All these factors and more combined to make me leave my plaster tubs and cross to Mr. Wilker, who, with the cot and the box it hid behind him, could not retreat. "Do you have a personal reason for broaching this topic, Mr. Wilker? Because if so, I would thank you to do me the courtesy of admitting it."

His face had been reddened by days in the sun, but I think he flushed still further. "Mrs. Camherst—"

I will never know what he would have said. I suspect, looking back, that he would have pointed out to me what the roaring of my heartbeat in my ears had obscured: Natalie's voice outside, greeting

the man approaching our tent, warning us that we were about to
have a visitor. But I did not hear it, and Mr. Wilker did not find his
tongue quickly enough, and so when light burst upon our dim little
scene, M. Velloin found me standing scant inches from my
companion, face tilted up toward him, and both of us red as beets.

We could only have looked more guilty had he caught us in an
embrace. We sprang apart with exclamations of surprise, me
retreating to my plaster. With Velloin silhouetted against the
brightness outside, I could not see his expression, but the way his
head turned from me to Mr. Wilker and back again said more
than enough. "I thought I would see how you're getting on," he
said, and I could have slapped him for the amusement in his tone.

"Quite well, thank you," I said, failing to sound at all polite.
"Thank you for the specimens."

He approached me and held out a sack. "The claws. I assumed
you would like to examine them."

Velloin offered them to me, not to Mr. Wilker, which under the
circumstances was not only decent of him but surprising. He had to
have been questioning my scientific purposes—men like him
generally do—and would question them even more now. "Thank
you," I said, this time with more sincerity. "I will draw these this
afternoon, while the plaster dries, and return them to you."

"No need to hurry," he said. "I'll be going out with the prince
in an hour or so, to see if we can't bring down a few lions. You're
welcome to join us, Wilker."

Mr. Wilker was not a hunting enthusiast, but I was hardly
surprised when he accepted. It would separate the two of us for a
time, which was good both for our own peace of mind, and for
quelling suspicion.

Or so I hoped—quite naively. As you may have guessed, this was the beginning of the long-lived rumour that Mr. Wilker and I were on intimate terms. At least, this is the point at which such whispers became common currency in Bayembe; it is possible that the simple fact of my departing on the expedition with him, especially in combination with the to-do over Natalie, began those rumours at home even before more specific word arrived from Eriga. A widow, by virtue of having been married, is protected from a degree of scandal that would ruin a maiden, but it does not mean that she can carry on in whatever manner she pleases without anyone taking notice.

I would like to say that I cared not a whit for the whispers. It would suit my dashing reputation for me to shrug off the concerns that burden more ordinary women. I was younger then, however, and apart from the damage to my own esteem, I cared a great deal for the effect the rumours had on those around me. It undermined Mr. Wilker, to have his scientific work overshadowed by impropriety; it reflected badly on Lord Hilford, to have given his patronage to two such scandalous people. But what enraged me the most was the foul elaboration of the rumour that said our indiscretions had begun in Vystrana, and that Jacob had either winked at it, or died because he did not.

All of that lay in the future that Gelis afternoon. The first stirrings of it, however, began during the hunt that night, when Okweme was (so I later heard) jocular with Mr. Wilker in a way that did not seem friendly at all. It continued for the remainder of the trip, and when we returned at last to Atuyem, the seed nurtured in water found fertile soil in which to grow.

NINE

*The rumours continue—Galinke's theory—Two months
in the bush—Reconsidering Edgeworth—Malaria—
Witchcraft—A letter from Lord Denbow*

One might have expected Okweme's interest in me to cool, with rumour saying I was already involved elsewhere. On the contrary, he pursued me more closely after that—but I did not like his reasons for doing so.

He said nothing directly, of course. But his manner shifted: friendliness taking on an oily sheen, warmth bringing him closer than I wished him to stand. I tried to describe this to Natalie, and could not find anything specific to point to; the problem was in the aggregate. "I cannot help but feel," I said in frustration, "as if my supposed misbehaviour with Mr. Wilker has, in his eyes, made me available to any man who chooses to claim me. One expects this sort of thing from a rake at a masquerade ball in Vickery Gardens, not from the son of a king."

"Some of those rakes at Vickery *are* the sons of kings," Natalie said dryly. "But I know what you mean. Well, I shall cease telling him where you are; perhaps that will help."

It did, but not enough. In desperation, I turned to Galinke. My irregularity meant I did not rejoin her in the *agban,* but I saw her after she emerged, and she invited me to stroll with her in the oba's gardens. As soon as I thought it reasonable, I directed our conversation to that particular knot. "There is nothing between myself and Mr. Wilker but professional matters," I told her, when the tale was done. "But I cannot see how to convince anyone of that."

"Sometimes women keep themselves to our side of the palace for a long time, and after that the rumours fall quiet," Galinke said. "But only sometimes. And you cannot do that, not without abandoning your work."

Which I would never do—though sometimes I had cause to be glad for the segregation the palace imposed. "Tell me," I said. "Okweme is your brother's son; have you any notion why he might be pursuing me? He did so even before I sullied my reputation. My skill with a pencil is hardly enough to make me a desirable catch, and I do not flatter myself that my beauty or charming manner has anything to do with his intentions. What political benefit might he gain, that I do not see?" Or what benefit his mother might gain, though I did not say it. I was beginning to think she had set her son on me, like a hunter putting a hound after a rabbit.

"Your people are currently very important in Bayembe," Galinke pointed out. "If they gain more territory and influence here, it could be to Okweme's advantage to have a connection."

"But *I* lack connections. My family, if they were Yembe, would not even rate chambers in someone else's compound up on this hill. My late husband's family would, but only barely. Unless—" The hypothetical I had described, the Hendemores and Camhersts as Erigan families, gave me a new idea. "Is it possible he thinks my children—*our* children, if he married me—would inherit something of value? We pass down such things in the father's line, not the mother's. My brothers' wealth, such as it is, will go to *their* sons, not mine."

Galinke had been shaking her head as I spoke, but the way in which she stopped told me a thought had come to her. She cast a surreptitious glance around and then, seeing no one, still took the precaution of drawing me down onto a bench, where we would be half-concealed by a stand of flowering reeds.

"It would be very strange," she said. "But—to your people, children belong to their father's lineage. Here, it is the mother's. *Your* people would expect Okweme's sons to inherit from *him*."

I began to see what she aimed at. "Is there something of value he has, that he cannot pass down to his own children?"

Galinke nodded. "Certain honours and property from his uncle, yes. And Okweme has no full sisters; all of Denyu's other children have died, so his heirs are more distant—cousins he does not like. He has two daughters from his wife, but that means nothing. They belong to her lineage, not his. But your children would belong to *your* lineage—and he could try to argue that, by the customs of your people, what is his should become theirs. To do otherwise would be to leave them with nothing."

It was almost enough to make me laugh. Okweme n Kpama Waleyim wanted me for my country's inheritance laws—or at least that was our speculation, though we had no proof as yet. But putting even a possible explanation on his behaviour renewed my incentive to escape it. "I shall have to contrive to be in the field more often," I said. "*Without* him, this time. Tell me, what happens if a woman becomes, ah, impure, while out in the bush?"

I will not say it was my desire to avoid Okweme and the *agban* that led to our second excursion, but they were among the relevant factors. He was not so shameless as to contrive a reason to join us again—not when there would be no hunting on our trip—and Galinke assured me that rural people were more flexible in matters of impurity, so long as we had ourselves cleansed appropriately.

Other factors included our first preservation attempt, which, while not a failure, had been less than perfectly successful. Mr. Wilker (who was exceedingly stiff with me, on account of our as-yet-unfinished confrontation) said the acidity of savannah snake blood differed from that of rock-wyrms, but thought he might adjust the process and achieve better results. And apart from the anatomical study of dragons, we had a great deal to learn about their behaviour and movement, which would require observation under conditions that did not involve Velloin shooting everything that moved.

We spent more time in the bush over the following two months than we did enjoying the comforts of Atuyem, which was exactly as I preferred. Mind you, I cannot pretend the environment of Bayembe is entirely pleasant: as in the previous volume of my memoirs, there is a great deal I am omitting regarding the heat, the dust, and the ever-present flies, whose buzzing I learned to hate beyond all reason. (One night a fly became trapped in our tent, and its aimless wandering in search of an exit brought me to the very end of my tether; only Natalie's intervention kept me from turning up the oil lamp and lighting the canvas on fire.) But on the whole, I find the hardships I suffer in warm climes vastly preferable to those of the cold—flies being the exception.

What pleased me was the understanding, for the first time in my life, that I was indeed a *naturalist*. Not the wife of a naturalist, brought along for her artistic and secretarial skills; not a hobbyist, collecting sparklings in her garden shed; but a scholar in my own right, engaging fully in my work. The tasks we set ourselves—to document the prey of savannah snakes, their breeding habits, their sexual differentiation, and so on—gave myself and Mr. Wilker sufficient distraction to pretend our unfortunate conversation had never occurred, and we fell into a rapport (at least for the purposes of our work) that was deeply and satisfyingly professional. I will not bore you with the minutiae of that work; anyone interested may refer to *Dragon Breeds of the Bayembe Region, Draconic Taxonomy Reconsidered,* or the articles eventually published in *Proceedings of the Philosophers' Colloquium* over the years following our expedition. As the second of those titles indicates, however, it was during my time in Eriga that I began to consider the question of what, precisely, constitutes a dragon.

At the time, of course, we were all still operating on Sir Richard Edgeworth's criteria, which were six in number:

1) Quadrupedalism
2) Wings capable of flight
3) A ruff or fan behind the skull
4) Bones frangible *post-mortem*
5) Egg laying
6) Extraordinary breath

Our voyage to Eriga had reminded me of the disputes over the great sea-snakes, which at the time constituted the main challenge to Edgeworth's model; I also thought about "draconic cousins" such as wolf-drakes, wyverns, and even my old sparklings. Furthermore, there were various theories regarding dragons in the Bayembe region, with some arguing for three breeds—savannah snakes, arboreal snakes, and swamp-wyrms—and others for as many as seven. (The latter came closer to the mark, though as it later turned out, for entirely the wrong reasons.) We could not see the swamp-wyrms without permission to visit Mouleen, but we applied ourselves to examining the distinctions between the grass-dwelling savannah snakes and tree-dwelling arboreal snakes, and found them to be entirely opportunistic: there is no meaningful difference between the two, beyond the simple matter of what territory each beast takes for its own.

Dry work to tell of, but it pleased me deeply—all the more so because it took me away from the strict and unfamiliar customs of Atuyem (of which the *agban* was only one), as it had previously taken me away from the strict and familiar customs of my own land. It was therefore a grave disappointment, as well as a cause for alarm, when Natalie fell ill.

I cannot say it was a *surprise*. Tropical diseases are legion, and we Scirlings are terribly susceptible to them. We all drank our gin and tonics as advised (I grew to like them, which of course made me a scandal when I drank them for pleasure back home), but one cannot haunt the bug-infested environs of watering holes without risking malaria.

We knew the signs to watch for. For Natalie to develop a headache was nothing of significance—we all suffered them, from the brutal strength of the sun and our appalling excuses for field pillows—but when she began to shiver, on a day when I was

having to exercise care lest the sweat dripping from my face mar
the page on which I sketched, there was no question as to the
cause. And Natalie, to her credit, did *not* attempt the foolishness I
have seen from others (men and women alike), which is to insist
that it was nothing, she could go on working, it would pass.
Malaria is nothing to trifle with, and we all knew it.

As soon as the porters we had hired could pack our camp, our
guide (a chatty Mebenye fellow named Welolo n Akpari Memu,
who knew the bush as well as I know my own library) led us to
the nearest village, where Natalie could rest in greater comfort.
That much, at least, went smoothly.

We ran into difficulty, however, when it came time to treat her
illness. I cannot fault the medical assistance she received; they
gave her water and herbs for the fever and the pain, which is all
we could expect from a small cattle-raising village in the Bayembe
bush. Erigans may be less vulnerable to such afflictions than
Scirlings and other foreigners, but their people still suffer malaria
often enough for it to be a familiar foe.

The assistance they offered, however, did not end at the
medical.

Natalie's treatment was being overseen by an old woman—the
oldest in the village, I think—whose name I never did get; they
only called her Grandmother. Between her rural accent and
missing teeth, I had difficulty understanding her speech, but I
soon picked a repeated word out of her explanation: *witchcraft*.

You will hear more of this later. For now, it will suffice to say
that there is a view common across Eriga which attributes most
or all trouble to the malevolent action of witches. These are not
necessarily the figures of intentional and blasphemous evil my

Anthiopean readers associate with the word; witchcraft can, as I understand it, be accidental, the result of ill will or unresolved conflict in someone's heart. Nor would Grandmother or her neighbours have claimed Natalie's problem consisted *solely* of witchcraft, and had nothing to do with our bizarre fondness for spending time in fever-ridden areas. But what sent us to such places, or weakened Natalie so that she fell ill? Witchcraft, clearly. And Grandmother, it transpired, wanted to bring a man from another village to treat Natalie's spiritual ills.

"Nonsense," Mr. Wilker said when I told him. "It won't do Miss Oscott one bit of good, and may upset her."

We were outside the house in which she rested, so she would not overhear our conversation. Beyond the edges of the small village, which hunkered down as if hoping the sun would cease beating on it so fiercely, the tree-spotted grass stretched forever. I felt very small and very insignificant: any one of us could cease breathing and this place would not care. "Grandmother believes she has one of the worse forms of malaria," I told him. "The sort that most frequently kills."

"Then we must get her back to Atuyem, if she can be moved. Sir Adam's doctor can treat her best."

This required us to time our journey very carefully. Most forms of malaria afflict the subject with periodic fevers (the interval of which is the primary means of distinguishing them), and during the respite the patient may be more capable of activity. That is not, however, the same thing as being well. Natalie suffered terrible joint pain, and this she *did* endure with admirable stoicism; she knew as well as we did that there would be no relief for her out in the bush. When her fever returned, we stopped until she could ride again. And so, by agonizing stages, we made our way back to Atuyem.

I expected our quarters there to have been given to another during our absence. (Those of you with good memories may recall we had been invited into the royal palace itself by the oba, supposedly because of his great interest in us; the man had ignored us completely since our arrival. There was every reason to think his interest had vanished.) To my surprise, they had not, and furthermore his own royal physician came with Dr. Garrett to examine Natalie and treat her. I was, in the meanwhile, given my own room, so that I might not have to share a bed with a sick woman.

Sir Adam, however, did not even do me the courtesy of allowing me a chance to sleep in that bed before he sent a message demanding my immediate presence at Point Miriam. I defied him long enough to bathe; you could have grown strawberries in the dirt caked on my skin. Then, wearing one of my non-bush dresses—which is to say, one of the only clean items of clothing I had left—I rode wearily down to Nsebu in answer to his summons.

Our resident ambassador had a fine office set up in one of the rooms, with heavy oak furniture totally at odds with their Yembe surroundings. The tired and therefore cynical part of me wondered if he had imported it so that he might plant his fists on the desk and loom at me across its polished surface in proper Scirling fashion.

"I have received," he said, biting each word off, "a letter from Lord Denbow."

My head was full of malaria and draconic taxonomy; it took longer than it should have to place the name. "Natalie's father."

"Yes. Miss Oscott's father. He is demanding I send his daughter home at once. Mrs. Camherst, what the devil have you done?"

"Nothing like you are thinking," I said, wishing desperately that I had ignored his summons until the following morning. A night of sleep would have been more precious than dragonbone, right then. "Unless you are thinking that I did as Miss Oscott wished, in which case you are correct."

Sir Adam slapped his hand atop his desk. "This is no subject for jokes, Mrs. Camherst. Lord Denbow is very angry."

I wondered how long ago his letter had arrived. Not that it mattered; Sir Adam would hardly be persuaded by the argument that leaving a baron to stew for a few more months would improve his temper. "Lord Denbow may be angry, but I will lay pebbles to iron that Lord Hilford is not. Or have you forgotten that the earl is our patron? He knows his granddaughter is here, and does not mind."

Acknowledging my sponsor's complicity may not have been my wisest move; I apologized to him for it later. It did no good in either case. Sir Adam launched into a diatribe about Lord Denbow, not Lord Hilford, being the legal guardian of Natalie Oscott, and furthermore the girl's own wishes not being of the slightest relevance. I suffered this in silence, but when he expanded his theme and brought up Natalie's illness, I lost my temper utterly.

"So you will blame me for her malaria? As others blame me for my husband's death—how very familiar. I cannot be permitted to make my own choices, as Natalie cannot either, but I am somehow to blame for the choices of others. What tremendous power I seem to have! But certain things are out of my hands, Sir Adam, and one of them is whether Natalie will even live to be *sent* home. I suggest you search your heart and find the decency to leave the matter of her disposition until *after* we know the answer to that question."

I had risen from my chair during this tirade, and by the look on Sir Adam's face, the last thing he had anticipated was for me to shout right back at him. (I think he expected me to break down crying—which only goes to show how little he understood this entire situation.) What he thought of the rest of my words I cannot say, but one part at least had clearly penetrated his mind, for he said, "Yes, well, everything of course depends on whether the girl recovers."

"Indeed," I said, mimicking the biting manner in which he had begun our meeting. "And if you should breathe even one word of this where she can hear, you and I will speak again." Whereupon I pivoted sharply and walked out of his office.

I must grant Sir Adam this: he had sufficient discretion that he had not said anything of Lord Denbow's letter prior to our return. (He would not want our internal troubles known among the Yembe.) He also was sufficiently chastened to leave the matter in peace during the weeks it took Natalie to overcome her malaria and regain a modicum of strength.

Before he had an opportunity to raise the matter again, someone else stepped in and, in the manner of one who takes a chessboard and flings its contents into the air, changed the game entirely.

TEN

The oba's interest—Ankumata's history—Legs of iron—
Royal greetings—Guard dragons—A mission to Mouleen—
The carrot and the stick

I said before that the oba of Bayembe had first invited us to the palace, then ignored us. I have never been a political creature, and so I can only guess at his motivation, but I believe he was testing our ostensible purpose in coming to his land. In short, he brought us under his eye, then left us to our own devices, in order to see what we would do.

The Scirlings who visited Bayembe came for a very narrow list of reasons. First there were the merchants, trading through the port of Nsebu even before it was established as a Scirling colony. After them came the diplomats, to represent our interest in Erigan iron, and they made arrangements for the soldiers (who equipped and trained the Yembe with Anthiopean guns against the Satalu and Ikwunde) and the engineers (who would build railways and dams, from which Scirland would subsequently profit). Beyond them were a handful of sheluhim and hunters like Velloin, and very few others.

My little group was therefore an aberration—and one that, as I came to understand, held particular interest for the oba. When it became apparent that Natalie would live, but while she was still recovering in her bed, he sent messengers to summon myself and Mr. Wilker to meet him at last.

This summons put a nervous chill in my heart. Given his previous neglect, I could only assume Sir Adam had spoken to him, and he was going to order Natalie at a minimum and possibly all three of us out of the country, lest Lord Denbow speak out in the Synedrion and cause diplomatic trouble. If he did, I could not think of a single thing I might say that would retrieve the situation.

Good grooming was unlikely to sway him, but I attended to my toilet with the finest care I could manage—much finer than I had ever troubled with before. (My Season does not count; Mama and the maids took care of it then.) Then, my heart fluttering with nervousness, I went to meet the ruler of Bayembe, in a courtyard before the golden tower of Atuyem.

Given the man in question, I must provide a certain amount of context first. Ankumata n Rumeme Gbori has been the subject of so much mythologizing during the course of his life that I feel it necessary to set the record something closer to straight before I proceed with any account of my dealings with him.

It is true that he was born to his father's fourth wife (putting him out of what was then the royal lineage), and that he was born deformed. The exact medical nature of his deformity I do not know, but it left his legs unable to bear his weight; though healthy in other respects, he was not able to walk until well into his childhood. Some sources claim he was seven when this changed, and others ten. The exact number does not matter.

What matters is that his mother died, and there is credible evidence to say that she was murdered by one of her co-wives. Ankumata would likely have died, too, except that a man of his father's court took him and raised him away from Atuyem, as his own son. And this man happened to be a blacksmith.

I cannot adequately convey the importance of that to a non-Erigan audience. For my Scirling readers, blacksmiths are a feature of village life: strong men, but not expected to be particularly bright. Their reputation in Eriga, and particularly in the eastern part of the continent, is a good deal more impressive. More than a few peoples there trace their origins back to a legendary blacksmith-king, and many more attribute magical powers to men who work in iron. It is part of the reverence they give in general to artisans, but it goes beyond that. An ethnologist could theorize for you whether this has something to do with the abundance of iron in Erigan soil, or whether it arises from some other aspect of Erigan existence; I can only report the fact of it. For Ankumata's subjects, it was as if he had been taken to be raised by a particularly wise magister, the sort who knows the secret of bringing golems to life.

And that is nearly what this blacksmith did. When Sunda n Halelu Gama took Ankumata into his home, the boy still could not walk; he rode there on his rescuer's back. But once there, Sunda—who, in the more dramatic version of this tale, is said to be Adu himself, the Yembe god of blacksmithing—set about crafting for him a set of iron leg braces that would do what the boy's own muscles and bones could not. So wondrously did he craft them, the story goes, that they weighed nothing at all, and no sooner did Ankumata don them than he leapt over the blacksmith's house to show his joy.

The truth is rather more prosaic, I am sure, for I never saw the oba leap any distance at all. But the braces do exist, and I believe he could not walk without them, which means Sunda deserves every bit of the credit he receives. He, perhaps more than any other save Ankumata's own father and mother, made the man who came back and claimed the rulership of Bayembe (a tale in its own right), and held it for so many years.

And what of the man himself? I found his age hard to judge; history told me he was fifty or thereabouts, though (as I have said) mythologizing has obscured some of the finer points of his life. He was broad of feature, as Yembe often are, and I think his shaved head was a disguise for natural hair loss (a bald scalp being more regal than a patchy one). He gave a sense of being both shrewd and good-hearted, which is an impressive combination, and not one many people of either sex can easily convey.

He greeted us sitting on a stool that made up in splendor for the deliberately simple appearance of his braces. The stool, as some may know, is an element of Sagao regalia adopted by the Yembe from their riverine subjects centuries ago, and although it is often likened to an Anthiopean throne, the truth is that its significance more closely parallels that of the crown. Yembe rulers are invested in their office by being seated upon the stool—and not just the oba, but the lineage chiefs as well, each with their own ancestral stool. This one was of sufficient size that I might have called it a bench instead, and moreover was crafted of solid gold, but it had its origins in the smaller and more humble wooden stool found in every home in the region.

Beyond that, much of the scene was a common one. I have, at this point in my life, met enough heads of state to know they are

almost always seated in some kind of frame—before a tapestry or painting or coat of arms, atop a dais, or, in this case, beneath a splendid awning—and surrounded by ministers, servants, and assorted hangers-on. How else is one to know that they are important? His wives were there, and various youths bearing enough resemblance to one of those women or to the oba himself for me to guess them to be his children; the olori Denyu n Kpama Waleyim and her son Okweme were in the group, and I was not glad to see them.

Nor was I glad to see Sir Adam and several of the army men. To my heightened nerves, this seemed like proof that we were all to be ordered back to Scirland. (The truly irrational part of me tried to combine this with one of my other problems, and invent a scenario in which Natalie and Mr. Wilker would be sent back, but I would be forced to marry Okweme.) But they could not command my attention now; it must all go to the oba of Bayembe.

A court functionary had instructed me beforehand that I would be permitted to show respect in the Scirling way (by curtseying) rather than the Erigan way (by kneeling and, before a personage as august as the oba, lowering my face to the ground). I have never been especially graceful at curtseying, and my knees have a regrettable tendency to go tremulous and unreliable when I am nervous; I almost wished they would let me kneel instead. It is difficult to fall over when one is already on the ground. But it might have looked a mockery if I tried, and so curtseying it was, with Mr. Wilker bowing at my side.

Our progress was marked by sonorous words from the *griot* at the oba's side. These learned men and women are sometimes called bards, but more often we use the Thiessin word, which serves as a synonym for a full dozen terms in different Erigan languages. I might equally use a dozen terms to describe them in Scirling: historians, storytellers, poets, musicians, praise-singers, and more. They are attached to aristocratic and royal families, and are often aristocrats in their own right, with all the power and wealth that implies.

I could not make out what the *griot* was saying; he spoke in the highly stylized form of Yembe used for his work, which bears as much resemblance to ordinary Yembe as Akhian or Yelangese calligraphy does to ordinary text, and is even less comprehensible to me. (Calligraphy at least will sit still and give you a chance to puzzle it out.) Knowing what I do now of their customs, however, I expect the bulk of it was a recitation of the oba's praise-names, his ancestors, his ancestors' praise-names, and other things meant to impress us with our insignificance in comparison to him.

One of those praise-names, rendered into English, is "he whose legs are made of iron"—or "Iron-legs," I suppose, though that lacks elegance, sounding more like the nickname sailors might give to a particularly salty captain. Certainly the braces, at least in their most recent iteration, deserved a degree of elegance. Gold had been inlaid along their sides in the characteristically geometric patterns of Yembe art, for it would not do to clothe the country's ruler in anything ordinary. But no effort had been made to gild the steel completely; to do so would defeat the purpose. Nor did he wear the lower-body wrap affected by many in his court that might have concealed the braces. Instead he wore an elaborate loincloth, for Ankumata n Rumeme Gbori understood the role of his own infirmity and its cure in his legend, and used them to his advantage.

This was a man who had taken weakness and made it strength. If you understand only one thing about him, that would be enough.

We minced our way through the opening formalities and the inquiries into Natalie's health. I half-expected this to lead into Sir Adam's demands, but no; the ambassador stayed silent (looking, if truth be told, a trifle bored), and the oba said nothing of Lord Denbow.

Instead he waved back the youth cooling him with a large fan and stood. I heard a quiet hiss as he did so: the braces contained cunningly engineered hydraulics. In a mild voice that did not obscure the weight of command, he said to myself and Mr. Wilker, "You will walk with me."

"Yes, *chele,*" we chorused. I suppose I might render the word as "Your Majesty," since an oba is the sovereign ruler of his nation (though in a different manner than a Scirling king); this, however, would obscure its derivation from *eche,* the Yembe word for "gold." Polite address for the oba meant something closer to "Golden One."

To my startlement, the invitation appeared to extend only as far as the two of us and his *griot.* By subtle signals Ankumata indicated to his wives and his servants that they would stay behind; the servants were less subtle in communicating this to our fellow Scirlings. Sir Adam's protest faded behind me as we followed the oba through a shadowed archway into a garden— the same garden in which I had walked with Galinke a few months before.

The oba walked slowly, though how much of that was his braces and how much the dignity of his rank, I cannot say. After we were well through the arch and out of earshot of the others (though not out of bow or rifle shot from the guards on the high walls), he addressed Mr. Wilker. "You have studied dragons. What have you learned?"

Unlike the boyar of Drustanev, who had once asked a similar question of Lord Hilford, Ankumata seemed genuinely interested in the answer. Mr. Wilker collected his thoughts and delivered a good précis of our findings thus far, adding—unwisely, from the perspective of my still-twitching nerves—the regretful coda that "Miss Oscott's illness forced us to suspend our work for the time being."

The oba nodded. Then, without warning, he spoke to me. "You have a desire to study the dragons of the swamp."

My heart gave a great thump in my chest. It was not precisely a secret, but I had only spoken of it to a very small number of people, and did not like the reminder of how easily gossip spread. But I could hardly lie to the man, and so I said, "Yes, *chele*. There is more we could learn about the dragons here—there will be more for years to come, I imagine—but comparison is useful; we might in some ways learn more about savannah snakes and other breeds by looking at Moulish swamp-wyrms than by studying the others alone."

We had reached the end of the garden, where a staircase led up the wall. One hissing, mechanical step at a time, Ankumata climbed; we followed, though not before exchanging a look of puzzlement.

At the top, with the guards standing respectfully aside, the oba gestured downward. "I have captured savannah snakes. But only their breath is of use; they cannot run with chains on, and if I remove the chains they escape."

I found myself looking down into a dry, sandy moat, at the

bottom of which two discontented dragons paced at the ends of their iron tethers. "You use them as guards?" I said.

"They impress people," the oba said. "They are not useful." He took a piece of dried meat from his *griot*'s hand and threw it to the sand below, where one of the snakes looked at it with resignation. (They will eat carrion, but prefer their meals to be juicy and running away.)

Offering advice to the sovereign of a country is a touchy affair, but his silence seemed to invite my thoughts. Cautiously, I said, "Were these captured as juveniles, or adults?" He indicated it was the former, and I rubbed one finger across my chin. "Hmmm. Perhaps if you raised them from the egg . . . some birds will imprint on the creature they see first. I do not know if it is the case with dragons."

Ankumata smiled. It should have been encouraging—a sign that I had not offended him. His expression, though, was not exactly one of pleasure; if anything, I would call it *satisfaction*. As if I had played into his hands.

He said, "You will go into Mouleen and get me swamp-wyrm eggs."

"I beg your pardon?" I said, echoed closely by Mr. Wilker.

"We have tried raising savannah snakes from eggs. It does not work. But the Mouri, the farmers on the edges of the forest, say the Moulish raise their dragons from eggs, and this is why swamp-wyrms eat anyone who tries to go into the swamp. You will bring me eggs, so that I may try it myself."

As royal orders went, this was a tall one. "*Chele* . . . who is to say *we* will not be eaten by the dragons? Or fall prey to disease, or to the Moulish. I am told they kill anyone who comes into their forest."

He dismissed this with a flick of his hand. "The forest kills people, not the Moulish. They dislike hunters, but you are different. And I will send Faj Rawango with you."

I had not forgotten the messenger who came to collect us on the docks. A short man, compared to the Yembe, and more ruddy of skin, nor was his name a Yembe one. He was Moulish? I briefly damned Yves de Maucheret for spending all his words on tall tales of the Green Hell, and none on describing that place's inhabitants.

Even with a guide, however, our survival was far from assured. Our success was even more so. "If you will pardon me for saying so, *chele,* your kingdom's climate is very different from that of Mouleen. I doubt whether any hatchlings would thrive here. And even if they did, this is quite a lot of work simply for a few palace guard dragons—" I stopped, my words cut short by understanding.

An understanding which, as it so often does, trotted out of my mouth without asking leave of my brain. "Ah. It isn't your palace you intend to guard, or not only. You are hoping to use them against the Ikwunde. Or the Satalu."

The oba's face hardened. In conversation with a sovereign, or anyone else of power, it is not generally advisable to say what they have chosen to keep unspoken, especially when it pertains to matters of state. But after a pause, he laughed: a long, hearty chuckle that called an involuntary smile from me. "You see? I am not wrong to send you. Your mind is sharp; you see things well."

I was also an outsider, not only to the Moulish, but to the Yembe. Such a person might die, and it would be no great loss to his nation.

Mr. Wilker and I exchanged looks. On the one hand, it was a

research opportunity, and one we both desired; nor were the physical risks appreciably worse than they would have been without the oba's involvement. On the other hand, it placed a burden on us, one we might not be able to fulfill. What if he was wrong about Moulish control of the dragons? Or what if they did indeed tame them, but we were not able to learn how? The warmth of our reception when we emerged from the Green Hell might depend heavily on what we brought with us.

I wondered how useful the eggs could possibly be. No large species of dragon reaches maturity in less than two years, and some take longer. Did Ankumata expect to still be at war two years from now? With enemies on both sides, I supposed he might. And even if he were not, it would be no bad thing to improve his country's ability to defend itself. I doubted this man, heir to centuries of Bayembe sovereignty, enjoyed his present dependence on Scirland.

Carefully, Mr. Wilker said, "What if we decline?"

One dark, gold-ringed hand waved this question away. "Is this not something you want? And your assistant, the young woman. You would want her with you, of course, once her strength returns."

This time I kept my thoughts behind my teeth. It was bribery, or perhaps I might more charitably call it payment: if we agreed, then he would block Sir Adam's attempts to claim Natalie. "But if we do not go . . ."

"Then I imagine the girl's father will retrieve her. Your ambassador says he is an important lord. I would not want to offend him."

First the carrot; now the stick. If we did *not* agree, Ankumata would do nothing to stop Sir Adam. It might even go further than that: if I protested or caused too much trouble, I might find myself evicted from the country as well.

"Might we have time to consider your generous offer?" Mr. Wilker said. "We would have to speak with Miss Oscott before we could make any decision."

"Of course, of course. Such choices should not be made rashly."

We descended the stairs. I saw Galinke in a far corner of the garden; she sat with three other women, but I knew from the angle of her head that she had been watching us on the wall. It confirmed my suspicion that her interest in me had not been entirely casual, and that her royal brother knew some of what we had discussed. Which operated to my benefit, at least in part; whether I would thank her for it or not remained to be seen.

ELEVEN

A nice idea—Consulting Natalie—Companions in my madness—
More preparations—The long rainy season

There was no privacy to be had in the palace. Mr. Wilker and I went into the lower town, ostensibly to visit the market, but in truth to talk away from interested ears.

"You are going to tell me I should not have brought Natalie," I said with a sigh after we had cleared the gate at the base of the hill.

Mr. Wilker shook his head, looking resigned. "That ship sailed from Sennsmouth months ago—and if it were not Miss Oscott, it would be something else. He did not quickly volunteer the threat, but he wanted and expected us to press for it."

"If I had enemies on my borders and allies only too eager to take advantage of my weakness, I suppose that I too might be ruthless in my use of tools." I sighed again. "Empathy, however, does not make the tool any happier about her use."

We entered the market. It was not the chaos of dockside Nsebu; this was laid out in an orderly fashion, though not the grid of streets common in many Anthiopean cities. The merchants and artisans organized themselves instead by lineage, each of which formed round clusters through which Mr. Wilker and myself wound. On all sides we were besieged by vocal and determined hawkers, selling everything from copper pots to religious charms.

Under the cover of this clamour, Mr. Wilker said, "What do you think?"

I shared with him my wall-top evaluation of the risks, and concluded by saying, "I won't deny that I've been trying to think of how we might convince the oba to allow us into Mouleen. I thought I might approach him through Galinke, his sister. To become involved in the affairs of Bayembe, though . . . not to mention that it may not be fair to the dragons. They did not ask to participate in this war."

Mr. Wilker's laughter briefly lightened the concern that weighted his expression. "I might have guessed you would fear for the dragons' well-being." Sobering, he went on. "It's a nice idea, conducting our work without getting tangled in local affairs. Maybe in twenty or fifty years it would be possible. But we chose to come here now, and having done so, I don't think we can escape politics."

We were talking ourselves into accepting. I wanted to see the swamp-wyrms of Mouleen; I had wanted to see them since I saw that runt in the king's menagerie. They were ugly beasts, and not known for their charming personalities—but they were dragons, and that meant I loved them.

I could not in good conscience make that decision, however, without first taking a certain precaution. "We shall have to talk to Natalie. Whether the oba would have found another lever or not, she is the lever he has chosen to use, and I imagine she will have an opinion on the matter."

At the beginning of our journey, I had thrown some sharp words in Mr. Wilker's direction regarding the validity of Natalie's wishes. Now their effect, and that of our trio's months of partnership, began to show. He nodded, with no hint of surprise or reluctance. "Indeed. Malaria may have dulled her taste for adventure—but if not, then I think we know our course."

Malaria had not, in fact, dulled Natalie's taste for adventure. "I knew it was a risk when I came here," she said cheerfully, despite the pallor that had overtaken her in the aftermath of the fever. "Pity it isn't one of those diseases where, after you've had it, you never need fear it again. But what is this you say about Mouleen?"

I explained the oba's requirements to her, and his halfheartedly veiled threat. She made a face. "I shan't ask you to go into the swamp for me. If my impending deportation is the only thing making you consider it, then don't worry about me; I'll find some other way to deal with my family. Hide behind Grandpapa's skirts, perhaps, or run away to join the circus."

She spoke lightly, but I could see that she meant it. Her resolve comforted me. It is one thing to decide that you are willing to risk leeches and fever; it is another entirely to drag someone else along with you.

What showed on my face in that moment, I do not know, but Natalie's smile faded and she reached out to take my hand. "Isabella, what is it?"

I could feel my answering smile waver. "Only reflecting on how fortunate I am, that I should not be alone in my madness."

It sounds like a platitude, but it is the honest truth. I found myself nearly overwhelmed with gratitude more than once over the subsequent days, as we prepared for our descent into the Green Hell. I was grateful for Natalie's companionship and enthusiasm; for Mr. Wilker's reliability and professional cooperation; for Lord Hilford, my patron, whose money made my presence in Bayembe possible; for Faj Rawango, without whom this escapade would have stood at best a minuscule chance of success. I was even grateful to Ankumata. Undoubtedly he was using us for his own ends—but he had also permitted us into his country, provided us with quarters in his own palace, and given us both the permission and the guide that made the next stage of our research possible.

The preparations were extensive, and unlike any I had made before. On our previous trips into the bush, we had been able to bring pack animals for our gear, but Faj Rawango warned us that horses, donkeys, and mules all tended to sicken in the swamp. Our supplies must be minimal, or we would find ourselves overburdened when the animals died.

The economies we made, however, were in peculiar places. Two tents (very small) and a minimum of clothing, but seemingly endless quantities of gin and tonic water, which would be our main protection against not only malaria but the parasitic infestations caused by foul water. (On no trip before or since have I carried more alcohol than undergarments.)

We also agreed, in a hurried conversation, to bring with us not only our chemical materials, but also the preserved bones we had gathered. Leaving them anywhere in Atuyem was not feasible; someone would be sure to find them. Destroying them would have been difficult, as the main feature of preserved dragonbone is its remarkable durability. If they became too burdensome to carry—in bulk, not mass, as savannah snake bones were even lighter than those of rock-wyrms—then we would bury them, with the hope of retrieving them later, but until then we would keep them under our watch.

One of the necessary tasks has become an oddly routine part of my life over the decades. I wrote letters to Lord Hilford, my parents, my brother Andrew, and my brother-in-law Matthew Camherst, explaining the alteration in our plans, with the unspoken understanding that this might be the last communication they received from me. Certainly it would be the last for a while; there was no postal service in the swamp, and even these letters would not go out until the next Scirling steamer came into port. I did not have to lay out instructions for what should be done if I perished—that, I had taken care of before my departure—but the implication whispered ominously between every line. I was only grateful that I would not be within my mother's reach when she read her letter.

Even that missive, however, was easier to write than the one to my son. I was painfully aware, with each line I scribed, that it might be the last he would ever hear from me. That had been the case with each letter, of course, but I felt it now more keenly than before. His brief note took me longer than all the others put together.

It was Seminis before we were ready to go. The calendar used in Bayembe, of course, is not the common Anthiopean one, and most of my Anthiopean readers will have no sense of what that means for the region. I will therefore make clear the significance, so that you may all appreciate our folly:

The long rainy season had begun.

At first the change was refreshing. Bayembe had been parched since our arrival; it was a positive delight to breathe air washed clean of dust, to see flowers bloom and gold things turn green. But the humidity in that season is dreadful—it is true what they say, that dry heat is more tolerable than wet—and, as you may recall, we were about to descend into a region known for its abundant rainfall.

Faj Rawango warned us. But he was a servant of the oba, and the oba wanted us to go; he did not warn us very strenuously. We, for our own part, were fools. None of us had experienced a rainy season in Eriga, let alone in the swamps of Mouleen, and Yves de Maucheret, the great Thiessois traveller whose writings were one of our only sources regarding the Green Hell, had not said much about the rain. We shrugged off Faj Rawango's warnings, loaded our pack donkeys (with a twinge of conscience for the fate to which we were about to subject them), and bade farewell—though we did not know it—to our last dry moments for a long, long time.

PART THREE

In which we suffer many privations
for the sake of our research, and
risk death by a variety of routes

TWELVE

An introduction to the swamp—The drakefly—
Moulish notions of property—Five visitors—We are tested

Words, I fear, will again fail me as I attempt to describe the environment into which we now entered. But words are what I have, along with my humble line drawings, and so I must employ my tools as best I can. For it is important that you have a clear sense in your mind of the world I inhabited for the better part of the next seven months, and keep it always in your thoughts as you read of the events that transpired there.

The first thing and the last, the thing that was there at dawn and still with me at dusk and present all through the day and the night, the thing that, it seemed, could not be escaped for even the briefest moment, was the heat. Even for a creature such as I, who passionately favors warmth over cold, it was oppressive and often foul. The high plateau that makes up much of Bayembe is arid and windy; these factors mitigate the tropical heat. But in the airless, low-lying swamp so aptly called the Green Hell, there was no such happy aid. In a region that humid, sweating brings no relief, for the air is as wet as your skin. You drip with sweat; it pours from your body; if you wipe it away then more comes to replace it in mere seconds, and all you achieve is to dehydrate yourself. So you endure the sweat, long past the point where you would give your left arm for a cool bath, and this becomes your new reality, until you cannot remember what it felt like to be dry, let alone cold.

I learned to survive it. I cannot tell you how. It is a trick of the mind, one I chanced upon when I reached my absolute limit of endurance and knew there was nothing I could do to relieve my state. Somehow I accepted the situation; I acknowledged it, then laid it to one side and went on with my work. I was still filthy with sweat and longed for a cool breeze, but these things no longer consumed my thoughts. (Natalie and Mr. Wilker, I presume, must have made their own peace with the heat, for neither of them ran mad with a shotgun or tore off their clothes in a futile quest to lessen their suffering.)

Other matters, however, could not be disposed of through tricks of the mind.

After the heat, there are the insects. Gnats, mosquitoes, dragonflies, butterflies, black flies, beetles, moths. Ants and spiders; my temperate-dwelling readers cannot *imagine* the spiders. They are every size, from too small to see to larger than my outstretched hand, and some of them are quite viciously poisonous. Others will lay their eggs below your skin, with predictable and gruesome consequences. The ants, at least, have the courtesy to advertise their hazard; there are some, fully three centimeters in length, that are the most amazing shade of electrical blue. They warn you, very clearly, that you will not be happy if you provoke their bite.

So your skin crawls not only with sweat but with insects and their effects. In the meanwhile, you stab yourself with thorns and spines if you are so careless as to lay your hand upon a tree; and you *will* lay your hand, because you will lose your balance on the rough ground, or slip in mud, or tangle your foot with an unseen branch or root. The wounds inflicted by flora and fauna alike risk infection, plus even the slightest hint of blood (and yes, my female readers will be thinking now of the occurrence that sent Natalie and myself to the *agban*) brings all manner of creepy-crawlies flocking to gorge themselves upon it. Leeches are not even the worst; I came to be quite sanguine about leeches, if I may be forgiven the dreadful pun. Once you overcome your disgust, it is easy to pull them off and cast them away—and this I did more times than I can count.

But not all the denizens of the forest are unpleasant. Such an environment teems with life not only on the small scale but the large: guenons and mangabeys and colobus monkeys, gorillas and chimpanzees, bongos and duiker and okapi, pygmy hippopotami and forest elephants and night vipers and more birds than a hundred naturalists could hope to catalogue in a year.

And, of course, dragons—but I will come to them in time.

Amidst this panoply of life, humans are not easy to find. Had I given in to the impulse I entertained from time to time and gone blundering into the Green Hell without proper guidance—and if I had, through divine Providence or sheer blind luck, managed to survive a month, which I doubt—I still might never have found the Moulish. There are fewer than ten thousand of them in an area more than fifty thousand kilometers square, and they shift camp regularly; it is like looking for a migratory needle in a haystack the likes of which you have never explored.

With Faj Rawango guiding us, we still could not find the Moulish. We could, however, go to a place where *they* might find *us*.

After leaving Atuyem, we traveled along the Bayembe border a hundred kilometers or so inland, keeping to the savannah, where our progress was easier. But we drew steadily closer to the broken land that fell from the plateau into the swamp, and the Green Hell loomed ever larger to my left; I stared frequently at it while we rode, even to the point of neglecting my other observations. Was it my imagination that supplied a distant sound of drumbeats? That emerald sea seemed an abyss to me, full of dragons and fevers, from which I might never emerge. Perhaps the sound I heard was only the pounding of my own heart.

But I had committed to this purpose. When at last we came to the region Faj Rawango sought, we bade farewell to the landscape that had been our home these four months, and which had grown almost comfortably familiar, and addressed ourselves to the forest below.

Our descent from the plateau was swift, but we were still some way above the swamp floor when we came upon a clearing. It had obviously been hacked out of the jungle more than once, but as swiftly as men cut the vegetation away, it grew back. "It is a place of trade," Faj Rawango said when we asked. "We—the villagers bring their harvest here, and the Moulish bring meat and ivory."

"How long will it be until they come?" Mr. Wilker asked.

Faj Rawango only shrugged. They would come when they came. It was not a formal market, to be held every four days.

We set up our tents. There is a hazard to having a party with multiple naturalists in it; we occasionally shirk our camp chores in our rush to observe the world around us. (I fear Mr. Wilker and I left Natalie to do much of that work herself.) Myself, I became distracted with only two tent pegs in the ground, because a buzzing, fluttering sound drew my eye to the trees.

The creature I observed was birdlike but, with my recent taxonomical efforts fresh in my mind, I hesitated to classify it as such. In size it was comparable to a bird, with feathers of a luminescent blue-green, and a drooping bifurcated tail. Its head, however, was distinctly draconic, with a muzzle in place of a beak.

I had only a moment to observe it; then it spread its wings to fly across the clearing, and I saw the reason for the buzzing sound.

Like a dragonfly, it had *two* long pairs of wings.

I exclaimed in delight, and then had to explain the cause to my companions, who had not seen the creature. Natalie is the one who coined the term "drakefly," on account of their insectoid wing configuration; Mr. Wilker objected to it, as the animals were clearly not insects of any sort, but it is the common designation even today.

We were still arguing this point the next morning, when Faj Rawango returned from the forest around our camp. His appearance stopped us short, and set both Natalie and myself to blushing, for he had discarded the wrapped garment of the Yembe, and in its place wore nothing more than the briefest of loincloths, held on his hips by a thin cord.

Dressed that way—I might better term it "undressed"—he seemed an entirely different man. With his Yembe trappings shed, those details which marked him as separate could no longer be overlooked: the smaller stature, the reddish cast to his skin, the leaner facial structure. He did not look like the other peoples who had surrounded us since our arrival.

Mr. Wilker broke the silence first, clearing his throat. "The

iron knives we brought. We'll be bargaining with those for their assistance?"

Faj Rawango shook his head. "No bargain. We will give them the knives. They will help us."

It sounded like sophistry, but he appeared to believe there was a genuine difference. "Why would they help us," I asked, "if not in trade? Is there something else we will be offering?"

He squatted down near us and picked up the pot that had contained our morning porridge. He had, I think, spent his time out in the forest not only changing his apparel, but considering how to explain the situation to us. "This," he said, holding up the pot, "isn't yours anymore. Not *only* yours. It belongs to the camp. Everything you have, you'll share. And they'll share with you. This is how they do things. It's how they survive."

I quote him as exactly as I can; if his meaning is not clear, that is because the kind of society he described is foreign beyond the ability of mere words to explain, at least for all who are likely to read this account. The Moulish have few material possessions, and little concern for personal property as most of us see it. Their way of living neither permits it nor derives much benefit from it. To own more than you can carry is folly; you will have to abandon it when the camp moves. But most of the things you own—if the "you" in this instance is Moulish—are easily replaced anyway, so their abandonment is no great loss. To try and hoard more than those around you have is a grave insult to social harmony and, I think, to the spirits; it invites ridicule from your fellows and, if that fails, more aggressive methods of forcing you to share. From this the Moulish get their reputation as thieves, but that word belongs to a different world.

Faj Rawango explained it as best he could, but we had little basis on which to understand him; and besides which, he was not Moulish—not precisely.

"My father came from the forest," he said, when Natalie pressed him for his story. "My mother was a villager in Obichuri. I went into the forest for a time when I was a boy, but came back and studied, and went to Atuyem."

He was an intensely private man; it took us months to expand that brief summary into something more like a story, one fleeting detail at a time. I will share the whole of it now, though—as much of it as I ever learned.

His mother had belonged to one of the Sagao lineages whose traditional role is that of the *griot*. To this day, I cannot tell you that lineage's name; Faj Rawango never shared it. Despite the matrilineal nature of Sagao society, he was not welcomed by his mother's people—likely out of distaste for his Moulish blood— and so he did not claim kinship to them. It was, I think, this same estrangement that sent him into the forest. But he declined to stay there, and upon returning to Bayembe, laid claim to the education that was his right. It did not suffice to make him a *griot,* but it won him a place in the civil service, and thus he came to us.

What lineage did his mother's family serve? Not the royal one, that much I knew. How did he end up with his name? It was neither Sagao nor Moulish; I found out much later that it came from the Mouri, the people dwelling at the northern edge of the forest, who are close kin to the Moulish. I had only fragments of story, never the full tale. He was a man who did not properly exist in any single world, but he seemed to have found a place between them, and that, more than his past, was who he was.

This, of course, is the judgment of later years. At the time, those fragments made my curiosity itch like mad. We thought we had discovered more, though, the day that a group of five Moulish—two men, one old woman, and two male youths—showed up in our clearing.

We heard them coming well in advance of their appearance. It is no advantage to be silent when traveling in the Green Hell; animals will attack silent creatures. The Moulish sing and stomp as they go, making themselves sound a far larger party than they are, to scare off beasts that might otherwise trouble them. We were therefore ready when they emerged from the trees.

All were dressed in the manner of Faj Rawango, in brief strips of barkcloth hung from their hips, and (apart from the occasional ornament) nothing more. The old woman was bare-breasted like the men—a sight that startled me a great deal at first, but soon became routine. (Nudity, I find, rapidly becomes boring when it is not treated as scandalous.) They looked at us with open curiosity, and listened with interest as Faj Rawango explained our purpose there.

Philologists say that there used to be a Moulish language unrelated to the Sachimbi family, that today only survives in some of their songs and chants. It was fortunate for our purposes, though perhaps tragic in other ways, that it has since been replaced with a language derived, through the Mouri villagers, from Yembe and other Sachimbi tongues native to the region. Because of this, while I had difficulty understanding Faj Rawango, the task of learning this new language was akin to learning Chiavoran when one has studied Thiessois. I could, by extrapolating from that common foundation, expand my vocabulary with good speed, although grammar took more time. For one such as I, with average skill at best on that front, this was a vital advantage.

I was therefore able to determine that Faj Rawango greeted the two adult men as "Brother," and the old woman as "Mother." "I thought he said his mother was a villager," Natalie whispered to me, confused.

"It may just be a title of respect," I whispered back. "The men, though . . . Mr. Wilker, can you understand him? It sounds like he's actually claiming to be their relative."

Mr. Wilker waved me to silence, the better to listen in, then nodded. "That's why he wants to join them in their camp. Because he's their brother. Half brothers, perhaps? They don't look much alike."

Indeed they did not, beyond the simplest resemblance arising from their shared heritage. Faj Rawango gestured at our camp, and as if that were a signal, one of the men and both of the youths began to prowl around, examining our tents and equipment. One of the boys approached the three of us and asked a question I could not understand.

"Your names," Faj Rawango said. We obediently gave them, which led to much merriment on all sides; the Moulish had great difficulty pronouncing them, as we did we with theirs. The old woman was Apuesiso; the men were Natchekavu and Eguamiche; the youths were Kisamilewa and Walakpara.

It was Kisamilewa who had approached us, and his attention soon alighted on the notebook I held. He extended one hand for it, in a manner that struck me as peremptory; but, mindful of Faj Rawango's comments on property, I handed it over. Not without misgivings: it was a fresh book, not the one in which I had recorded my savannah observations, but it did have my sketch of and notes on the drakefly, as well as sundry less memorable creatures. I did not want to lose them.

And lose them I did. Kisamilewa smiled broadly and walked off, notebook still in hand. (I did not regain it until nearly a month later.) It was, of course, a test: would we share as we were expected to? My notebook was not the only thing the Moulish claimed that day. Much of it, I realized in time, was not even "sharing" by their own standards; they pushed as far as they could think to go, beyond the boundaries of their usual sense of propriety. We were strangers to them, more so even than the "villagers" (a category encompassing not only Mouri, but every Erigan who is not Moulish), and it was necessary to see what we would do.

We handed over pots and pans, notebooks and compasses, an entire crate of gin. (A drink they returned as soon as they tried it; the taste was not at all to their liking.) I began to wonder where it would end, and no sooner had the thought but found my answer: Walakpara pointed at my blouse.

I almost did it. The heat was intense—I understood why the Moulish wore so little clothing—and I had been insisting to myself so vehemently that I must cooperate that I almost began to undo my buttons. Mr. Wilker's gaping stare stopped me, though, as did the understanding that I would be eaten alive by insects if I stripped. (And although I had an undershirt beneath the blouse, would they not ask for that next? Would it end before I was naked?)

"I'm afraid not," I said firmly, in Yembe, and vowed to take the consequences.

My refusal was met, not with anger, but with laughter. Apuesiso said something to the boys; it had the sound of calling them off from the hunt. My blouse stayed on; some of our belongings were restored; and so we packed up and went to join their camp.

THIRTEEN

Entering the Green Hell—Moulish society—
Hunting and other tasks of daily life—Geguem—Trousers—We go deeper

Faj Rawango had given us other warnings on the ride to that clearing, chief among which was to show no fear of the forest. The villagers fear it—with good reason; they do not know how to survive in it—and the Moulish scorn them for this; to show fear, therefore, is to mark oneself as a villager, and not welcome.

Is the swamp frightening? In some ways, yes. I have mentioned the great variety of creatures that live within it; what I have not yet said is that they are invisible to the untrained eye. You hear them on all sides, but the dense growth conceals them, sometimes even when they are scarcely two meters away. It is also as near to trackless as makes no difference. The clearing in which we had camped persists only because the nearby villagers maintain it; Moulish camps vanish almost as soon as their inhabitants depart. I never did acquire the skill by which they find their way, and so following our quintet of guides felt like plunging into an abyss from which I might never return. I had been far from home before, but never had I felt so strongly that I was in a different world entirely. I could only trust to those around me, and hope it would be enough.

Contrary to some of the more foolish reports that have been made about my time in the Green Hell, facing the swamp with courage does not make one an "honorary member of the tribe." It may suffice to win acceptance in a camp, and from time to time I did wonder whether the Moulish around me recalled any note-worthy difference between us, apart from my childlike incompetence with various tasks. ("Childlike" is a generous term. I might better be compared to the victim of a head injury. Moulish children are astonishingly competent, on account of not being coddled, as offspring in Scirling society are.) But the basic assumptions of life in the swamp are not those of life outside it, and although I reached the point of being able to navigate them with a degree of ease, they never became habit, much less un-thinking reflex. I misstepped time and time again, and was toler-ated only because of my willingness to learn from my mistakes.

As an example of this: when we came to the Moulish camp, perhaps two hours' walk from our clearing, I assumed we would be taken before some kind of chief or headman. It took me days to understand how erroneous this assumption was. The elders of their people are looked to for wisdom and advice, and their youths for judgment in times of conflict (a fact which startles me deeply even now, depending as it does on a view of the cosmos I do not share), but there is no single leader, nor even a formal council.

How could there be? If there are eight elders in camp today, there may be only six tomorrow, two having wandered off to spend time in another camp. This, also, is a source of the odd acceptance we encountered: membership in a camp is not at all a formalized thing, like the lineages of the Bayembe region. A member is someone who eats and sleeps near the others, and contributes to their work. As soon as that person leaves—and they do leave, very often, while others show up—that membership ends, until the next time.

This, we came to understand, was the source of our confusion over Faj Rawango's greeting to the others. Natchekavu and Eguamiche were his "brothers" in the sense that they were men of his own generation, nothing more. Claims that the Moulish have no concept of "family" are not true; they acknowledge that some people are the sons and daughters of the same parents, and such relatives often work together when they are in the same camp. But all those of a given age group within the camp are brothers and sisters, as all those above them are mothers and fathers, or (if older still) the camp's elders. Faj Rawango calling those two his brothers was simply a way of claiming the right to join their camp, and to bring the three of us with him.

It sufficed to get us in the door, metaphorically speaking. Those presently belonging to the camp—about fifty altogether—gathered on the open ground at the center, where Kisamilewa and Walakpara, the youths who had brought us in, explained our situation. We distributed the iron knives and a few more things besides, and assured them, through Faj Rawango, that we did not at all mind doing our share of the work. There was a stretch of time during which he was drawn in for further questioning, and the rest of us shooed to the edge of the camp. This was nerve-wracking on two accounts, the first being that we worried about the closer examination they were giving him, and the second being our inability to cope in more than the most atrociously broken Moulish with the questions we still received during that time.

I cannot give you a full report of why the camp chose to accept our presence that day, any more than I can recount who said what and to whom. At the time they were all strangers to us, apart from our quintet of guides, and even those five I could only understand in snatches. I felt, indeed, as if I had suffered a head injury, and lost all comprehension of the world around me. Curiosity had a great deal to do with it, I know; the Moulish were largely unfamiliar with pale-skinned Anthiopeans. But there were deeper reasons I never fully uncovered. The decision having been made, the Moulish frowned upon us questioning it, as that might disturb the harmony created by their agreement—and they prize harmony to a high degree.

What I can tell you is that we were allowed to stamp out our own bit of forest, not quite a part of the camp but near to it, rather like the clearing in which their children played. Instead of building temporary leaf-walled huts as the Moulish did, we pitched our tents in that space, stacking the supplies and equipment between them and using a few crates for seats and tables. After some discussion with Faj Rawango, the Moulish slaughtered the donkeys who had carried our belongings from Atuyem (our horses having remained in a nearby village). Both creatures were mild-tempered enough that I did regret their fate, but as Mr. Wilker pointed out, the alternative was to wake up some morning and find nothing but a bloodstain where they had been. Better that our hosts should get the benefit of their meat, rather than some nocturnal predator.

His logic was sound, but I could not help seeing the poor donkeys as our last link with the world outside the Green Hell.

With their deaths, we were committed to this course, for good or for ill.

If we wished to be successful in the mission Ankumata had given us, then we could not pursue it immediately.

We could not even pursue our broader agenda of research. If we went gallivanting after swamp-wyrms straightaway, the Moulish would have dismissed us as antisocial lunatics, more concerned with our own inexplicable desires than with the well-being of the camp. At best they would have lectured us on our lack of consideration; at worst they would have abandoned us, solving an intractable conflict in their usual manner, which is to simply walk away from it. A group as small as ours does not survive well on its own in the swamp, even with guns to help. We had to prove our worth to the camp first.

Fortunately, proving our worth was far from incompatible with the work of naturalism. The morning after our arrival, a deafening chorus of cicadas and other insects roused us from our sleep, followed shortly by Faj Rawango. "Today is a hunt," he said, and nodded at Mr. Wilker. "They'll expect you to come and help with the nets."

"What of Natalie and myself?" I asked.

He shrugged. "Here with the children, or making noise to drive the game into the nets. They will tell you."

It was a near thing that morning; the children were fascinated by everything from my clothing to my hair, and wanted the chance to study me. But I, of course, preferred to study the swamp, and so we compromised: Natalie remained behind, and I came to do my part in the hunt.

This entailed walking past what I later learned to identify as the sacred hunting fire, whose odorous smoke—nearly as foul as a swamp-wyrm's breath—must touch all those who go out for that task, and then navigating the intricate maze that is the natural environment of Mouleen. We were still close enough then to the swamp's edge that the land was mostly dry; farther in, one seemingly cannot go ten feet without crossing a waterway. Here I only had to wade through two narrow streams before we came to the area chosen for our day's work.

It was as Faj Rawango had said. The men (with Mr. Wilker among them) strung nets between the trees in a broad arc; then the women (myself among them) beat sticks together and shouted at the top of our lungs to frighten the game from us into that arc. Now I began to see all the creatures only my ears had detected before: tree hyraxes, talapoin monkeys, delicate little duikers. Where larger animals charged, the nets were pulled aside to let them through; the Moulish will hunt such beasts, but by different means than we used that day. The smaller ones, once caught, were clubbed or stabbed with fire-hardened spears.

I had not brought my notebook, but I recorded all that I could in my memory, for commitment to paper that evening. This became the standard mode of my work for much of my time in the swamp; although we did have excursions wholly for the purpose of observation, a great deal of our data was gathered in the course of participating in the daily labors of our Moulish hosts. It is excellent training for the memory, if not quite as good for scholarly progress, which prefers to commit things to paper straightaway.

I could not, however, resist asking questions. (Nor could I resist paying attention to things the Moulish considered entirely uninteresting. They are fond of giving nicknames to people; mine was soon Reguamin, which translates to something like "woman who stares at things." Natalie was Geelo—"builder"—for her good assistance with huts and other such structures, and Mr. Wilker was ignominiously dubbed Epou, "red," for his permanently flushed face.)

On our way back to the camp, when we reached the first of the streams, I gestured at the water. Grammar was beyond me as yet, but I knew from Faj Rawango the word I wanted. *"Legambwa?"*

The girl leading me laughed. She was no more than sixteen, I judged; her name was Akinimanbi, and in all my time with her I rarely saw her other than cheerful. Her answer meant nothing to me, but she was quickly adapting to my ineptitude, and bent to splash her hand in the water, indicating its shallowness. By way of similar motions and a few Yembe words I inquired as to the depth a swamp-wyrm would require, and got a shrug; her explanatory gesture seemed to indicate a variety of possibilities, from little more than half a meter to a channel that would merit the name of river.

I pantomimed jaws latching onto my leg, and pretended to scream. Akinimanbi laughed again. That much I understood; she thought me foolish for worrying about such a thing. The significance of her waving arm, however, was opaque to me, as it seemed to indicate the trees. I had thought swamp-wyrms aquatic, but I had not forgotten the so-called arboreal snakes of Bayembe; were their lowland cousins similarly opportunistic, and known to climb? I might be eager to see dragons of any sort, but the prospect of having one drop on my head was alarming.

No dragons fell on my head during our return to the camp, nor in the days that followed. We were about three weeks in that location, with hunts every few days, and smaller excursions to gather food every morning: nuts, berries, roots, frogs, whom the Moulish ate in vast quantities, without ever seeming to dent the supply.

(Because someone always asks: yes, I ate termites. Also ants, beetles, caterpillars, and the cicadas whose cacophony woke me every morning. If one is to live without the benefits of agriculture beyond sporadic trade with villagers, every source of food becomes vital. I will not, however, pretend I ever became fond of the practice. Insects are too crunchy for my taste.)

During those three weeks, we applied ourselves assiduously to being good members of the camp—a task made easier by the absence of dragons, at least that we saw. Moulish came and went, some of them drawn from other camps after word reached them of our presence; others moved to visit kin, or to get away from neighbours who vexed them. It meant constantly learning new names and, as our command of the language improved, explaining ourselves again and again; I began to feel we would never truly settle in, but be trapped forever in this limbo of novelty. But in time the questions stopped.

With the fluctuation of the camp (most of which I will gloss over here, except where it becomes pertinent), you might rightly ask whether we stayed with the same people our entire time in Mouleen. For sufficiently small values of "the same people," the answer is yes. Akinimanbi, I discovered, was newly married, and she and her husband Mekeesawa shared a fire with her grandparents, Apuesiso and Daboumen. At all times except a few I will note in due course, we were always in camp with one or the other of those two couples, and often both.

As in the previous volume of my memoirs, I will not force you to toil through broken sentences that would more accurately represent my early lack of skill with the Moulish tongue. You may simply imagine that when I said to Akinimanbi, "I've heard that the dragons here are rather bad-tempered," one morning shortly before we left that campsite, my phrasing was not nearly so fluent.

She shrugged, cracking nuts with great efficiency and throwing the shells into the fire. "A hippopotamus is worse. The dragons usually won't chase you."

I had less faith than I might in that "usually," owing to my experiences with the "usually" approachable rock-wyrms of Vystrana. "Do you ever hunt them?"

Akinimanbi stared at me as if I'd suggested throwing a baby into the fire along with the shells. "*Hunt* them? That would be"—and she finished with a word whose meaning I could not guess. (*Geguem,* which I suspect is a term left over from the older language.)

"I don't understand *geguem,*" I said, apologetically.

She looked to her grandmother, Apuesiso, who was squatting on the other side of the fire. I could not imitate their posture; a lifetime of chairs has trained me out of the position. I sat on one of our crates, having discovered that sitting cross-legged on the ground meant unpleasant visitors crawling up my skirts.

Apuesiso was braiding a rope from some fiber I had not identified. Without pausing in her work, she sang a song, at least half of which was in the older tongue. I could not understand a word of it, and prepared to say so. But Apuesiso knew that; I think she began with the song for reasons of tradition or propriety. When it was done, she shifted without pause from music to speech. "A long time ago, a man killed a dragon. He was ashamed of what he'd done, so he tried to hide it by getting rid of the body. He ate the meat, used the skin, and turned the teeth and claws into tools. But it was no good: the spirits knew what he had done. *Geguem.*"

Murder, then; or perhaps sin. "Did they punish the man?"

By her snort, I might have asked whether rain fell from the clouds. "Because of him, we die."

The broken quality of our conversation meant I had to ask several more questions before I properly understood what Apuesiso meant. The death of the dragon was, in their view, the reason human beings are mortal.

I am more a natural historian than an ethnologist; my immediate thought was to wonder how hungry that man must have been to resort to eating foul-smelling and fouler-tasting dragon meat. But of course such myths change over time; the exact phrasing owed more to the usual hunting practices of the Moulish than to the actual disposition of a dragon's body. (Indeed, I later heard another rendition of the story wherein the bones were also said to have become tools. I was far too excited about that one, until it became apparent that, no, the Moulish ancestors did not have their own method for preserving dragonbone.)

But if I have relatively little interest in the religious practices of other people, there is no surer way to draw my attention than to bring up dragons. "Why did he kill it? Was it for food, or did the dragon attack him?"

They laughed my questions off, as well they might. It was a myth; such narratives are not known for their exploration of the human psyche and its motivations. As well ask why Chaltaph refused the gifts of Raganit in the Book of Schisms: scholars may think up interpretations, and those are enlightening in their own fashion, but in the end the story itself gives no clear answer. But the taboo against further dragon killing was clear.

I brought this up with Natalie and Mr. Wilker that afternoon, as we went through the tedious routine of washing our clothes in buckets of water collected for the purpose. (We could not use groundwater, as it was too often muddy. Fortunately, the storms that came every afternoon as regularly as clockwork made it easy to collect rain.)

"So they won't look kindly on us killing a dragon," Mr. Wilker said, wringing out one of his shirts. It is a credit to the man that he never once asked Natalie or myself to do his laundry for him— though on reflection, it may be more a discredit to our own clothes-washing skills, or lack thereof. We were both too gently reared to have firsthand experience with such matters; Mr. Wilker, with his working-class childhood on Niddey, knew more than we.

"About as kindly as we would look on someone pulling another fig from the Tree of Knowledge," I said, trying, with less than total success, to scrub mud from the hem of one of my skirts.

Natalie was hanging the clean articles from a line to dry (inasmuch as they could, in the eternally damp air of that place). "No tests on bone, then, unless you want to try and do it in secret."

Mr. Wilker and I exchanged glances, then both shook our heads. "Not yet, anyway," he said. "Too much risk of being found out and losing their goodwill."

"Besides," I added, "it works, with modification, on both rock-wyrms and savannah snakes, who cannot possibly be related except in the most distant sense. I think we can assume it would work on swamp-wyrms as well. And as much as I would like to be able to study samples for reasons other than preservation, Mr. Wilker is right; it would lose us their goodwill, which would do more harm to our work in the long run."

I had gone on with my skirt-washing efforts while I spoke, but my thoughts had drifted from that task; it startled me when a pair of hands appeared and took the skirt away. Mr. Wilker set it against the crate lid he was using for a washing board and began to scrub it, doing in mere seconds what would take me minutes to achieve, if indeed I could at all.

"Thank you," I said, blushing. "Would it scandalize you terribly if I cut that apart after it dries and turned it into trousers?"

"Oh, *please* do," Natalie said, with vast relief. "Then I won't feel guilty for doing the same. Skirts in this place are sheer madness."

Mr. Wilker had seen me in trousers before, in Vystrana. He had not liked it at the time—but then, we had not liked each other at the time, either. He said, only a little stiffly, "It seems the practical choice, yes."

Natalie and I accordingly spent the evening cutting up and restitching our clothing, much to the amusement of our hosts the following morning. The only differentiation they observe in clothing the two sexes lies in how they hang their loincloths; skirts versus trousers meant little to them in that regard. But Natalie and I both felt awkward in such masculine garb, and it showed. We soon adjusted, however, and this is the origin of my practice of wearing trousers whenever I am on an expedition, which has been such an article of gossip over the years. (Whatever the scandal-sheets may claim, I do not wear them at home, though I have considered it once or twice.) (The incident at Booker's Club should not be counted; I was *extremely* drunk at the time.)

Our decision was timely, as we moved camp the very next day. I have spoken already of the tendency for the Moulish to come and go from a camp; there is also the migration of a camp wholesale, when they have been long enough in an area to exhaust the nearby sources of food, and must move elsewhere to find game and wild fruits.

This created a spot of difficulty for our expedition, as we had known it must when they slaughtered the donkeys. With no beasts of burden, the Moulish carry all of their belongings with them, in baskets strung from tumplines on their heads. Although this is quite an effective method for those whose neck muscles are conditioned to it, the four of us (Faj Rawango included) could not be so described, and also had more equipment than we could carry in such fashion.

Our best guess at conversion from "distance a Moulish man carrying a burden can walk before noon" to Scirling units told us they intended to move about fifteen kilometers farther into the swamp. Some of our things we could abandon, having discovered we had no real need of them. (A proper Moulish sentiment, and one that has become habit for me over the years.) Others we could get rid of, so to speak, by encouraging members of the camp to take them; they rarely resented us borrowing things back when we needed them. But some items—foremost among them the crate of gin and the box containing our preserved dragonbone—posed a genuine problem.

"Well," Mr. Wilker said with a sigh, "I suppose we could conduct another experiment. Bury the bones, and see how they fare in this muck." He kicked at the wet soil.

That box was nailed firmly shut; the Moulish did not know

what was in it, and I preferred to keep matters that way. "Will we be able to find it again? I feel I've come to know this area quite well, but I'm sure that a week from now it will look like every other bit of swamp to me."

"They know the spot," Natalie said, fishing a machete from among our baggage. "And I think Faj Rawango could find it again. We'll just have to ask for help. I fear, though, this is the closest thing we have to a shovel."

We dug the hole with two machetes and our bare hands, which would not have gone very well in more solid earth. In that terrain, however, it was more a matter of hacking through a mat of roots, then scooping away what muddy dirt remained. (And then pausing with every handful to shake off the small creatures crawling up one's arms.) This, of course, attracted an audience, but we were able to satisfy their curiosity by saying we only wanted to spare ourselves the effort of carrying the box's contents with us.

Everything else went into packs and baskets and so on. Akinimanbi talked her husband Mekeesawa into taking our bottles of gin, removed from their crate and wrapped in clothing for protection; he grumbled at carrying a tumpline-hung basket "like a youth"—grown men carried their nets and spears, not other burdens—but agreed without much rancor, as the rest of us were taking on substantial loads of our own. And so, shouldering our loads, we went with our hosts to their next camp.

FOURTEEN

*The heart of the swamp—Leeches—
Egg-hatching season—Hunters of knowledge*

I thought I had seen the Green Hell during our weeks in that first camp, but I was wrong.

Compared to the swamp proper, those upper reaches are dry and scrubby, with dwarfish vegetation (however much it may tower above the trees and brush of the savannah). Once you descend into the heart of the Green Hell, you find yourself in a land of water and giants.

The trees there soar forty or fifty meters high, as if they were the pillars of some great temple. Their roots form great bladelike walls, bracing the trunks in the soil, sometimes growing closely enough that earth accumulates in between and a smaller tree begins growing in the cup thus formed. The space beneath is emerald and dim, save for where a stray beam of sunlight breaks through the many layers of vegetation to strike the ground. There the swamp grows even warmer, but at the same time the light is a glorious thing, as if it carried the voices of angels.

Most of the light is to be found where the waterways grow

wide enough that branches cannot fully bridge the gap. But these are rare; storms and floods along the three rivers that feed the swamp can change the landscape enough that what last year was a minor stream has now become a main artery of the delta. "Rivers" in Mouleen therefore have trees growing in them like islands, and are patched with sunlight like a piebald horse.

When we came to a waterway deep and broad enough to be troublesome, or (more often) turned to follow one for a substantial distance, the Moulish paused to make simple rafts, on which they floated their belongings for ease of transport. "Tuck the hems of your trousers into your stockings," Mr. Wilker said, suiting action to words. "It will reduce the chance of you finding a leech on your leg."

"I think trousers just became my favourite thing in all the world," Natalie said.

We tucked our hems into our stockings and half-waded, half-swam downstream. When we came out again, our hosts picked leeches off their limbs with an unconcerned air. We Scirlings examined ourselves and one another; Natalie circled behind me, and I felt her tug on the fabric of my shirt. Then she made a most peculiar noise—a sort of strangled moan.

"Ah, Isabella?" she said. "You, ah—your shirt—"

My shirt had come loose from my waistband during our exertions. I put my hand to my back, very unwisely, and felt the soft, disgusting mass of a leech just above my right kidney.

I fear it may damage my reputation to admit this, but I yelped and promptly began to dance in a circle like a cat chasing her tail, trying to see the leech and also to get away from it. The latter was futile; it had fastened onto me, and slapping at it with my hand was hardly persuading it to let go.

The Moulish were no help, as they found my antics utterly hilarious. Finally Akinimanbi took pity on me; while Mr. Wilker held me by the shoulders, stopping my dance, she lifted my shirt and pried the thing off. I shuddered at the sight of it, and kept shuddering for a good while afterward, obsessively running my hands over various parts of my body to make sure I had no more bloodsucking passengers, at least none of any size larger than a mosquito. (I did, as I have said, eventually become accustomed to leeches, but this being my first encounter with them, it did not proceed so calmly.)

On we went, until we came to the place the camp had agreed upon for its next site. How they identified it, I do not know; with the landscape as changeable as the shifting waters, there seemed no guarantee a location would still be where one remembered it, even if one could find it again.

With what remained of the day (and our energy), we helped the others cut away brush and saplings from the new site, trimming the detritus to make huts for them to sleep in. Pitching our own tents took longer, and when it was done, I had no will even to eat. But Natalie insisted we feed ourselves, so I swallowed a plantain and some starchy root whose name I had not yet learned, then collapsed face-first into my pillow.

This was the basis of our routine for the next several months. The camp—or rather, the portion of it that consisted of us and Akinimanbi's family—never stayed more than three or four weeks in any one place. We were in the depths of the rainy season now, which meant a daily deluge each afternoon, and often showers at other times of day; it is not the near-constant rainfall seen elsewhere in the world, but it is more than enough. The mountains farther inland had melted their snowcaps by now, feeding the three rivers; it began to seem that the swamp was eighty percent water and twenty percent land. Campsites were wherever the ground rose high enough to have a chance of staying above the flood. Nor were such places accidental: Mekeesawa told Mr. Wilker that they piled branches and planted certain vegetation in what passed for their "dry" season to ensure these miniature hillocks would persist.

There was, I began to realize, more organization to their society than met the eye—though it is still nothing like as structured as those which develop in less ecologically hostile regions. The Moulish cannot afford stratification by class, nor even much in the way of gender roles; all must do what they can. But they not only understood their environment, they shaped it in small ways to suit their purposes. They also maintained a surprising degree of connection between camps, firstly through the constant migration of people, and secondly through the use of talking drums.

Natalie was fascinated by these. For a people with so few material possessions, and most of those temporary, the drums were treasures: carved with elaborate designs, and carried with reverence each time the camp moved. Their use is too complex for me to explain, but the Moulish have a way of translating their language into drumbeats, which can then be used to send messages between camps. By passing a message from one camp to the next, they are able to communicate from one end of the swamp to the other, much faster than any human could carry a message. The drums therefore permit them to stay in touch with kin far away, and are often used to ask or tell where someone is, so that another may find them.

Mekeesawa explained this to me one afternoon, while Natalie was questioning the current drum bearer about the method of translation. He added, "It is very useful during this season. No one wants to wander for too long."

By now my command of the language had improved substantially, such that I could converse with him in more than my early mixture of nouns and mime. I laughed and said, "Because of the rain? I can understand that."

"The rain," Mekeesawa said, "and the dragons."

We were not busy with any task for the camp; I judged it safe to question him, without fear that my interest would seem selfish. "What makes them more dangerous in this season than another? Do they object to this much water?"

He grinned. "They love it. Full of things to eat. But this is when the eggs hatch."

I attempted not to perk up like a scent hound that has come upon the trail of a fat, juicy rabbit, but I fear my success was middling at best. It was easy to forget that a world existed outside the Green Hell: a world, and perhaps a war. Had the Ikwunde backed off from the rivers, or were Scirling soldiers and Bayembe warriors fighting them as we spoke? I had no way of knowing.

Even if open conflict had broken out, nothing I did here could affect it—or so I thought. Eggs would not help Ankumata immediately. Even so, Mekeesawa's words reminded me that the oba would be waiting for us to deliver on our promise.

If the eggs were in the process of hatching, though, he would have to wait a while longer, until there was a fresh set. "Do the dragons lay them in the water?" I asked. "Or on dry land, and they hatch when they become submerged?"

It was not, I thought, an alarming question. Mekeesawa, however, clapped his hands together, which I recognized as a sign to ward off bad luck or evil spirits. "I don't know about such things," he said.

The peculiarity of his response arrested me. The key factor distinguishing the Moulish from their neighbours—even the closely related Mouri—is not physiognomy or language; it is their relationship to the swamp they call home. They know every plant that is useful and every one that is hazardous, every insect that can poison you and every one that can be eaten for lunch. They hunt a wide variety of creatures, even hippopotami and forest elephants (against whom they use some of those poisonous insects), and are as well versed in the behaviour and life cycle of those beasts as any naturalist could hope for.

Now a Moulish hunter claimed to me that he did not know where swamp-wyrms laid their eggs. You may understand, gentle reader, when I tell you this made me suspicious.

I considered several possible responses and settled on, "Many animals become quite violent if they believe you might threaten their young. I should like at least to know what to watch out for, so as not to stumble upon swamp-wyrm eggs." Of course I would go *looking* for them eventually, but this made for a more discreet way of questioning him.

Much good it did me. "They've all hatched by now," Mekeesawa said.

"Yes, but if we are still here when the next set are laid—"

I should have known better. Yves de Maucheret had claimed the Moulish worshipped dragons; I had seen no sign of it thus far beyond that one myth, the tale of how humans became mortal, but

I should have known that *something* gave rise to that claim. I had clearly stumbled upon a taboo subject, and it is my fault for letting my intellectual curiosity drive me into pursuing it too directly.

No more would Mekeesawa say on the topic, and I had to restrain the urge to question others in the camp, in the hopes of finding someone more willing to speak. Instead I passed this along to the others, and we discussed how we might proceed.

"We have a fair bit of time to spare," Mr. Wilker said. The rainy season meant the Moulish had only to drop a net in the water to get their supper; they spent much of their day at leisure, singing and dancing, when they were not occupied with household tasks like pounding out fresh barkcloth or weaving baskets. "We've gathered useful information for the general purpose of naturalism, but perhaps it's time we devoted ourselves more strictly to dragons."

I nodded in agreement. We had caught distant glimpses of a few, and likely been closer to more; a swamp-wyrm who wishes to remain concealed is not easily spotted. But those glimpses had taught us very little so far. I said, "Not pursuing eggs, of course; not immediately. But we know virtually nothing of what swamp-wyrms eat, or how they hunt, where they sleep, the differences between male and female, their mating habits . . ." I ticked each item off on my fingers, and stopped when I ran out on that hand. I could have kept going. My understanding of what a naturalist *did* had greatly deepened in the years since Vystrana.

"We don't even know how one might safely observe them," Natalie pointed out; and that became our first question to answer.

For some time we had been agreeable if moderately inept members of the camp, mostly going along with the day-to-day activities of our hosts. Now that we reared our heads as naturalists, however, we met with more difficulty. Not hostility, per se, but simple confusion.

"This is the lazy season," Akinimanbi said, suiting inaction to words. At her side, Mekeesawa was stripping the bark from a branch to make a new spear, but his movements were desultory. He might have been a Scirling farmer, whittling wood to give his hands something to do. "Why would you go out when you don't have to?"

"We *do* have to," I said, and then stopped. Most of the reasons I could give her were so foreign to the world in which she lived, I might spend the next hour explaining them and still not convey my point. There was nothing like the Philosophers' Colloquium here, nor journals in which one might publish, nor acclaim given for that sort of thing. And simple scientific curiosity, as I had learned in Vystrana, rarely meant much to the people for whom my object of curiosity was their daily and sometimes disagreeable reality. (One need look no further than Scirland for proof of that: while we have naturalists who study local birds and bugs, they are far outnumbered by those whose interest lies in more distant lands—myself chief among them.)

Akinimanbi waited patiently while I considered how to explain myself without seeming like a madwoman. At last I said, "If you consider the three of us to be hunters of a sort, then what we are hunting is knowledge."

Her eyebrows went up at this, and I realized my error. "Except it's not like your story, where the man did wrong by killing the dragon! We don't want to kill anything. Forget what I said about hunting; we *gather* knowledge, as you gather food. To, ah, feed our minds. Or—"

At this I stopped, because Akinimanbi and Mekeesawa both were laughing at me, slapping their thighs and rolling back where they sat. I deserved it, for the way my words had tumbled over one another; I might have explained myself, but the part about not seeming like a madwoman had been a resounding failure.

Belatedly, I thought of a better way to make my point. "Your people understand the forest: how the animals behave, where to find them, and so on. I want something similar—but instead of the forest as a whole, I want to understand dragons. They are not only here, you know; there are dragons in the savannah—" Mekeesawa nodded. "Well, there are more than that, all over the world. They live in the mountains and on the plains and maybe even in the ocean. I want to know them as you know the creatures of this forest."

"But why?" Mekeesawa asked. His eyes were still merry with laughter, but his question was serious. "You don't live in all those places."

With the amount of time I have spent traveling in my life, one might make the argument that I *do* live in all those places, if only temporarily. But Mekeesawa's point was a good one, and not easily dismissed. The Moulish understood the creatures of the Green Hell because their survival depended on it; my survival did not depend on my traveling the globe to find dragons. (Indeed, it has on more than one occasion nearly been detrimental to my life expectancy.) How could I answer him?

Thinking back on the matter now, it is possible my only true answer to that question is now in its second volume, with more to come. These memoirs are not only an accounting of my life; they are an accounting *for* it.

But that day in the Green Hell, I could hardly present these books to Mekeesawa. I gave the matter my final try. "There is a man—an elder of my camp, in a manner of speaking. He has asked me to do this for him." That was the best explanation I could give for Lord Hilford's role as my patron. "And if *that* does not make sense to you, then I can only ask you to tolerate the madwoman."

I suspect that last suggestion was the one they accepted in the end. One way or another, we got the freedom to continue with our work—and, at long last, an explanation for Akinimanbi's overhead gesture so many days before.

FIFTEEN

Traversing the flood—Moulish engineering—Swamp-wyrms on the hunt—
I miss my footing—My misfortunes—Witchcraft, again

I have described to you how the inundation of the Green Hell made the place almost more lake than land. We had gained two newcomers to the camp since settling there, and lost five others; I had assumed they went by raft while I was otherwise occupied. But travel by raft is too dangerous during that season: apart from the usual predators, swamp-wyrms not excepted, the water swarms with small, eel-like creatures we had dubbed fang-fish, which are rapacious carnivores. To avoid these hazards, the Moulish traveled by other, more exciting means.

Three of us went out with Mekeesawa; Faj Rawango elected to stay in camp, I think to mitigate any sense that we were being antisocial by pursuing our own ends. Mekeesawa took us to the end of the long spit of land on which we had pitched our camp, and we waded across a shallow stretch to another spot that was not so much island as tree. It was one of the great forest giants, tangled about with smaller parasitic trees, and he indicated to us that we should climb.

Tamshire's rocky soil does not support much in the way of good climbing trees; nor do Tamshire's gentry support much tree-climbing in girls. Mekeesawa clambered up with no trouble, and Natalie followed him with surprisingly little, but I required Mr. Wilker's assistance. My face, I am sure, was flamingly red by the time we reached the others; in part because of the heat, but much more because of the indelicate physical contact his aid required. We had swept aside our conversation on the hunt—or rather, swept it under the rug—but it is difficult to ignore questions of propriety when a man places his hand on your posterior to help you up a tree.

He, at least, could blame the redness of his skin on his Niddey ancestry. (I am not sure Mr. Wilker had stopped being red since we arrived in Nsebu.) And we were both soon distracted by what Mekeesawa had brought us up there to see.

The giant tree soared higher still, but here the parasites that clung to its trunk branched outward. In front of us those branches tangled with others from another tree; then I looked more closely, and saw the tangle was no accident at all.

It may have begun that way. But just as the island on which we camped had been built up by human action, so too had this tangle been fostered, with creeping vines binding the branches together and shaping them into—

"A bridge!" Natalie said, grinning from ear to ear.

In Scirling, I said to her, "You truly have the soul of an engineer." I did not mean it as a slight, though. Nor did I mean to denigrate the bridge, especially once I discovered it was part of a semiformal network extending across various parts of the swamp. During most times of the year this elevated system is more trouble than it's worth to use, but when the waters rise high, it allows the Moulish to traverse the places where dragons and other predators are likely to lurk.

As works of building go, it may not be as obviously impressive as a Nichaean aqueduct or a Yelangese highway. But I defy anyone to stand at the end of a Moulish tree-bridge and not be impressed.

I also defy them not to be the slightest bit nervous about committing their weight to such a structure. Mekeesawa went first, examining the bridge and pausing occasionally to weave a branch in where it would grow to reinforce the whole. While the process was fascinating to observe, it did not exactly foster confidence.

We three Scirlings exchanged dubious looks. "There are two ways to approach this," Natalie said. "Mr. Wilker, you are the heaviest of us. If you go first, the bridge will be the least damaged and most able to support your weight; however, that may increase the risk for Isabella and myself. If *we* go first, you will have some warning as to its structural integrity ... but it may also be damaged, and therefore unsafe, by the time you cross."

Mekeesawa was by then on the other side, and waving impatiently for us to come. "It must be quite safe," I said, and made myself approach the end of the bridge. "The Moulish cross these things all the time."

"The Moulish," Mr. Wilker muttered, "weigh half what I do"—which was only a minor exaggeration.

I drew in a deep breath and set my foot on the branch, gripping a nearby vine as if my life depended upon it (which I hoped it would not shortly do). The structure I faced was to what I would call a "bridge" what a rope ladder is to a staircase: it might support my weight, but that did not make it reassuring. Sparing a moment to bless once more the decision to dress in trousers, I slid my other foot past my ankle, settling it just beyond the point where another branch crossed my main support. Bare feet, I realized, would be much better for this task, being able to bend and grip the surface— but only if those feet belonged to a Moulish woman, mine being far too tender for the task. The branches and vines I gripped were, at least, blessedly thorn-free; at this height, they had much less to fear from passing herbivores. Step by step, I proceeded.

It is inevitable, I suppose, that halfway through such an undertaking, one *will* commit the error of looking down.

Beneath me lay a lacework of branches and vines too thin to support my weight if I fell; beneath *that*—vertiginously far below—the water was a murky, green-brown plate, broken only by the wake of something swimming just beneath the surface.

I forced myself to look away and breathe through my nose, preventing the hyperventilation that would have made me dizzy. When I finally forced myself to take the next step, my shoe slipped a few centimeters: not enough to imperil me, but more than enough to set my heart racing. The half-dozen steps it took to reach Mekeesawa seemed to take forever—but then, at last, I was safe.

Whether Natalie and Mr. Wilker had similar difficulties, I cannot tell you, for I was busy restoring strength to my now jellylike limbs. Once we had recovered, Mekeesawa led us onward to a place where he said we could likely observe the dragons— including some of their young.

This was an area low-lying enough that it had been thoroughly drowned by the flood, with only the tips of underbrush poking up here and there in the water to show there was anything between the trees. Swamp-wyrms love such territory; it is full of fish, frogs, and other bite-size snacks. Much of their diet comes from these sources, but they do also pursue more substantial targets; and here, as in the savannah, we did not have to wait long before we saw this demonstrated before our eyes.

The manner of it was quite similar; only the environment differed. In the trees across the way from where we sat, a troupe of colobus monkeys had begun a chattering argument amongst themselves. One of them so offended another that the second took to flight, branch to branch across an overhanging tree; and so it met its end.

A ripple of disturbance made a traveling V along the water's surface, our only warning of the dragon. And scant warning at that; an instant later, the swamp-wyrm burst above the surface, lunging into the air with jaws extended—snap! And the monkey was gone. A great wave spread as the wyrm splashed down. The colobus troupe fled in a panic, but one of them missed his grip upon the next branch and fell. He floundered only briefly in the water before the lithe, mud-green body eeled over to him and sent him to join his brother.

This is not the only way swamp-wyrms hunt, of course. They will, like crocodiles, snap up creatures that wander too close to the water's edge, as well as those in the water with them. In the drier reaches of the forest, they will behave more like arboreal snakes, concealing themselves beneath brush or twining around a tree. This semi-aerial hunting, however, is their most striking characteristic. When they swim, they fold their wings up into something like a fin that helps them steer at speed; then, when they are ready to strike, they extend their wings and use them rather like the arms of a ballista to propel themselves into the air.

Sometimes one will lurk beneath his prey and bring his mouth just to the surface of the water; then he will patiently expel his extraordinary breath (which readers of the first volume may recall is a noxious fume) until the creatures above are so overcome that they drop. The result is rather like manna from heaven—at least if you are a swamp-wyrm.

"It's very like a savannah snake," Mr. Wilker said when the dragon had subsided once more. "They may be more closely related than we thought."

Natalie's mind was on more immediately physical matters. "I've never seen a wing *fold* like that. How on earth are those joints structured?"

Without killing and dissecting one, answering that question would be difficult. But we had more than enough to occupy us, trying to estimate the size of the beast (from our brief glimpse of it), querying Mekeesawa about how that compared to the usual run of swamp-wyrms, and guessing at the number of colobus monkeys a dragon would have to eat each day in order to keep itself in good health.

Mr. Wilker climbed a tree to study the water, calling down observations regarding the movement patterns of the creature, while Natalie exhorted him to be careful he was not eaten himself. I took my sketchbook from the small bundle I had lashed to my back and put down a loose collection of lines, but what I had observed thus far was grossly insufficient to let me make a good drawing. I had seen the one Velloin captured, but it was a malformed runt, and much inclined to curl into a sullen ball. I remembered well enough that the legs were set more like a crocodile's than those of a terrestrial dragon, but not their exact disposition, and of the jointing of the

wings I had little idea, on account of the runt's deformities.

Indeed, it took many observational trips before we had good data on such matters. But those trips took longer than they should have, because of the difficulties we—or more precisely, *I*—encountered.

It began on the journey back to camp, when I fell into the swamp.

We had crossed two tree bridges on the way to that spot; those traverses had been enough to reassure me that the structures would bear our weight. Perhaps that reassurance made me careless; I cannot say. I believe I was still as cautious as any woman might be who is trusting her life to a few branches woven together with vines. But on the second bridge, not far at all from camp, I misstepped, and found myself off balance. I reached for a vine—it tore—I windmilled my arms, trying to recover—I struck a nearby branch—and then I was falling.

The instinct to flail for support was still active, and it saved my life. My right hand caught a lower branch, and if its bark tore half the skin from my fingers and palm, it slowed my descent. Slowed, not stopped: when the limb finished bowing beneath my weight, my arm was nearly yanked from its socket, and I lost what grip I had. Like that second monkey, I fell into the water, and you may recall that the purpose of these bridges is to lead the Moulish safely past the areas where dragons and other perils may lurk.

I hit the water with a slap, driving down hard enough that I sank almost to my knees in the soft mud below. That came as near to killing me as the fall or any predator did; had I not managed to pull myself free, I might have drowned in short order. But pull I did, with all the strength that a good dose of panic can bestow. Then I kicked to the surface and sucked in a great gulp of air, and at that point I was home and dry, apart from being in the middle of some dragon's possible hunting pool.

A commotion off to one side was the two men hurling themselves down the tree as fast as they could go. I struck out toward that sound, trying not to splash too much. My thoughts kept returning to that smooth ripple across the water, and the swift death that had followed. Would a swamp-wyrm attack something as large as a human woman?

The general answer to my question is yes. But as it turned out, that was the least of my worries.

My fall had sent everything in the water darting away, but now they were returning. I felt movement past my limbs, and then a sharp pain on my left arm: one of the eel-like fangfish had found me, and buried its sharp teeth in my flesh.

It had already been imperative that I get out of the water, but with this, my situation became dire. Fangfish will come to the scent of blood, and a school of them could tear me to pieces, leaving nothing but a skeleton behind.

As with the leech, I reacted on terrified instinct, seizing the fangfish and ripping it free. My blood made a dark ribbon in the muddy water. I retained sufficient presence of mind to shout for Mr. Wilker to stay out; he had reached the shore, and was plainly about to throw himself in, but it would help not at all for both of us to be chewed on. Heedless now of splashing, I redoubled my efforts, and soon came within reach of his arm; he gripped my wrist and hauled me from the water.

My breath sobbed in my chest, from exertion and fear alike. But I was safe now—or so I thought, until I heard Mekeesawa shouting in alarm. Heart pounding, I turned to look over my shoulder, expecting that narrow and graceful V.

What I saw instead was the charging thunder of a pygmy hippopotamus.

You may laugh; hippos are absurd-looking creatures, and the term "pygmy" suggests a pocket-size version. But your average pygmy hippo weighs more than two hundred kilograms and will beat the living daylight out of anything that trespasses in its waters. It is smaller and less vicious than its savannah-dwelling cousin, but this is like saying that a tornado is smaller and less destructive than a hurricane. While true, that does not mean it cannot wreak havoc.

Mr. Wilker and I prepared to run. But Mekeesawa, knowing what we did not, urged us back up into the branches instead.

Which is how I came to be treed by a furious, porky creature that would have cheerfully employed its silly little legs to stomp me into the mud. Once roused, hippos cannot be trusted to stop at defending their waters; they will chase the intruder, and can often outrun him. The one benefit of the entire debacle was that the creature's bellows of rage drew the attention of the nearby camp, and some of the hunters came and killed it; we dined upon hippo meat that night.

(This, you may be interested to know, is the incident which pesuaded me to wear trousers at all times while in the field. I no longer cared what others thought proper; I was all too aware that I never knew when I might have to swim, run, or climb a tree to escape an angry beast. I may risk my life on a regular basis—or I did in my youth— but I will not do so in the name of mere propriety.)

* * *

I had torn a great deal of skin from my hand, wrenched my shoulder, and thoroughly jammed my legs with my landing in the mud. This slowed our progress, and as I indicated above, it was only the first of many setbacks.

To this day, I maintain that the difficulties we suffered were only the natural consequence of doing strenuous work in a hazardous environment. I have been in other hazardous places before and since—Vystrana; the Akhian desert; anywhere politicians may be found—but I think only the Mrtyahaima peaks equal the Green Hell for sheer lethality. Even the Moulish, who know the region better than any, suffer a great deal of hardship as a result of living there. Had we *not* encountered difficulties, it would have been a clear sign of supernatural blessing.

But I cannot deny that the dragon's share of those problems fell upon my head. It was I, not Mr. Wilker or Natalie, who fell from that bridge. I am the one who, on a subsequent day, was bitten by a venemous snake; I am the one who fell inglorious victim to an intestinal parasite, which had to be purged with a careful dose of strychnine. I broke two fingers on two separate occasions, attracted leeches like iron filings to a magnet, and knocked one of my sketchbooks into the campfire one night. I was, in short, a recurrent disaster.

The effect of this upon my mood was if anything worse than the incidents themselves. In Vystrana I had ostensibly been my husband's companion and secretary to the expedition; here I was supposed to be an equal partner with Mr. Wilker, yet I felt incompetent in comparison. It raised the spectre of our old strife—less, I should say, through any fault of his, and more through my own self-doubt. I tried harder to prove my worth (which led to things like the broken fingers), bore an unjustified grudge against Mr. Wilker for seeming proof against all perils, and generally made an utter shrew of myself. (How the two of them never gave in to the urge to chuck me into the swamp, I will never know.)

The most detrimental effect, however, was upon our pursuit of a certain goal.

I had not forgotten the matter of dragon eggs. Remembering Mekeesawa's reticence on the subject, I tried asking Akinimanbi; Natalie's theory was that the Moulish had a gender taboo, and such things were considered the proper province of women.

As theories go, it was not a bad one, but in this case it was incorrect. It might have been a seasonal taboo—eggs not to be spoken of in the season of their hatching—but I did not know enough to suspect such a thing, and in any event that was not it either. This frustrated me enough that I began to press more sharply than was polite.

Which did not earn me an answer, but did give me something else. Akinimanbi rounded on me at the edge of camp and said, "Why should I tell you? You're cursed!"

By then the "camp" had dwindled to Akinimanbi, her husband, her grandparents, and our crew of four. This was usual for the season; later they would come back together in larger groups. I had cause to be grateful for the smallness of the camp, as it meant the embarrassment of our argument was seen only by a few. "What do you mean, I am cursed?"

"All these accidents," Akinimanbi said, gesturing at my

splinted finger. "A witch has put an evil spell on you, Reguamin. Everyone knows it. No one will tell you anything until you deal with it."

Before the last division of the camp, some of the youths had been telling stories in my presence—quite loudly—about people under the influence of witches. I had not realized their stories were meant as a coded message to me. It was the same notion I had gotten from the grandmother in that village, when Natalie became ill with malaria; and I had as little patience for it now as I did then.

"No one has put a spell on me," I said, "evil or otherwise. It's simply bad luck. Or who are you saying has done this? Your husband? Your mother? One of the people who has been with us in camp?"

"The witch doesn't have to be here," she countered. "It could be a villager. Or someone in the land you come from."

That struck me as very convenient. Blame misfortune on someone not even present: it was the same as saying the Lord did it, with an extra helping of blame. "No one in my land practices witchcraft," I said. "If anyone does such things, it's your own people."

"*Everyone* practices witchcraft," Akinimanbi said forcefully, stepping closer. With my advantage of height, she should not have been able to glare *down* at me, but somehow she gave the impression of doing so. "They practice it in their hearts, when they become angry or upset. Maybe your brother here in camp lusts after you, but you won't marry him, so his heart works witchcraft against you. Maybe you have a child who wasn't mourned properly, and so its spirit has cursed you. Who have you wronged?"

I thought of the tension between myself and Mr. Wilker, my

mother's disapproval, Lord Denbow's fury at Natalie's disappear-
ance. But if he were working witchcraft, would it not target his
daughter instead?

It was all nonsense, just like the legend of Zhagrit Mat. I even
wondered for a moment if one of the Moulish might be responsible
for my misfortunes. But no; it was simply bad luck, and I said so.

"Bad luck has a cause, Reguamin," Akinimanbi told me darkly.
"If you spent your time staring at the right things, you would
understand. Until you take care of it, the bad luck will not go away."

And she would not tell me what I wanted to know. Controlling
my impatience and frustration as best I could, I said, "Assuming for
a moment I believe a word of this . . . how would I take care of it?"

Even the hypothetical possibility of my cooperation made her
look relieved. "Find the cause. Think who you've wronged, and
make peace with them. Undo the witchcraft."

I could hardly go back to Scirland for a tearful reconciliation
with my mother. "I will think about what you've said," I told
Akinimanbi, and hoped that would be the end of it.

But the worst, of course, was yet to come.

SIXTEEN

Yellow jack—The dragon roars—Akinimanbi's argument—
The ritual—Natalie and Mr. Wilker—My confession

You may recall that I praised Natalie Oscott in an earlier segment of this narrative, for not being so foolish as to attempt to press on with her work when she suspected that she might have contracted malaria.

I was less sensible than she.

My excuse—and it is a poor one—is that I already felt a keen sense of my insufficiency, owing to the string of misfortunes I had suffered. My broken fingers had healed enough for me to be of use once again; I did not want to delay us more, or put my share of the burden on Mr. Wilker and Natalie. (No, that phrasing is too noble, though I shall leave it for posterity. I did not want to surrender to others' hands what contributions I might now make.)

When I felt the first stirrings of a headache, therefore, I shrugged them off. The ache in my body I attributed to the ongoing lack of a proper bed; stiff muscles were a familiar problem, and if they pained me more now than before, surely that did not mean anything. Nor did my lack of appetite, which could be attributed to weariness with a diet of hippo meat, honey, and termites, and a craving for the familiar comforts of home—never mind that I felt no such craving, not even for foods that were ordinarily a pleasure. Part of me recognized the peril in these signs, but I was not yet ready to admit their significance, not even to myself.

That stage of my denial may, perhaps, be excused. But as the day wore on, I began to shiver, and then I acted like a proper fool: I strove to conceal my shudders from the others, knowing they would insist we return to camp at once. The three of us had found a swamp-wyrm wrapped around a tree, lying in wait for unwary prey, and I had at last a good opportunity to draw it; I told myself that the opportunity should not be wasted, and that evening would be soon enough for me to lie down and rest.

But soon my hand began to shake badly enough that it affected my work. And Natalie, who had been crouched where she could study the jointing of the dragon's wing, noticed.

"Isabella," she whispered, in a tone of concern.

Before she could say anything further, my lack of appetite abruptly asserted itself in the other direction. I dropped my sketchbook and vomited into the underbrush, and from there matters only got worse.

The dragon fled, which brought Mr. Wilker back to us, and he wasted no time in lecturing me as I deserved (though at the time I was bitterly angry with him for it). He insisted we return to camp on the spot, and I was no longer in any condition to argue; indeed, I was in no condition to walk. Before long he resorted to carrying me, and by such ignominious means did I find myself back in my tent.

Once laid on my pallet, I moaned and curled into a ball. Mr. Wilker, about to depart, stopped and turned back. "What is it?" he asked.

"My back," I said. "It *aches*."

He dropped to his knees and rolled me over against my protests, peeling back my eyelids with careful fingers. Whatever he saw there made him recoil. "God almighty. This isn't malaria."

"What?"

I will never forget the look of abject fear in his eyes. "I think you have yellow fever."

And so I did. The early stage is much like malaria; the back pain and sometimes a yellowing of the sclera in the eyes are what distinguish the two. For the next three days I shuddered and sweated on my pallet, alternately attempting to take sustenance and refunding it a short while later. It was like a dreadful case of the 'flu—dreadful first because it was so physically unpleasant, and second because I knew the peril I was in. Yellow jack rarely kills Erigans; they most often contract it in childhood, and afterward are immune, as we Scirlings are with measles or the pox. But for those of us not exposed to it from an early age, it can be very hazardous indeed.

I knew all this, and yet when my fever abated, I still fell prey to the unfounded optimism that accompanies the course of the disease. "I feel quite better," I insisted, and ate a hearty meal to prove it. "We shall be back at work tomorrow."

But Mr. Wilker would not let me take refuge in hope. "If you remain healthy for a week," he said, "then we may consider it. Until then, you rest."

He was, of course, correct. Some people escape yellow fever

that easily, but I was not among them. Shortly after my apparent recovery, I entered the second, and far worse, stage of the disease.

I can tell you very little of what happened during those days, at least from my own perspective. I was delirious with fever and pain, which rendered my memories little more than a hallucinatory smear of impressions. Natalie told me afterward that Akinimanbi's grandmother Apuesiso stripped me bare and coated me in cool mud, changing it as necessary to bring my fever down; this explains why, when I came to my senses, I was filthy and naked even by the minimalist standards of the Moulish. She also told me I vomited black bile, which is a terrible sign and heralds death more often than not. I dreamt of the talking drums, pounding out my doom. I shook and I raved; I sweated blood out my pores, and where the mud did not cover me my skin was gold with jaundice. In short, I nearly died—a phrase I can write with equanimity only because it was so long ago, and because I have the reassurance of knowing I survived. (As you can plainly tell, for I am not writing this memoir from beyond the grave.)

But at the time, it was nothing short of terrifying, even once the worst was past. Knowing that, having recovered, I was thereafter proof against further infections comforted me little; I had thought myself recovered before, only to be dragged under once more by the second stage of the fever. I lived in fear that this new reprieve was likewise temporary, and I would soon succumb entirely.

My will to live was sufficient to make me bathe, so that I could dress once more in something other than mud. But my enthusiasm for our research was shattered by the conviction that the Green Hell was going to kill me.

In this fragile state did the dragon find me.

If you have never been seriously ill, you cannot understand how sensitive your mind is afterward, how easily jarred by the world around you. But remember that state, if you have experienced it, and imagine it if you have not.

Now imagine that a sound begins in the forest, beyond range of your sight. It is a snarling, roaring sound, which your tired, sensitive mind immediately tries to identify, fitting it to one beast or another you have seen. You fail, because this is nothing like any animal call you have heard before, and this failure makes you afraid. Is the creature something new, or is your mind going to pieces?

Before you can answer that question, the sound changes. It draws closer, in a trampling rush that paralyzes you where you sit. And then *something* comes bursting between the trees, a beast like none in all the world, with a terrible maw and a seething, many-legged body behind it, which snarls and rages in a swift circle around you, then turns its fury upon your camp. It knocks down tents, flings your belongings into the dirt, scatters the fire and stomps your clothing into the ashes. It is chaos and noise incarnate, and if you were healthy and well rested you would recognize it as nothing more than someone wearing a wooden dragon mask, with others trailing behind it under cover like a Yelangese festival puppet.

I was not healthy, nor well rested, and I had never seen such a puppet. I shrieked and cowered, the noise and destruction too much for me to encompass. The dragon saw my fear and fed it, rushing at me again and again—and then, with one final snarl, vanished back into the forest.

Silence fell, more complete than any I had heard since coming to the Green Hell. The display had shocked even the natural beasts of the swamp into quiet.

Just as I began to regain my breath, Mr. Wilker broke the silence. Red with rage, he stormed forward, to where Apuesiso was picking herself up from the dirt. He swore the air blue in Scirling, then mastered his tongue enough to speak in a language she would understand. "What is the meaning of this? Your people have just destroyed half our things! They've terrorized Isabella—is this how you treat a woman only barely recovered?"

"It is how we warn those who do not listen."

The voice was not Apuesiso's. I turned, still trembling, and saw Akinimanbi standing a little way behind us. She and Mekeesawa had not been with our camp in some time—not since before I fell ill. When had she returned?

Only just now, by the surprise with which Mr. Wilker and Natalie faced her. Akinimanbi nodded to her grandmother. "She sent word of what happened, through the drums. We brought the *legambwa bomu*. It is a thing we do, when people ignore the advice of those around them."

That gave me the strength to rise to my feet. "You are saying I brought this upon *myself*? How? And what is this—this *destruction* supposed to teach me?"

"It teaches us all," Akinimanbi said, gesturing around the camp. Following her hand, I saw that Apuesiso and her husband Daboumen had not been spared the pseudo-dragon's wrath: it had torn leaves from the roof of their hut, smashed their meat-drying rack, broken the new spear Daboumen had been working on. "We have made noise in the world, and so it comes back to us. We are all to blame for letting it reach this point." Her gaze came back to me, its weight almost palpable. "You know what the noise is, Reguamin. You must root it out, before it kills you."

Noise, to the Moulish, was not simply unpleasant sound. It was a disruption to social harmony. And Akinimanbi directed her words to me, as the pseudo-dragon, the *legambwa bomu,* had directed its roars.

Even with my body and spirit exhausted by fever, I did not believe in witchcraft. But I had submitted before to foreign rites, in order to reassure those around me—could I not do the same here?

It depended on the rites in question. The Vystrani might have been Temple-worshippers, but at least they were Segulist. I did not know what might be required of me here.

There was a simple way to find out. I drew in a deep breath, stiffening my weak knees, then went forward so I could talk to Akinimanbi without others listening in. "What would I have to do, to rid myself of this ill?"

She said, "Witchcraft is caused by the evil in people's hearts. It unbalances the world and makes problems for everyone. What-ever evil is in your heart, you have to let it go."

I could not contain a weary snort. "It's that simple? I decide to let go of whatever troubles me, and all will be well?"

Akinimanbi shook her head. "Maybe others resent you. Maybe your brother and sister"—by which she meant Mr. Wilker and Natalie—"or people who aren't here. Have you done something to offend them?"

"I can hardly mend bridges with people all the way back in my homeland."

"Apologize to them anyway," she said. "Here, in camp. We will hear you, and so will the spirits."

Her advice struck me as oddly Segulist. The New Year lay several months off as yet, but she was urging me to repent of and atone for my errors. Had I not known better, I would have wondered whether sheluhim had come to the Green Hell after all, or some shred of our religion filtered through into the Moulish world. I think, however, that such practices are simply a basic human impulse. If we cannot ask for and receive forgiveness, how can any society survive?

I have never been a very good Segulist, though, and I still did not accept the notion that following Akinimanbi's counsel would end my misfortune. With all the dreary pessimism of my half-dead state, I told her as much.

Her reply was pragmatic and eye-opening. "Is that a reason to stay silent?"

There was no good answer to that. All the things I feared—giving in to superstition, humiliating myself in front of others, tearing the scabs off wounds I was happier ignoring—did not outweigh Akinimanbi's point. My spirit was *not* easy; it ached under the weight of all the things I had not said, even to myself. Even if that was not the cause of my woes, would it not be better to lay that burden down?

And—lest you think my motives were purely noble—I suspected that going along with her plan would also remove the barrier that stood in the way of my research.

(Admitting to such mercenary thinking will not reflect well on me, but I do not want anyone thinking I am one of the Righteous. The driving force in my life has always been my passion for draconic research, and although I have tried to be fair in my dealings with others as I pursue that goal, my motivations are not what you could call selfless.)

"Very well," I said, resigning myself to this fate. "Show me what to do."

I did not speak of what followed for many years after the fact. It was too personal, not only for myself, but for Natalie and Mr. Wilker, and while I may choose to expose my every flaw here in this text, I have no right to decide the same for them. Before he passed away, however, Mr. Wilker gave me permission to tell others what he said that day, and everything Natalie said became public eventually, in its own fashion. What Faj Rawango and our Moulish hosts said was, to their way of thinking, behind them as soon as the event ended; they do not object to others mentioning it later, so long as it is not done to encourage further discord. Furthermore, it feels contrary to the spirit of the event itself to dishonestly recount what we said. I will therefore set it down with as much precision as memory permits.

The Moulish, of course, have ceremonies for such things. The youths who had made up the *legambwa bomu* rejoined us, as did Mekeesawa, and we all seated ourselves around the central fire of the camp—a significant place, as it is both literally and metaphorically where they come together as kin. Certain leaves were thrown into the fire, creating fragrant smoke, and we scooped this smoke with our hands as if we were hunters departing with our nets. The leaves may have soporific qualities; I cannot say for sure. It is possible that the feeling of quiet contemplation that settled over me was simply the consequence of my choice.

I began by making my apologies to the camp. "We came here not to aid you and act as kin, but to learn about dragons. We want this knowledge for our own people—" I caught my phrasing, stopped, and began again. "*I* want this knowledge for *my* people. They will respect me more if I learn things they do not know. But they will not respect you for knowing it, because you are of a different people. I was going to present the knowledge as my own, even though you helped me gain it. That is not fair to you, and I am sorry."

Our hosts clapped their hands, to banish the evil in my words. Then Akinimanbi said, "I have been impatient with your ignorance, Reguamin. You try, but you are like a child; I have to spend much of my time telling you what to do or what is going to hurt you. It makes for more work." She cupped one hand over the bare skin of her belly. "But I carry a child now, and teaching you has prepared me to teach my son or daughter. I should not have resented you."

Dutifully I clapped my hands, but my cheeks heated with embarrassment. I was a world traveller, a natural historian, and beginning to think of myself as intrepid, even if that sense had taken a beating of late. Being called an ignorant child put me quite neatly in my place.

Mekeesawa spoke next. "My brother left to join another camp because he did not like having you among us. I had not seen him since before the floodwaters rose. I thought about going to visit him, but I did not want to leave Akinimanbi, and she did not want to leave you. Finally I insisted we go, and she agreed—but while we were gone, your troubles grew worse. She might have stopped it, if she had been here. I took that from you; and I was angry at you for being the reason I have not seen my brother, and for claiming so much of my wife's attention. Forgive me."

On it went, through Akinimanbi's grandparents and the others in camp. It was an eye-opening experience; despite living among them all these months, we had not seen the effects of our presence very clearly. Our willingness to do our part, however ineptly, had won us a degree of tolerance; but our ineptitude, and the burden it imposed on those around us, was greater than we had realized. I saw that understanding dawn on Natalie and Mr. Wilker, even as it did on me. They were not the focus of this undertaking, being not the ones supposedly targeted by witchcraft, but the arrangement of it was such that we could not help but all be made aware of some of our errors.

Faj Rawango kept his words simple, because of our Moulish audience. "You made a promise," he said. "You have not yet carried it out. If you are set on keeping your word, then I do not believe witchcraft will come on you—but if you are reluctant in your heart, it will."

My promise to the oba. Was I set on keeping my word? I honestly did not know. I should not have made that promise so blindly; I had sworn to give Ankumata something that belonged to another people, without understanding its value to them. I still hoped that, when I learned more, a solution would reveal itself—but what if it did not? Which obligation would I honour: my promise, or the debt I owed to the people around us now?

When it came time for Natalie to speak, she hesitated and looked around the fire. "I—I don't think I can say this in your language. Not easily."

Daboumen flapped one hand at her. "Your words are for your sister and for the spirits. They will understand you."

I confess I felt relief at that. The Moulish might be watching, but what we Scirlings had to say, we would say only to one another. Natalie looked equally glad. In our language she said, "The truth is that I'm not sure *what* to say. I think you were an idiot not to admit you were unwell, but apart from that, there's very little I resent you for, and far more to make me grateful."

"Your father would not agree," I said ironically. "If there is anyone minded to curse me, I think it may be him."

Natalie shrugged. "Apologize to him if you will, but not to me. While I do not think this is the life for me—I miss my bed too much—it has given me the courage, and I think the freedom, to pursue the life I *do* want."

"What is that?" I asked, curious.

She blushed and glanced sidelong at Mr. Wilker. "I—do you remember what I said to you before we left Scirland? About things I was not interested in?"

Her reddened cheeks directed my memory. She did not want the touch of a man. "Yes, I remember."

"While we were in Atuyem, I found out that sometimes co-wives will . . . provide one another with affection. I have wondered, from time to time, whether *that* is what I want. But I—well. Suffice it to say that I have tested my theory, and proved it false. I enjoy the company of women a great deal, but I honestly do not think I want anything, ah, *more*."

By now her blush was fierce, despite her oblique phrasing, and Mr. Wilker's expression far too stiff to pretend he had not caught her meaning. Sometimes a widow's companion provided her with more than just a friend, though such arrangements were not spoken of in polite society. I wondered with resignation whether *those* rumours had begun making the rounds as well.

"I understand, Natalie," I said. "And you are welcome to stay with me for as long as you please. If you do not want to join me on expeditions—"

"I honestly think I would like to work," she said. "At a proper career, I mean. But that is something we can talk of later."

Given a choice, I would have preferred to go on talking about whatever career she had in mind, rather than continuing with this ceremony. But the Moulish were waiting, and Mr. Wilker had not yet had his turn. Natalie and I clapped; the others followed suit; and now I had nothing left with which to delay.

He sighed. "Where to start."

"Oh dear," I said involuntarily, glad all over again that we were speaking Scirling. "That bad, is it?"

Mr. Wilker scrubbed one hand across his face. "No, not *that* bad. But we have never been very good at saying things to one another, have we?"

I had to grant the point. "We resented one another in Vystrana, for certain. I thought you low-class—which was entirely arrogant of me, and I'm sorry for that. But I also resented you for being a man, and not having to justify your presence on the expedition. You were skilled, and that was enough. *I* had to ride my husband's coat-tails."

"No coat-tail could have brought you in if Lord Hilford did not think you qualified," Mr. Wilker said. "Which I did not see at first. But even once you had proved yourself . . . I mean no slight against the earl, who has been exceedingly generous to me. But my position is far from secure. I feel the necessity, every day, of proving myself to him and to the world, and I have spent far too much time worrying that . . ." He trailed off, and I could tell he had gone further into the truth than he meant to. But having gone that far, he could not retreat, and so he finished what he had begun. "Worrying that I would lose my place to you."

Startled, I said, "But you have so much knowledge I lack!"

"Yes—but *you* amuse him. I don't mean to belittle you by saying that, either. Lord Hilford likes to shock people, and he likes other people who do the same. Getting as far as I have, though, has depended on caution, on never offending those whose toleration and aid I need. I may be a good assistant for him, but I am not what he looks for in a protégé."

We were indeed headed for territory through which our command of the Moulish language could not have borne us. I said, "I have wondered from time to time which of us faces the more difficult obstacles. A lady can be taken as an exception to the rules, if her breeding is good enough; mine will carry me this far, at least. You cannot escape your own breeding as easily. But I think that, in time, the quality of your work will win you a place in the Philosophers' Colloquium; they have taken men of your class before, if not often. They have never taken a woman. So there are doors that will open for you, which remain firmly nailed shut for me."

For the first time, I saw Thomas Wilker unbend enough to grin at me. "Shall we storm them together?"

"That sounds like a splendid plan," I said, and extended my hand. He took it in a firm grip, the way he might have taken a man's hand, not a lady's. The very frankness of the gesture made me say, "You—do not have an interest in marrying me, do you?"

A laugh exploded out of him. "For God's sake, no. No insult intended—"

"None taken. To be perfectly honest, I have little interest in remarrying." I sighed and released his hand, returning my own to my lap and studying it as if it were of great interest. "I would give a great deal for Jacob to still be alive. But with him gone . . . a widow has freedoms a wife does not. I could wish for greater financial security, but apart from that, what would I gain from having another husband?"

"It would provide a father for your son," he said.

That swiftly, the scab was torn off. Little Jacob: he did not deserve to be thought of as a wound, but there it was, and with my defenses lowered by illness and this ritual, I could no longer pretend otherwise. A sudden jolt rattled my shoulders, as if something—a laugh, a sob, a shout—wanted to burst free. "My son. Oh, God. What am I to do with him?"

"What do you mean?"

The words came forth, slowly at first, then increasing until they formed a flood. "How could I risk coming here, when I have a son? Of course, few people ask that question of men who leave *their* sons behind to go abroad—because those sons have mothers to care for them. But even if the man is a widower, he does not face a tenth the censure I have received. Should his child be orphaned, everyone will pat the boy on the head and praise his father's courage. Should *I* die, Jacob will grow up knowing his mother was an unfeeling madwoman who got what she deserved."

I could not bear to look at anyone, whether they spoke my language or not. I fixed my gaze on the fire, as if its flames could burn this tangle out of me, and leave me free of such conflicts. "I *resent* my son. There—I have said it. I resent him because he shackles me; I cannot live the life I want, not without feeling guilty for devoting my heart to the thing that makes me happy. Surely it is selfish of me to care so much about the contributions I could make with my intellect; surely the greatest contribution to society a woman can hope to make lies in raising her children. No sacrifice she might make is too small, in service to that great cause.

"And all the while I have people telling me, *at least you still have something of your husband.* Do they mean the book chronicling our work in Vystrana? No, of course not—never mind that we undertook that work together, with intent. That cannot *possibly* be as valuable as the accidental consequence of biology."

Very quietly, Tom said, "Is not a child worth more than a book?"

"Yes," I said violently. "But then for God's sake let us value my son for *himself,* and not as some relic of his father. When he is grown enough to read, I will be delighted to share his father's legacy with him; it is my legacy as well, and I hope he has inherited our curiosity enough to appreciate it. I would not mind a motherhood where *that* was my purpose—to foster my son's mind and teach him the intellectual values of his parents. But no; society tells me my role is to change his napkins and coo over the faces he makes, and in so doing abandon the things I want him to treasure when he is grown."

At long last I brought my gaze away from the fire. Akinimanbi sat with one hand on her belly; she was bearing, and seemed glad of it. I was happy for her—but I had never particularly wanted that for myself, and at least half of my disinterest in remarrying stemmed from that fact.

"'Would that I were a man,'" I said, quoting Sarpalyce's legend. "Except that I do not wish I were a man. I only wish that being a woman did not limit me so."

The fire crackled quietly. Then, nodding—in understanding or acceptance, perhaps both—Tom Wilker brought his hands together in a clap.

The others followed suit. I did not cry; I have rarely been prone to tears. But I felt purified. There is a word I learned later, a term from Nichaean drama: *catharsis*. I had, at long last, said what was bottled up tight in my heart, and while I still did not believe in evil spirits, I felt infinitely more free for having spoken.

Of course, others believed in evil spirits. Daboumen gestured me out of the way. I obeyed and watched, mystified, as he dug in the soil beneath where I had been sitting. I had chosen the spot of my own free will—no one directed me there—but a few inches below the surface, he found a twisted, ugly piece of wood. (Cynic that I am, I believe he placed it there by sleight of hand, though I am uncertain how he managed that when his only garment was a loincloth.)

"The witch put this there," he said, and gave it to me. I did not need his gesture to guess my part in the script: I threw the twisted thing into the fire.

"Now," Akinimanbi said, "you are free."

PART FOUR

In which I make several discoveries,
not all of them related to dragons

SEVENTEEN

Improved fortune—A newcomer in camp—The "pure"—
The Great Cataract—Yeyuama's challenge

When I have related an abbreviated version of this tale to others, every last one of them has asked the same question: did the ritual work?

I am not sure how to answer that. Did we suffer no more mishaps in our research? Of course not; we were still in the Green Hell, which had not transformed itself into the Garden of Paradise simply because my companions and I voiced our woes. Furthermore, I doubt there is a single person reading this account who is not aware of the even larger problems I was to encounter before long.

But it is true that I no longer felt myself jinxed. In part, I attribute this to the improvement of my mood and my concentration; I no longer made the sorts of careless errors that had caused me trouble before. The rapport between myself and my companions improved, and so did the coordination of our efforts, with concomitant good effects. And since human minds are very good at finding patterns, and ours had recently shifted from looking for bad luck to looking for good, we wrote off setbacks as expected, rather than proof of misfortune. This is how I explain it, at any rate; our Moulish hosts, of course, viewed the matter differently.

What mattered was that both groups were in better spirits, and as a result my companions and I soon found ourselves offered the very opportunity we had been looking for.

It began with the arrival of a newcomer into camp, a man I had never met before. Mekeesawa introduced the man as his brother Yeyuama, and I soon realized he was an *actual* brother: related by blood, not merely by age, as the Moulish measure such things.

Yeyuama was not like the other Moulish men we had known, in any age group. "Did he go out hunting with you yesterday?" I asked one morning, about three weeks after I had purged myself of the witchcraft taint.

The intimacy of the ritual had changed matters between Thomas Wilker and myself; he was Tom to me now, and I was Isabella. (Natalie remained "Miss Oscott" to him, I think because of his situation with her grandfather. I found myself much more aware now of his little deferences, the ways in which he acknowledged his lower-class origins and made certain no one would think him trying to rise above them.) Tom said, "Not that I saw. Was he here in camp?"

"Not that *we* saw," Natalie said. And that was peculiar indeed, for it did not fit any of the patterns we knew for Moulish responsibilities.

Yeyuama did not keep us wondering for long. He came over to

the fire we had built in front of our much-bedraggled tents and squatted on his haunches with the ease of a man who has sat thus his entire life. "You follow the dragons, Reguamin," he said.

Followed, and stared at. "With caution, yes," I said, hoping my humourous tone would come through. Yeyuama had an air about him that intrigued me: both gentle and watchful, as if he could spring into action at a moment's notice. He was *extremely* fit; the Moulish are not a fat people, as a consequence of diet, behaviour, and natural physique, but Yeyuama had the compact musculature of a man who both eats well and exercises often.

He cocked his head at me. "Have you killed?"

"A dragon? No, of course not. I know the story."

Yeyuama waved that away. "Not only dragons. Anything."

My thoughts raced back to the savannah snakes we had hunted, the rock-wyrm in Vystrana, the wolf-drake I had shot (but not killed) when I was fourteen. "With my own hands?" He nodded. I was about to say no—I *wanted* to say no, as it was clear which answer Yeyuama was looking for—when I remembered the Great Sparkling Inquiry.

Both ethics and pragmatism prevented me from lying to him, the latter because my face fell before I could stop it. "Yes. In my homeland, there are these creatures . . ." I held out my fingers to indicate the size of a sparkling. "Like insects."

(Lest anyone accuse me of dishonesty, I must assure you that my taxonomic speculations had not yet gone so far as to change my thinking about sparklings. Would I have admitted it to Yeyuama, had I begun to think of them as members of the draconic lineage? I do not know. The honourable answer, of course, is yes—but I am not certain my ethics would have carried me that far.)

Yeyuama brushed this off as being of no consequence. Everyone in Moulish society killed things like insects, but only grown men were hunters. He looked next at Natalie, who denied killing anything, and Tom, who confessed it. Yeyuama nodded, as if he had expected that. "What I have to say is not for you," he told Tom. "Only the pure may hear it."

The pure: those who had never hunted and killed. Yeyuama was pure; he never went with the other men. He was, I realized, the closest thing to a priest one might find in Moulish society. This must be what Yves de Maucheret had meant.

With our recent conversation so fresh in my mind, I could easily read Tom's expression. Here, where there was no stratification of wealth or birth, he had expected to be able to participate in full; to be refused, as the Colloquium refused him, cut deeply. On impulse, I said to him in Scirling, "You've shot animals with a gun. Perhaps that doesn't count as 'with your own hands'?"

That provoked a rueful, bitter laugh. "No, I imagine it counts. And besides, when I was fifteen I cut the throat of my family's carthorse after he broke his leg. Don't offer," he said, forestalling the next words out of my mouth. "It may upset them if you share what he says afterward. If this is a research opportunity, then you two should make the best of it." He got up and left.

As it transpired, the core of what Yeyuama told us was not so secret that I feel obliged to leave it out of this narrative. (There would be a great gaping hole if I did, as if you walked in at the tail end of some tremendous anecdote being told over drinks. Everyone in the room would be goggling and laughing and you would wonder where the elephant came from.) I may elide some details, but the bulk of it should be clear to you.

"There is a test," Yeyuama said, once Tom was gone. "Before you can touch the dragons. This test is dangerous; sometimes it kills those who try."

A Moulish man—a lifelong resident of the Green Hell—was telling me something was dangerous. I said before that the Moulish do not fear their home, because they know how to survive it; this does not mean, however, that they fail to respect its perils. I asked, "Do we have to say now whether we will try? Or may we decide after we know what the test is?"

Yeyuama laughed, breaking the atmosphere of hushed secrecy. "Only a fool would agree without knowing. I will show you. There is no shame in refusing; most boys do."

For there to be men like Yeyuama, who have abstained from killing in order to remain pure, this test must be offered while they are still young—before they, as youths, join the men on the hunt. I use male terms; virtually all of those who "touch the dragons" (a phrase whose meaning will become apparent later on) are men, though the Moulish denied any prohibition against women when I asked. It is simply that the challenge is a strenuous one, and few women choose to undertake it. But there was no resistance to Natalie and I trying. Merely a great deal of curiosity, to see how the Scirling women would do.

This challenge required us to go with Yeyuama on a lengthy journey. He would not name our destination, but we knew it lay west, toward the cliff from which the three rivers fall. It would take us the better part of a month to get there and return, he estimated, and no one could go with us who was not also pure.

Which meant leaving behind both Tom and Faj Rawango. The latter said, "After this, you will get eggs for the oba."

The way he phrased it, I wasn't sure whether it was a statement or a command. "After this, I may finally have some notion of how to *do* that. But much will depend on when the egg-laying season is." I thought about how long we had already been gone, and added, "Would you like to go back and report to him? He must be wondering."

"No," Faj Rawango said. "I will stay here." (A decision which I chalked up mostly to his unwillingness to report so little progress. He did not seem to be enjoying his sojourn among his father's kindred.)

Tom was another matter. "You'll be going from camp to camp," he said, having queried Yeyuama for details. "Not going entirely on your own. Still . . ."

"You do not like it," I said.

"First that business with witchcraft, now this test of theirs. I didn't expect you to embrace so many of their ways."

I had not *embraced* anything. In the case of the witchcraft ceremony, it was more "shoved unwillingly," and as for this—"We require doctors to obtain certification before they can practice, and lawyers must sit examinations before they can pass the bar. Whatever this test may be, think of it in that light. It is a matter of qualification, nothing more."

"Passing the bar," he said dryly, "rarely threatens one's life. But you're right about one thing: it appears to be necessary. We can observe dragons all we like, but there are some secrets we won't know unless you go through with this. I'm not trying to stop you. I only wish we had another way."

For my own part, I wished he could come with us, though I had wit enough not to pain him by saying so. Natalie and I packed up what we could; it was not much, as neither of us had the strength of neck to carry a basket on a tumpline. Then we made our farewells to Tom and Faj Rawango, Akinimanbi and Mekeesawa, Apuesiso and Daboumen, and ventured deeper into the swamp.

I will gloss over the process of our journey, in favor of coming more quickly to its end. Suffice it to say that we did, as Tom had predicted, go from camp to camp, meeting both strangers and people who had formerly been part of our own camp, and enduring a thousand questions when they discovered that Yeyuama was taking us on this pilgrimage. I soon realized our destination was not secret; it was merely taboo, a thing not spoken of except when the occasion arose. Those we passed seemed to have at least a general understanding of what Natalie and I faced, and few of them seemed to think we stood much chance.

There is no faster way to harden my determination to do a thing than to assume I will fail at it. But when I saw at last the challenge Yeyuama intended, the revelation shook even my self-confidence and will.

We had left the last camp behind two days before. My sense of geography was sorely addled by the tracklessness of the swamp, but Natalie and I, making estimates of the distance we had traveled, could guess where Yeyuama was taking us. We were drawing near to the western border of the Green Hell.

The noise grew by subtle degrees as we traveled onward, at first remaining faint enough that my conscious mind did not notice it. Then it rose high enough to attract my attention: the steady, rushing thunder of falling water. "We must be near," I said, and got a bright grin from Yeyuama in response.

This I took to be agreement, only realizing my error after we had slogged at least another mile onward. We were not yet near at all. I had simply underestimated the magnitude of what we had come to see.

The Great Cataract of Mouleen.

As I have said before, the three rivers of Girama, Gaomomo, and Hembi come together west of the Moulish swamp, a confluence of the sort that happens in many parts of the world. But here, as nowhere else, the rivers are stopped shy of their peaceful meeting by a fault in the earth that dropped the land of Mouleen not quite a hundred meters below the rivers' previous beds. Along this curving and irregular edge, the three rivers spread out and break up their flow, plunging downward in a roar of countless waterfalls.

Yeyuama brought us to the very edge of the great lake which forms the base of these falls, an expanse of water large enough to give me an unobstructed view of much of the Great Cataract. Even at this range, I could feel the force of it: the constant thunder of the water, torrents of it crashing endlessly down, threatening to drive the air from my lungs. Everywhere I looked I saw rainbows, light refracting from the mist thrown off by the falls. I might have stepped through some portal into a magical place—the homeland of wild-hearted faerie creatures grander and more terrible than any human could hope to understand.

My face opened with exhilaration, in an expression that was not quite a laugh. I could not help myself; the madness I felt at the mere sight of this place could not be held in. Natalie looked much the same. Yeyuama was solemn by comparison; but then, of course, he had been here before. And this place, clearly, was sacred to his people.

I could not imagine a place less like the sober Assembly Houses I associated with religion; but I could, with no difficulty at all, understand why one might attach such a word to this place. Such sublime grandeur seemed very much like a thing of the gods.

The cataract itself was too breathtaking to behold for long, even though the height of the floods had passed and the waters of the swamp were beginning to subside. My eye sought out more restful sights. I saw that the lake was the hollow pounded out by the falling water, and surmised that it must be quite deep. From there the mingled contents of the three rivers spread out through the low-lying region we called Mouleen, and thus gave rise to the swamp; indeed, from here we could no longer speak of it in a meaningful sense as a river, whether singular or multiple, for the waterways branched and recombined into the mazelike delta which I had been inhabiting for the last five months.

But for what purpose had Yeyuama brought us all this way?

Such was the noise that I had to raise my voice almost to a shout in order to be heard. "Is this the place of the test?" I asked, gesturing at the entire stunning scene: cataract, lake, and all.

Yeyuama grinned again. "*That,* Reguamin, is your test!" And he pointed.

The broken curve of the Great Cataract was not a single fall, but many. Here and there along its length, islands persisted on the edge, dividing the whole into its parts. It was not, however, to one of these that Yeyuama directed my attention, but rather to an island *within* the cascade itself.

It jutted out from the white thunder perhaps two-thirds of the way between us and the plateau above. It was framed by falling water all around: the rivers tumbling down one stage behind, then parting to plummet the remaining distance on either side. Thinner trickles, some of which might have been respectable falls in other parts of the world, ran through the island and emerged from its front like strings of diamonds. And the whole of the island was thickly covered in verdant growth, trees finding purchase on the stone, vines falling in elegant curtains below.

"You must visit that island," Yeyuama said, his voice strong over the roar of the water. "Then you will be ready to touch the dragons."

I understood why many boys refused, and few women tried. Visit the island? How was one to get up there, or for that matter to come back? It stood in the midst of the falls, nowhere near the border of the lake. To go over the first edge in a boat (or the more stereotypical barrel) would only result in missing the island, or being dashed to pieces if one did not. Swimming the lake would be both hazardous and difficult, as the current pushed one away from the base, and once that obstacle was surmounted one still had the challenge of climbing the rock face.

Yes, these were the thoughts in my mind as I stared at the Great Cataract of Mouleen. Of course I had begun to ponder how it might be done. If you know anything of my life, you will not be surprised.

Natalie and I discussed it, once we had retired far enough to be able to converse in more normal tones. "I expect it used to all be like that," she said, sketching out a shape with her hands. "Multiple tiers—you can still see fragments of it, apart from that major island. But the force of the water would, over time, knock down the lower tiers, leaving that one remnant as the only piece of significant size."

The geologic history of the place interested me less than the navigational opportunities it afforded. "I don't suppose there are likely to be caves behind? Perhaps it's a mystery of sorts, with a tunnel that offers safe passage. Those who pass the test are the ones who find it."

"And those that don't are the ones who die," Natalie said, with a decided lack of optimism. "It would be lovely if there were a tunnel, but somehow I don't think you will be that lucky."

I noticed her choice of pronoun. Somehow, without ever saying so directly, we had agreed that I would be the one to attempt this thing, not both of us together. There was no particularly good reason for it, and several against; indeed, others were quick to point out later that only one of us had a small dependent child at home, and that one was not Natalie. But only one of us was mad enough to try, and that one was not Natalie, either.

Because I could not look at that island, overgrown and floating in the midst of rainbows, and not want to experience the triumph of standing on it with my own two feet.

Yeyuama caught frogs and roasted them while the two of us discussed the matter in Scirling. There was no need to speak in the Moulish tongue for his benefit; he had made it clear that he would offer no advice, and he was good enough at maintaining his poise that no twitch of alarm or satisfaction would steer us in one direction or another. We were entirely on our own.

"Why is this the test?" I asked at one point, when our speculations had ground to a halt. Then I repeated myself in Moulish, for this, at least, was a question Yeyuama might answer.

But he shook his head. "You will see—or you will not."

Meaning that only those who passed the test were fit to know the answer. I ground my teeth in frustration and renewed my

determination to reach that island.

We scouted the area for another two days, circling the edge of the lake to view the island from different angles. It seemed likely that the best approach was from above, coming down from the rivers onto the island; without viewing the land up there it was hard to be certain, but it seemed more promising than any attempt to come at it from below. But then how to return? "If I had a long enough rope . . ." I began, then shook my head. "It would have to be absurdly long, and I have never been good at climbing."

Natalie opened her mouth to answer, then stopped.

"No, it's foolish," she said, when I looked at her inquisitively.

I laughed. "And I am, of course, the *last* person to entertain foolish notions. Out with it, my dear."

"You would break your neck," she protested.

"And I am unlikely to do so by the means we have already discussed? You have my curiosity up now, you know. There is no help for it; you will have to tell me."

She sighed. "We don't even have suitable wood, so it couldn't be done anyway. But I was thinking of those glider wings."

Her obsession back in Scirland. An untested design, though recently improved by that enthusiast in Lopperton.

A chance to *fly*.

I tried to throw a halter over the nose of my sudden, wild hope and hold it back from galloping away. It was reckless. It was impossible. Natalie was right; we did not have suitable wood.

We did, however, have something else.

EIGHTEEN

A need for dragonbone—Sketches in the air—
An angry dragon—More truth—"We have the forest"

C

an you not tell me what you need them for?" Tom asked, as we waded across a shallow stream. "Even the slightest hint."

I could have told him that I didn't want to offend Yeyuama and the others; it had the virtue of being true. It was not, however my chief reason. "If I tell you, then you will try to talk me out of it."

He stopped on the bank and stared at me. "Is that supposed to set me at ease?"

Our time in the swamp had left him a scruffy thing, his clothing stained beyond repair, his hair grown shaggy and his jaw darkened by stubble. Likely my own appearance was little better (although I was at least spared the stubble). Had we wandered the streets of Falchester in this state, we would have been thought lunatics—which was, I imagined, not far off the mark. Long residence in harsh and unfamiliar conditions does strange things to the mind. You swiftly learn not to heed irritations that would be unbearable in the normal course of your affairs, and you embrace notions that would be unthinkable at home.

"It is supposed to be honest," I said. "I do not want you chiding me afterward for hiding more from you than I must."

Tom's first response to that was inarticulate. Then he said, "I have asked myself, time and again, what possible need you could have for dragonbone—*dragonbone,* when we're among a people for whom dragons are in some way sacred. You don't mean to impress them with it; that wouldn't be as dangerous as you've implied. What, then? Everything I can think of is worse than the previous idea."

He would not have thought of Natalie's wings; I was fairly certain he had no idea of her interest in the subject. I considered asking him what he *had* thought of, but decided it would only upset him further. Instead I fell back on the only recourse available to me, which was simple persuasion. "Please, Tom. If we are to proceed with our research, and fulfill our promise to the oba, I must do this. And it will go better with your help."

He sighed in frustration, but said, "I am here, am I not?"

"Yes," I admitted. "For which I thank you."

By then the others had caught up to us: Natalie and Yeyuama, Mekeesawa and Faj Rawango. The rest of our camp was not far off, but we six were making a side journey to retrieve something left behind during our earliest days in the Green Hell.

The box was still where we had buried it. Already the wood was somewhat worse off for being buried in the wet earth, and the fabric that wrapped the bones was half-eaten by insects, but the bones were still wholly preserved.

"Will it be acceptable to use this?" I asked Yeyuama, holding out an alar humerus for him to see.

He frowned at the bone. "Who killed this dragon?"

"A hunter," I said. "But not in the way that your brothers are hunters. He kills animals only for the pleasure of proving himself stronger than they, and takes trophies to prove his strength to others." Yeyuama indicated the bone, and I shook my head. "He does not know we have this, and would try to take it if he did. We kept the bones so we could understand dragons better."

Akinimanbi had explained to him our purpose in the swamp. Her rendition had made us sound more like priests than scholars— but that was not entirely unfitting; or at least it was useful to our cause. Yeyuama said, in a cool tone masking something I could not read, "Dragon bones fall to dust. How is this one still solid?"

We had been cautious in who we shared that information with, but I had no fear of sharing the truth with him. Not because he lived far from Vystrana and would never trouble the dragons there; not because he lacked the chemical equipment to imitate our work. Those things were true, but also irrelevant. Yeyuama was pure: he would never kill a dragon for its bones. Nor would he help others do so.

I therefore told him everything, as much as my command of his language allowed. The mourning behaviour of rock-wyrms; Rossi's experimentation; Frederick Kemble's struggle to synthesize a replacement for the bones, which might be aided by Tom's efforts with the savannah snakes. Yeyuama listened in silence, and when I was done he sighed, gesturing at the bones. "You should not have done this before facing the island. But you may use it."

I wondered if the Moulish had funerary customs for their own dragons. Was that what Yeyuama meant by "touching the dragons"? Well, I would find out soon enough—if I did not break my neck.

Natalie sorted through the bones, chewing on her lower lip.

"Mr. Garsell insists a curved surface is better, but still, I could wish some of these were straighter. The ribs, though, will be useful for the center of the frame, and we can make cords . . ." She trailed off, sketching in the air.

Tom had a good visual imagination. He followed the movement of her finger with narrowed eyes. Before I could divert him, his jaw sagged in disbelief. "You—Isabella, *please* tell me she isn't planning to build some kind of wing."

My mouth opened and shut a few times, while he stared at me. Then, helplessly, I said, "Would you like the truth, or a comforting lie?"

"What in God's name are you *doing?*" he demanded. We were speaking Scirling; the three Erigans looked on in interest, no doubt speculating as to what we might be saying. "Do you have to fly with the dragons to prove your right to study them? Moulish swamp-wyrms don't even *fly!*"

"They do glide, though—and I shall do the same. It's an unconventional solution to the problem I've been set . . . but Tom, I believe it will work."

He squeezed his eyes shut, hands frozen in midair as if, should he just concentrate hard enough, he could make this entire conversation not have happened. Then he opened his eyes and fixed his gaze on Yeyuama. In Moulish, he said, "I know I am not 'pure.' But please, for the love of—of whatever spirits you worship, let me help with this. If she is injured, I'll never forgive myself."

His concern touched me, all the more so because he made no reference to the consequences he would likely face in the event of my death. Jacob had once told me he would be blamed if anything happened to me in Vystrana; Tom, I suspected, now occupied the role of "man responsible for my well-being" in the eyes of society. I said to Yeyuama, "He has some knowledge of healing injuries. I hope, of course, that his skills will not be necessary, but if they are . . ."

Yeyuama sighed, looking resigned. "If I don't agree, he will probably follow us." Tom did not deny it. "Very well, Reguamin. Your brothers and sister may assist you. But they may not go all the way with you."

(At the time, it surprised me that Yeyuama agreed to let anyone else be involved. In retrospect, I think Tom was not the only one dumbfounded at my chosen approach to the problem of the island, and Yeyuama did not want to be responsible for killing me, however indirectly. That is only speculation on my part, though.)

We bundled up the bones Natalie deemed useful and took them with us back to camp, but we would not be with our hosts for much longer. As I proposed to come at the Great Cataract from above, and was bringing bulky equipment with me for the task, it would be easier for us to make the journey along the top edge of the swamp, rather than in its depths. So long as our paths lay together, however, we would travel with the other members of the camp, who were shifting to a new location.

It was by then becoming a larger group once more, as the seasonal round brought the Moulish back together, and they sang as they walked. Natalie had been singing with the Moulish for some time, but now Tom joined in; his voice was rough but tuneful. "You should sing," Yeyuama prompted me; when we left the camp, he would break off on his own to wait for me at the base of the Great Cataract.

"Oh, no," I said hastily. "The frogs are more melodious than I."

He seemed puzzled by my protest. "Why does that matter? It makes harmony."

The word he used, *ewele,* has the same double meaning as its Scirling translation: not only the effect produced by music, but a concord among people. Judging by the way he deployed it now, he meant the latter sense—or rather, he meant the latter produced the former. Still—"I would be embarrassed to try."

But Yeyuama would not accept my refusal. Nothing would do but that I sing. And so I did; Natalie gave me an encouraging pat on the shoulder, and Tom did his best not to wince. But the Moulish all smiled: however out of tune I might be, now I was harmonious.

Our harmony, alas, did not last. It was broken by a furious, coughing snarl, and the sound came from some distance ahead.

All singing fell silent. The hunters, who carried few burdens other than their spears and nets, dropped anything else they held and vanished into the surrounding growth. Mothers and elders boosted children into the trees, and within a few seconds I could not see them, either. Even after my time among them, I was startled at the speed with which they all concealed themselves.

Yeyuama had gone stiff at my side. He met my gaze, and I saw him make a decision. "Dragon," he said, and I nodded. "An angry one. Come."

That seemed to be extended to all three of us—three, because Faj Rawango had gone with the hunters. Tom stepped forward, but Natalie shook her head and grabbed the bones tied to his back. "Leave these with me. I'll hide them."

As I went forward with Tom and Yeyuama, I wondered uneasily whether those bones might be the cause of the disturbance. It was the death and theft of their kin that had made the Vystrani rock-wyrms angry; we had not observed anything of the sort here, but the absence of evidence is not the evidence of absence. Moulish dragons were sullen and hostile creatures under the best of circumstances, but I had never seen one in a fury. Had we inadvertently provoked this one?

I had my answer soon enough, in the shouts and curses of men.

They were not speaking the Moulish tongue. I picked out Yembe words here and there, but the part that came through the most clearly to me was an unholy admixture of Thiessois and Eiversch. And although I had not heard that voice in months, the language of the profanity told me who the speaker must be.

M. Velloin had come into the swamp in search of newer and more exciting prey.

Yeyuama's expression hardened as I gave him this explanation in a quick, worried undertone. "We will not let him kill a dragon," he said—leaving unspoken what measures they might take to prevent him. Yeyuama himself might be pure, his hands unsullied by death, but the same was not true for the hunters.

I half-expected to hear screams before we even reached the scene. The hunters, after all, had gone before us, and must already be in place. I also expected the raging of the dragon to subside, for Velloin was assuredly armed with a good rifle, and had shown pride in the swift kill. But neither shift came, and as we crept to the edge of the scene behind Yeyuama, I saw for myself what was happening.

Five or six Yembe hunters were ranged around the dragon, spears at the ready—but it was spears they held, not rifles, and they used them only to keep the dragon at bay. Three other men were engaged at closer range, hauling with all their might on ropes that had been looped about the swamp-wyrm's limbs. Velloin stalked around this fray, protected, as the others were, by a kerchief tied over his mouth and nose in addition to a pair of goggles, to keep the noxious gas from his eyes. He held another lasso in his hands, and as I watched, he flung it over the dragon's muzzle and dragged the loop tight.

"God almighty," I whispered, staring. "They're not trying to kill the dragon. They're trying to *capture* it."

Velloin had done it before, and had said he wanted to try again. But the swamp-wyrm before us was no runt; it was a splendid beast, one of the largest I had seen. Even with four men trying to bind it, the creature still thrashed. It was difficult to imagine Velloin could drag it ten feet like that, let alone into a cage.

As it transpired, he didn't intend to. Velloin passed his rope to another man, then picked up a bow. The arrow he nocked was too light to have any chance of killing the creature, but before he put it to the string, he dipped the head in a small clay jar. Poison of some kind, I assumed. Something to weaken and slow the dragon for easier transport.

He did not get the chance to try. Yeyuama had been watching the scene with narrowed eyes; when he saw the poisoned arrow, he lifted his hands to his mouth and made a sound like a birdcall. Like, but not the same: clearly it was a signal, and just as clearly, this was what our own hunters had been waiting for.

I would have sworn my oath on the Holy Scripture that there were no Moulish in the immediate vicinity of this struggle, but on Yeyuama's call, half a dozen nets dropped from the trees to snare the men below. Spears thudding into the ground at the feet of the Yembe caused several of them to leap back. Ropes slipped free of hands, and then the dragon spun about, smashing men to the ground with its muscular tail.

What followed was chaos. Half-restrained as it was, the swamp-wyrm could not move easily, but it was determined to crush its tormentors; then Yembe spears began to stick in its hide, and it changed its intent to flight. This most of the Yembe seemed willing to let it do, but as the dragon slipped away, I saw Velloin raising a rifle.

"*No!*"

I did not even realize I was the one who had shouted until I had already flung myself forward. Then there was nothing to do but continue. "Hold your fire, sir!" I commanded, staggering across the trampled ground, coughing on the foul air.

One of the Yembe caught me. But I had caught Velloin's attention; for a moment that rifle was pointed at me. Then the hunter saw me properly, and jerked in surprise.

"Well," he said, tugging down the kerchief that covered his face. "Mrs. Camherst, I presume. My God—you still live."

"I was not aware my status was in question," I said, trying and failing to pull my arms free of my captor. "Will you tell this man to unhand me?"

Velloin grinned, not pleasantly. "I do not give orders to the son of a king, Mrs. Camherst."

Confused, I twisted to look up at the man holding me. He released one arm and uncovered his own face, revealing Okweme n Kpama Waleyim.

"Is this your scheme?" I asked him. "Or Velloin's? I have a hard time believing it is his; surely he would prefer to kill his prey, rather than snare it."

Okweme's grin was as unpleasant as Velloin's. Had I ever thought the man friendly, let alone attractive? "We are here at the request of my royal father. He will not be glad to hear that you interfered."

"It wasn't just her," Velloin said. He resettled his rifle on his shoulder. "Those nets and spears must have come from the swamp rats. Come out!" he shouted, turning to scan the trees. "We know you are there."

Tom needed no encouragement; indeed, I suspected Yeyuama must have been holding him back. Yeyuama himself followed a step behind. One might have mistaken his slow stride for relaxed, but to my eye, it had more the character of focused anger. The hunters stayed hidden, and I blessed them for it.

I had grown accustomed to measuring people according to Moulish stature, against which Tom, whose height was middling at best, seemed a giant. Facing Okweme and Velloin, Yeyuama was almost childlike in his smallness. There was nothing childlike, however, in the look he directed at the interlopers. "You are not welcome here."

"Speak Yembe," Okweme snapped.

Yeyuama merely raised his eyebrows at the man. "He doesn't know your language," I said, remembering my own experience with the Moulish tongue. "He might pick a few words out from what you say, and vice versa for you—no more."

"Then you translate," Okweme said.

However little I wanted to follow his orders, an interpreter would be necessary. "Unhand me, and I will."

Scowling, Okweme complied. I explained my position to Yeyuama, then repeated his original message and his subsequent expansion. "You have tried to harm one of the dragons. Because

he is feeling merciful, he will let you go, but you must not return."
(His actual phrasing had been "Because you are ignorant," but I
softened it; proverbs about shooting the messenger kept dancing
through my mind.)

"Harm?" Velloin said, with half a laugh. "That is rich. How
many have you harmed, Mrs. Camherst, pursuing your research?
Or are you still reliant on others to do your butchery for you?"

"I can learn by observation alone—and so I have," I said.
Yeyuama looked to Tom for a translation, but Tom was rigid with
tension, watching the rest of us. Gritting my teeth, I conveyed
what Velloin had said.

Velloin saw my discomfort and pressed the advantage. "Have
you stolen any eggs yet? *Eggs*," he repeated in Yeyuama's direction,
very loudly, making sure he noticed the word. "Tell your friend
about your own orders—that the oba sent you to take away
something even more precious than a living dragon. See how he
likes you, when he hears that."

He had me over a barrel. I was not good enough at lying to
make up something else to say to Yeyuama; even my hesitation
gave too much away. Desperate, I looked at Tom, and saw him
open his mouth, perhaps to lie on my behalf.

No, I thought, very distinctly. Perhaps I was like these two, in
that I had come here for the oba's gain as well as my own. I would
not further compound that by trying to conceal anything. That
was witchcraft, at least in the nonsupernatural sense; it was evil.
And such evil must be purged with truth.

I relayed Velloin's words as faithfully as I could, then said, "It
is true. The ruler of Bayembe sent me here to take eggs, though I
have not done it. If these men do not shoot us, I will explain more

later; but the explanation will not supercede the apology I give you now. I made my promise to the oba in foolish ignorance, without first learning what its consequences would be. I am sorry. And I am doubly sorry for not telling you sooner."

Yeyuama listened without blinking, without any hint of reaction. When I was done, he remained silent a moment longer, while my nerves wound tight. Then he said, "You will be tested. After that, we will see."

Tested? Another witchcraft ritual, perhaps. Okweme interrupted my speculations. "What did he say?"

I translated both that and Yeyuama's next words. "You are noisy—he means something more like 'disruptive'—and ignorant, and you do not care to learn. You must leave now."

Velloin snorted. "How does he think to make us leave? We have rifles."

"And we have poisoned spears," Yeyuama said, through me. "We have nets and traps. We have the forest. You are villagers, and our home will eat you. Go now."

The other Yembe heard my translation and looked uneasy. They were indeed villagers, outsiders to this place, and although they had spent this entire time looking for the hunters they *knew* must be about, they had not yet spotted a single one.

It was a fragile threat. These people could easily kill Yeyuama; the Moulish, however, could kill more than a few of them. Then the oba might send a larger force, this one hunting not dragons, but men. However well the Moulish knew the Green Hell, they were safe here largely because no one cared to face the difficulty of coming after them. If they gave the oba a reason to change his mind, they would lose.

But those were future possibilities; the present was this confrontation, and I could see that the other men were not eager to gamble their lives against the demons of the forest.

"I recommend you take his advice," I said. "The Moulish are quite fierce in defending what they hold sacred. Please assure the oba that I will have useful information for him soon; he must, however, be patient a while longer." Information, of course, was not the same thing as eggs, nor was "useful" the same thing as "encouraging." But it would, I hoped, buy us a little more time.

"Very well," Velloin said, and shot a look at Okweme that silenced whatever the prince had been about to say.

Tom spoke, for the first time since this entire affair began. "I don't recommend trying to come back at a different point. By this time tomorrow, the entire swamp will know of your hunting party, and I doubt they'll be so generous a second time." The talking drums. The Moulish were not a unified state, but at times like this, they could act in concert, and would.

I did not know whether Tom had convinced Velloin or Okweme, but it at least gave the other Yembe something else to be worried about. The two leaders might have a mutiny on their hands, if they tried to come back.

They left for the time being, at least, and I sagged in relief when they were gone. But not for long: there was still Yeyuama to deal with, and the revelation Okweme had forced upon me. As little as I wanted to return to that topic, delaying would be even worse.

But when I tried to explain further, he stopped me with the same answer as before: "You will be tested, Reguamin. Then we will see."

Ominous words. Unfortunately, I had no choice but to accept them.

NINETEEN

Into the open—Constructing the glider—Wishbones—
Across the river—Abseiling again—The waterfall island—
Movement in the water—Bees—Strangely regular stones—My great leap

Given the dangers I had already faced in my short life—
deadly disease, attacks by wild beasts, kidnapping, and
other threats from human sources—you would not
think that leaving the forest for the more open ground of the savannah should be frightening. Yet so it was.

The villagers of the Moulish border fear the forest, and when I
went into the Green Hell, I experienced a taste of their fear. But
the reverse side, which I have not yet mentioned, is that the
Moulish themselves fear the land outside the forest. It does not
quite go so far as what physicians term agoraphobia—the fear of
open places and crowds—but after a life lived in the close
embrace of the swamp, the savannah feels like a desiccated
wasteland by comparison, one in which there is no shelter to be
found. You are exposed: the sun beats down without mercy, the
scattered trees providing only tiny oases of shade, and everything
can *see you*.

Being not Moulish, and only a visitor to the Green Hell, my reaction was not so extreme as theirs; but I did gain a degree of sympathy for it. My months in the swamp had acclimated me to an environment never further away than my elbow. Now I felt as if I teetered atop a small and unstable perch, and might at any moment go tumbling away into the emptiness.

This feeling was all the stronger because I knew I would only be in the open air for a short while, after which I would tumble (or, one hoped, serenely glide) back into the confines of the swamp. I was not particularly eager to return to the Green Hell, but at the moment it felt familiar—and besides, I hoped, great discoveries awaited me there.

Having departed from our Moulish hosts, Tom, Natalie, Faj Rawango, and I picked our way across the broken land where the fault that created the Great Cataract began. It was not easy going, but moving out onto flatter land would bring us too near the villages, and the men who fortified and held the rivers against Ikwunde advances. We did not want their attention and their questions. In due course, however, we came to the bank of the Hembi and settled down, under Natalie's guidance, to build a pair of wings.

I would not be able to fly with them, of course, in the sense of achieving the kind of lift and maneuverability that most breeds of dragons can manage. I lacked the thoracic muscles necessary for such a thing; the best I could hope for would be to glide. Even that was the fulfillment of a girlhood dream, though, and so I threw myself into this task with goodwill.

The center of the frame was an oval shape, made by lashing ribs together, with a division where they could be pulled apart for easier transport. Two femurs reached out from this to form the leading edges of the wings, the surface itself consisting of canvas stretched over fans of alar cartilage. I painted that canvas with the sap of the rubber vine to make it airtight, while Tom helped Natalie lash the bones and cartilage together with gut and cord.

I myself would hang feet-down from the center of this affair, just behind the femurs, with a crossbar for me to grip. Natalie was going to use a fibula for the crossbar, but I had, out of nostalgia for my childhood, insisted that a wishbone be among the pieces we preserved, and it seemed too apt not to employ here. (Apt and—I must admit—superstitiously lucky. If wishbones were a thing of flight, and I wished to fly . . . an irrelevant connection, of course, as it would not be serving anything like the anatomical function of a furcula in this instance. But when one is going to fling oneself off a cliff, these little superstitions become oddly vital.)

Tom and I had spent enough time studying the mechanics of flight for me to need little instruction in the use of my glider. By leaning my weight to one side or another, I could turn; by throwing it forward or back, I could direct myself down or up. But only so far: the control offered by such a design is limited in the extreme, as enthusiasts of more advanced designs are no doubt shouting at the page even now. Furthermore, while I might not need instruction, to undertake such a thing without practice is little short of suicidal. But the art was in its infancy back then, and that meant there had been no dramatic accidents (such as the one that claimed the life of Mr. Garsell, Natalie's Lopperton friend, three years later) to instil the proper fear in me. I therefore had only enough fear to make myself terrifed—not enough to turn back.

While we did this work, Faj Rawango scouted the river. He soon returned with good news. "If you can cross the Hembi," he said, "and come at the falls along the spit of land between it and the Gaomomo, I think you will be almost directly above your island."

"That sounds ideal," I said. "I would prefer not to have to glide along the waterfall any farther than I must, as the air currents there are likely to be unpredictable." (We had, in those days, a general sense that air currents were relevant to flight; the specifics had not yet been tested with anything more complicated than a kite. If they had . . . but it is quite useless to second-guess my own actions at this late date.)

To cross the Hembi, I would need some sort of vessel. Faj Rawango accordingly went out again, and while he was gone, I held my final conference with Tom and Natalie.

"There's a good vantage point a mile or so back," Tom said. "We'll watch from there—though to be honest, it will make no difference one way or another."

A born gentleman would not have shown his nerves at the thought of what I faced. I was glad Thomas Wilker was not a born gentleman; it made me less ashamed about the storm of sparklings dancing in my stomach. "I will feel better for knowing you are watching," I said, and shook his hand.

Natalie embraced me. She had been all efficient concentration during the building of the glider, but with that task done, she had nothing to distract her from the situation. "I think the design is good," she said into my shoulder, "but if it is not—"

"I have every confidence," I told her. "Come, though—we must give my conveyance a name. What shall we call it?"

A dozen possibilities fluttered through my mind as I said that.

I had named my son after his father, but to call a glider after them both seemed a bit much. *Greenie,* after my beloved sparkling trophy? *Ankumata,* in an attempt to flatter the oba, or alternatively *Lord Hilford? Draconean,* in honour of the ancient civilization?

Tom made a sound I had never heard from him before, which I can only call a gurgle, as if he almost swallowed his tongue laughing. "Furcula," he said.

I had related the story while we built the glider, of how I dissected a dove in my childhood to discover the purpose of a wishbone. "It *is* vital to flight," I admitted. "And if it breaks, well, that is supposed to make my wish come true. *Furcula* it shall be!"

And so it was that, with the wondrous *Furcula* in two pieces athwart my lap, I came to be rowed across the Hembi River near the border of Bayembe, for the purpose of flinging myself over a waterfall.

Faj Rawango rowed the small boat, and studied me with an unblinking gaze as he did so. "What is it?" I asked, when I could bear the silence no more.

He did not answer immediately, to the point where I thought he might not do so at all. At last he said, "You could have gotten eggs more easily than this."

"Perhaps," I said, after some reflection. "We still know nothing about dragon mating: when it happens, where eggs are laid, even how to tell a female swamp-wyrm from a male. I would have had to go searching. That would have upset the Moulish, possibly to the point of violence—which is a different sort of cost, and one I am not eager to pay. And then there are other things I would not have learned. They may not be entirely relevant to natural history; tree-bridges, for example, are not directly concerned with dragons, but rather with how humans coexist with them. That is, however, something I am interested in knowing. As is this priesthood, or whatever term I should use for it, that Yeyuama belongs to. So perhaps I pay in difficulty, but I believe I gain more than enough in return."

Faj Rawango pulled steadily on the oars, not taking his eyes off me. "You do not do this for them."

The Moulish. In all honesty, it took me a moment of thinking to understand what he meant. Some years later—after stories of my exploits aboard the *Basilisk* began to filter back home, and the outrage over my Erigan deeds had faded somewhat—there were those in Scirland who romanticized me as some kind of champion of the Moulish, nobly aiding them with no desire for my own gain. This is entirely false, and I cannot decide if its falsity is too flattering to me, or perversely insulting, to myself and the Moulish both. One could imagine that I approached my research the way I did out of respect for our hosts and their traditions, but insofar as that is true, I cannot claim credit for it. It was the accidental consequence of my true reasoning, which was concerned with how to achieve the best results with a minimum of fuss. Flinging myself off a waterfall was, in my ledger, less fuss than Velloin's approach; that is as noble as I can claim to have been.

We were nearly to the far bank of the Hembi. The Moulish had not been on my mind, not in that fashion, but now Faj Rawango had put them there, reminding me of a conversation in Vystrana years ago, about what good our expedition could do for the people of Drustanev. This time we had done better; we had not held ourselves aloof from those around us, but had assisted in their daily work, contributing where we could in repayment for their hospitality. Still, it was not as much as we might have done.

Now was hardly the time to be thinking about such matters, when I needed all my concentration for the task of not dying. I said to Faj Rawango, "I hope I have at the very least not been detrimental to our hosts. But if you know of any way I can be more beneficial to them—"

The prow of the boat scraped against the bank. Faj Rawango did not answer me. It was, I think, not his place; I was asking about the Moulish, and although they were his father's people, they were not his own. Furthermore, the point was not so much to effect a trade, wherein I gave them a particular thing in exchange for what I had received thus far, and would receive in the future. The point was to make me think about the question.

I did not intend to think about it right then, not when I had more immediately perilous concerns at hand. But as I turned to brace myself against the boat's edge and step out, I swept my gaze across the long, shallow valley where the three rivers came together, just to reassure myself the Ikwunde were not even now sneaking a raiding party across.

They were not. The waters here were too treacherous to make a good crossing, and the close spacing of the rivers meant they could too easily be caught with their forces strung out in a vulnerable line. But as those thoughts went through my mind, I remembered something I had heard Natalie say.

The Royal Engineers were planning a dam, somewhere in the west.

I knew the geography of Bayembe passably well by now. More than well enough to be certain that there was only one part of the country with a river that might usefully be dammed, and that was this western region, the border with Eremmo.

Speculation froze me where I stood, with one foot in the boat and one on the bank. They could try to dam the Hembi—but if they did so anywhere in this valley, it would spill over into the nearby Gaomomo and Girama, with very little profit to anyone.

If one were to dam all *three* rivers, though . . .

Faj Rawango said something to me, but I did not hear it. My mind was racing across the landscape, wishing desperately that I had one of those survey maps on hand, or that Natalie were there to answer a few questions. *Could* all three rivers be dammed? And what would happen if they were?

It would create an enormous, shallow lake all through this valley. One which the Ikwunde would find much more difficult to cross than these three rivers; they would need a fleet of boats, or else—if the lake stretched far enough—they would be forced up into the western hills, which offered difficulties of their own. Provided the thing could be built (which would be easier said than done, with the Ikwunde making forays into the area), it might substantially improve the defensibility of this border. Had Galinke not said something about that, when we were in the *agban?* And with the water turbines Natalie had been so excited about, it could supply power for a number of industrial purposes, which I was sure would be very useful to our commercial interests here.

But what would it do to the swamp below?

I turned, staggering a little as the boat shifted beneath my foot, and looked toward the Great Cataract. I was no engineer; some of the ideas that went through my mind then were utterly false. (The dam would not, for example, cut off all water to the Green Hell; it must perforce allow the rivers through eventually.) But I was correct in my basic assumption, which was that a dam would interfere with the flow of the water, and that would, in turn, have untold consequences for the creatures and people of Mouleen.

By then Faj Rawango had stood and reached for my arm. "Are you all right?" he said, awkward in his concern. "If you do not wish to do this . . . I'm sure there's another way."

He thought I was paralyzed by my impending doom. "No, that isn't it," I said, then belatedly added, "Thank you." I finished disembarking and bent to retrieve the pieces of the *Furcula* out of the boat; they were light enough that it was easy to carry one in each hand. "But please do me a favor. Ask Natalie whether those engineers were talking about building a dam *here*."

Whether they had admitted it to her or not, I was convinced that was their intent. If memory served, Lord Hilford had said something about an attack on the Royal Engineers in this area. This might also explain what Sir Adam had meant, the night we dined at Point Miriam; he had said something about how the Green Hell might not always defend Bayembe. Oh, he knew what this would do—I was certain of it. Certain, and seething mad, that he would dismiss the "backwater" as an unimportant casualty in pursuit of this goal.

It seemed Faj Rawango knew nothing of such plans; he frowned in puzzlement, but nodded. Then he handed me my small, waterproof bundle, which I strapped to my back. It held a notebook and pencils, a bottle of water and a few strips of dried meat, a coil of rope, a penknife, and bandages with which to strap up any joints I might sprain along the way. A few other small odds and ends. They would, I hoped, be enough.

Faj Rawango blessed me in the Yembe fashion, which I

acknowledged with gratitude. They say there are no atheists in war; I tell you that pantheists abound at the edge of a cliff. I would have taken the blessing of any god I could get.

Then there was nothing left to say. I put the dam out of my mind; it should have been difficult, but preparing to risk one's life concentrates the mind wonderfully. Natalie had a letter in her pack, addressed to my son, in case I should not survive this. Jacob was too young to read it, or even to understand its meaning if someone else read it to him, but the words needed to be set down for posterity. (His posterity, not that of the world; I will not share its contents with you here.)

I hesitated: this was my last chance to turn back. Then, with what I hoped looked like a decisive nod, I left Faj Rawango and walked toward the edge of the cliff.

Rocks broke the smooth flow of the water here, making treacherous rapids no boat could approach. Now that I was atop the cliff, I could see those rocks went very near to the edge—no, all the way to it; there was a perch from which I could survey the (vertical) terrain. Leaving the wings of the *Furcula* on the ground with my bundle to pin them in place, I went to see what I faced.

From the ground, the mist of the falling water had been an exquisite thing, veiling the cataract in rainbows and mystery. From here, it veiled the ground instead—which was a mercy. I had vertigo regardless, the world reeling around me as I gazed over the cliff. But it did not reel so badly that I failed to find the island for which I aimed.

It was not so far away. In fact, from here it looked quite different: not so much hovering as dangling, as a pendant dangles from its chain. The chain on the far side was broken, inasmuch as

I could see through the thunderous mist, but a rough string of rocks, some of them overgrown with vegetation, appeared to lead from my perch down to not very far above the island's surface. Was this how the Moulish made their own journey?

(In fact it was not. But I will not tell you how they did it, for I do not want hordes of curiosity-seekers to try that path for themselves. Suffice it to say that their way is far easier than my own—which accounts for Yeyuama's willingness to permit me some assistance. Fortunately, few people are reckless enough to imitate what I am about to detail.)

This presented me with an interesting choice. The intent had been to fly the *Furcula* down to the island, and then to fly a second time from the island to the swamp below. But that, of course, was to commit myself to the hazard twice, and furthermore to do so when my first jump, of necessity, must be the more difficult of the two. The wind whipped about me quite strongly, and my target was small. It seemed I had another option, however, which was to try to climb down by terrestrial means, and then to use the *Furcula* for the second, and much easier, stage.

Of course this had its own hazards. The rocks were wet with spray. I must climb with the two pieces of the glider strapped to my back, which would not be easy; they might act as a sail to carry me off. I could not even be certain that the path I thought I saw would take me all the way; it might prove more broken than it seemed from this angle.

But with a choice between those perils and the ones attendant upon flinging myself from the cliff, I found my answer was clear.

The first part of the descent was relatively easy, save that I had to watch the edges of the glider's wings, lest I damage them against the stone. (The dragonbone, of course, would survive any knock I might give it; the bindings and canvas, however, might not.) The stones were indeed slick beneath my hands, but there were also pockets of dirt and small plants; for a wonder, none of them were thorned, nor occupied by anything worse than a confused beetle or two. I had to make a sideways traverse that was worryingly narrow, and the wind was indeed tugging at my unused wings, but the difficulty grew the closer I came to the island.

I will not pretend I navigated this challenge with aplomb. My heart was racing, my hands cramping with tension, and I knew that the mist was a blessing; without it I might have seen exactly what awaited me if I fell. As it was, I kept my gaze glued to the rock no more than a few feet away. Unfortunately, I could not do so forever: there came a point where my so-called path ended, and I was not yet at the island.

From above, it had looked complete. As I had feared, however, the view had been deceptive. The path brought me *laterally* to the island, but not *vertically*. I stood above it, with no easy way to close the gap.

Evaluating this required me to look down, which promptly rendered me certain that my foot would slip, the wind would seize me, the very stone would fling me off. I clutched the cliff face as if it were the dearest thing to me in the world; indeed, at that moment no thing could have been dearer. But I could not stay there: one way or another, I had to move.

To go up would be as hazardous as coming down had been, with a flight still waiting at the end of it, and my body exhausted by this trial. Would the others see me, and send Faj Rawango back?

The alternative was no safer. I had a coil of rope wrapped

about my body, and Jacob had taught me to abseil in Vystrana. Even presuming I could do so again, however, it would cost me my rope; I could not untie it once I was at the bottom. And to try abseiling with my bundle and wings strapped to my back . . .

I am a scientist, and fond of thinking matters through in a rational fashion. On some occasions, however, rational thought is not one's friend. Before I could weigh the circumstances in great detail, I edged back along my path, to a space where a larger outcropping gave me a bit of safety to move.

There I unstrapped my wings (nearly losing one to a gust of wind) and my bundle, tying them together with my belt. This achieved, I went back to the end of my pseudo-path and, hoping with all my might that I was not committing an act of abject stupidity, dropped them over the precipice. They tumbled a bit in the air, but landed on the island as I had hoped. Whether they had been damaged in the fall would remain to be seen: first I must try not to damage myself.

I had kept my coil of rope, which I fixed about a stone, blessing Tom and Mekeesawa for teaching me knots during my time in the swamp. There was no time for questioning whether the rope might slip, or my weight pull the stone loose; such questioning would only paralyze me. I wrapped the rope around my body as Jacob had taught me, and committed myself to the void.

It was not like abseiling in Vystrana. Here there was mist, which softened my hands and made the rope burn them unmercifully; here there was also an unpredictable wind that tried to spin me about like a top. I cracked not only my knees against the wall but also my shins, my hips, my shoulders, my elbows—every part of me, including my head, though fortunately that blow was glancing. I felt I had gone a hundred meters, but I was not yet at the island; I dared not let myself look down to see how much farther I had to go.

As a consequence, the ground beneath my dangling left foot took me by surprise, and I thumped onto my posterior when my grip loosened for an instant. Fortunately the rope, wrapped about my body, kept me from rolling off the nearby edge, which I might otherwise have done.

Some minutes passed before I could force my mind to work again, and more before I could persuade my body to unwrap itself and crawl away from that edge.

But I had done it—half of it, at least. I was on the island.

Not without damage. I was bruised and scraped, and my wings, when I collected them, had suffered three small ruptures in the canvas. I had needle and waxed cord with which to repair that, however, and they were (I hoped) not large enough to endanger me. I was not eager to contemplate the perils of getting *off* the island, however, not when I had only just arrived.

Instead I set myself to discover why Yeyuama had sent me here.

The island was not large. I estimated it to be no more than thirty meters across where it met the cliff face, and less than that in depth. Here and there the rocks projected through the vegetation, but much of it was thickly overgrown, and rivulets from the thin falls behind traced paths through and under the green. It was a beautiful place, and I intended to draw it before I left, but I saw nothing that looked like an answer.

So I went to the edge of the island, where it projected into the air. My gaze went first to the cliff above, to the place from which

I thought Tom, Natalie, and Faj Rawango might be watching. Between the distance and the mist, however, I could not spot them. Next I looked down (with a careful grip on a stone to make certain vertigo did not send me over), but there was no hope of seeing Yeyuama. He should be watching for me, though, and we had arranged to meet by a particular large and identifiable tree.

I did, however, see something else.

There was movement in the water below that was not turbulence from the falls. It moved crossways to that turbulence, in a smooth and sinuous curve, shifting as I watched. The curve was not large relative to the lake as a whole but, measured against the bank, must have been at least ten meters long. It reminded me of nothing so much as a serpent I had seen eeling through the muddy, still waters of the swamp.

Serpent. Sea-serpent. *Dragon.*

Heedless of my lofty perch, I dropped to my knees, then to my stomach, so I could lean out in greater safety and get a better view. The movement I had been watching faded—dove deeper, perhaps?—but there was more to the south. A second disturbance. Watching, scarcely daring to blink, I counted three in all, that I could be certain were distinct from one another; there might have been more.

This, I was certain, was what Yeyuama had sent me to see. There were dragons in the lake below.

(I was glad all over again that I had not chosen to try and swim those waters in my quest for the island.)

Dragons in the lake. What might it mean? They were not swamp-wyrms; of that, I was sure. They were too large and too mobile, eschewing the stalking tactics of their downstream kin. Kin—that was an intriguing notion. How did these dragons relate to the other local breeds? Surely the lake could not support a large population. How did they propagate, with so small a number?

The chain of thoughts that followed was not, I confess, entirely scientific. My astonished mind leapt from one idea to another with the speed and unpredictability of a grasshopper, making connections and then discarding them. But the picture formed by those it did not discard *felt* right; it explained the data, albeit with some intuitive leaps along the way.

I had been asking about dragon eggs. Mekeesawa put me off. Akinimanbi told me I would get no answers so long as I was under the baleful eye of witchcraft. I duly got myself out from under it, and Yeyuama appeared. He brought me here, saying I would understand once I saw.

And our expedition, in all our observation, had not managed to record the differences between male and female swamp-wyrm anatomy.

Humans have a small degree of what we term sexual dimorphism, with males generally a bit larger than females, and slightly different in form. Other species have more. And in some insects, for example bees, the number of fertile females is extremely low, with all others being males or infertile females.

In Vystrana, I had speculated briefly about the existence of a "queen dragon." Rock-wyrms had no such thing... but lying full-length on that waterfall island, I became convinced that swamp-wyrms did, and they were in the lake below me.

The full shape of the thing did not become clear to me until later, when Yeyuama, satisfied by my achievement in reaching and returning from the island, shared with me the details of his calling. (Details I will, out of respect for his wishes, leave incomplete here. The biology is of concern to my audience, and that I will share; the rituals and geographic specifics will remain with the Moulish.) But my theory was correct in its general outline, which is that what lived in the lake were the females of the breed, and those we had seen until now were exclusively male. And while I might have seen that from the shore—with difficulty, on account of the turbulence in the water—this rite of passage served a multifarious purpose, not only showing me the female dragons, but testing the qualities necessary for carrying out the work of Yeyuama and his brethren.

I sat back, breathless with speculation and delight. A thousand questions wanted to burst from me, about the dragons, about how the Moulish interacted with them, and what I might do now that I understood.

Alas, the man who could answer them was a very long way below me, and I had not yet passed his test. First I had to return to the ground in one piece.

Newly energized by my excitement, I retrieved the pieces of the *Furcula* and set to work stitching closed the holes that had formed in my wings. My needlework has never been impressive, but the necessity of repairing our clothing, not to mention modifying my skirts into trousers, had made it functional, and I included patches cut from my shirt-tails to cover the seams for extra reinforcement.

When that was done, I drank some water and ate a little, surveying the island with an eye toward sketching it before I departed. It was only partially a delaying tactic, putting off the moment when I would have to test the glider; but I am glad for that delay, as it led me to notice the oddity of my surroundings.

Some of the island's stones were too regular in shape.

Not *very* regular; they had been badly weathered by the elements. But here there was something like a row, and there, a corner. Heedless of my raw palms, I began to dig at the covering growth and dirt, hacking away with my penknife when the roots and vines resisted my pulling. And I uncovered enough to confirm my suspicion.

There were ruins on this island.

Ruins of ruins: if Natalie was right, and there had once been a more continuous ledge interrupting the progress of the Great Cataract, then the rest of what once stood here had gone tumbling down with it. But there was enough for me to be certain that what I saw was not natural.

The Moulish do not build in stone. There is no reason they should; the Green Hell is not well supplied with it, except at the edges, and stone houses cannot move with their owners when the nearby food runs out. Anything they might build would be lost to the jungle by the time they came back, and so it is far easier and more sensible to simply fashion a new hut at need. The peoples of Bayembe use some stone, but much more mud brick, whose raw materials are abundant and cheap. And with these ruins so weathered and overgrown . . . it was not the work of anyone recent.

My instant thought, of course, was that the ruins were Draconean. Yeyuama had sent me up here as a rite of passage, so that I might "touch the dragons"; it seemed obvious that this should be a relic of the civilization that had once worshipped them, the civilization to which Yves de Maucheret had compared the Moulish religion. There was nothing here, however, to indicate a Draconean connection, apart from their apparent great age—and I was no archaeologist, to estimate more precisely than "thousands of years old." No great walls stood on this island, no striding statues or other characteristic pieces of Draconean art.

Nonetheless, it was intriguing enough that I felt obliged to document the remains. In several places the overgrowth was too thick for me to pursue the remnants of the walls, but I sketched as much as I could uncover, working my way methodically across the island. This systematic approach soon brought me to another suspicious regularity: an alcove in the cliff, where the water of the falls parted around the promontory of the island. It was nearly my height, and oblong in shape—almost like a door.

"I will feel like an idiot if I was right," I remarked to the air. If there truly was a tunnel to this place, and I had simply failed to find its entrance . . . but at least that would save me jumping off the island when I left.

Closer inspection told me I was not so lucky as to be an idiot (at least not where this matter was concerned). The alcove was far too overgrown and silted with dirt to be the means by which the "pure" reached this place, and my probing hand, reaching through the leaves, found stone beneath.

Smooth stone. Far too smooth to be natural.

Thrusting both hands into the greenery, I found more smoothness—indented with lines, as if it were carved.

The vines resisted my tearing them away, as they had a good foothold in the dirt along the sides. But I was stubborn, and my curiosity was up; and once I had torn enough out to see what lay behind, nothing short of the island dropping out from beneath me would have turned me from my task.

The entire back of the alcove was filled with a vertical slab of granite, much discoloured by the ages, but inscribed from top to toe, except where a gap in the middle broke the text into two portions.

I stared at it, mouth open. This was not, I felt sure, what Yeyuama had sent me to see; it was too thoroughly buried. No one had laid eyes on this in a long time. But then what *was* it? The writing in the top half reminded me of Draconean—well, truth be told, it reminded me of chicken scratches, which had been my first impression of that ancient script when I saw it as a child. But I had seen enough Draconean writing since then to know this was far more chicken-scratchy, as if a child had tried to imitate their work.

Or had been in the process of developing it. Could this place be older than the Draconean ruins we knew? I wished I were archaeologist enough to guess. Regardless of the truth, I had no idea what to make of the text in the lower half, which was quite different in appearance: little rounded blocks, which I might have thought decorative had there not been so many, in tidy lines.

I take the time to describe this stone to you, even though many of my readers have likely seen photographs (or the thing itself, in the Royal Museum or a touring exhibition), because I want you to understand what I found that day. I did not know what I was looking at, other than a puzzle. And one which, alas, I could not take with me: had the Lord Himself given me the strength of ten men, to pluck that slab from its sheltered pocket, I could not have taken it off the island. The weight would have sent the *Furcula* straight into the lake. Nor did I have any large sheet of paper with which to take a rubbing.

I briefly contemplated tearing all the blank pages from my

notebook and making a kind of mosaic, but it would have taken an age, and my sunlight was rapidly vanishing. As nervous as I was about trying my wings, darkness would make that task neither easier nor safer. I must do it now, or wait until the morrow, and I did not relish the thought of a night spent up here in the thunder and the cold spray.

Were it not for that ticking clock, I do not know how long I might have dithered. Instead I set to work, slotting the two pieces of the glider together, tightening their lashings, tying my bundle to my back.

That sufficed to get me physically ready. My mind was another matter entirely.

The wind tugged at my wings as I went toward the edge of the island, though not so strongly as to risk lifting me off my feet. I almost wished it had; that would have reassured me that this contraption was indeed capable of supporting my weight. But no: like a baby bird, I must hurl myself into the air, and see only then whether or not I could fly.

(I had always thought baby birds adorable beyond words. Now I found myself admiring them for their courage.)

Have you ever stood at a precipice and felt a sudden fear, not that you will fall, but that you will fling yourself over? That the instincts which preserve our lives will fail you for that one vital moment, and in the gap, you will, for no good reason, step forward and seek your own end? I have, on more than one occasion. That afternoon in Eriga, however, I discovered that it is not so easy as your fears would have you believe. I had *reason* to step forward; flinging myself over was my purpose in being there. Yet my legs stood frozen. They might have sunk roots into the ground, so little capable was I of lifting my foot even an inch. With the harness of the *Furcula* wrapped about me—a promise that I would not die—I became convinced of my own doom, and could not move.

The wind jarred me from my paralysis. A stronger gust knocked me a little sideways, slightly off balance, and before I could regain my inertia, I ran forward and leapt from the island, into the rainbows and mist.

TWENTY

On dragon wings—Air currents—Demise of the Furcula—
Journey downward—I spend a miserable night—
Movement in the forest—Labane—The use of a Scirling woman

And I flew.

Glided, rather—but it was enough. Instead of falling to my death, I hung suspended in the air, floating on currents and the carefully measured physics of my wings.

It was a miracle.

An uncomfortable one, I must say. We have invented better harnesses since; the one I wore dug unmercifully under my arms, and I held the crossbar in a strangulation grip out of fear that I would somehow slip free. This dragged the nose of the *Furcula* downward, and I began to descend more rapidly; a hasty shove sent my nose upward once more, leveling me out. My heart pounded so hard it seemed in danger of leaping from my chest, but I was *flying*.

My panicked gyrations had not only changed my altitude; they had altered my direction. I was headed swiftly for the northwestern corner where the Green Hell met the Great Cataract and the plateau above, and while the dragonbone struts might survive the collision, my own bones would not. I attempted to turn right, over the forest, but something—a wrong shift in my weight; a trick of the air currents—fought me, so that it was easier to go left instead. I skimmed along the falls, back toward the center and the waterfall island, though too low now to make a landing where I had begun.

Landing there was not my aim regardless. I had lost sight of the tree where I was supposed to meet Yeyuama, but was more concerned with finding a safe place to alight. My original intent had been to plunge myself into the lake, in preference to crashing into a tree; now that I had seen the queen dragons, such plans seemed less wise. If I could direct myself to the edge of the lake, though, it might be safe enough.

No one, man or woman, can take into account factors they do not know in the first place. So it was with me and the behaviour of air currents.

Hot air rises. Birds take advantage of these drafts, which we now call thermals, to gain altitude. The air near the falls had been cool, owing to the mist thrown off by the water and the growing shadows of the setting sun, but over the forest proper it was the full blazing heat of a tropical afternoon.

The *Furcula* rose. I was trying to direct it downward, but my control was minimal and my skill even less; I was, even more than I had realized, at the mercy of the elements around me. Instead of settling, my glider lifted me up, up, above the shorter trees near the lake's bank, above the giants beyond. Glorious as flight might be, this was not at all what I wanted.

As before, I would have to turn myself about and head back the way I came. I threw my weight to the side . . . and lost stability altogether.

Some unexpected draft—from the Great Cataract or the slopes of the Green Hell, I do not know which—sent me veering sharply to the side. This sudden shift in my balance made my legs swing wildly, turning my course still more erratic. The attempt to bring my lower body under control caused me, by reflex, to draw my arms in; the *Furcula* tipped downward. My toes slapped a high branch. I forced my hands outward again, and the glider lifted, but by then there was no hope of regaining control.

I was going to crash.

I knew this, very clearly. I felt I had all the time in the world to know this fact, to study it, to imagine what the consequences would be. I saw the forest below me and tried to evaluate one spot or another for its desirability as a crash site. A foolish waste of time: the emerald sea that was the canopy of the Green Hell had little to offer in the way of variation, and I had not the slightest control over where I would fall. I saw the top branches approaching, and had the presence of mind (though it threw my glider off even more) to draw my legs up, so I would be less likely to catch my ankle somewhere and dislocate a joint.

Then I struck the branches, dragging through them for a short distance before the resistance grew enough to stop my forward momentum.

And then I fell.

I did not fall very far. I was strapped into a dragonbone glider; the wings were too large to pass easily through the trees, and too strong to break. But they dragged some distance through the branches before catching against a few sturdy enough to hold, and then I jolted to a halt.

I almost kept going. The *Furcula* had stopped at an angle that left me dangling from the crossbar, my weight only partially supported by the harness, and the jolt caused my grip to falter. I made an undignified noise, half yelp, half squeak, and clutched for dear life at the wishbone. My devout wish at that moment was for it *not* to break.

The bone held. But my grip would not; sooner or later it would give way. Thinking to support my weight by some other means, I glanced about, saw a nearby branch, and attempted to hook my leg over it.

This jarred my glider loose from its precarious angle. With a cracking of branches, the *Furcula* and I slid free once more. For a moment we were in relatively open air, and I, driven by terrified instinct, dragged the glider's nose down as hard as I could, lest I lose the support of the harness entirely. The *Furcula* struck another branch, nose first, and flipped entirely upside down—and there, again, it stopped.

Once my heart slowed to something like a sustainable pace, I realized that I had inadvertently improved my situation. I still sat above a lethal fall, but at least the glider was now between me and my potential demise.

Moving carefully, I persuaded my hands to let go of the wishbone, extricated my arms from their harness, and shifted myself around until I sat atop the bones that formed the central frame of the glider. The branches beneath me might give way, but the bones, at least, would hold.

There I sat for several long moments, concentrating on nothing beyond my breathing and my pounding heart. When at last I achieved a semblance of composure, I opened my eyes and looked about.

I was still in the forest canopy—a fortunate thing indeed. Beneath the level on which I sat, the branches became much more numerous, and might have speared me through the canvas. Below *that* would be a gap in which there were few branches at all; had I plunged through the understory, I would not have stopped until I reached the ground thirty meters below, and there I would have died. As it was, I had suffered nothing worse than an assortment of scrapes and bruises, and two wrenched shoulders. For an uncontrolled landing in a glider, I considered myself virtually unharmed.

Of course, I still had to reach the ground alive.

I thought longingly of my rope, left dangling above the waterfall island. I could have used its aid now. Lacking such, I faced a long and hazardous climb—one I was not at all certain I would survive.

What did I have that might serve as a rope? My clothing, if cut apart; but I did not relish the notion of climbing naked, nor surviving in the Green Hell that way afterward. I was neither as hardy nor as resistant to disease as the Moulish. The bindings on the glider frame, but they were too thin to grip, and too firmly lashed into place. The canvas of the glider wings.

That, clearly, was my best prospect—compared against the alternatives, which was not saying much. I would not call it ideal. I had to balance on the branches of the tree in which I had landed and use my penknife to cut through the tough, rubber-painted fabric. My harvest, such as I could collect without endangering myself, was not very large. But I had seen the Moulish use vines to support themselves when they climbed trees, wrapping them about the trunk like straps, while bracing their feet against the bark.

Where the tree afforded no good branches, I could try the same.

My descent to the forest floor was nothing short of grueling. As I said in my description of the tree-bridges, I was not much of a climber (though I was a much better one by the time I reached the ground). I slipped often, and had to rest a dozen times along the way. I strained my fingers and my ankles, scraped my left knee raw, and was stabbed by countless thorns before I thought of wrapping a length of rubberized canvas around my palms to protect them.

The only saving grace was the chance to observe the life of the forest from this new vantage. (If you doubt that I had any care for such things when my own life was in danger, understand that it was a means of distracting myself from my peril.) Birds and insects buzzed about me, and monkeys danced through the trees. I saw a drakefly alight on a nest not ten feet away, and discovered that in addition to eating insects, they are thieves of eggs.

I would have taken notes on this, but the light was failing me. As I neared the lowest rank of branches, I was forced to consider my situation. Should I finish my descent to the ground or not?

I hardly relished the notion of spending the night in a tree. But I was exhausted in body and mind, which would make the remainder of the climb even more perilous; furthermore, this would be my first night in the Green Hell without the shelter of a tent or hut and the warning light of a fire to keep animals away. There were nocturnal predators in the swamp, some of which would certainly be bold enough to prey upon a lone, helpless woman.

No, the tree it must be. I lashed myself in place with the strips of my poor, butchered *Furcula,* and attempted to get some rest.

As you might imagine, this was easier said than done. I had

grown accustomed to the sounds of the forest, but they seemed different when no wall, however flimsy, stood between me and the creatures making them. Furthermore, my bindings did nothing to convince my brain that I was not going to tumble off the branch if I so much as breathed too deeply. Nor could I help but think about my companions, who would have seen me go careering off over the swamp. They might have even seen me crash. The thought of their fear made my heart ache.

How far had I gone? I had the vague sense that my course had taken me southward and east, but beyond that, I had lost all sense of distance or direction.

My sense as a naturalist reasserted itself. I was not in the heart of the Green Hell, that wet, tangled delta. The ground beneath me was drier, which meant I must be on the slope—but not *too* far up it, as the vegetation was not the scrubby stuff we had camped in while first waiting for the Moulish. ("Scrubby" by the standards of Mouleen; it would have been a respectable forest, albeit fantastically overgrown, in Scirland.) And I had not been in the air so long as to come anywhere near the bay. I was therefore somewhere in the southwestern quadrant of the swamp, and if I headed west and perhaps a bit downslope, I would come once again to the Great Cataract, which was a place my companions might find me—if I did not come across any Moulish first.

If I did not *perish* first. I had only a little water and food; my survival was far from assured.

Fear of my state kept me awake long into the night, but exhaustion can trump many things. I did at last snatch a bit of sleep, and woke with a start around dawn.

My disorientation was profound. I did not know where I was,

and felt for an instant as if I were about to fall. I clutched the branches around me, then hissed in pain at the pressure on my abused hands. Every part of my body *ached*; I had not felt this poorly since my bout of yellow fever. This, I realized when my heart slowed down, was the flaw in leaving the last of the climb until morning: my various injuries were all much the worse for a night spent rigid and terrified in a tree.

But there was nothing to be done for it now. I worked my way methodically through my body, easing cramped muscles and warming stiff joints as best I could without unbinding myself from the tree. (That, I wanted to leave for as long as I could.) This done, I considered the food and water still tied to my back. Should I consume them now, for strength? Or conserve them for later?

Before I could decide one way or another, I saw movement down below. My instant thought was *predator,* and I froze—but then I saw the movement had a human origin.

I was exhausted and terrified, and did not yet have my bearings. Moreover, I had no reason to expect anyone but Moulish here, on the southern side of the Green Hell.

"Hello! You there, down below! Oh, thank heaven you're here. I was so worried I would—"

The men froze, raising their spears as if to attack. Then, far too late, I took in all the details that should have warned me.

These were not the short, slight figures of Moulish hunters. They were taller and darker of skin—nearly as dark as the Yembe. They wore fringed bands about their arms and calves, carried shields of hide stretched over a frame. And they journeyed in silence through the swamp, as the Moulish rarely do.

They were strangers, men of a people I had never seen

before, and by the looks of their armament, their purpose here was not peaceful.

You may blame me for being so slow to recognize them, and I will grant that as fair. I had seen no accurate images, only the caricatures then current in Scirling news-sheets, which were exaggerated for the purpose of whipping up support for the Nsebu colony and our alliance with Bayembe.

They were Ikwunde warriors.

On the other hand—and I can laugh about it now, when the event is years behind me—it took them a comically long time to spot *me*. They had no reason to look for a woman halfway up a tree. When one of them at last turned his gaze upward, he leapt back a full pace in shock.

By then I was wishing I had untied myself, so I might at least have tried to hide. But I was still bound in place, and could not take back the unwise words that had drawn their attention to me. The one who had seen me pointed his spear, directing the others' eyes, and they began to talk in quick, low voices amongst themselves.

Their language is wholly unrelated to the Sachimbi family; I could not understand a word of it. The tone, however, and the hostile looks I received, told me their conversation was not one of pity. With fumbling fingers, I began trying to unbind myself.

They saw the movement, and it seemed to hasten their decision. One of the men yanked the spear and shield from my spotter's hands, giving what was clearly an order for him to climb the tree. I redoubled my efforts—to what end? Did I think I would escape them? But I had to try. Whatever these men were doing here, I wanted no involvement with it.

I soon discovered why my spotter had looked grumpy upon

being ordered after me. Ikwunde, of course, is a nation of desert and grassland; they are a herding people—or they were, before the inkosi Othaku Zam redirected their efforts toward conquering his neighbours. My spotter was as bad a climber of trees as I. He got one of his companions to give him a boost up, but then had to contend with the parasitic tree wrapped around the base of my own, and did very poorly.

Not that I fared much better. I got myself untied at last, but nearly fell in trying to change my position. I could not go groundward, not with that man below me, nor could I leap across to another tree like a monkey. Up once more? I could not reach the stripped frame of the *Furcula,* and it would not do me any good if I did.

I was, I thought, too high for them to throw a spear at me. (I did not know how far an Ikwunde warrior can throw a spear.) Given how badly my pursuer climbed, I might simply outwait them on my branch—for surely they had pressing business elsewhere.

But I underestimated the determination and agility of the man sent after me. He drew close below me, close enough that he would have caught my skirt, had I been wearing one. Frightened, I kicked out, trying to deflect his hand or even strike his head.

I should not have tried. The attempt destroyed my precarious balance, and I fell.

My panicked grab at the branch slowed me, as did the smaller vegetation I crashed through on the way down. It was brake enough that I escaped a fracture. But I landed hard, driving all the breath from my body—and even had I not, they would have been upon me before I could flee.

The Ikwunde surrounded me. There were five of them, and

very terrifying they looked, from my perspective on the ground. One barked a question at me, which of course I could not answer. He asked again, his voice growing steadily more angry, and I feared he would kill me simply for my lack of comprehension.

I held out my hands as if they could ward off such a fate. "I am unarmed. You see? I am no threat to you. I—"

They, I think, understood me no more than I did them. One seized the bundle on my back and wrenched it away, upending its contents onto the ground. Notebook, needle, thread; what remained of my scant rations. He picked up the notebook and began to page through it. "I am a scholar," I said, even though I knew the words were useless. "Surely you must see. I am only here for study."

But it mattered naught what I was there for. The fact remained that I had seen them. Ikwunde warriors, in the Green Hell, where they had no business being.

No more than they had business at the rivers, which was territory Bayembe supposedly controlled. But our soldiers were on guard for them there, and so I supposed it was inevitable that they should try their luck here, despite the lethal reputation of this place. I had heard nothing from the Moulish of previous attempts; this must be their first.

There were only five of them, though, with no sign of more. Five men might be dangerous to me, or to the Moulish, but not to Bayembe. Not even *these* five, whose distinctive regalia I now recognized: they were Labane, some of the most elite troops the Ikwunde possessed. Chosen as young as ten, they were taken into intensive training, and lived the next twenty years in a regiment with their new brothers, according to their shared age. A Tsebane (for that is the correct form of the singular, though one never saw it in Scirling papers at the time, and rarely sees it now) cannot marry while he still serves; there is nothing in his life except loyalty to his brothers and to the inkosi, the ruler of Ikwunde. And the task to which the inkosi set him was war.

Such men had no need of a captive. I would only slow them, threaten the secrecy of whatever they sought here. I knew, as clearly as I knew my own name, that they stayed their hands only out of confusion, that a battered, trouser-clad Scirling woman should fall out of a tree at their feet; once their confusion was satisfied or grew dull, they would kill me.

What reason could I possibly give them for sparing me?

Innocence would not avail. Neither would a plea to their compassion. I seized upon the only thing I could—which was my notebook, dropped in disgust just a moment before.

When I reached out to collect it, three spears whipped down to point at me. I persevered, taking the volume in my hand and paging to a suitable sketch. This I held up for one of the Labane to see: the one I thought must be their leader, for he had ordered my pursuer up the tree. "You see this? The dragon. *Legambwa*," I added in Moulish, for there was a greater chance they would recognize that word than the Scirling one. Belatedly, I thought to switch to that tongue, and proceeded in a mixture of it and Yembe, in the hope that some fragment or other would be familiar to my captors. "They are all over this swamp. Very dangerous. They will attack you. But I—I can show you how to avoid them. How to be safe."

I illustrated my words with pantomime, pointing repeatedly at the swamp-wyrm sketch, then using my hand, clawlike, to suggest a draconic attack. My palm I pressed to my heart, indicating by

warm and hopeful tone that I offered a way to avoid such perils.

Perhaps someone among my captors spoke a rudimentary amount of Moulish or Yembe; perhaps my pantomime was effective. Perhaps something else passed among them, during their brief conversation. I had, as some readers may recall, been caught by strange men in a foreign country once before, but on that occasion I had been able to parse their language as a dialect of Eiversch, which made communication possible, if not easy. This was as opaque to me as Draconean, and that, as much as the warlike nature of the men who had caught me, made this incident far more terrifying. I felt as if I were in the grip of yellow fever again, the world around me making no sense, and I my next breath potentially my last.

Something persuaded them, whether it was any part of my plea or a notion of their own making. All I knew was that the one who came for me did so with a length of vine rather than a spear, and so I did not resist as he bound my hands together behind my back. Nor did I protest when he ripped apart the fabric of my bundle and used it to gag me, though I dearly wished for a drink of water before he did. I was not dead yet, and that was more than I had expected a moment ago; everything else could wait.

When they dragged me to my feet, someone worked at my wrists for a moment, and then I felt a tug on my bound arms. They had tied another length of vine to the first, making a kind of leash to prevent me from running.

As if I *could* run. You have an image, I hope, of the treacherous terrain that makes up the Green Hell; now try to imagine traversing it at speed, with your hands behind you to disrupt your balance. I would not get ten paces before I fell. I nearly fell when a Tsebane shoved me forward, but through sheer determination not to squander my reprieve, I managed to keep my feet.

They placed me in the lead, as if I were the canary whose demise would warn them of danger. I dearly wanted, once I could think straight, to lead them into just such a situation; there were predators out there, patches of sucking mud, even perilous insects that might be persuaded to attack. Unfortunately, my previous luck with such tactics notwithstanding, I could not be sure I would survive the trap myself—and besides, they did not yet trust me. Any attempt to lead them astray would result in a spear between my shoulder blades.

In order to survive, I had to prove my worth as a guide.

I therefore bent all the knowledge I had gained of the swamp to the task of impressing them. This was difficult to do, bound and gagged as I was, but I led them ostentatiously away from a thicket of underbrush whose thorns housed very unpleasant ants, then veered again, nodding my head upward, to avoid a serpent dangling from a branch.

Step by step, hazard by hazard, we proceeded into the depths of the Green Hell.

TWENTY-ONE

The safety of the Moulish—Another party—Something in my pocket—
The loss of my knife—Refuge on high

I had some hope that a friend might find me. Tom, Natalie, and Faj Rawango had promised to watch from the plateau above; they, unfortunately, were on the north side of the swamp, and could not quickly reach me, the descent from that point being more or less impassable. But Yeyuama had promised to watch from the lake. He knew this place as well as I knew my own garden, and might even now be on his way toward me.

Which, I soon realized, might get him killed. One against five was terrible odds, and worse when the one is sworn to nonviolence. But surely his sharp eyes would spot the Ikwunde before they saw him? And if not, I had seen for myself how easily the Moulish could conceal themselves when they chose. Perhaps he could gather hunters to help. They had followed his lead against Velloin and Okweme—though I suspected that was because the conflict there was dragon-related. Would the camps here stir themselves to help me? We had met briefly during my first journey to the Great Cataract, but these were not the Moulish who had been a part of my larger social world these past months.

Such were my thoughts, chasing in anxious circles like a mouse trapped in a box. It was preferable to thinking about the alternatives.

Unfortunately, the Labane were driving me northeast: deeper into the swamp, but away from the lake. With each step, the chances of Yeyuama finding us decreased, and the chances of us stumbling across a Moulish camp increased. I had once likened finding them to searching for a migratory needle in a haystack, but now, with such risk attendant, I feared a needle behind every straw.

It was possible the Moulish would be safe nonetheless; they might hear the Labane before they drew near, might hide themselves before one of these warriors struck. That possibility was not one I could rely upon: to do so would be despicable, a callous abrogation of what I owed them for their shelter and aid.

I therefore had to escape.

The skill and courage of the Labane are praised even by their enemies, but they were not foolhardy enough to travel the Green Hell in darkness. When it came time to halt, I meekly advised my captors away from what I recognized as a trail nocturnal predators would follow; this I did not only for my own safety, but to convince them of my sincere aid. We camped in as secure of a location as I could find, and I was, with reluctance, ungagged long enough to consume what remained of my own water and food. Whether they would give me any of their own the next day, I could not tell.

They bound me, of course, feet as well as hands, before sitting me against a tree and tying my body to it for good measure. One of the five kept watch, too. I had expected it, but still I cursed inwardly. How could I escape, with such measures in place?

In time I had to give up that question, for exhaustion claimed me, like falling over a cliff. In the morning my captors held a conference in which they seemed to be debating my continued use; I could scarcely breathe until one came to untie me. I would live another day. But how many more would I have?

This day proceeded much like the first, except that I did my best to guess where the Moulish might be, and to guide the Labane away from such places. This made for a fair bit of wading through inhospitable muck, but my captors could scarcely fault me for that; as far as they knew, inhospitable muck was what the Green Hell was made of. At one point I smelled a foul odor clearly recognizable as the lingering effects of a swamp-wyrm's extraordinary breath, but the dragon itself—both fortunately and otherwise—was nowhere to be seen.

We did, however, find something else. And as wretched as it was to be a captive, a part of me is glad I had not escaped the previous night, for I would have missed my chance to learn more about what the Labane were doing in Mouleen.

I feared at first that we had come across Moulish hunters, or worse, a camp. But the sound and movement that made my captors go into ready crouches proved to have another source: a second group of Labane.

This was a group of three, but I saw that they carried extra equipment, and some of it was bloodstained. From this I guessed that their brothers had met with misfortune along the way. I cannot be glad for the death of men, even my enemies, but it reassured me that my captors would see my value as a guide. Indeed, I hoped that was what they were telling the second party, as the two exchanged information in low tones. By his gestures, it seemed the other leader was vastly annoyed at his men having gotten turned around in the swamp.

For my own part, I was busy thinking. Two groups: that made it likely there were more than two. Both of them small. None of them carrying guns, whose crack would advertise their presence for kilometers around. Everything about this arrangement spoke of stealth. I was certain now that these were scouts, looking for a path across the Green Hell.

I was no military strategist, but I knew that if they succeeded, it would mean dreadful things for the defense of Bayembe. It was more imperative than ever that I escape and warn someone.

The second group did not join our own, strengthening my belief that these were scouting parties. I wished them ill fortune and damnation in their search. *Our home will eat you,* Yeyuama had said. For the sake of those to the north, I prayed that it would.

We continued on. I stumbled often with exhaustion; the leader finally unbent enough to allow me more water, without which I believe I would have died. But the various scrapes I had taken were hot and tender, and my joints ached; I was not sure how much farther I could go. Only the prospect of escape gave me strength . . . but I knew that the later such escape came, the more likely I was to fail.

Oddly, it was a fall that gave me hope. I tripped over a tangled fern and landed hard on my right side—hard not only for the force of it, but for the object in my pocket that dug painfully into my hip. It was, I realized, my penknife: the same penknife I had once nicked from my brother Andrew, so many years ago, which had accompanied me faithfully ever since.

With that knife (and a bit of flexibility), I might be able to cut myself free. That was one hurdle cleared, at least potentially; and the relief of it gave me conviction that I could clear the others, too. I would need a distraction, something to divert the man keeping watch that night, and then I would need an escape route.

Both meant choosing our campsite wisely. I forced my tired mind to focus, and was rewarded with the observation that there were quite a few drakeflies about. I mentioned before that they are insectivores; from my research I knew that, for drakeflies to be present in such numbers, there must be a hive of some sort nearby, to provide a suitable concentration of potential meals.

Finding what I was looking for without being obvious about it was difficult, but at last I spotted what I had hoped for: a wasps' nest, not too high above the ground. The wasps would ordinarily be dormant at night, but I knew—from painful experience—that they were easily disturbed.

I contrived to get my knife out of my pocket while taking care of biological necessity—the one task for which my captors unbound me, as none of them wanted the job of assisting me. (They did not, however, grant me any privacy during the process.) I kept it folded in the palm of my hand while one of them re-bound me, and breathed easier when the task was done. I was, as before, tied to a tree, and then I watched as they ate their evening meal.

They carried some rations of their own, but supplemented them with hunting as the occasion arose. (Hunting only, never gathering; I cannot blame them for fearing what plants might be poisonous, nor for distrusting the advice I tried to give them.) Earlier that day I had discovered how far a Tsebane can throw a spear, when one of them skewered a duiker at a distance I would have thought impossible. It raised the very real possibility that, in my flight, I might catch a spear between the shoulders . . . but I screwed my courage tight. I *must* do this thing.

This thing, however, had to wait for them to settle in for the night. The evening before, the leader had checked my bonds before bedding down; I could not risk him noticing any change. Once the camp was silent, though, with only one man keeping watch, I unfolded the knife and set to work.

The vines binding my wrists were first, and the most difficult. I cut my hands several times, and once dropped the knife—a loss that put my heart in my mouth, for what if I could not find it again? But I did, and resumed my task, feigning exhausted sleep the whole while.

The next part posed a different set of challenges. I waited, eyes closed to slits, until the watchman looked the other direction; then I slid my right shoulder (the one farthest from him) out from under the vines. Now I must be swift, for if he looked closely, he would see that I should not be able to slump so far in my bonds. With my right hand I felt about for something I could throw: a stone, a branch, *anything.*

Nothing came to hand. There are few stones lying about in Mouleen, and fallen branches are too often tangled with whatever has grown about them. With a sinking heart, I realized I would have to throw what was, right then, my most precious possession: my knife.

Before I did that, I would need to get one more use out of it. Working quickly, trying not to pant with fear, I transferred the blade to my left hand, blessing the undergrowth that gave a tiny amount of cover to my movements. I drew my ankles up as close as I could, wincing at the sound; the guard glanced my way, but did not react. With the penknife I cut through the vines on my ankles (and also cut my calf, for I was clumsy with fear and insufficient ambidexterity).

Perhaps I made a sound. Perhaps the Tsebane was simply that wary. But he turned then, half-rising from his crouch, as if to come investigate me.

I yanked myself free of the last of the vines and threw my knife at the nest. My arm had not the range of a Tsebane's, but I had spent their entire meal calculating the arc from me to that nest, repeating to myself again and again that I *would* strike it true. And so, through blind luck, divine providence, or sheer conviction that I would succeed, I threw right on my first try.

I did not stay to see the results, though I heard them as I fled. I dodged around the tree, and knew I had chosen right when the watchman's spear thunked into the wood; then I was off, through the forest, running desperately (but not at all quietly) for the closest thing I had been able to approximate for a safe escape route.

A nearby waterway.

I dove in without a single thought for leeches, snakes, fangfish, swamp-wyrms, or anything else. I exhaled a portion of my air, so as better to sink down, and began to push my way along the muddy bottom, trying not to shriek in fear when I felt things brush against my body. With my eyes shut, I could not see where I was going; I could only hope that by me moving underwater like this, in the darkness, the Labane would not be able to see me to throw a spear. (Or, better still, that they were too occupied with the wasps to pursue—but I could not take that risk.)

My intention was to stay underwater for as long as I could; and so I did, but that was not very long. The pounding of my heart soon drove me to the surface, where I tried to gasp in a new breath as quietly as I could—partly to keep from being heard, and partly because I wanted to listen for the Labane. I thought to hear curses and shouts from the direction of the camp, on account of the wasps. The silence that greeted me caused my muscles to clench in fear. The Labane were not ordinary soldiers; they were trained from childhood to accept pain and privation without complaint. They might die of the wasp stings, but they would not scream.

It meant I had no idea where they were.

I continued along a short distance, diving when I could, but fear kept using up my air. My progress was maddeningly slow, and when I surfaced for the fourth time, I saw movement on the bank I had left.

Whether it was a Tsebane, I cannot tell you. I believed then that it was, and did not stay to confirm my suspicion. I flung myself toward the opposite bank, not caring now how much noise I made, and plunged into the forest on that side, praying the water would delay them, praying some creature might eat them, praying for *anything* that might aid me.

What I found was a tree.

There were many trees about, but this one was of a particular sort: one of the forest giants, its trunk well wrapped in parasitic growths, standing alongside what a few months ago would, I knew, have been a flooded region. It was, in short, the kind of tree often used for tree-bridges—and that gave me an idea.

I dragged myself up with the panicked agility of a squirrel, clawing my way from one handhold to another, too driven by fear of what lay behind to even squeak when my footing slipped. The farther I went, the more apparent it became that I had chosen correctly: this tree and its parasites had been cultivated by the Moulish, which meant there was a bridge somewhere above me.

When at last I reached it, I crawled out a little distance, until I was something like halfway along the span. Here I lay, flattening myself as best I could amidst the twined branches and vines of the bridge, far away from any tree the Labane might expect to find me in.

They did not know the forest. They would not think to look for the bridge.

Or so I prayed.

My decision was rewarded when I heard a quiet voice below. Whether it had been a Tsebane on the other bank, one was here now—no, two, for I heard a response from not far away. They were indeed searching for me. And I had no doubt that if they found me, they would not take the chance they had before, that a Scirling woman was too useless to pose a threat.

But they did not find me. They searched in the area for a time; I heard them going back and forth, though they were surprisingly silent for men in darkness, in terrain totally unlike their homeland. I was well concealed by the structure of the bridge, though, and from the ground the bridge itself looked like nothing more than a particularly thick tangle of branches. One had to know what to look for to spot it, and they did not.

Nor did they know what hazards to look for. I heard a coughing roar, familiar to my ears, and knew they had woken a swamp-wyrm.

I heard no shouts of pain to tell me the creature had taken a bite out of a Tsebane, nor any equivalent sound from the dragon. I did catch a faint scent of its extraordinary breath, drifting up from the ground below, and was glad to be out of range. More distant sounds might be the Labane fleeing; I could not tell. But I stared into the darkness above me and blessed the forest which had cut and scratched and stung and battered me—and, ultimately, protected me.

I lay rigid and frightened for what seemed like an age before light began to filter through the green, and then lay for a time longer before I could persuade myself to move. Even then, I peered through the vines in all directions, picking off leeches while reassuring myself (insofar as I could) that the Labane had not laid a clever trap that I was about to spring.

They had not. Eventually I climbed down, aching from head to foot. But I could not permit myself the luxury of collapse: quite apart from my ravenous hunger and need for water, I had to warn the Moulish.

TWENTY-TWO

*The drums speak—Others are missing—Ikwunde plans—
Point Miriam—Politics—Wisdom and foolishness—
Moving the eggs—Fangfish*

I would not go so far as to say I found the Moulish; it would be more accurate to say they found me. I did, however, correctly read my surroundings to the extent of guessing where there might be a camp, so of that I can be proud.

My grammar, I fear, suffered terribly from my exhaustion and distress. It took far longer than it should have to explain the situation to them, while an elderly man fed and watered me. Then one of the hunters, an energetic fellow named Lumemouwin, wanted to go out with the others to look for the Labane. "They will *kill* you," I said helplessly. I knew the Moulish were perfectly capable of moving in stealth, but that did not change the fact that I would feel any deaths as if they were my fault. "Please, will you not warn the other camps—"

"We will," said one of the grandmothers, a woman called Ri-Kwilene. "But first we must know what to tell them."

She meant rather that they wanted to make sure what I said

was true, before they alarmed anyone else. I suppose I did not look like the most reliable messenger, and foreigners have been known to run mad in jungles before. That did not make me any calmer as they sent hunters out to investigate.

But the men returned before long with confirmation that they had seen what few signs the Labane camp had left behind. (No bodies; it was too much for me to hope that the wasps or the dragon had done them in.) Then the elders took to the drums, pounding out the message that would soon spread from one end of Mouleen to the other.

The drums brought Yeyuama to me a few days later. As grateful as I was to see him, I immediately noted that he was alone—or rather, accompanied by two young men I did not recognize, both of them Moulish fellows. "Where are the others?" I asked, my hands twisting about one another. "Has something happened?"

Yeyuama shook his head. "I do not know. They never came down from the cliff."

My first thought was that the Labane had captured them. Then I told myself that was foolishness; the Labane were coming from the southern side of the Great Cataract, and my friends had been on the northern. Still, it did little to reassure me. (It would have done even less had I known that the Ikwunde pressed an attack along the Girama River the very day I went over the waterfall—I think to divert attention from their scouts in the swamp.)

If I would feel guilt for the deaths of any Moulish, how much more would I feel if anything happened to my companions? I bore a great deal of responsibility for their presence here in the first place. I looked from Yeyuama to Rikwilene. "Can a message be sent out, asking after them?"

She frowned and shook her head. "The villagers will wonder, if they hear too much speech from the drums." (The "villagers" in this case were the Labane scouts.) "Someone will send word if your brothers and sister are found. The other camps know you are here."

I argued, but could not budge her. Which was, I suppose, practice for what followed, when we began to discuss what to do about the Labane.

With the aid of a map laid out in sticks and leaves, I explained the larger situation: the impending war against the Ikwunde, of which the Moulish knew only a little, and what might happen if the people to the south could bring their army through the swamp. Here, however, I ran into immediate objections. "As many villagers as all the people of the forest together?" Lumemouwin said skeptically. (I had told them there were more Ikwunde than that, but they simply had no personal experience of human crowds on that scale.) "Impossible. They could never bring them through. The forest would eat them."

"The forest might eat some, yes—but even if two in every five die, it could be disastrous," I said. "For you as well as for the peoples of Bayembe; I assure you they would not hesitate to kill Moulish along the way. Though I wonder . . ." My words trailed off as I stared at my own map. Yes, the Ikwunde could march through, if they were prepared to accept such attrition. But could they do so *effectively*? I had heard military men talk about the importance of supply lines, and my own experience with the logistics of carrying equipment through the Green Hell made me doubt an army would fare well. A small, mobile group like the Labane could manage—but a small, mobile group would not be good for much more than harrying villages along the northern border. Was the aim to distract the defenders stationed along the rivers? Surely this was too much trouble for something so small. Unless they had a more valuable target . . .

My map was incomplete. I had focused on the Great Cataract and the northern and southern edges of Mouleen, but I had not paid much attention to the eastern end. With one hand I fumbled blindly for another stick, and jammed it into the soft dirt.

"Point Miriam," I whispered.

It was a fort—but one built to defend the harbor. The Ikwunde were not great seafarers; they had, however, conquered enough coastal towns that they might conceivably mount an assault on Nsebu and Atuyem. That was why the Scirling colony had been placed there: our defense of the harbor was part of our agreement with Bayembe. We had built our walls and placed our guns, and *all* of that effort was focused on the sea, which they believed to be their only point of vulnerability.

But the eastern fringes of the Green Hell came very close to Point Miriam. And if an attack came from the fort's *landward* side . . .

How many men would they need to take it? I was not tactician enough to guess. A small force might do it, though, if they had surprise on their side; and undoubtedly it would be a great surprise if the Ikwunde appeared out of the swamp to assault the fort. My mind spun out possibilities for what would follow: an invasion force by sea, perhaps, once the harbor's main defense was gone, or perhaps an attempt to hold the fort itself. All of the possibilities were dreadful.

Swiftly I laid out for the others what I envisioned. "Can you warn the fort?" I asked when I was done. The Moulish carried out some amount of trade with the villagers along their borders; surely that was true along the bay as well.

Those around me exchanged glances. "We can tell the camps in the east," Rikwilene said. "But will the villagers listen?"

The villagers, or the Scirling officials at Point Miriam. "If the message was from me . . ." I dismissed this thought before it was even complete. "They'd have no reason to trust such a claim. Even if they believed the words came from me, they would doubt my judgment." Sir Adam would hardly be inclined to vouch for my reliability. And while I wanted to believe they would take precautions regardless, I knew they were just as likely to laugh it off. No one could assault Point Miriam through the Green Hell. No one.

If I went in person, I might have a chance of persuading them. But the scouts were already in the swamp; the army could not be that far behind. My odds of making it the length of Mouleen before they mounted their attack were even worse than my odds of Sir Adam listening to a transcribed drum message.

But there were people who *would* listen to the drums. And I had seen for myself how effective they could be, the day we found Velloin and Okweme trying to kidnap a dragon.

I looked around the circle at the gathered camp, youths and hunters and elders, with the children slipping between legs to listen. "Please," I said. "You can stop them before they even get to Point Miriam. You can save any number of lives in Bayembe. If you send a message to the camps—I have seen how strong your hunters are. You can fight the Ikwunde. Not head-on, of course, but from the shadows—"

Even before I started, I knew it was a lost cause. Heads were shaking all around, men and women drawing back in disapproval. "This is a villager fight," someone said; I did not see who.

Ikwunde against Yembe, Scirlings interfering, Satalu in the wings. What did any of that mean to the Moulish? Even if the Ikwunde conquered Bayembe, enclosing the Green Hell on three sides, it would have little consequence for the people here. Oh, perhaps someday that would rebound ill upon them—but vague fears of "someday" would persuade no one to put himself in harm's way. Indeed, from their perspective it might be better if the Ikwunde triumphed, for that would destroy or at least set back the Scirling colony, and take with it the plans for a dam above the Great Cataract.

Not that the Moulish knew of the dam . . .

"What does this mean?" Yeyuama asked, snapping his fingers.

I stared at my hand. I had not even realized I had done that, so caught up was I in my thought. "It means I've had an idea," I said slowly. "One I should perhaps share only with you—to begin with, at least. It concerns the dragons."

He nodded and beckoned the two fellows who had arrived with him to join us off to one side. "They are pure," he said, when I looked quizzical. "I brought them for the ceremony, but what you have to say comes first."

I would have been happier sharing this only with Yeyuama, who at least was familiar to me. But I was in no position to object. "It concerns what those hunters said," I told the three of them. "I needed permission to come here, from the oba of Bayembe, and he required a promise from me in return."

This tale I kept as short as I could, stressing at every point my ignorance in making that promise, and my apology for having done so. "But," I said, and then took a deep breath. "If it is not wholly blasphemous to suggest this . . . then I think, should that bargain be kept, it would help save the forest from a very great danger. One your people are not yet aware of."

Explaining the dam was both easier and more difficult than I expected, first when I told Yeyuama and the other two, then again when I repeated my words for the rest of the camp. The Moulish understood dams well enough; they created their own in certain seasons, to aid in their fishing. But a dam large enough to control the Great Cataract? Nothing in the world could be so powerful.

"I assure you it can," I said, with all the conviction I could muster. "And if this is built, it will change your forest forever. No longer will the floods rise as before; the swamp will always be in its dry season. The waterfall itself will be changed, and Yeyuama fears what the consequence of that may be for the dragons." This had not been in my original speculations, when I stood on the bank of the Hembi, for at that time I had not yet seen the queens in the lake. Yeyuama's hands had trembled when the possibility came to him. After that, he had given his full support to my plan.

I said to my assembled listeners, "If you stop the Ikwunde from crossing the swamp and attacking Point Miriam, I will tell the oba that in gratitude for your help, he must not build this dam. It will be an agreement between his people and yours, sealed by the giving of a gift. The specifics of that gift are a matter for the pure, but I truly believe it will gain you this man's friendship. And that friendship will protect your home for generations to come."

They needed time to consider it, of course. Such a thing could not be decided on a whim. I chafed at every minute of delay, but Yeyuama took pity on me; he and the other two pure drew me aside for the ceremony acknowledging my safe return from the island, which also served as distraction.

It should have been done on the bank of the lake, but we could not spare the time to go there. They built a hut away from the camp, then put me inside it with a small fire, onto which they threw the leaves whose scent was so reminiscent of a swamp-wyrm's extraordinary breath. It was the same material used on the fire the hunters passed when leaving camp, but whereas they were only required to walk through the smoke, or perhaps scoop it onto themselves with their hands, I was left inside the hut until I nearly asphyxiated. When Yeyuama finally let me out, I was glad enough of the fresh air that I hardly minded his insistence that I strip naked (yes, in front of all three of them) and bathe myself in a quiet and predator-free part of the swamp.

"The smoke purifies us," he said when I was done and clothed once more. "Nothing can undo the harm caused by that first death, but we come as close as we can."

Yeyuama's distraction had served its purpose, with pefect timing. A boy came running up just then, summoning the four of us once more back to camp.

The other pure were drawn into conversation briefly after we returned, while I waited apart. Then I was beckoned over, and Rikwilene delivered their answer. "You speak wisdom on some things," the old woman said, "and foolishness on others. We will not attack the Ikwunde."

My heart sank. All that hope . . . but this was too much to ask of them, and the possible reward too uncertain.

"Our hunters can be hunters of men when there is no other choice, but what you ask—for us to stop their camps so directly—

that would only result in death on both sides. *But,*" Rikwilene said, and my breath stopped, "we have agreed to try other ways."

On the instant, my imagination filled with new possibilities, each one madder than the last. The hunter Lumemouwin stopped me, though, with a cautionary hand. "You do not know the forest, or our people. Not well enough. We will be the ones to make these plans."

He was right. I was no tactician, nor was I Moulish; I did not know how they might be most effective. What I had to offer was information, and assistance with the world outside when this matter ended. "If it would be useful," I said, "I can tell you things about Point Miriam, and the weapons the people on both sides carry."

Yeyuama laughed. As tense as I was, it shocked me that he could be so cheerful. "We will have to think how to translate that for the drums, but yes. And you can do more than that. You are one of the pure now."

As pure as a hut full of foul smoke could make me. "Yes," I said. "The promise I made—"

"Not that," Yeyuama said, grinning. "Come. This, too, is only for a few ears."

The ears in question were those of the pure: those who had qualified themselves to "touch the dragons."

That category, you may note, does not include *your* ears, nor your eyes neither. (Unless you have undergone that test yourself and passed, in which case you will not need me to tell you what I am about to omit.) As before, I will speak only of those things which I believe are safe to be shared with others, based on the judgment of my more experienced Moulish counterparts. I may have gone to the island and returned, but that was only the barest part of what it meant to join their ranks.

"If we move the eggs now," Yeyuama said when we had drawn apart, "they will hatch early. And then they may feast upon those who come into their waters."

I received these words in wide-eyed silence. He spoke the way my parents' housekeeper in Tamshire might, suggesting that it would be advisable to shift the winter shutters into position a few weeks early. As if "moving the eggs" were a common task—just one not usually done at this time.

While the other fellows considered it, Yeyuama explained to me. And this, suitably edited, is what I learned.

The dragons I had seen in the lake were, as I have said, queen dragons, the females of a species for which I had heretofore only seen the males. Now I learned that the chief task of the pure was first to bring suitable males up to the lake for breeding, and then to disperse the eggs after they were laid, to various points around the swamp.

The ramifications of this have been laid out extensively in my more academic works; I will dwell on only one now, as many of you are no doubt anxious to leave the dusty byways of natural history and get back to the invading army. The eggs so distributed were *not*, as is common among other draconic breeds, large and few in number. They were myriad, and shockingly small: less than ten centimeters in length. I thought of swamp-wyrms and their usual habits, and asked Yeyuama how on earth newly hatched dragons could be of much use in stopping an army, however many of them there might be.

He grinned from ear to ear, as delighted as a magician pulling back the curtain to reveal his great trick. "You have seen them, and feared them. But you have called them fangfish."

The tiny, eel-like predator that had taken a bite out of my left arm back in Floris; the entirely aquatic creature we had thought at best to be a draconic cousin. In reality it was the infantile form of the great swamp-wyrm. They hatched in abundance, and were eaten in abundance not only by snakes and other creatures, but by their own, more mature kind; those who survived grew and changed, eventually becoming the full-grown dragons to which we had devoted the bulk of our attention and study.

(Despite the unsightly scar on my arm, there was a part of me that thought in delight: I've been bitten by a *dragon*!)

Then I remembered the swarms of fangfish that had roiled the waters during the flood, the avoidance of which had spurred the construction of tree-bridges. If the Ikwunde attempted to wade through on their way to Point Miriam—and they could hardly avoid it—then the consequences would be very bloody indeed.

"You will help," Yeyuama said, still grinning. "Your way of going to and from the island was madness; I have never seen anything like it. Most of us go a much easier way! We should call you Sasoumin instead."

Sasoumin—"woman who flies."

Yeyuama went on while I was considering my new appellation and fighting the urge to giggle with delight. (Even now, I believe that is the name by which I am best known in the swamps of Mouleen. It is much more flattering than some of the sobriquets I have born in the news-sheets of Scirland.) "I will show you where the eggs are, and you will help move them; that is your work now. We will use the drums to tell others to do the same."

I will, of course, not tell you where the eggs are initially laid, save to say that they are not *on* the island; the purpose of that challenge is to give a view of the queen dragons, and to test the mettle of those who will henceforth be taking their unhatched offspring from their original place of laying to new locations deeper in the swamp. This stage of the process I did not do, for it was not the correct season for newly laid eggs. Although the experience sounds hair-raising—queen dragons are decidedly unfriendly—it is one of my great regrets that I never had the chance, for my time in Mouleen was drawing to an end, and I have never been able to return for more than a few days. To come so close to one of the queens . . . I have had other breathtaking experiences in my life, some of which (others would say) surpass even that one. But one does not cease to treasure a gem simply because one owns another that is larger. I would have loved to place that in the jewelry box of my memory.

I did, however, go with Yeyuama to where the current clutches of eggs were buried, in soft swamp muck. This is where they do much of their incubation, before being shifted to the water for hatching. The history of how this process developed has been discussed at greater length by the Yembe historian Chinaka n Ofiriro Dara; I advise those interested in such matters to read her work, and to consult my own monographs for analysis of its effect on draconic development.

But enough of such matters: there is an invading army to attend to.

Drums had passed the requisite messages through the Green Hell, faster than any messenger could carry them. The four of us (myself, Yeyuama, and our two companions) were not the only ones shifting eggs; indeed, ours were likely to be the least relevant,

for the Ikwunde were almost certain to make their crossing farther to the east. To hatch only some of the dragons now would, however, disturb the balance of the swamp. As it was, Yeyuama admitted that the effects of this would be difficult, as it was not the season of flooding, when food would be most abundant. "I hope they get a good meal off the Ikwunde, then," I said.

He shrugged philosophically. "If necessary, we will make another queen egg next year"—and that is how I discovered that part of the egg-handling process fosters the sexual differentiation between the queen dragons in the lake and their male suitors in the swamp.

I keep diverting to matters of natural history. This is, I suppose, because what followed was akin to a large number of dominoes toppling over where I could not see them. Much of it I only learnt about afterward, or pieced together from what I was not told; altogether, the picture it made was very complex. As is only fitting, I suppose, for the chain of events that led to me being accused of treason against the Scirling crown. I shall have to give you the larger picture first, and then my humble strand within it that stitched these events together.

TWENTY-THREE

Nagoreemo's message—Tom, Natalie, and Faj Rawango—
The Ikwunde cross the swamp—Captives of war—My army

The Moulish had, as per my request, sent a messenger to
the fort at Point Miriam. In their generosity, they did not
even recruit a coastal villager to carry the word on their
behalf; this was deemed important enough that they sent one of
their own, a man who spoke Yembe, an elder named Nagoreemo.

He left the Green Hell and climbed the rocky slope up to Point
Miriam, drawing many stares, I imagine, from Scirlings
unaccustomed to seeing a man in nothing more than a loincloth.
At the gate to the fort he was stopped by one of the soldiers on
guard, and in his careful Yembe, conveyed the news that an
Ikwunde force intended to pass through Mouleen and attack
them from the landward side.

What words he used to explain this, I do not know. My own
conjecture had been translated into the language of the drums,
which is (of necessity, owing to how that language functions) both
long-winded and limited in its specifics. But the Moulish are
practiced at sending a message the length of the swamp without

distorting it, so I have faith it arrived at the coast in much the same shape it left our own drums in the west. Once there, however, it was interpreted by the local camps, then given to Nagoreemo, who then translated it into Yembe and relayed it to soldiers whose own grasp of that tongue was, I suspect, less than fully proficient.

Small wonder that no one believed him. One of the officers at the fort, an army major by the name of Joshua Maitland, believed Nagoreemo was a defector from his own people, come to warn them about an ill-advised *Moulish* assault on the fort. Others thought him simply mad. The result was that he was turned away—with, I am ashamed to say, many jeers, and even a few blows from rifle butts. That venerable elder deserved better from us.

In the meanwhile, events at the far end of Bayembe had become quite warm, to distract all eyes from anything that might be happening along the bay. The Ikwunde mounted a series of assaults along and across the Girama, including one that nearly made it to the Hembi before our forces caught them. This, as you may imagine, raised alarms all through that region, with the consequence that our side instituted new patrols to watch for any Ikwunde advance scouts. They not only found some of those; they also found Tom, Natalie, and Faj Rawango.

Had the patrol that found them been composed of Bayembe forces, all might have been well, for Faj Rawango was experienced enough in the ways of the oba's court that he could have demanded, and likely received, a proper hearing. They were, alas, found by Scirlings—and promptly taken prisoner.

Did the lieutenant think those three were Ikwunde spies? No, of course not; only one was Erigan, and even the blindest Scirling private could see that the short, slight Faj Rawango was nothing like the tall, well-knit men in the Ikwunde army. But they were something inexplicable, and so they had to be detained. (The fact that Tom and Natalie both explained themselves to him at length did not dissuade him from this course.)

They were soon transferred into the care of a captain—but this fellow, alas, had heard complaints of their activities from the despicable Velloin, who had given a highly biased account of our meeting in the swamp. As a result, they were read a lengthy diatribe on civilized behaviour and the necessity for them to reflect well on Scirland; following this, they were summarily packed up with the wounded from the river fighting and shipped back across toward Nsebu. All three of them were somewhere in the middle of the savannah when the rest of this matter resolved.

The Ikwunde, from what we can determine, were following a plan more or less like the one I had posited, though with a great many subtle flourishes I could never have imagined and honestly cannot recall. (Those interested in such things can find an exhaustive discussion of all aspects of the Ikwunde War in Achabe n Kegweyu Gbori's ten-volume work *Expansion and Retreat of the Ikwunde,* translated into Scirling by Ezekiel Grant.) Scouts like the ones I encoutered had been sent into Mouleen all along its length in the hope of locating a waterway suitable for transporting their army by boat; needless to say, this failed. The Ikwunde therefore took the information gathered by their scouts—including, I fear, some I provided myself—and sent five companies of Labane by the shortest route possible, from Osheth on the Eremmo border to Point Miriam.

Toward Point Miriam, at least. They encountered some difficulty along the way.

I saw with my own eyes how rapidly the swamp-wyrm eggs hatched once placed in water, the "fangfish" wiggling free like the eels they resembled. They are a disturbing sight then, soft and almost helpless looking, but with mouths already full of teeth. We took great care in crossing the waterways as we traveled from egg cache to egg cache, and even more care after that task was done, when Yeyuama and I set out for the eastern edge of the Green Hell.

For although I esteemed the Moulish greatly and knew they would be of more use than I in opposing the Ikwunde, I could not bring myself to sit idly by while this matter played out. If nothing else, I needed to see enough that I could accurately inform the men at Point Miriam of what had transpired.

Which meant I was there to see one of the Labane companies— already much worse off for their travels to that point—attempt a crossing of fangfish-filled water.

They had searched for a way around it, and been thwarted by creative Moulish troublemakers; now they had no choice but to build rafts and attempt to pole across. Yeyuama had refused to try and provoke any fully grown dragons into troubling them, because these Labane carried guns, but he could not stand in the way of a swamp-wyrm's own inclination. One took great exception to the Labane trespassing upon his territory, and rammed a raft before anyone aboard it saw him there.

I had thought to feel triumph at watching the forest eat those who would trespass in it. When the moment came, I merely felt sick. There was no pleasure to be had in the screaming—for even a Tsebane will scream when a dozen infant dragons latch onto him. It is a horrible way to die, and yet those who did may well have been luckier than those who were merely bloodied, for the latter faced near-certain infection, which in many cases was only a more protracted way to go.

But I knew better than to think we could warn them off their course; these were, after all, the most dedicated troops the inkosi possessed. And when my resolve faltered, I had only to remind myself of the casualties my allies suffered. Despite warning and care, the Moulish had not been able to stay entirely safe; Labane scouts had caught some of them, and one camp was overrun as they tried to move out of the army's line of march. All in all, twenty-one Moulish died, which is a massacre for numbers as small as theirs.

Because of this, some among the western camps argued in favor of actively hunting and killing those the forest had not disposed of. But the youths brought out the *legambwa bomu*, the dragon mask, and charged around with it, reminding all that killing was what cursed humankind with mortality; and while killing for food might be a tragic necessity, killing these men was not. They therefore took the surviving Labane prisoner.

Prisoners were not something they had much experience with. The Moulish deal with their own internal problems by talking it out or walking away to a new camp, not by waging war. Tying people up was something done only when a person had run mad (or, as they would put it, was targeted by serious witchcraft). What should they do with their captives?

Had I not just spent seven months in the swamp, flung myself off a cliff, crash-landed in the trees, been a captive myself, and then run the length of the Green Hell, I might have thought my answer through more thoroughly. As it was, I asked whether they would be willing to send enough hunters with me to escort the prisoners to Point Miriam, and the Moulish, glad to be rid of them, agreed.

This is how I marched out of the jungle toward the fort with what, at first glance, might understandably be mistaken for a small invading army.

Our slow pace (limited to the speed of hobbled Labane) and general disorganization went some way toward establishing us as no threat. Soldiers, however, are apt to get nervous around armed strangers, even when the weapons in question are nets and fire-hardened sticks of wood. I placed myself prominently at the front of the group, intending to draw the eye and give the soldiers something like a familiar (by which I mean a Scirling) face to reassure them.

This might have been more successful had I looked less a scarecrow. I had been in the same clothing since the morning I parted from Tom and Natalie, and it had seen a great deal of abuse in the interim. I was unwashed, underfed, and giddy with the success of our plan. So it was that when rifles were leveled in our direction, I waved my arms above my head, hallooed the fort, and cried out in a loud, laughing voice, "Do you believe us now?"

It was of course my luck that Major Maitland answered me from the wall (though I did not know he was the one who had misinterpreted Nagoreemo until later). He shouted down at us, "You and your army of savages can stop right there!"

"*My* army?" I looked at the Moulish with exaggerated surprise. "These do not belong to me, sir. Unless you mean our prisoners? I would not claim them if you paid me, for it was their intent to sneak up on you from a direction you did not expect—as I believe you were warned, though you did not listen. Fortunately for you, the Moulish believe in sharing what they have, and they have wit and common sense in abundance. More than enough to make up for its lack elsewhere.

"I, by contrast, am Scirling, and less well schooled in generosity. I therefore say that if you and your masters do not promise to clap these Ikwunde in irons and then reward these brave people as they deserve, then we jolly well may just let these fellows go, for they are not worth the nuisance of keeping."

(In hindsight, I can see how this may have been construed as a threat.)

Maitland went quite purple. I think he might have given the order to fire—a few warning shots to put me on better behaviour, at least—but by then Sir Adam had attained the top of the wall and seen what lay outside. "Mrs. Camherst?" he called down, shocked, and I answered, "What is left of her."

"What the devil is all of this?" he demanded, gesturing at the mass of people I stood with.

This time I answered him with more decorum, although Maitland provoked me sorely with his own interjections. Sir Adam continued to question me—how had we captured them; how many there were; what on earth did I think I was wearing—until I said, "Sir, I will answer everything to your satisfaction, but not by shouting it up at you. This is dreadfully public, and my voice will give out. Will you take the prisoners, and give your surety that the Moulish will be rewarded? They, not I, have done the work of capturing these Labane, and have killed a great many more besides, at no small risk and cost to themselves."

Maitland snorted loudly enough for me to hear it, even at that range. "You expect us to believe that your savages killed Labane warriors with—with what? Sharpened sticks?"

"No, Major," I said coolly. "They killed the Labane with dragons. As a gentlewoman and natural historian, I assure you it is true."

I suspect it was my declaration more than anything else that opened the gates of Point Miriam to us, for everyone wanted to know what I meant by *they killed the Labane with dragons*. We shuffled in, me at the front, the Moulish surrounding the hobbled prisoners, and I made sure to find a soldier with good Yembe to serve as an interpreter before I let Sir Adam take me off for questioning.

If that strikes you as a phrase that might be applied to the suspect in a crime, you are not far wrong. Sir Adam was deeply suspicious of my tale; he called in a doctor to examine me before anything else, so certain was he that I had lost my reason. (I blame the trousers.) Much tedious back-and-forth ensued after that, but the important moment came when I told Sir Adam what I intended going forward.

"In return for their work in saving this colony and Bayembe," I said, mustering what remained of my energy, "the Moulish do have a price."

"Gold?" Sir Adam asked. "Guns? Out with it, Mrs. Camherst; tell me what you have promised them."

"Nothing so mercenary, I assure you. But it is the forest known as the Green Hell that has protected Bayembe and this colony; it must be protected in return. I understand that you intend to build a dam in the west, across one or more—I presume all three—of the rivers. The plans for this must stop."

The governor shot to his feet. "Mrs. Camherst, I do not know where you have gotten your information—"

Under no circumstances was I going to name Natalie. "Do you

think no one knows what your engineers are here to build? Do not fear for the defense of Bayembe, Sir Adam. Even without your lake, I assure you, this country will be safe."

I was extraordinarily lucky that he stopped me before I said anything more.

"Damn the defense," he growled. "Our soldiers can stop the Ikwunde. There are *contracts* depending on that dam, Mrs. Camherst—blast it, what do you think the point of this colony is?"

"What do you mean?" I asked, mostly to purchase time to think.

He made a disgusted noise. "Power, of course. Of all kinds. Power from the dam, and we have contracts saying that eighty percent of it will be ours for a period of fifty years after construction is done. With that and Bayembe's iron, our profits will be enormous. Think of what the effects of *that* will be. And you expect us to throw all that away, simply because a few naked savages stopped a raid?"

My hands were shaking; I clutched them tight in my lap. "I knew nothing of this."

"Of course you didn't. You are nothing more than a reckless young woman—"

"Who just saved this colony from invasion and possible destruction." My voice wanted to shake, too; keeping it steady made my words come out loudly. "You should perhaps consider keeping the young ladies around you better informed, Sir Adam— but in this case I am glad you did not. Can you not see the headlines now? SCIRLING GENTLEWOMAN SAVES NSEBU. DARING FLIGHT REVEALS DASTARDLY PLAN. SWAMP NATIVES DEFEAT LABANE WARRIORS. HUMILIATED PRISONERS BROUGHT IN CHAINS TO FORT. And then can you imagine the response if people learn that you turned your back on those who kept Labane spears out of it?"

He did not go purple as Maitland had; he turned pale instead. "Are you threatening me, Mrs. Camherst?"

"No, Sir Adam," I said. "I am merely explaining how people back home will see this. If you hear a threat in that, it is only because you fear the inevitable consequence."

"It is *not* inevitable," he said, his voice trembling. "It is something you intend to bring down upon me. It is a threat, Mrs. Camherst, however you try to disguise it with pretty language."

I sighed. I was weary; I was filthy; I had entirely spent the energy which had sustained me on the way here, and wanted nothing more than to sleep for a month while my various wounds healed. "Very well, Sir Adam. Call it a threat if you must. I gave my word to the Moulish that I would do everything I could to assist them in this cause, and I intend to keep it. Lock me up if you wish; it will not help you, for I have already written down my tale, and made arrangements for it to be shared with friendly ears."

It was the last inspiration of my tired brain: an utter fabrication, invented on the spot to forestall the house arrest I otherwise saw in my future.

It failed.

Sir Adam strode to the door. "Find a room for Mrs. Camherst. And see that she does not leave."

TWENTY-FOUR

Royal displeasure—Eggs for the oba—Overly frank questions—
Accusations of treason—Life outside the Green Hell—
Farewells, and a reflection on sorrow

B ut of course I did leave in the end—courtesy of Ankumata n Rumeme Gbori.

I do not know what precisely he said to Sir Adam,
but I believe it had something to do with the promise I had
made before departing for the Green Hell. He wanted to know
why I had failed him, and refused to let a Scirling question me
in his stead. It was not freedom; armed guards accompanied me
from Point Miriam to Atuyem, and took me back again
afterward, too. Still, it was the salvation I needed. Sir Adam's
outburst had stopped me before I admitted that the success of
my plan depended on me speaking with the oba, and so he let
me go.

This time there was no public ceremony, no hangers-on. The
oba preferred to express his displeasure in private. Apart from the
guards who stood both outside and inside the chamber, there was
only his *griot* for company, and his sister Galinke.

"The Golden One grants you what you desire," the *griot* said, "and in return, you betray him."

It was not a good sign that the *griot* spoke to me. This is a thing they do in Bayembe, to underline the exalted status of the oba; he speaks to his *griot,* and the *griot* speaks to whatever lowly soul is unworthy to receive the words directly. Mr. Wilker and I had previously been honoured by Ankumata's friendliness, but I had now lost the privilege.

Galinke sat with her hands folded and eyes downcast. This rebuke was for her as well as for myself; she had suggested me to her brother as a tool, and so she too had failed him. And I, in a sense, had failed her.

My curtsy was as deep and respectful as I could make it. "*Chele,* I thank you for bringing me here today. There is more you have not heard, but Sir Adam would not release me to tell you."

Ankumata gestured at his *griot,* who said, "Speak."

I had rehearsed the words all the way from Point Miriam. "You asked me to bring you eggs. Whether you meant me to collect them, trade for them, or steal them outright, I soon discovered that for me to do any such thing would have been a grave insult to the Moulish, and dishonourable repayment for their generosity, without which I certainly would have died in the swamp. My promise was a blind one, and I will know in the future not to repeat that mistake.

"But blind although my promise was, I have found a way to keep it."

Alert readers may recall that Yeyuama had told Okweme that he would address my intended theft of eggs after I had visited the island. I thought at the time that he was referring to my possible death in the attempt; had I perished, it might well have been seen as proper judgment upon me for my intended crime. But when we debated the possibility of stopping the Ikwunde and the dam alike, he told me his true meaning—which was not at all what I expected.

It is the privilege and responsibility of those who touch the dragons to move the eggs where they are needed. Prior to the island, any attempt on my part to interfere with that process, whether by theft or trade, would have been a blasphemy grave enough to ensure my death.

But *after* the island . . . if I wanted to move eggs somewhere, then it was my right to do so.

"The Moulish have agreed to let me offer you eggs," I said. "I do not have them with me; you will have to wait for more to be laid. But when the time comes, certain men among them will bring you eggs and instruct you in their care. When one of those dragons perishes, they will bring you another—for the ones they supply will be incapable of breeding. This is not meant as a slight against you; it is the unavoidable consequence of swamp-wyrm biology. But if you place those dragons in the rivers above the Great Cataract, you will have a defense like that which has just protected Point Miriam."

The oba listened to all of this impassively, hiding his thoughts behind the mask of a man who has survived political waters more dangerous than those the Labane tried to cross.

I swallowed and went on. "For this arrangement to work, however, the Moulish will require something in return. They have sheltered your land, at no little risk to themselves, and now offer you a treasure; moreover, what they require is a necessity for that treasure to thrive. I hope your generosity and wisdom will see the value in granting their wish."

Here I paused, until the *griot* prompted me to continue. This was the most delicate point, for if I angered Ankumata as I had Sir Adam, I might be locked up and never let out again.

But I could hardly stop now. "The dam," I said. "The one planned in the west. Its effect on the swamp would be catastrophic for the Moulish and their dragons both. If you wish for the arrangement I have described, then you must not allow the dam to be built."

Silence fell. Ankumata propped one hand against his leg brace, unblinking gaze never wavering from me. I fought not to squirm under its weight. Eighty percent of the power, Sir Adam had said; that was the dragon's share of the benefit, and I had no doubt that most of the cost in labor and material would come from Bayembe, not Scirland. It was not a deal that favored the oba. But could he abandon it? And did he wish to?

The next words did not come from the *griot*. They came from Ankumata himself.

"There is no profit for your people in this trade."

"We have already had our profit," I said, "in the safety of those who would have died in the Labane attack." My mouth was very dry. Surely it was a good sign that he was no longer speaking through his *griot,* but his words reminded me that my peril came from multiple directions. "As for the rest..." I shrugged helplessly. "I can only do what I think is right, *chele*. For as many people as possible. This seems better to me than allowing the dam to be built. But perhaps my judgment was incorrect."

More silence. I do not know whether Ankumata was still thinking, or merely waiting, to make certain no one would think he rushed into his decision.

I nearly jumped out of my skin when he said, "The gift is good. There will be no dam."

Muscles I had not even known were tight suddenly relaxed. Then my traitor mouth betrayed me, saying, "Are you certain? Sir Adam, I fear, will be angry—"

Ankumata's eyes gleamed with what I think was suppressed amusement. "Your country has promised assistance in defending Bayembe. I accept the assistance you have provided on their behalf."

That was undoubtedly *not* the wording in the treaty—but if he thought he could get away with that argument, who was I to disagree? I asked, "Is that why you sent me to the swamp, instead of one of your own? Because you could call it Scirling aid? No, that cannot be it. I thought at the time that you would not mind as much if we died. Later, it occurred to me that you could more easily disavow our actions if we caused trouble. But if that were the case, you could have sent Velloin. Or both of us together, but I am sure someone has informed you of how I detest the man. I cannot think why you did not send him instead, before me, unless it is because I am Scirling and he is not."

This is why I have declined all offers of diplomatic postings. As I have grown older (and in theory more sedate), various government officials have thought to take advantage of my experience and international connections by sending me as an ambassador to one place or another. But I have at all ages been too prone to speaking my mind, and not always judicious enough in who I speak it to.

The oba of Bayembe, however, chose not to punish me for my frankness. He said, "If Velloin were a woman, he would not have gone into the *agban*."

I did not immediately parse his meaning. I looked to Galinke, who smiled; I thought of the days she and I had spent in conversation there. My seclusion had been less than entirely willing . . . but I had gone, rather than risk offense to my hosts, which might have jeopardized my ultimate purpose.

Velloin would not have bent to such concerns.

Understand: this is not the same thing as saying I was perfectly respectful of Yembe traditions, or Moulish ones, either. Romantics of various sorts over the years have painted me as a kind of human chameleon, adapting without difficulty or reservation to my social environment; this is twaddle. (Flattering twaddle, but twaddle all the same.) As I indicated during my account of the witchcraft ritual, my driving concern has always been my research. In pursuit of that, however, I have generally believed that it is more to my advantage to cooperate with those around me than to ignore them. Sometimes this has been a nuisance, and on occasion an outright mistake, but overall this philosophy has served me well.

And on this occasion, it explained why my solution to the problem had appealed to Ankumata.

I curtseyed again and said, "Thank you, *chele*." Then one final thought occurred to me. "If—if I may ask one more thing—"

He made an exaggerated show of wariness, but gestured for me to continue.

"Have you ever killed anything? Not flies and such, but animals or humans."

His hand had come to rest again on the iron of his braces. They made him strong in some ways, including a few that healthy legs would not have, but they could not do everything. Ankumata said, "I am no hunter."

I nodded. "Only those who have never killed may do the work that will bring swamp-wyrm eggs to you. There are other requirements as well, which you cannot fulfill . . . but I think it would please the Moulish to know that they are giving their dragons to a man who is in that sense pure. You may wish to find others who have not killed and recruit them to assist." My gaze flickered briefly to Galinke. "Women as well as men."

This audience had used up more than enough of the oba's time. He dismissed me with a wave of his feather fan. "I will read your research notes before you depart."

None of the secrets Yeyuama had shared with me were written down, so agreeing was easy enough. "I will see to it that you have copies of what is printed afterward as well," I promised, and retreated from his presence with a sense of profound relief.

The natural effects of the agreement to transplant swamp-wyrm eggs into the border rivers of Bayembe did not become fully apparent for a number of years after my departure, and so I will not address them here; that is a matter for later volumes.

The political effects, however, played out more rapidly, as I found myself accused of treason against the Scirling crown.

These accusations came in three distinct waves. The first was immediate, following on the rumours that I had brought an army to the walls of Point Miriam and threatened the soldiers there. That, I think, prepared the soil for the later rumours; it made for a good story, and a pleasingly scandalous counter-narrative to the tale of Isabella Camherst, savior of Nsebu.

The second wave was a product of my argument with Sir Adam and subsequent house arrest. He had the good sense not to share the specifics of our conversation, but a great many people knew I had done *something* dreadful enough to warrant being locked up, and later marched under armed guard to see the oba. When that selfsame oba intervened to have me released, whispers began to fly that my loyalties lay not with my own homeland, but with our colonial ally. No one could say for certain what action I had taken on their behalf—that awaited the third wave of accusations—but rumour supplied any number of scurrilous possibilities.

As for the third wave, it did not take shape immediately. Ankumata was too experienced a politician to tell Sir Adam of his arrangement with the Moulish before he had to; I was safely back in Scirland by the time that matter came to light. (And a good thing, too, or I might never have escaped with my life.) But eventually it became known that there had been plans for a dam, and that Bayembe had backed out of those plans, in favor of some arrangement with the Moulish. This damaged the trade agreements with Scirland, which led to other foreign parties taking an interest in Bayembe, and ultimately weakened our influence in that country. I would not say this damaged Scirland, in the sense of inflicting harm upon my own nation; but it robbed us of a profit we might otherwise have had. This was more than enough for some to declare me a traitor to my own people.

All of this was inadvertent on my own part—but it does little good to cry, "I only wanted to study dragons!" Science is not separate from politics. As much as I would like it to be a pure thing, existing only in some intellectual realm unsullied by human struggle, it will always be entangled with the world we live in.

(That is a lie, though I will leave it in. Not the entanglement—that much is true—but the notion that I would like it to be otherwise. If science were only some abstract thing, without connection to our lives, it would be both useless and boring. But there have been times when I wished that I might snip a few of the threads tying it to other matters, so they would stop tripping me as I went.)

The effect of these accusations, along with others acquired during the expedition (such as the rumours of intimacy with Tom), was to drive all interest in my scientific discoveries out of the public mind in both Bayembe and Scirland. While my companions and I recuperated from our trials—in Nsebu, for Sir Adam had refused to allow us to return to Atuyem, even after my house arrest ended—we endured endless questions, not one of which had to do with natural history. On Tom's advice, I answered as few of those as my indiscretion and the status of my inquirer would allow. The political negotiations played out with a minimum of our involvement, which was as I preferred; I devoted myself instead to making better notes of my observations in Mouleen, since swamp conditions had made proper efforts there impossible.

It was a peculiar time. If I had felt odd briefly leaving the Green Hell for the savannah during our trek to the Great Cataract, how much stranger was it to sit on a chair in a Scirling-style house, to sleep in a bed, to wear skirts once again? The air felt positively cool and dry after the oppressive humidity of the swamp, and the sky seemed impossibly huge. Things that had become routine to me these past months reasserted themselves as unthinkable: had I truly eaten *insects*? Conversely, things which had once been shocking were no longer so. When every woman one has seen for half a year, only Natalie excepted, goes about wearing nothing more than a loincloth, the Gabborid custom of leaving one breast bare seems positively modest.

Over it all hung the certainty that we would not be in Eriga for much longer. "They'll drag us home," Tom predicted, shortly after we were reunited. "The soldiers were talking on the way here; they said the government might recall all civilians from Nsebu, if the

Ikwunde continue to press. Except for the trading companies, of course. And now, with what you've done . . ." He shook his head, bemused. "There will have to be an inquiry."

Natalie laughed. The recent surprises seemed to have done her in; her manner was that of a woman who had washed her hands of everything, and now was merely waiting to see what would happen next. She said, "Well, I've ruined myself thoroughly enough to avoid marriage, and if I am *very* stone-headed I may yet avoid the madhouse. I suppose I am ready to go home."

I was not. Now that I knew fangfish were immature swamp-wyrms, I wanted to study their life cycle in greater detail, perhaps get an estimate for what percentage survived that infantile stage and grew to adulthood. I wanted to see the seasonal mating of the swamp-wyrms in the lake below the Great Cataract; I wanted to watch the great queen dragons lay their eggs, and distribute them through the forest alongside Yeyuama and the others. I wanted to document how the hatchlings fared in the river environment of Bayembe (and that was *before* I knew what would happen after their transplantation).

But I have never once left the site of an expedition feeling that I have learned everything, answered every question there is to ask. My curiosity always finds new directions. Despite that, I was honestly not certain I could face the Green Hell again—not so soon. Like a man undertaking strenuous labor, I had thought myself fit enough while I was still working, but now that I had stopped, a profound weariness set in, as much psychological as physical. A mattress might feel strange beneath my back at night, but I was not eager to trade it for a damp pallet again.

Regardless, the choice was not ours to make. Tom was right:

before the month was out, Sir Adam informed us that we were to return to Scirland. "Are our visas revoked?" I asked.

I meant the question politely enough, but Sir Adam was not inclined to read anything I said in a charitable light. He said, "They will be, if that's what it takes to get rid of you."

"That won't be necessary," Tom hastened to assure him, and we left his office.

We did obtain permission to return to Atuyem—under escort, of course—so that we might make our farewells there. I had already parted from Yeyuama two weeks before; the Moulish did not tarry long in Point Miriam after handing over the Labane. I sent gifts with him, as lavish as I could arrange: more iron knives, foodstuffs not found in the swamp, anything I thought the Moulish might find of use. They wear little jewelry, but I sent a carved wooden pendant for Akinimanbi, a charm made in Bayembe to protect infants from sickness. I had no belief in its supernatural efficacy, nor would Akinimanbi necessarily think much of an item that invoked a Yembe god, but it was the best gesture I could think of to express my gratitude for her aid and forbearance.

In Atuyem, I met with Galinke and clasped her hands. "Despite all the trouble and confusion that has come of it," I said, "I am still more grateful than I can say that you recommended me to your brother. I only wish there were something equally vital I might do for you in return."

She smiled broadly. "In a way, you have. The more secure Bayembe is, the less likely it is that I will be sent to the mansa as his wife."

I had not forgotten our early political discussions in the *agban,* which had played no small role in affecting my decisions. "Then I am glad to have been of service," I said.

Galinke was not the only one who benefited from our expedition. Faj Rawango had, on account of his ancestry, been appointed to a prominent role in the new contact with Mouleen. And of course Ankumata had gotten what he desired, though he did not bid us farewell in person.

When people speak of the tragedies in my life, they ordinarily mean the deaths: not only Jacob, but all those around me who have perished, whether in direct consequence of danger or simple misfortune and the passage of time after our friendship has formed. At times, though, I think these partings should be accounted as highly, if only in the ledger of my own sorrow. Akinimanbi did not die on a Labane spear, but I never saw her again after leaving for the Great Cataract; in that sense I lost her as thoroughly as if she *had* died. So it was with Yeyuama as well. I only saw Faj Rawango once more, years later, and although Galinke corresponded with me, we could not be friends the way we might have been had we dwelt in the same land. So it has been, again and again throughout my life, as I form connections with people and then lose them to distance and time. I mourn those losses, even when I know my erstwhile friends are safe and happy among their own kin.

But the only way for me to avoid such losses would be to stay home, to never journey beyond the range of easy visitation. As my life will attest, that is not a measure I am willing to take; nor would I forgo the pleasures of my transient friendships if I could.

So we made our farewells, packed our things, and boarded a steamship in the harbor of Nsebu. Much browner, thinner, and more worn than we had been when we arrived, we made our way back to Scirland.

TWENTY-FIVE

Reactions at home—A stranger to me—Conversations and apologies—
No longer a recluse—The thief—A small bar—The cost of the world

There was indeed an inquiry, and a flood of articles in the news-sheets, and gossipmongers swirling in the social waters like so many hungry fangfish.

That I survived these things at all owes a great deal to Lord Hilford, who was my tireless champion in venues ranging from Society to the Synedrion. He defended me against Sir Adam's report, accusations of fornication, and his own son (who had not forgiven me in the least for absconding with his daughter). Natalie was disowned, and took up residence with me as my permanent companion.

She proved surprisingly able with Jacob, once she was a resident of my house rather than a visitor to it. "I would not want one of my own, I think," she said with a laugh, "but I do not mind borrowing yours for brief spans of time."

My son. Now three years old, he had grown tremendously in my absence; I might not have recognized him, had his resemblance to his father not become even stronger. He, I think, barely recognized me at all, shrinking into Mrs. Hunstin's skirts when I crouched down and held out my arms for him to come.

His diffidence struck me like a blow. It was not only his youth that made him forget me, or the fact that I had been absent for a third of his short life; it was the distance between us before that. I was, I thought wryly, as remote a figure in his world as a queen dragon was to a fangfish, dwelling far away in the clean, turbulent waters of the lake. (Of course I thought of it in those terms. My head was full of plans for the book I would publish, which I had been using as a distraction from the prospect of a Synedrion hearing. And I had begun to think about motherhood as a naturalist might—which made it much more interesting to me.)

The witchcraft ritual had purged some of the tension and pain from my thoughts, though, and on the journey home I had realized that I was eager to see my son once more. I vowed, as Mrs. Hunstin coaxed him toward me, that I would find some means of improving matters between us. I still had no desire to be the sort of mother society expected me to be; but surely I could be *some* kind of mother to him, in my particular way, to a greater extent than before.

My own mother . . . I will not go into detail regarding the conversation between us, save to say that "conversation" is an exceedingly polite name to give it. She had heard the rumours about Tom Wilker, and drawn very erroneous conclusions from them, not the least of which was the notion that I had only gone to Eriga for his sake. I took great exception to her readiness to condemn me, and after that I no longer had to ignore her letters, for she wrote me none.

Andrew I apologized to for the loss of the penknife he had given me when we were children. He listened to the tale of its demise with all the wide-eyed excitement of the eight-year-old boy he had been, and afterward clapped me on the back as if I were a man. "It fell in a noble cause," he said solemnly, and then demanded to know whether Erigan women really went bare-breasted.

I had expected to return to my life as a recluse, albeit for different reasons than before. I imagined myself rising each morning to write papers on our observations, Tom and I having agreed to bombard the Philosophers' Colloquium and other scholarly bodies with material until they were forced to acknowledge our existence and our merit. We had plans for another book as well, which ultimately turned into two: *Dragon Breeds of the Bayembe Region* and *Dragon Breeds of Mouleen*.

But I had not accounted for my celebrity, which brought a flood of mail and even some curiosity-seekers to my house in Pasterway. Natalie dealt with these, but I could not (and did not) refuse all invitations to events and house parties; if I wanted the Colloquium to acknowledge me as a scholar, it was to my benefit to present myself as such in public. (This also lent strength to my assertions that any scandals, real or imagined, associated with my time in Eriga were secondary at best to my true purpose there.) I set to work making a place for myself in Society, even if it was not the place Society intended for me.

And, one Athemer morning in early Pluvis, I sat down in Kemble's parlour with Tom, Natalie, Lord Hilford, and Frederick Kemble himself, to discuss the matter of dragonbone.

"It was Canlan," Lord Hilford said. "I have no proof of it—nothing I could take to a court, not with a marquess as the defendant—but I'm certain he is the one behind the break-in. The man I set to investigating wrote to me recently, reporting that Canlan received a very large sum of money from a company in Va Hing. A new outfit, one whose members include several chemists and industrialists."

Tom frowned, drumming his fingers on one knee. "But why sell the information, when he could profit more by exploiting it himself?"

The earl snorted. "Because he needed ready money. The Canlan estates are not what they once were; to invest in this research himself would require more funds than he can spare. And also, I suppose, because he's lazy. Gilmartin isn't a chemist himself, which means he would need to hire men who are, which means dividing his profits, and also a great deal of work I doubt he's inclined to undertake. Much easier for him to hand it off to someone more energetic."

I thought of the accusations against me, that I had betrayed Scirland by helping Bayembe do without *our* help. That had largely been inadvertent on my part, but Canlan had sold this knowledge to Va Hing with malice aforethought.

Of course, I could hardly throw stones, not when we had stolen the seeds of it from a Chiavoran working for a Bulskoi lord in Vystrana. Whatever came of this would be an international collaboration, against the will of all involved.

"What do you have for us, Mr. Kemble?" I asked.

He rose and unlocked his desk, taking from it a small oblong wrapped in canvas. Because I was the one financing his work, he handed it to me first.

My hopes were too high; I nearly dropped the thing, surprised by its heavy weight. This was not the feather-light material from which we had built the *Furcula*. I unwrapped it nevertheless, and found in my hands a solid bar the color of dragonbone, no longer than my palm.

"Chemically, it's the right substance," Kemble said. "Which is more than I had a year ago. But the structure is entirely wrong. It's too dense; it weighs more than lead. Though it's stronger than lead, for what that's worth."

His tone said he did not think it was worth much. "If it has the strength of dragonbone, surely that is of use," I said, giving Tom the bar to examine.

Kemble grunted. "Only if you could produce it in large quantities, easily and cheaply. Which, right now, you can't. Or at least I can't. I gambled on making that; it cost all the funds you gave me for the next year. I had to know if it would work. But you might as well build your machines out of firestones as use that for any industrial purpose."

I could not contain my wince. His funds for a *year*? I could not fault him for the experiment, but even so . . .

Kemble proceeded to outline the method by which he had created the bar, while Tom and Lord Hilford asked intelligent questions. I followed none of it, but slouched in my chair in a most unladylike fashion and chewed on my lower lip. It was progress, though not success. And I was determined to follow through until it *became* success, even if it bankrupted me—but far better, of course, if it did not. With Natalie now a part of my household and Jacob steadily growing, I would need a greater income.

Up to that point, my sketches had only been for private pleasure, and later for field notes and scholarly illustrations. But news of what transpired in Eriga had ignited public interest: all the world knew the Moulish had just defeated the mightiest warriors of the Ikwunde with dragons. Might there not be a market for pictures? Several news-sheets had offered me money for the "true story" of what happened in Eriga, and while I did not trust them to report my experiences honestly, it suggested I might profit by selling a non-scholarly book as well. Something of more substance than *A Journey to the Mountains of Vystrana*, but less density than what I would present to the scholarly community.

I had more reasons than just Kemble's research and the maintenance of my own household to spur me. Lord Hilford had been my patron for this expedition, but I could not depend upon his generosity forever; he had his own financial security to consider, and besides which, he was not a young man. By the time I was ready to begin the project I had in mind, he might not be in a position to fund it.

The sea-snake we had seen on the voyage to Nsebu; the lack of difference between savannah snakes and arboreal snakes; the drakeflies in Mouleen; the swamp-wyrms and their queenly kin and the fangfish I had not known were related. Wolf-drakes and sparklings and wyverns, and all the other creatures that we classed as mere cousins. I was increasingly convinced that our entire draconic taxonomy needed to be rethought—but to do that properly, much less persuade anyone to heed me, I would need a great deal more data than I had now. For all my reading, there were still woeful gaps in my knowledge, particularly where the scholarship was in another tongue; and once I had remedied that lack, I would need to undertake a much larger study than anyone, so far as I knew, had ever attempted.

Tom saw me chewing on my lip and leaned over. "Something troubling you?"

"Not troubling, precisely," I said, keeping my voice down so that I might not interrupt Kemble and Lord Hilford.

He raised one eyebrow, inviting me to elaborate.

A slow grin crept over my face, against all rationality and common sense. "How much do you suppose a voyage around the world might cost?"

ABOUT THE AUTHOR

American fantasy writer Marie Brennan habitually pillages her background in anthropology, archaeology and folklore for fictional purposes. She is the author of the Onyx Court series, the Doppelganger duology of *Warrior* and *Witch*, and the urban fantasy *Lies and Prophecy*, as well as more than forty short stories. The first memoir of Lady Trent, *A Natural History of Dragons*, was critically praised and received a starred review in *Publishers Weekly*, who hailed it as being "[s]aturated with the joy and urgency of discovery and scientific curiosity."

A NATURAL HISTORY OF DRAGONS

BY MARIE BRENNAN

"You, dear reader, continue at your own risk. It is not for the faint of heart—no more so than the study of dragons itself..."

From Scirland to the farthest reaches of Eriga, Lady Trent is known to be the world's preeminent dragon naturalist, who brought the study of dragons into the clear light of modern science. But before she became the illustrious figure we now know, there was a bookish young woman whose passion for learning defied the stifling conventions of her day. Here at last, in her own words, is the true story of a pioneering spirit who risked her reputation, her prospects and her fragile flesh to satisfy her scientific curiosity; of how she sought true love and happiness despite her lamentable eccentricities; and of her thrilling expedition to the perilous mountains of Vystrana, where she made the first of many historic discoveries that would change the world forever.

VOYAGE OF THE BASILISK

BY MARIE BRENNAN

"Wonders terrestrial and aquatic, ancient ruins, near drownings, and more kinds of dragon than you can shake a wing at..."

Devoted readers of Lady Trent's earlier memoirs, *A Natural History of Dragons* and *The Tropic of Serpents*, may believe themselves already acquainted with the particulars of her historic voyage aboard the Royal Survey Ship *Basilisk*, but the true story of that illuminating, harrowing, and scandalous journey has never been revealed—until now.

Six years after her perilous exploits in Eriga, Isabella embarks on her most ambitious expedition yet: a two-year trip around the world to study all manner of dragons in every place they might be found. From feathered serpents sunning themselves in the ruins of a fallen civilization to the mighty sea serpents of the tropics, these creatures are a source of both endless fascination and frequent peril. On the way Isabella must cope with storms, shipwrecks, intrigue, and warfare, even as she makes a discovery that offers a revolutionary new insight into the ancient history of dragons...

IN THE LABYRINTH OF DRAKES

BY MARIE BRENNAN

Even those who take no interest in the field of dragon naturalism have heard of Lady Trent's expedition to the inhospitable deserts of Akhia. Her discoveries there are the stuff of romantic legend, catapulting her from scholarly obscurity to worldwide fame. The details of her personal life during that time are hardly less private, having provided fodder for gossips in several countries.

As is so often the case in the career of this illustrious woman, the public story is far from complete. In this, the fourth volume of her memoirs, Lady Trent relates how she acquired her position with the Royal Scirling Army; how foreign saboteurs imperiled both her work and her well-being; and how her determined pursuit of knowledge took her into the deepest reaches of the Labyrinth of Drakes, where the chance action of a dragon set the stage for her greatest achievement yet.

WITHIN THE SANCTUARY OF WINGS

BY MARIE BRENNAN

The conclusion to the thrilling memoirs of Lady Isabella Trent and her legacy of dragon evolutionary research and anthropological adventures

After nearly five decades (and, indeed, the same number of volumes), one might think they were well-acquainted with the Lady Isabella Trent—dragon naturalist, scandalous explorer, and perhaps as infamous for her company and feats of daring as she is famous for her discoveries and additions to the scientific field.

And yet—after her initial adventure in the mountains of Vystrana, and her exploits in the depths of war-torn Eriga, to the high seas aboard the *Basilisk*, and then to the inhospitable deserts of Akhia—Lady Trent has captivated hearts along with fierce minds. This concluding volume will finally reveal the truths behind her most notorious adventure—scaling the tallest peak in the world, buried behind the territory of Scirland's enemies—and what she discovered there, within the Sanctuary of Wings.

For more fantastic fiction, author events, exclusive excerpts,
competitions, limited editions and more:

VISIT OUR WEBSITE
titanbooks.com

LIKE US ON FACEBOOK
facebook.com/titanbooks

FOLLOW US ON TWITTER
@TitanBooks

EMAIL US
readerfeedback@titanemail.com